MARATHON GROUPS

THE CENTURY PSYCHOLOGY SERIES
Kenneth MacCorquodale, Gardner Lindzey
and
Kenneth E. Clark, *Editors*

MARATHON GROUPS
Reality and Symbol

by
ELIZABETH E. MINTZ

with contributions by
LORELLE SARETSKY
BARRY SHERMAN

NEW YORK

APPLETON-CENTURY-CROFTS
Educational Division
MEREDITH CORPORATION

Dedicated
to Alex, Ann, and Harvey

CONTENTS

PREFACE

This is not an impartial book. I have attempted to report what I have seen in marathons as accurately as possible; every episode and every quotation from marathon participants can be documented by their written or recorded words; and I have attempted to present the limitations, the drawbacks, and even the possible risks of various types of marathons in different settings and for different purposes. Also, it must be acknowledged that the accumulation of objective data, difficult here as in other areas of human interaction, is only beginning.

It may take years for research to provide conclusive answers to such questions as: Is the marathon encounter primarily a useful adjunct to other forms of psychotherapy? Or, is it a worthwhile treatment method in itself? Is it psychotherapy at all, or rather an opportunity for men and women to widen their horizons of feeling and experience? Is it a solution to our widely recognized problem of social alienation? Can it help to resolve antagonisms between subgroups in our society? Awaiting the reply of research, only the testimony of marathon leaders and marathon participants (no more unanimous here than with most other questions asked by human beings) can be invoked to support my personal conviction that the encounter group, in Carl Rogers's words, may be "the greatest social invention of our time," and that the marathon is the most potent form of the encounter group.

This power of the marathon encounter group, it seems to me, is related to its simultaneous functioning as a reality experience and as a symbolic experience. The principle of the marathon is simple: it provides an opportunity for the participants to be together, for a prolonged period of time, in a situation in which the basic value is the honest expression of feelings. In its requirement that the participants confront one another and themselves as honestly as possible, without social pretenses, it is more real than most social institutions. In a successful marathon, an immense range of human feelings emerges with more intensity and authenticity than can usually be seen in any conventional social setting. In this sense, the marathon is a microcosm of human reality.

At the same time, the marathon has a symbolic quality. To many members of the group, it represents a second chance for a fulfilling childhood. To others—or indeed to the same individuals at different times—it represents a situation of competition among peers. It is a playground and a battlefield.

The marathon offers each participant an opportunity to test and validate his private symbols against the group consensus. Symbols are mediators between the world of inner reality and the world of outer reality. They bridge the gap between the lonely, unique experience of each individual and the realities around him. In a marathon group, an atmosphere usually develops in which words, our customary symbols used both for communication and concealment, are supplemented by other symbols, not always verbal. The offer and acceptance of a cup of milk may mean "I can take care of others and can let them take care of me." The outpouring of rage against someone who temporarily represents a hated figure may not only provide catharsis but may change the idiosyncratic, individual symbol into a more valid perception, "I am sometimes angry at people because they represent someone I once hated." The fantasied descent into a black maelstrom whose conquest represents the overcoming of an ancient childhood terror may, through the power of the symbol, drain some anxiety permanently away. In a marathon such nearly universal human symbols as the milk and the black maelstrom derive even more power from being recognized and shared by others in the group. It is far easier to descend in fantasy into the childhood nightmare when others say, "This is like some of my own experiences," so that there is companionship instead of fearful solitude.

The marathon is not an artificial love feast. Its participants bring in and express the anger and frustrations and fear carried over from childhood experiences or evoked by present dissatisfactions. Often they arouse feelings of hostility in one another. According to the basic principle of the encounter group, every feeling may be freely expressed. The expression of hostility may be frightening at first, then in the prolonged intimacy of the group the members gradually cease to fear each other.

As time goes on, an extraordinary phenomenon takes place. The participants begin to care about each other. After a full expression of great irritation toward another participant, a group member may discover suddenly that the irritation has dissolved and that he feels affection in its place. After an intense expression of almost infantile helplessness and rage, a woman becomes tender and perceptive with the other members. After exposing what he sees as his own guilt or shame, a member finds that he is still accepted by the group, and that his honesty is valued. The most frequently repeated words of marathon participants are, "I have found out that I can be myself."

At this time, my own experience includes well over a hundred marathons. Every participant is different, every group is different. Not all groups are equally successful; some participants remain relatively unmoved, and some depart unsatisfied. But for most participants, and in most marathons, the experience culminates in a sense of mutual acceptance and joyous human communion. In one marathon, a participant who happened to be a clergyman spontaneously ended with the benediction, "May the Lord watch between me and thee, while we are absent one from another." Although I have no personal religious allegiance, these words seemed to me totally appropriate. Nonreligious and even antireligious participants also responded to the blessing, certainly not because of its specific religious connotations, but rather because of the implication that the feeling of being part of humanity might be sustained after the ending of the marathon.

This is a time when many men believe that the survival of humanity itself is threatened. Occasionally it seems to me that the concern and loving acceptance for one another which most participants feel as a successful marathon approaches its end is perhaps only the transient flickering of a campfire about to be put out by the gathering forces of war and violence and pollution. A beautiful young man, recently dismissed from a hospital where he was diagnosed as a paranoid schizophrenic, and admitted to the marathon only at the urgent request of his psychiatrist, justified the psychiatrist's judgment by giving and receiving a great deal in the group; he expressed my own recurring pessimistic thought in the vivid language of psychosis when he said, "The devil lets these good things happen sometimes."

Yet more often I have a different conviction, shared by many others who have had the privilege of working with a marathon encounter group. Here we observe how self-revelation can bring growth in self-respect instead of shame; we see participants move from preoccupation with their defenses and pretenses to an awareness of their common humanity; we are repeatedly impressed by the emergence of their warm feelings for one another. Is it, then, possible to believe that open communication not only among individuals but among social groups and perhaps even among nations might be threatening at first, but in the end less dangerous? Is it possible that the potential for human affection is greater than the potential for destruction? Perhaps there are ways of developing methods to extend the basic encounter principle of honesty within our own culture, and even beyond it.

This hope perhaps sounds sentimental and unrealistic, but the language of humanism is likely to sound sentimental, especially in contrast to such practical terms as overkill and fallout and defoliation.

What other hope do we have?

Hastings-on-Hudson, N.Y.   E.E.M.

MARATHON GROUPS

1 THE NATURE OF A MARATHON

Time is a basic dimension of human experience. From habituation, we are almost unaware of how automatically we think in terms of hours, days, weeks; of the endless scheduling imposed by social needs; of our measurement of education and achievement and earnings by time units. With the exception of our immediate families and sometimes with not even this exception, our relationships with others are broken up by our obedience to time.

From habituation, also, most of us are partly unaware of the paradox that, despite our subservience to time, we live emotionally in the past and the future to an extent which damages our ability to savor the present. From the past we retain grudges and regrets, and we are preoccupied with fears and ambitions for the future.

A marathon group is an island in time. It is a group of people who remain in continuous involvement with one another for a prolonged period of time, typically at least twenty-four hours. There are no interruptions. The group does not deal with anything except its chosen task, which usually is the expression and exploration of immediate feelings. These conditions create in the marathon, for most participants, a sense of timelessness which makes the present moment very real and intense. And for most participants, the intensity of the marathon experience operates to bring about personality changes, in the direction of self-understanding and self-acceptance, which often endure.

Intensity seems to be the common denominator of marathon groups, but the groups can vary greatly in terms of purpose, setting and techniques of leadership. In an uncarpeted office adjacent to a meat-packing plant, staff executives and line supervisors, some in heavy-duty working clothes, meet for eight consecutive hours to improve communication and ventilate anxieties over a recent reorganization. In a beautiful wilderness setting, nude marathon participants with lighted candles in their hands file along a woodland path in silence, seeking an ecstatic peak experience. At Synanon and Daytop, ex-drug users meet voluntarily without formal

This chapter is in part adapted from articles published in *Psychotherapy; Theory, Research and Practice* (Mintz, 1967); *The Journal of Contemporary Psychotherapy* (Mintz, 1968); and *The American Journal of Psychotherapy* (Mintz, 1971).

leadership, sometimes for as long as thirty-six hours without sleep, ruthlessly exposing and assaulting one another's weaknesses in an effort to strengthen themselves and each other. There is a different drama and a different atmosphere in every group. But whatever the variations, the observation of many hundreds of marathon groups, now reported by many leaders (Bach, 1966; Stoller, 1968; Alexander, 1969), suggests that the dimension of prolonged time brings about an identifiable sequence of events.

First, an atmosphere develops, usually fostered by the marathon leader but also created by the extension of time, in which the participants gradually become aware of their own social pretenses and begin to question whether or not these pretenses are necessary. Next there is time to test how it feels to relinquish the social pretenses, whether disaster actually follows the unmasking or whether it is possible to be liked and respected for one's natural self. And finally, there is time to assimilate the experience and to consider whether or not it is necessary to assume the same old social role upon returning to the outside world. Because the individual participant is allowing himself to feel and behave with more sincerity and spontaneity than in his usual daily life, and because his companions in the group are also undergoing the same experience, there arises in nearly every marathon a feeling of warmth, intimacy, and mutual acceptance which is experienced as unique and beautiful and which is usually carried away from the group in the form of enhanced self-regard and enhanced regard for others.

"People are beautiful, and for the first time in my life I hope for happiness." [1]

"I went back home and realized how much I love my wife and children."

"The feeling of exhilaration just lasted a few days. Then I was a little bit depressed for a day or two. Down to earth. Then I just started feeling good, plain solid good, glad to be alive and working. It's lasted for months."

"It's really true that when you find out what you're really like, it's not so bad. I'm not a stinker. How about that!"

"Something wonderful happened, something to do with closeness and openness with others, taking off the armor, throwing away the shield."

"I always used to think that I had to be dignified with my students,

---

[1] Quotations throughout this book, except for a few reconstructed from memory immediately after a marathon, are taken verbatim from tape recordings or from letters to the writer. Names and identifying data are disguised.

Most of this data was sent to me spontaneously by participants; in other instances, if a marathon experience seemed especially significant, I requested the participant for written follow-up. Specific research results (Mintz, 1968) are discussed in more detail in Chapter 10.

stay aloof, or else they wouldn't respect me. Monday after the marathon I went into my class and it was different. I didn't plan it; it was just different. It was the first time they ever came up after class to ask me questions. One boy just came up to talk to me. It never happened before."

These are representative examples from a file of about 500 letters received by me after marathons, describing changes in feelings and behavior which frequently follow the sequential experiences of heightened self-awareness, increased honesty of self-expression, and intensified intimacy with others which can occur in the time-extended group.

Marathon groups have other distinctive values related to their various purposes. For instance, in a black-white confrontation group the prolongation of time affords a dramatic opportunity to recognize human similarities and environmental differences. In a therapy group the prolongation of time provides leeway for regressing to the full expression of primitive infantile feelings and thereafter integrating them with the mature personality. But to a greater or lesser degree there is always observable the movement away from artifice and self-deception toward spontaneity and truth.

Sometimes it is suggested that a marathon group is efficacious because it exerts prolonged and unendurable pressure which finally breaks down psychological defenses.[2] This is true for some participants. One man, anticipating a marathon with some dread, wrote: "In thirty hours can I conceal/The secret feelings which I feel."

For most participants, the reverse is true. The marathon offers a growing sense of safety rather than of stress, because it is a situation in which genuine self-expression is not only permitted but rewarded. Never yet have I observed an instance in which a marathon group attacked any honest expression of feeling, and never have I seen any effort to intensify guilt which was already being experienced by a participant. On many occasions, a participant tells the group about a shameful action, sometimes an action which has never before been acknowledged. Invariably the group deals with the situation realistically and constructively, not with specious reassurances, but with an effort to help the self-accusing member put the past behind him and regain his self-respect.

Far more typical, however, is the exploration and relinquishment of social and individual pretenses which often have become so ingrained that the individual is almost unaware that they are contrary to his own inner feelings. Our society stresses conformity to sex-role stereotypes, socioeconomic, occupational, and ethnic stereotypes. Behavior which apparently is inconsequential often symbolizes acceptance of the stereo-

___

[2] Typical of this viewpoint, though more characteristic of the lay press than of professional contributors, is the caption "Marathoners hope to change their behavior almost instantly by breaking down their defenses through simple fatigue and strong pressure" (Lamott, 1969).

type. A few years ago, women who did not wear high-heeled shoes might be perceived as unwilling to accept the feminine role; still longer ago, women's use of cigarettes and lipstick was seen as a defiance of propriety. Today in some subcultures it is a signal of rebellion for young men to wear beards; but the beards in other subcultures signify conformity. Such signs are widely recognized, though not always consciously so. It is not by chance, and not entirely for the sake of comfort, that as a marathon progresses the men remove their neckties, the women become less punctilious about renewing lipstick, and all the participants take off their shoes.

In addition to role stereotypes, most of us must somehow reconcile double messages from past and present environment. For example, most people now in their middle years were trained to be embarrassed about sexual feelings but now live in a subculture in which lack of sexual enjoyment is deplored. Children are trained to inhibit their aggressiveness but are expected to compete vigorously when they grow older. These inconsistencies turn into inner conflicts. Here again the time extension of the marathon is priceless, enabling participants to experience and examine both sides of such conflicts in a neutral, permissive setting.

There are also role demands once placed upon the growing child by the idiosyncracies of his family situation and now internalized, which are not socially necessary and often are actually maladaptive. The marathon group, because of its prolonged intimacy, functions as a new family, which encourages movement toward more flexible and realistic behavior.

At the moment when a participant realizes that he has been living under the pressure of standards which do not really represent his own values and feelings, there is often a sense of aliveness and delight. Many people become aware that they are suddenly breathing more deeply and easily. Occasionally people report an experience of seeing forms more distinctively and of colors becoming more vivid, a phenomenon for which some therapists have borrowed the Buddhist term *satori,* meaning enlightenment. Often the emotional experience comes first and is verbalized subsequently. Overt behavioral changes are usually less noteworthy than the subjective feelings which accompany them.

"I honestly believe this is the first time in my life I was ever able to stop being a nice guy. My God. Does it feel great. My God!" This participant had expressed a degree of anger and resentment which for him was unprecedented, but which did not distress or frighten anyone in the group.

"I thought I couldn't look good without eyelashes and makeup." This young woman lacked essential confidence in her attractiveness, and gave an impression of artificiality which was commented upon by the group.

"Got cured of Uncle Tomming." A black participant.

"Always felt uneasy about hugging another man—I thought that it might be considered homosexual." In nearly every marathon, one or more men express pleasure at being able to show physical affection toward other men.

"Suddenly it dawns on me that I can be strong without being un-feminine." A common marathon theme is the exploration of the validity of sexual stereotypes.

Such insights can, of course, occur under various circumstances, including group therapy meetings on a conventional weekly basis. The marathon, however, is unique in providing a sustained role-free atmosphere. Participants need not experiment with spontaneity and authenticity and then leave the room and feel compelled to don their masks again until the next session. They can experience a freer way of living and feeling long enough to become at home with it, and in most instances long enough so that the new freedom can be crystallized into words.

"I feel like I've been in jail and didn't know it. Put myself in jail and didn't even know it." The jail was this participant's excessive self-control.

"But I do look better with them, most of the time." She is not inclined to give up her false eyelashes, but apparently they have changed from a symbol of safety to a decoration.

"Now I know I was Uncle Tomming, I won't do it anymore. I won't. I couldn't."

"It's great to be warm with other men. It's great to show it and feel it."

"I can be everything I really am." This was the young woman who had been taught that true femininity was associated with weakness. She had just arm-wrestled with a man and had been able to put forth her full strength. He won but had enjoyed and appreciated her vitality.

Movement from conscious or unconscious role-playing to authentic self-expression takes place in any form of effective therapy. Indeed, an analogous sequence of events takes place not only in conventional group therapy but also in classical psychoanalysis: recognizing that a defense exists, relinquishing the defense, and achieving a new integration of the personality. There are other unexpected but striking resemblances between classical psychoanalysis and the marathon. The isolation of the marathon group from external stimuli parallels the traditional stimulus-free arrangement of the psychoanalytic use of the couch. Although the stimuli to which marathon participants are subjected certainly are far more rich, varied, and intense than those which the analysand experiences as he explores his inner world, there is the common denominator that a situation is created in which there are no distractions to be used as defenses—no television, no cocktails, no social chitchat. The requirement that marathon participants express themselves as honestly as possible is dynamically equivalent to the basic rule of free association in psychoanalysis, except that any physical expressiveness is forbidden in the latter situation. These dynamic similarities can easily be overlooked by behavioral scientists, in part because of other obvious differences between the two situations, and perhaps also in part because behavioral scientists, whether they are orthodox psychoanalysts or encounter group leaders, are human beings with human loyalties to their preferred methodology and their professional associates.

Such personal loyalties may also be in part responsible for an exaggeratedly sharp distinction sometimes drawn between therapy groups and encounter groups, even to the point of maintaining that these two orientations are not only at variance but even in opposition to one another.[3] If this distinction is accepted, therapy groups are viewed as following the medical model, in which group members seek treatment because they are suffering from mental or emotional illness, treatment being directed toward the alleviation of pathology. Encounter groups, on the other hand, are composed of normal people who seek group experience to enhance their social skills or further their personal development. Leadership is directed toward providing stimuli for growth, especially through encouraging participants to express their feelings toward one another. If such a clear differentiation is really valid, it would become important to consider it in examining the nature and the values of marathon groups, which are customarily thought of as part of the encounter movement. The question would arise: Is a marathon primarily a growth-enhancing experience for healthy people, or is it a therapeutic experience for people with emotional difficulties? This question, however, is based on a spurious dichotomy between encounter and therapy, a dichotomy which in my opinion is not only naïve but obsolete.

Most psychotherapists in outpatient practice today find that a high proportion of their patients are not classifiable according to any psychiatric taxonomy. Many of them, as has often been noted (for example, May, 1969), can function well in society but suffer from a vague sense of purposelessness and alienation. Also, psychotherapists are frequently consulted by people who function in society better than the average person, but who wish for help in fulfilling their maximum personal potential. Even the nature of psychosis is questioned today (Laing, 1967), although probably most clinicians would still accept as its criterion the inability to distinguish between external and internal reality (Fenichel, 1945, ch. 18). The disappearance of the clear demarcation between mental illness

---

[3] A three-day workshop entitled "Encounter Versus Psychotherapy" was held in October, 1969, under the auspices of Interactional Dynamics (a group of psychological consultants) in New York City. Leaders of the encounter movement and recognized psychotherapists compared their viewpoints. Some, like myself, saw no essential clash of purpose; others considered their respective positions incompatible.

and health is indicated by the contemporary uncertainty among psychotherapists about the appropriateness of the term "patient." [4]

It seems questionable also to draw a sharp distinction between an experience which is therapeutic because it is directed toward the removal of symptoms and an experience which is therapeutic because it helps to release the individual's potential for enjoyment and achievement. Whether a symptom is regarded primarily as an ineffectual effort to cope with instinctual demands, or as a maladaptive reaction to the environment, it represents limitations or inhibitions or divergences of the energy which ideally would be devoted to the quest for self-fulfillment. In psychoanalytic theory, a fundamental goal of psychoanalysis is seen as the liberation of energy which was hitherto bound up in the maintenance of defenses, so that this energy can thenceforward be used by the ego to seek satisfaction in work and in love. Thus the dichotomy of "Healing Versus Growth" appears as artificial as the dichotomy between mental health and mental illness.[5]

There is, of course, a striking difference between the thoughtful atmosphere of a traditional therapy group, in which the leader is often called Doctor and physical contact may be forbidden as acting-out, and the colorful, lively, uninhibited atmosphere of a successful encounter group. A traditional group usually encourages the reconstruction of personal histories as well as the expression of immediate feeling; an encounter group stresses the here-and-now. A traditional group places relatively more emphasis on cognition, an encounter group on feeling. The leader of an encounter group is likely to be comparatively active and self-revealing. Physical contact and nonverbal communication are accepted or encouraged in an encounter group. Goals are similar; methods are different.

The spontaneity and intimacy sought in an encounter group develop readily in the marathon situation. Encounter groups are held with other time arrangements, but the encounter-marathon combination seems especially powerful. It can be adapted to a wide spectrum of human needs, including not only personal growth but the well-being of communities,

[4] In this book, the term "patient" is used for someone who is undergoing group or individual therapy outside a marathon, and generally the terms "participant" or "group member" for people attending a marathon. Occasionally "protagonist" seems the most suitable term for the central figure in a psychodramatic scenario. The expression "client" to me connotes a cold, technical relationship. It has been tempting to introduce the term "candidate" in the sense of "candidate for growth" because marathon episodes so often resemble mythological or primitive ceremonies in which a candidate is prepared for or helped to accept a new phase of life, such as puberty, marriage, parenthood, or leadership.

[5] The title of a panel discussion sponsored by the American Academy of Psychotherapists (1960).

most typically by focussing upon the resolution of conflicts between various subgroups. Here the value of the marathon format is that it facilitates the recognition of members of the opposite faction as human beings with human needs and feelings. This creates an emotional climate in which it becomes easier to differentiate between real, objective clashes of interest and apparent clashes of interest which actually stem only from prejudice and anxiety. Black-white encounter marathons and labor-management marathons are examples. It is possible, though optimistic, to imagine groups directed toward the diminution of international hostilities.[6]

Special applications of encounter techniques are useful here. For instance, Mr. Black and Mr. White might engage in a role reversal, exchanging positions and trying to exchange personalities and points of view, thus hopefully arriving at a better comprehension of one another's feelings. This kind of group is usually conducted with a modification of the marathon's time format. Several meetings are held over a period of two or three days, each lasting for several hours. In this way the intensity and intimacy of the marathon are attained to some degree, but there is opportunity for reflection between the sessions, in keeping with the relatively greater importance of the cognitive aspect of the situation. Such groups develop an atmosphere very different from that of the traditional conference model, with participants seated formally around a table and maintaining protocol in a way which tends to strengthen identification with their own group and exacerbate hostility toward the other group, thus maintaining the original power struggle (as tragically exemplified by many "peace talks").

Among encounter marathons intended for personal growth rather than for conflict resolution, it is possible to make a broad differentiation between those which are structured, in that the group as a whole is requested to participate in activities specified by the leader, and those which are unstructured, in that interaction is allowed to develop spontaneously and the leader intervenes in response to the immediate, varying needs of the participants. These two approaches may be combined. The entire group may be put through an activity and may then separate into small subgroups to discuss the individual reactions to the group experience. However, in comparing the two approaches, their relative merits and limitations become clearer if they are considered separately.

Structured groups, although they may be limited in number, may

---

[6] A three-day conference between five Palestinian Arabs of recognized public distinction and five Israelis of similar prestige was held in August, 1968, under the sponsorship of *Israel* magazine, which published a taped transcript of the proceedings (*Israel*, 1968). The transcript reveals a discernable movement from fixated hostility toward the recognition of common human denominators.

also accommodate up to several hundred people.[7] The activities in which they are asked to engage are variously known as exercises, encounter techniques, or games. The purpose of these activities may be to increase self-understanding, to enhance self-acceptance, to facilitate interpersonal intimacy, or to cultivate an atmosphere in which peak experiences can occur.[8]

Highly structured activities, used primarily for the purpose of increasing self-understanding, are exemplified by many of the exercises developed by the NTL (National Training Laboratories) Institute for Applied Behavioral Sciences, associated with the National Education Association, which throughout the year offers a series of two-week groups for individuals seeking personal growth, educators and community leaders wishing to develop their interpersonal skills, and businessmen whose participation is frequently supported by their firms in the expectation that their effectiveness at work will be improved. These groups are called "laboratories," "sensitivity-training groups," or "T-groups" (for training). The leaders are called "trainers," are not considered psychotherapists, and have not necessarily undergone advanced formal professional training. A specific statement is made that NTL "does not design or conduct programs to cure or alleviate pathological mental or emotional conditions" (NTL, 1969). Groups usually meet for several two-hour sessions each day, a variation of the time-extended marathon format. Representative exercises include: asking the participants to write down something about themselves which they have never told anyone, reading it aloud, then discussing in the group the meaning of trustfulness; exchanging feedback on mutual impressions by asking participants to select which members of the group they would choose for a boss, for a helper in serious trouble, to send on an important mission, and so on; and instructing participants to spend three minutes with eyes shut and fingers pressed over their ears considering the question "Who am I?" and then sharing their thoughts and fantasies.

Very different in emotional quality, but similar in that the activity is structured and directed by the leader, are procedures designed to enhance self-acceptance through physical nudity in the group. This approach was initiated in 1967 by Bindrim (1968) and has since been used in many of the growth centers which have developed throughout the

---

[7] An example is an all-day demonstration group conducted by William Schutz at the 1968 meeting of the American Psychological Association in San Francisco, attended by approximately 500 people, who were divided into small subgroups and asked to engage in various exercises.

[8] The expression *peak experience* is used by Maslow (1964) to denote an event of such subjective emotional intensity that it is felt as transcending ordinary life experiences. It does not necessarily imply a feeling of religious significance but often has a mystical or spiritual quality.

country after the model of Esalen Institute in California, a residential community which offers a varied program oriented toward personal growth and including many experimental innovations. A typical procedure is that in the nude group, each member in turn names whatever part of his or her body seems least acceptable, usually receiving reassurance from the group in response; a man might be told that he is handsome despite his pot belly, or a woman that her breasts are not really too small or too large for beauty.

Intimacy among the group members is likely to develop naturally as the group engages in such exercises as these, but other games are intended specifically to promote intimacy, often through physical contact. An extreme example is an ice-breaker game which can be used with either small or large groups. Participants are asked to walk as close together as possible into the center of the room, then unexpectedly told to sit down on the floor, so that they find themselves suddenly in close physical touch with strangers, eliciting feelings of embarrassment, amusement, or enjoyment. Time may be allocated thereafter for discussion of the experience, or it may be assumed that cognitive integration will take place naturally without discussion.

Structured procedures for the cultivation of peak experiences are most likely to be effective in a time-extended group and are used most often at weekend workshops given at various growth centers. Typical of these methods is a directed sequence of experiences (Bindrim, 1968) in which participants are first required to select and bring with them to the group as sensory stimuli whatever objects they most enjoy hearing (such as a record), eating, smelling (such as perfume or a flower), touching (perhaps fur or velvet), and seeing (such as a favorite picture); former peak experiences are recalled and discussed; partners are chosen and asked to gaze into one another's eyes; instructions are given for deep breathing and muscular relaxation; individuals are asked to experience and enjoy the sense-stimulating objects which they have brought with them; there is another period of eye-to-eye gazing and meditation; and finally the group discusses whatever experiences were induced. Silence is enjoined throughout most of the session.

Procedures such as those described above, and the marathon format itself, elicit a spectacularly wide diversity of opinion among behavioral scientists. It has been suggested that "latent or borderline psychotics . . . may, under the stress of such groups and the complete giving up of defense, jump the barrier between sanity and insanity" (Slavson, 1969). In rebuttal, NTL (1969) offers records to indicate that of 14,200 participants in its programs over a twenty-year period, only thirty-three people found the experience so stressful that they left the program before its completion. It is my own conviction that any participant who can be pushed into open psychosis by his experience in an encounter group would probably have responded in the same way to a terrifying movie, a family crisis, or perhaps even an ill-timed interpretation in individual psychotherapeutic treatment. Indeed, it seems likely that there would be a purely statistical probability of at least thirty-three patients out of 14,200 becoming psychotic during the course of conventional psychotherapy.

More specific criticisms can be made of the structured group procedures. The NTL exercises, for example, could be seen as fostering a childlike attitude of compliance with the directions of the trainer which might appear to be directly at variance with the spontaneous self-expression usually regarded as a basic goal of encounter groups. The technique of reassuring a nude group participant about the acceptability of his or her body can be misused if the reassurance is insincere (Blanchard, 1970); a man or a woman may be likeably human and appealing despite a pot belly or unattractive breasts, but it does not seem probable that a genuine, lasting enhancement of self-esteem would result from insincere efforts to persuade the nude participant that his or her body is esthetically beautiful. Procedures designed to foster intimacy through physical contact may be useful in preparing participants for fuller emotional involvement in the group, yet mere physical proximity can hardly be regarded as genuine intimacy, which is based on mutual knowledge and acceptance. There is something paradoxical, also, about the cultivation of peak experiences through a prescribed routine, suggesting the possibility that participants, in an effort to attain the rapturous awareness which is expected of them, may deceive themselves about what they are actually feeling. The phoniness which encounter groups seek to overcome may reappear in the guise of pretended spontaneity, false rapture, and pseudointimacy. The deliberate attempt to attain an intense emotional experience through structured procedures could result in a temporary euphoria which might actually deter the participant from seeking harder but more realistic paths toward self-fulfillment. Many leaders of encounter groups do allow adequate time for the spontaneous sharing of feelings in combination with the use of prescribed group exercises, in which case the movement from social role-playing to authentic self-recognition and self-expression can take place. However, this movement is most unlikely to take place if there is an implied pressure upon the participants to feel the way the exercise is intended to make them feel. In this case there is the danger that group members may simply adopt a new social pretense of being intimate and spontaneous. The mystique of the group may come perilously close to "If you can't be spontaneous, fake it." This tacit pressure resembles the familiar and destructive child-rearing tactic of insisting that a child should not only behave but feel in the way his parents regard as socially appropriate. Thus Perls (1969, p. 1) warns that "instant cure, instant joy, instant sensory-awareness . . . often becomes . . . another phony therapy that *prevents* growth." One growth center, recognizing that for some people it has become a way of life to move from one marathon encounter group to another each weekend, and that addiction to such groups can become a means to avoid confronting whatever personal limitations prevent the development of lasting and rewarding personal relationships, offers a special weekend workshop for "people who are over-grouped." Quotations from contemporary announcements of weekend workshops at various growth centers include the phrases: "a joyful human reunion"; "breakthroughs into new depths of inner strength, beauty, and human understanding"; "joyous sensory explorations . . . into the open energy flow of your feeling body"; "experience trips into the inner self"; "techniques for increasing trust and compassion."

From the point of view of social needs, even the highly structured encounter group can nevertheless be seen as providing experiences which contemporary society fails to offer. A comparison has been made between encounter groups which offer "restitutive experiences in emotional requirements" and the replacement of nutritional elements in devitalized foods (American Group Psychotherapy Association, 1970). The extraordinary proliferation of these groups indicates the existence of a powerful need. Growth centers multiply to such an extent that a popular magazine published a cartoon entitled "Encounter Groups: New Hope for the Post Office." Commercially sold games for use at parties are entitled *Group Therapy*, advertised as "a guide, an excuse, and a structure for frank communication," and *Sensitivity*, advertised as "an experience that can break down the bars of alienation and anxiety."

If a distinction is made between pathology which is characteristic of our culture, and pathology which has arisen because of unique personal difficulties, the value of a highly structured encounter group can be seen more clearly. Most social critics (Maslow, 1968; Fromm, 1941; May, 1969) agree that our society produces a syndrome which does not deviate from social norms but is intrinsically pathological. The syndrome is marked by fear of intimacy and longing for intimacy; difficulty in relating to others without role-playing; and conflicts between assertiveness and dependency. It is a syndrome succinctly described as alienation. A highly structured encounter group can deal with this alienation on a group basis. The ceremonial nature of some group encounter techniques and the way in which they are performed in unison gives many participants a sense of unity with others which is generally lacking in our culture, except for people whose beliefs and temperament enable them to obtain it through membership in a religious congregation. In addition to the longing for this sense of unity, there is also in many people the longing for a transpersonal, spiritual experience. For people in whom this yearning cannot be fulfilled through religion, encounter groups holding out the expectations of peak experience may have a particularly strong attraction. Because highly organized, highly structured group activities can often provide these various values, and because they make it possible to conduct large groups, it is my personal opinion that the usefulness of such activities far outweighs their limitations and potential risks.

These dangers and drawbacks can be minimized if ethical standards for the conduct and leadership of encounter groups, especially marathon encounter groups, are established and recognized. It has been pointed out (Blank, 1969) that at present the demand for encounter groups so far exceeds the supply of trained professional leaders that anyone with minimal experience, obtained at a single workshop or through reading, can offer an encounter group by means of commercial advertising. Some highly experienced group leaders conduct marathons of a hundred people or more, dividing them into subgroups which are led by less experienced assistants, and spending a few hours in turn with each of the subgroups. Since encounter groups are not proffered as psychotherapy, it is difficult to enforce either legal or professional standards of conduct. The establishment of ethical standards must come from within the encounter movement itself. If a group is announced as open to any participant who wishes to attend, any public announcement should include an accurate description of whatever procedures are intended and what they may reasonably be expected to accomplish, without exaggeration. The leader should have sufficient understanding of psychodynamics to recognize and handle any emotional disturbances arising during the session.[9] A qualified psychotherapist should be available to any group member who becomes distressed after the group terminates. All these precautions are triply important if the group is a marathon, which because of its intensity has a higher potential for destructive as well as for constructive experiences.

However, if the purpose of the group is clearly determined in advance, if each group member understands that he is fully responsible for himself, these safeguards may be less important. Some behavioral scientists (Gibb, 1969) are so impressed with the therapeutic potential of the group under these circumstances that they question whether any professional leader is necessary. Leaderless marathon groups are regarded as highly effective in rehabilitation of drug addicts (Yablonsky, 1965). A serious, long-term research study of small-group dynamics resulted in the development of Planned Experiences for Effective Relating (PEER) which is a program of prerecorded audio tapes enabling a group to function without a leader "to help people learn to relate more fully and effec-

[9] The American Psychological Association, the American Psychiatric Association, and the American Group Psychotherapy Association are currently taking under consideration what level of training and experience constitutes an adequate background for the understanding of group and individual dynamics.

tively to the world around them" (Berzon, Reisel, & Davis, 1969). Typically these groups meet for a two-hour session twice a day for five consecutive days. The activities of these groups, as directed by the tape recordings, are carefully planned to allow members complete freedom of choice as to whether or not they will choose to take part in any given activity. This absence of pressure probably minimizes the possibility of emotional disturbance.

Unstructured marathon groups offer considerably more leeway for individual growth and also offer an extraordinary opportunity to observe the ways in which growth takes place. Because my approach is probably representative of most therapists who conduct unstructured marathon groups, and because I have conducted well over 150 groups lasting two days or more, this book (except for chapters contributed by other writers) is based primarily on my own observations, corroborated by taped or written data from participants.

Any comfortable, informal setting will do for a marathon. For two-day groups, my office is used, its floor strewn with cushions. For groups lasting several days, a woodland setting is pleasant and adds the dimension of closeness to natural beauty, which in some participants may evoke a spontaneous peak experience. Coffee and snacks are always available. Some marathon leaders, aware that eating can be used to alleviate anxiety, forbid snacks. My conviction is that there is a greater advantage to offering participants the deeply primitive symbolic communion and security represented by food. Clothing is informal. First names are used. Observers are not permitted.

The group begins at a definite time, usually around noon on Saturday. It ends at a definite time, usually late Sunday afternoon, but makes its own decision as to when to break up for sleep late at night. Members make their own sleeping arrangements, unless the meeting is held in a residential setting.

The question of selecting participants has not, to my knowledge, been experimentally explored by comparing homogeneous with heterogeneous groups. My own impression is that teenagers work best in groups of their peers but otherwise a wide age range is practicable and valuable. An effort is made to select an approximately equal number of men and women, but such variables as diagnosis, occupation, and educational level do not seem relevant. A participant who at first appears below the group's general level of sophistication may make an outstanding contribution before the end. People with deviant approaches to life, such as homosexuals, occasionally inquire anxiously whether they can "fit into" the group; my conviction, based both on marathons and on conventional therapy groups, is that both homosexuals and heterosexuals can benefit by recognizing their similarities and by exploring and accepting their differences. The presence of black participants enriches the group and, unless the group is planned to focus specifically on interracial encounters, most racially mixed groups seem to become almost unaware of color in rather a short time. Similarities between human beings are infinitely greater than differences, and the emotional impact of recognizing these similarities is more powerful in a broadly heterogeneous group.

There is one possible exception: professional psychotherapists often work more spontaneously in a group of their own. This is not because of intellectual or emotional superiority, nor are their personal problems by any means unique. However, an attitude of therapeutic responsibility becomes very deeply ingrained after years of clinical practice. Many therapists, even if they enter a group with a firm intention not to use their professional knowledge as a defense, find themselves unable to refrain from taking a professional attitude if someone in the group becomes distressed. Professional groups usually show at the beginning a slightly greater tendency to overintellectualize, but show little or no difference from other marathons after the first hour or so. Indeed, most therapists are especially quick to note and attack any effort on the part of their colleagues to avoid immediate here-and-now confrontation by defensive intellectualization.

Whether or not a screening interview is indicated depends upon the circumstances. Colleagues often refer a patient who is in concomitant individual psychotherapy, either because treatment has reached a plateau or because the patient needs an opportunity to try out freer and more intimate ways of relating in a permissive setting. Former marathon participants often refer friends or family. Such a recommendation, either by a colleague or by a well-informed layman, is accepted without screening. Otherwise a brief interview or a lengthy telephone conversation is usually sufficient to identify the exceptional individual who is confusedly seeking a sensational adventure, or who seems too fragile to tolerate the challenge of a marathon.

In general, people who comprehend the nature of a marathon are quite capable of deciding for themselves whether or not they have the strength and stamina to meet its emotional and physical demands. In my total experience, by now including over 1,000 participants, only five people have been so overwhelmed by the marathon situation that they left prematurely. One of these was able to return later to another marathon with success; none of them suffered a psychotic episode. Occasionally either my judgment or the judgment of the referral source is overoptimistic, and someone enters a marathon who is thrown into a panic by the emotional pressure. In these cases, the group works very skillfully to provide support and comfort for the frightened member. Thus far, the threatened psychotic break has always been prevented, but at considerable expense to the group itself, whose other members give up their time and energy to the needier participant. It is for the well-being of the group, rather than because of anticipated danger to the fragile individual, that some preliminary screening for marathons is advisable.

If I am working alone, I find that fourteen participants is the maximum number which permits me to feel in contact with all participants, and ten is the minimum number for varied interaction. With a co-therapist, a larger group is practicable.

The sequence of events in a typical marathon has been described as involving first the recognition of social pretenses, next their gradual relinquishment, and finally a deepened acceptance of self and others. This sequence can be further broken down into discernible phases, each of which is seen in the group as a whole although not necessarily in every participant, and each of which requires appropriate modifications of the leader's behavior.

The initial phase is marked by apprehensiveness. If some of the participants are aware of their feelings, and courageous enough to express their anxiety, the group moves toward openness and intimacy quickly, often within the first two hours. More frequently, there is a beginning phase of defensiveness, which in psychoanalytic terms can be seen as a manifestation of characterological defenses, and which in social terms can be seen as clinging to familiar socially stereotyped modes of behavior. Participants inform one another about their work, their family situations, and their problems, but problems are presented for the sake of imparting information rather than with emotional involvement. In response, the participants usually ask for further information, give advice, or offer interpretations. One participant wrote, "I did not know why I was so afraid—of my feelings? Of other people? Or just afraid they wouldn't like me? I had made up my mind to be myself but wasn't sure just what myself might be. Perhaps this is what scared me." It is generally recognized that openness and intimacy are the basic values of a marathon encounter, and the participants have come in search of these values, but their decision does not remove the fear and shyness.

Tension builds. The group is sometimes actually dull for the participants and anxiety-producing for the leader, who also has a social stereotype to maintain—the stereotype of the successful leader. Participants often express irritation at the feeling that time is being wasted and may be openly critical of the leader for not being more directive. It is easy to avoid this arid phase by introducing encounter games at the beginning. My own policy is to avoid this strategem unless the group seems really unable to tolerate the tension. Used as ice-breakers, encounter games undoubtedly relieve tension and provide a sense of intimacy, but in my opinion the apparent relief is only a diversion and the intimacy is an illusion. Until people have some knowledge of one another, it seems to me that the directed exercises of touching hands and telling secrets offers merely a new way to avoid true confrontation, a ritual which may express good will but which is as far from genuine interpersonal contact as are most conventional handshakes. Therefore, unless a group member shows signs of intense anxiety, it is my practice to remain rather passive during the initial period of resistance, except to make clear certain requirements: that the group must function as a group at all times, without one-to-one relationships or "subgrouping"; that social chatter and history taking are not useful; that after the ending of the group any personal data which has been revealed is to be treated confidentially; and that any reaction which one group member has to another is to be expressed openly and directly.

During this same phase, anxiety or uncertainty is often shown about the extent to which physical contact is regarded as appropriate, to which I usually respond by telling the group, casually or humorously, that physical contact is permissible short of murder or sexual intercourse. The purpose of this is not so much to set limitations against activities which presumably would not occur in any case, but rather to reassure participants that they may feel free to engage in physical contact without fearing the loss of self-control, since in our society many people suffer from largely unconscious fears that touching except in highly conventional ways may release uncontrollable impulses. Many other marathon leaders, especially when conducting nude marathons, prefer to set limitations by asking participants to sign a statement in advance that they will not engage in inappropriate sexual activity, a precaution which probably is less important to prevent impulsive sexual behavior than to forestall community criticism.[10]

As others have observed (Rogers, 1969), the first outburst of spontaneous feeling, which may take place very early in the group or be delayed for several hours, is likely to express hostility. We may speculate that this is because hostility is the most precariously repressed drive in our society, because it is used as a defense against the threat of self-revelation, or because (in psychoanalytic terms) a regression is taking place from ego-defensiveness to the earlier anal-sadistic phase of psychosexual development. Most often, the anger breaks through between two group members, but sometimes it is directed toward the therapist and sometimes toward someone altogether outside the group, a family member or co-worker on the job.

Usually this is the first point at which I become active as a leader. Unless several participants have had previous marathon experience, the

[10] At present a few encounter group leaders are privately offering marathon groups in which sexual intercourse, not necessarily between married or previously acquainted couples, is encouraged and facilitated through encounter techniques adapted to suit this purpose. The question of whether or not such groups can be valuable for society or for the individual or might become valuable in the future raises issues which are outside the scope of this book.

group if left to its own devices is likely, in these first hours, to minimize the intensity of the hostility either by seeking further information or else by tacitly trying to persuade the angry participant to be more reasonable. Since insight and self-control rarely occur until after the release of repressed feeling, the goal in dealing with anger in the group is to facilitate its full expression, along with the expression of any accompanying guilt or fear.

When several of the participants have expressed and partly worked through their hostile or competitive feelings, a new atmosphere gradually begins to fill the room. Some of the participants, although not all at the same time, begin to express the most primitive of all human feelings —the longing to be cared for and loved and the terror of being abandoned or destroyed. Childhood memories of pain often emerge, without the self-pity which under other circumstances frequently accompanies descriptions of childhood traumata. Many participants weep, sometimes for their own remembered pain, and sometimes for the grief of others. It is possible to see this phase of the marathon as the consequence of increased trust which has been developing with the increase of intimacy, or as a further regression to the oral-dependency stage of psychosexual development.

After undergoing a full regressive experience of either rage or grief, a participant almost invariably reintegrates his feelings on a mature level. Relief, relaxation, and joy are usually expressed. A participant who has regressed and grown up again is almost certain to show a special understanding of the emotional conflicts of other group members, and a special sensitivity in dealing with them.

The regressive experiences of anger and pain lead naturally to the next phase of the group, in which participants draw physically and emotionally close together, expressing a deep appreciation and acceptance of one another. At this time, during the last few hours, if any participants have remained withdrawn or defensive, the entire group is likely to turn in their direction and work, often with great skill, to help them express whatever they are feeling. At this stage the group itself is such a powerful therapeutic force that it is hardly ever necessary for the leader to intervene in order to protect the withdrawn member or help him preserve his defenses.

In most marathons, and for most participants, there is a sense of radiant intimacy in the group's last few hours. But it is commingled with separation anxiety. The time for breaking up, set in advance, is punctiliously kept, thus giving participants an opportunity to experience a clear-cut separation. My policy is to give warning of the impending break-up about an hour before the time, and to ask for any reactions, especially resentments, which group members may have kept to themselves. They also express feelings about returning to their daily lives, in which zestful anticipation is mixed with apprehensiveness about missing the warmth of the group. The last few minutes are in most groups poignantly beautiful. Participants spontaneously clasp hands, or put their arms around one another in a circle, or embrace in pairs and trios. After these moments of difficulty in parting, the actual separation usually seems easy, and the group members go off briskly.

My policy of passivity at the beginning, and of working with un-expressed resentments and separation anxiety at the end, is typically consistent from one marathon to another. Other leadership activity varies according to the infinite variations of the groups. The events of a mara-thon group, and the demands placed upon its leader, are reminiscent of Freud's comparison of psychoanalysis to chess, in which the endgame and the beginning game can be described, but "the endless variety of the moves which develop from the opening defies description" (Freud, 1933, p. 342). Certain cardinal technical principles can, however, be described.[11]

1. Feedback, or immediate face-to-face interaction, is encouraged. Its purpose is not for group members to exchange criticism in order to help one another alter their social behavior, but rather to facilitate a full and free exchange of feeling.

Group members are asked not to speak about how they feel about one another but to tell one another directly. They may be asked to gaze unwaveringly at the person to whom they speak, or cross the room and place a hand upon his shoulder, in order to reduce emotional distance. They may be asked to communicate feelings without words, but only through sounds or gestures.

Nonverbal communication is used in many ways. As an example, the technique of arm-wrestling is invaluable in dealing with conflicts center-ing around fear of competitiveness, difficulties in expressing hostility, and fears of physical contact, and also greatly heightens the spontaneity of interpersonal relating.

2. There is a continual focus on the here-and-now. If anyone speaks of someone outside the group, in past or present tense, an effort is made to bring the feelings directly into the room.

"You're talking *about* your mother. Talk *to* her. Pretend she's sitting in that chair. What will you say?"

"Who here can represent your mother? Then talk to her."

Here are two different approaches to the task of bringing the par-ticipant closer to his feelings for and about his mother. The former approach is taken from Gestalt therapy, the latter from psychodrama. In general it would seem that the Gestalt method might be preferable for

[11] The work of Perls (1969), Moreno (1946), and Schutz (1967) was most in-fluential in the development of these principles. Further examples of their applica-tion are given throughout the book. Chapter 3 offers an extended description of encounter games.

someone who tends to avoid experiencing his own feelings by turning attention to the world outside, and the psychodramatic method preferable for someone who tends to avoid confronting outside reality by turning his attention constantly inward.

Complex memories, fantasies, and dreams can be turned into scenarios to help focus on the here-and-now. A man who has never been able to mourn the death of his father, and who consequently suffers from a persistent sense of loss, is finally able to cry with great relief when he goes through the drama of visiting his father's grave and talking to his dead father, in the presence of the group. A girl who is phobic about becoming ill and requiring hospitalization enacts a traumatic surgical operation to which she was subjected as a child, with group members playing auxiliary roles, and reports a noticeable diminution of the phobia.

Every therapist, not only the contemporary experientialist but also the classical psychoanalyst (for example, Fenichel, 1941, p. 20), is aware that a patient may escape from immediate feelings by speaking of his childhood; conversely, he may avoid dealing with painful episodes from his past by concentrating on the immediate situation. By bringing material from the past or from the outside world into the here-and-now of the group, it is possible to facilitate the integration of an individual's past experience with his present self.

3. General characterological attitudes toward the self and toward others are translated whenever possible into interaction with the group, often involving the physical representation of the attitude. Generalizations are made specific by this means; impulses and their corresponding defenses become clearer; and self-awareness is heightened. The procedure of going around the group, relating to each member in turn, is particularly effective here, and there is an infinite variety of possible applications.

A participant who speaks about one of his attitudes toward other people may be asked to demonstrate it in the group. Thus, a man who says that he has a problem of becoming easily irritated is asked to go around the group and say to each member "You irritate me because . . ." finishing the sentence in accordance with his feelings toward each individual member.

A participant may be asked to exaggerate a trait which he regards as a problem. Thus a woman who complains of being diffident is asked to go around and behave in an extremely shy, fearful way toward each group member. By becoming aware of her different reactions to different types of people in the group, she may gain increased understanding of what situations elicit her shyness and may also increase her control over the shy behavior by this conscious caricature.

A participant may be asked to act out an attitude which has been observed by the group but of which he is unaware. Thus a man who is perceived as domineering and is unaware of this behavior may be requested to relate in a domineering way to each member. When he tries consciously to be domineering, he may identify the elements in his manner which are perceived by others in this way.

A participant who is afraid of a certain kind of interaction may be requested to act it out on a physical level. Thus someone who is afraid of being let down by others may be asked to face this fear in literal terms by falling backward and being caught by another participant, or by permitting himself to be lifted and held by the group.

A characteristic way of relating to others can sometimes be translated into bodily movement. A young man typically went halfway to form a relationship and then drew back. He was asked to approach each member in turn, wait until he felt an impulse to relate to them nonverbally, act it out halfway, and then draw back. He discovered that toward most of the group members he felt an impulse toward an affectionate embrace which was mingled with an impulse to slap or strike them. We inferred that this ambivalence, of which he had been only dimly aware until it was experienced physically, was a factor in preventing him from becoming emotionally close to anyone.

A participant may be asked to act out a way of relating to others which is the exact opposite of his habitual way. Thus a woman participant who is ordinarily hypersensitive about the possibility of hurting someone's feelings, to the point where she has difficulty in being natural, is asked to go around and make a cutting, rejecting comment to each group member. The assumption here is that her anxiety about hurting someone else is a characterological defense against unconscious hurtful impulses, in accordance with the psychoanalytic theory of reaction formation. By acting out the repressed impulse, she may become aware of it and gradually bring it under conscious control.

4. If a participant is dealing with some personal problem, an effort is made to involve other group members, or the group as a whole, whenever possible. In any activity, such as the going-around procedure, after the central figure has expressed himself adequately, other group members are asked to share their responses to him. Often their empathic experiences are deeply meaningful even though they have not expressed their feelings overtly.

5. If a participant goes through a cathartic emotional experience, such as often happens after a scenario, or acts out an attitude toward himself or others, as in going-around, an effort is made to help him understand the experience and integrate it on a cognitive level. Most participants verbalize the meaning of such an experience with minimal help from the leader. If they do not do so, a sentence or two either from myself or from another participant is usually all that is necessary.

"Now can you see why you've been unwilling to visit your mother?"

This participant, in talking to a mother surrogate in the group, found himself expressing anger of which he had not been previously aware. He had been avoiding his mother in order not to express the anger which would have made him feel guilty over hurting her feelings.

"You're like me—you're afraid to face the pain. So you close up." This is the man who was finally able to cry over his father's death, speaking to another group member who also was avoiding the grief of mourning. Participants often deepen their own self-understanding in trying to help other participants.

"Well, you were nasty and sarcastic, and nobody dropped dead." The young woman who was asked to act out her repressed hostility, which she had concealed behind an oversolicitude about hurting others, was greatly relieved after she had forced herself to make a biting remark to each member of the circle. Several participants commented that she actually seemed more real and likeable after she abandoned her air of sweetness. The experience, with my concluding comment, demonstrated that her hostility was not actually capable of destroying its target.

In these procedures of the unstructured marathon, the individual participant in one way or another takes the initiative by speaking of a feeling or a problem or a wish. The group as a whole is never guided toward the exploration of any specific area. Nor is a participant required to engage in any encounter which he wishes to decline. However, an effort is made to explore the reasons why he chooses to decline that particular encounter, an approach adapted from the psychoanalytic technique of resistance analysis.

Perhaps the greatest value of the unstructured marathon, as opposed to one directed by the leader, is that most participants, with or without professional background in psychodynamics, become deeply and genuinely helpful to one another, and frequently show extraordinary creative ability in dealing with one another's conflicts. Reassurance and advice, which characterize the initial defensive phase, give way to empathy. A circuit is thus established within the group; ideally, each participant not only undergoes the experience of feeling accepted for his real self by the others but also obtains the satisfaction of knowing that he is capable of offering them help on a meaningful, mature level.

REFERENCES

Alexander, E. From play-therapy to the encounter marathon. *Psychotherapy: Theory, Research and Practice,* Summer 1969.

American Group Psychotherapy Association, *Conference program,* 1970.

Bach, G. R. The marathon group: Intensive practice of intimate interactions. *Psychological Reports,* Vol. 18, 1966.

Berzon, B., Reisel, J., & Davis, D. P. PEER: An audio-tape program for self-directed small groups. *Journal of Humanistic Psychology,* Spring 1969.

Bindrim, P. Facilitating peak experiences. In H. Otto & J. Mann (Eds.), *Ways of growth.* New York: Grossman, 1968.

Bindrim, P. The nude marathon. *Psychotherapy: Theory, Research and Practice,* September 1968.

Blanchard, W. H. Ecstasy without agony is baloney. *Psychology Today,* January 1970.

Blank, L. *The use and misuse of sensitivity and other groups.* Paper presented at 1969 convention, American Psychological Association.

Fenichel, O. Problems of psychoanalytic technique. *The Psychoanalytic Quarterly,* Albany, 1941.

Fenichel, O. *The psychoanalytic theory of neurosis.* New York: W. W. Norton, 1945.

Freud, S. *Collected papers.* Vol. II. London: Hogarth Press, 1950.

Fromm, E. *Escape from freedom.* New York: Holt, Rinehart, & Winston, 1941.

Gibb, J. R., & Gibb, L. M. Emergence therapy. In G. M. Gazda (Ed.), *Innovations to group therapy.* Springfield, Ill.: Charles C Thomas, 1968.

Israel Magazine, Vol. 1, No. 8, Philadelphia, Pa.

Laing, R. D. *The politics of experience.* New York: Pantheon, 1967.

Lamott, K. Marathon therapy is a psychological pressure cooker. *New York Times Magazine,* 13 July 1969.

Maslow, A. H. *Religious values and peak-experiences.* Columbus: Ohio State University Press, 1964.

Maslow, A. H. *Toward a psychology of being.* Princeton: Van Nostrand, 1968.

May, R. Love and will. *Psychology Today,* August 1969.

Mintz, E. E. Time-extended marathon groups. *Psychotherapy: Theory, Research and Practice,* May 1967.

Mintz, E. E. Marathon groups: A preliminary evaluation. *Journal of Contemporary Psychology,* Winter 1969.

Mintz, E. E. Therapy techniques and encounter techniques. *American Journal of Psychotherapy,* January 1971.

Moreno, J. L. *Psychodrama.* New York: Beacon House, 1946.

NTL Institute, *News and Reports,* November 1969.

Perls, F. S. *Gestalt therapy verbatim.* Lafayette, Calif.: Real People Press, 1969.

Rogers, C. The group comes of age. *Psychology Today,* December 1969.

Schutz, W. *Joy.* New York: Grove Press, 1967.

Slavson, S. R. Speech presented to American Group Psychotherapy Association, February, 1968.

Stoller, F. H. Marathon group therapy. In G. M. Gazda (Ed.), *Innovations to group therapy.* Springfield, Ill.: Charles C Thomas, 1968.

Yablonsky, L. *Synanon: The tunnel back.* Baltimore: Pelican, 1967.

2 THE PATH TOWARD MARATHONS

The encounter marathon of today is closely related to the spirit and thought of humanism. As a philosophy, humanism emphasizes the values of love, creativity, and self-fulfillment which is viewed as including an active concern for the welfare of society as well as for the self and which also implies an awareness of values transcending the search for immediate material satisfaction. As psychology, humanism departs from the nineteenth-century mechanistic model of the human being and from the attention to pathology rather than health which characterized traditional psychology. Instead, humanistic psychology (although it has by no means abandoned the tools of scientific research) views man as striving toward self-fulfillment rather than merely toward comfort; as essentially responsible for the direction of his own fate; and as potentially capable of using the technological knowledge of today in the interests of mankind as a whole.[1]

It is important to recognize the basic humanistic orientation of the encounter marathon because, historically speaking, its format and techniques grew principally from various efforts to resolve social or individual pathology. Although individual pathology can often be recognized and dealt with appropriately in an encounter marathon, these groups increasingly appear as a growth experience rather than solely as a corrective therapeutic experience. Nevertheless, their historical development goes back to interpersonal sensitivity training as pioneered by the National Training Laboratories in an effort to approach social problems more effectively; and to several innovative approaches to psychotherapy, including group therapy in its various forms, Gestalt theory and techniques, and the utilization of nonverbal communication. To this I would emphatically add, though many psychoanalysts and encounter group leaders would differ, the understanding of unconscious factors in the human psyche which sprang originally from Freudian psychoanalytic theory.

My own professional life experience and the shaping of my approach

---

[1] Readers are referred to the *Journal of Humanistic Psychology*, founded in 1961; to *Manas*, a weekly review of contemporary thought and literature; and in general to the work of Erich Fromm, Rollo May, Abraham Maslow, and Carl Rogers.

to encounter groups has included direct contact with these influences. In some respects, I believe that the evolution of my thinking is representative of a general movement in psychology toward humanism. Hence I shall emphasize those aspects of its development with which I have had personal experience. My professional biography, I believe, in many respects typifies the experience of other psychologists who now find themselves at home in the humanistic movement.

From my academic work toward the doctorate in clinical psychology at New York University, I recall little or no recognition of the existence of group psychotherapy, although in the late 1940s its development was well under way.[2] Indeed, in those years training in clinical psychology was focussed primarily upon research and diagnosis. Many psychologists and most physicians regarded psychotherapy as treatment for disorders of the brain and nervous system, hence it was viewed as a branch of medicine in which nonmedical people should not engage except perhaps under close medical supervision.

To some extent this question (discussed in *Professional Psychology*, Winter, 1970) still exists, as indicated by the reluctance of many psychoanalytic institutes to train candidates other than psychiatrists. Humanistic psychology, however, is almost entirely free from interdisciplinary controversy. Among its well-known figures, Frederick Perls came from psychiatry; Abraham Maslow, Carl Rogers, and William Schutz from psychology; and Virginia Satir from social work. The American Academy of Psychotherapists accepts people who have been well trained in psychotherapy regardless of theoretical orientation or disciplinary background, as does the American Group Psychotherapy Association. To me, it seems primarily a historical accident that psychoanalysis is in general identified with the medical tradition, while behavior therapy is associated with learning theory and is usually identified with psychology.

However, until the last two decades, advanced training in psychotherapy had to be sought by psychologists primarily from private groups. My own training, focussed upon psychoanalytic theory and technique, was with the National Psychological Association for Psychoanalysis (NPAP) in New York City. This was a controversial group because it trained nonmedical candidates, basing its right to do so upon an explicit statement of Freud (1927). Thus, indirectly, NPAP was related to the trend of thought which regards emotional disturbances as consisting of difficulties in living rather than as a disease entity (Szasz, 1961; Laing, 1967). Paradoxically, the medical model was nevertheless followed at NPAP, in that the psychoanalyst was regarded mainly as an impersonal expert upon whose technical skill the patient's cure depended.

---

[2] A comprehensive account of the historical, scientific, and philosophical background of the development of group therapy is found in Durkin (1964).

Yet to an extraordinary extent, as I hope to show, many essential psychoanalytic concepts are directly applicable to the understanding of what happens in an encounter group. Freud's great central contribution, his discovery of the extent to which behavior and conscious feelings are influenced by unconscious feelings and ideas, is relevant throughout each marathon group for every individual. The social masks which participants wear when the group begins, which they gradually doff with apprehension and relief and finally delight, were not really assumed on the basis of a conscious awareness of what society expects. They were donned and retained primarily on the basis of childhood experiences, many of which were repressed from awareness, which have left all of us still somewhat afraid of being punished for "wrong" impulses or behavior even though the fear is no longer realistic. In the free-association technique of traditional psychoanalysis, these fears are manifested by reluctance to speak freely. In a marathon encounter group, the same fears (sometimes conscious, sometimes unconscious) are manifested by a reluctance to engage in self-expression and spontaneous exchanges of feeling. The neutral and permissive attitude of the psychoanalyst is regarded as intrinsic to the therapeutic process; similarly, the warm although not neutral acceptance of the group (usually though not invariably extended to each participant as times goes on) is an essential part of the value of the marathon for growth and healing.

Other basic concepts of Freudian theory are so universally valid and lend themselves so well to flexible application both in working with people and in understanding personality, that they can be recognized, though in different terminology, in the theoretical formulations of many group therapists. The familiar Freudian division of personality into the three systems of ego, id, and superego is paralleled by Berne's more easily understandable terms of the Adult, the Child, and the Parent (1966). Schutz (1958), who has logically integrated Freudian concepts with group dynamics, sees needs which emerge in the group as involving inclusion, which corresponds to Freud's state of oral dependency; control, which corresponds to Freud's anal phase of development; and affection, corresponding to the Oedipal and genital phases.[3]

Transference, in the sense of distorted perception of others, is clearly visible in groups, as members misperceive other members initially, often on the basis of subtle resemblances to childhood figures. Oedipal rivalries, fears, and wishes appear with transparent clearness. Specific defense mechanisms, such as repression, projection, and denial, appear at least as

---

[3] Even within the psychoanalytic tradition, I believe that today most clinicians tend to view the oral, anal, and Oedipal stages of the original libido theory as referring to ways of relating to other people developed at certain stages of biological development, rather than as referring to the shifting of sexual excitation from one body zone to another.

clearly in the lively interaction of the group as in free association on the analyst's couch. In particular, an understanding of regression (see Chapter 4) seems to me invaluable when working in depth with an unstructured group.

What I could never accept in Freudian theory, and what indeed is rejected today even by most traditional psychoanalysts, is the image of man as a being who essentially strives for the reduction of tension, the "Nirvana principle" (Fenichel, 1945). Anyone who has ever seen a baby clap its hands or ecstatically take its first steps must recognize that there is a human delight in activity simply for the joy in feeling alive. Nor could I ever accept the implicit autism of the classical instinct theory, which looks upon relationships between people primarily as means by which various physiologically determined instincts can be directly or indirectly gratified. Clinical observations and personal experience seem abysmally far away from this approach, unless the instinct theory is broadened to denote an instinctual need to relate to other human beings, as the British ego-psychologists maintain (Fairbairn, 1952; Guntrip, 1961).

A more specific concept of psychoanalysis, which is of both theoretical usefulness and immediate practical value in dealing with group phenomena, is the discovery that the infant perceives his mother alternately as a good, tender, caretaking mother goddess, and as an evil, depriving, destructive mother witch. In several of the following chapters, I describe the fantastic rage which a marathon participant may feel in perceiving me as the incarnation of the witch, which is transformed into a perception of me as kind and motherly after the anger is expressed. Without my rigorous psychoanalytic training, it seems to me that it would have been difficult for me to accept, and use for therapeutic gain, the violent reactions of rage, resentment, and exaggerated admiration which come my way in a marathon—in their intensity far beyond anything I ever experienced in conducting individual psychoanalysis.

A convincing application of this psychoanalytic discovery, in relation to the dynamics of the total group, has been made by Durkin (1964, Chapter VII). She points out that, at its beginning, the group as a whole is likely to be perceived by individual members as threatening and suggests that this anxiety arises because, in an intimate but new situation, the participant unconsciously views his unexplored new world of people as the cruel and rejecting mother. This hypothesis is based on the assumption that the combination of unfamiliarity and intimacy brings about a regression to the misperceptions of infancy. It would account for the apprehensiveness which almost everyone feels at the beginning of a marathon, even people who have undergone rewarding experiences in previous marathons, and even people who usually possess considerable social poise.

It still seems to me that psychoanalytic theory, if the contributions of contemporary ego-psychologists are included, offers in general the most useful theoretical framework within which to study personality. However, like some other psychoanalysts and like many of the younger clinicians, I soon became discontented with the mystique of the couch, the many-times-a-week sessions, the prescribed impersonality of the analyst, and especially the quasi-religious attitudes of some of my colleagues toward psychoanalysis as a goal in itself rather than a method of treatment.[4] At case conferences, where the presenting analyst discussed a patient, the remark "But you're not really doing analysis" was an implied slight, which could best be forestalled by the preliminary acknowledgement, "Of course, I realize that I'm not really doing analysis." Theodor Reik, the founder of NPAP,[5] taught the value of a flexible, intuitive contact between analyst and patient, but among some colleagues I found attitudes which at times seemed a debasement and almost a caricature of what Freud had originally taught.

At times the mechanical application of psychoanalytic formulae seemed to lead away from emotional fulfillment rather than toward it. There was, for example, the myth of the "completely analyzed person" who could no longer be disturbed by emotional conflicts. There was an exaggerated attention to verbal communication which often impressed me as quibbling; for example, it was seriously proposed that a patient whose favorite store was Macy's was probably a voyeur (may see). Some colleagues considered it resistance if the patient moved on the couch, instead of confining his activities to free association, and if he turned his head to look at the analyst. A control analyst with whom I worked for a short time rebuked me for accepting daffodils brought to me by a young woman who, as a child, had never been able to express affection toward her mother. This patient's gift was seen by me as an experiment in giving, but I was told that the gift should have been declined on the grounds that the patient must know the impropriety of offering gifts to her analyst, hence she was really showing hostility and not affection.

Not only was the patient required to accept a completely impersonal analytic situation, but the analyst was expected not to express feelings toward the patient, and indeed not even to have such feelings. The ideal analyst, one of my colleagues said in all seriousness, would be a

---

[4] Since the following observation is not substantiated by research but is based only on personal experience, it must be made tentatively: I am impressed by the frequency with which marathon participants recover repressed memories or experience an intense catharsis of repressed feelings, after failing to achieve these results in long periods of traditional psychoanalysis. At the same time, it should be reiterated that, as psychotherapy, marathon experience seems most effective for people who have undergone individual treatment, even if this has been only partially effective.

[5] With whom I had the privilege of working for several years in a small private seminar, under the auspices of Dr. Ruth P. Berkeley.

computer. Another colleague, supervising the work of younger therapists, maintained that counter-transference was never an appropriate
topic for discussion in supervision, which should deal exclusively with
technical procedures. If the analyst had personal feelings toward the
patient, it was an indication of unresolved emotional problems, for which
the only remedy was that the analyst himself must return for further
analytic treatment. Later, when I myself became a supervisor, one of
my first students presented a problem to me. With some embarrassment,
she said "I think I have some trouble here. I think I have a counter-transference."

"What do you mean?"

"Well, I . . . I . . . I *like* this patient!"

All this, it seemed to me, created a situation in which the autism
and inner loneliness from which most patients were already suffering
must be exacerbated rather than healed. I shared this viewpoint with colleagues, many of whom agreed, and we acknowledged to one another
that we no longer sought to maintain the blank-screen detachment we
had been taught.[6] Other colleagues suggested that I had not acquired sufficient self-discipline to maintain the requisite psychoanalytic impersonality (which was quite true) and that therefore I was "incompletely
analyzed" (which was also true) and should seek further treatment.

In those same years, other therapeutic viewpoints were being developed. Rogers was advancing his concept that the therapist's "uncon-
ditional positive regard" for the patient was the essential curative factor
(1961). The experiential school was maintaining that effective therapy
required a mutually spontaneous interaction between therapist and
patient (Whittaker & Malone, 1953). Some writers went so far as to advocate complete self-revelation by the therapist (Jourard, 1964), in the
conviction that the patient, now usually called a client, would thereby
learn the courage to reveal himself in turn.

At that time I had little personal contact with these other viewpoints and was able to work out for myself the principles which I still
seek to follow in individual and group therapy and also in conducting
marathons. Therapy, as I see it, is intrinsically a one-sided relationship.
Anyone who comes to me, whether for treatment or for the life experience of a marathon, is seeking for personal growth or help and is
paying a fee, not only for my specialized knowledge but for my time and
attention. Therefore I seek to reveal my own feelings, and to share my

---

[6] Of course, not all psychoanalysts working in the classical tradition apply the
blank-screen formula. Racker (1968, p. 31), for example, writes "Freud's counsel that
the analyst should be a 'mirror' has . . . been carried to an extreme. Freud gives
this advice against the habit, prevalent among some analysts of the early period, of
relating facts of their own life to patients. 'Be a mirror' thus meant 'speak to the
patient only of himself.' It did not mean 'stop being of flesh and blood and transform
yourself into glass covered with silver nitrate.' . . . For only Eros can originate Eros."

own experiences, only insofar as in my judgment they will be helpful in the therapeutic situation. Often I am completely spontaneous in my reactions to the people with whom I am working. But if I am struggling with boredom or antagonism or irritation toward an individual patient or a marathon participant, this may well be a reflection of my own personal problems, hence I do not necessarily express these feelings. Only when it seems essential to the maintenance of an intimate relationship with a patient or with a marathon participant, do I share my own emotional problems. I am free to laugh with patients, and sometimes to cry with them, but I do not ask them to weep with me over my personal griefs; I acknowledge that there are problems both in my external life and in myself, but I do not seek to use the therapeutic relationship to solve them.

Because I wish to integrate this theoretical discussion of the patient-therapist relationship with examples of how transference reactions can develop even when the real personality of the therapist is disclosed, I shall skip ahead chronologically and offer examples taken from a later period, when I was offering combined group therapy and individual treatment, and from my past six years as a marathon leader.

It is my conviction that the therapist's willingness to behave naturally actually facilitates and illuminates the development of transference reactions, rather than inhibiting them. This is especially true in a group. If a group member expresses a reaction toward me which seems transferential, it can be checked out against the perceptions of the other members.

In one ongoing therapy group, to my amusement and amazement, I was simultaneously perceived by one young woman member as a rigid, inhibited, asexual person who "would never wear perfume" and by another as a "dizzy dame who must have got her Ph.D. by smiling at professors." Had I maintained an air of consistent aloofness, I do not believe that either of these reactions (both of which eventually proved useful in helping the women understand their own projections) could have been voiced and perhaps would not even have been evoked.

Especially in marathon groups, it would be impossible for me not to reveal my own personality even if I sought to be reserved. Yet in marathon groups I have elicited and worked through, on many occasions, transference reactions of a depth and intensity which I do not recall from any individual session. This is in part due to the prolonged time extension, which in a single weekend allows the development and working through of a transference distortion; and in part due to the presence of the group, which provides peer support and thereby diminishes fear of rejection, punishment, or excessive dependency upon the leader.

Two examples of unmistakable Oedipal transference reactions to me can be offered. With dramatic clarity, they show how unconscious childhood attitudes can emerge and be worked through even in a setting where there is considerable social and personal interaction. Both Alice and Gordon, with whom these episodes occurred, were in treatment with me on an individual basis in addition to attending marathons, but similar episodes have occurred many times with marathon participants whom I was not seeing for individual therapy.

Alice was a woman in her middle forties. Attractive and successful, she was nevertheless hampered in both her personal and her professional life by a deep self-defeating attitude which was related to her identification with her pathetic, masochistic mother and her fear of being treated by men as she had been treated by her overbearing father. She chose me as her therapist, she told me, because she had met me at a professional gathering where I was wearing bright clothes and was evidently enjoying myself, in direct contrast to her self-denying mother. She had two goals: she wanted a doctoral degree, which she had been unable to acquire despite her general capability; and she wanted to marry, which she had been unable to do despite her ability to attract and enjoy men.[7] In treatment with a previous analyst, she had almost been persuaded that her age made both of these goals unrealistic and that she must relinquish them. Here is Alice's written account of her marathon experience:

> At one of the marathons in which I participated, there was a man to whom I felt drawn and impelled to establish a relationship. I didn't know why at the time but something kept me feeling this way. Then I realized that in spite of his arrogance and pomposity I still liked him. I also saw through this to his vulnerability and realized that this combination of qualities was what I had seen in my father. I was drawn to what I had known as a child. Through this man I was able to get to feelings of hurt and rejection I had as a little girl toward my father and was able now to verbalize these feelings.
>
> Near the end of the marathon this man (who also was a therapist) said "You've been a little girl long enough. Why don't you come over here and relate to me as a woman." I went to him, sat on his lap, but couldn't get beyond the little girl. It appeared that there was still a residue of feeling toward my father that I couldn't reach.

Alice, seated on Robert's lap, looked stiff and childish and embarrassed. She had already expressed her feeling that he represented her father; but as a psychoanalyst I knew that the Oedipal conflict, which we had discussed frequently in her individual sessions, involved not only fear of incest with the father but fear of being punished by the mother. And I knew also that, despite our peer relationship on a professional and

[7] Alice's history has an over-the-rainbow ending, which does *not* invariably occur in the combination of individual therapy and frequent attendance at marathons which I now believe to be the treatment of choice for most people. In the course of about four years of individual sessions, plus six marathons, she obtained her doctorate, and she later married a man who was extremely congenial and devoted.

social level, she must also unconsciously see me as mother. I said "Let's see what happens if I leave," and walked out of the room.

Waiting in the adjacent room, I heard somebody in the group say "Wow!" and then heard friendly laughter. For several minutes, I remained away. When I returned, Alice was embracing Robert in a way which stopped short of actual sexual foreplay, but which was unmistakably sensual on an adult level. After the embrace, Robert and Alice both told us that the instant I left the room, she had become sexually responsive to him, and Alice wrote:

> To my astonishment, since consciously I had never seen Elizabeth as forbidding, I felt different the moment she was gone. As soon as she was out of the room, I was able to relate to Robert as a woman.

This episode opened up a whole new area of awareness about her relationship to her mother as a factor in her difficulties with men,[8] which we worked through in individual treatment.

The episode of Gordon occurred during a four-day marathon conducted in a woodland setting, where we all danced and swam together when we were not working. Gordon in certain ways resembled Alice. He functioned adequately both in business and with women, but he was unable to commit himself to marriage. An early marriage had ended after a year, and while he wished consciously to marry again and have a family, he always found himself withdrawing from a girl if the relationship became prolonged and intimate. In treatment with a previous analyst, and also in his individual sessions with me, Gordon had learned that to him every woman represented his mother, but this remained an intellectual understanding rather than an emotional reality. He was tortured by an obsession to think of a woman as "little whore" in moments of sexual intimacy but could not relate this to his Oedipal bitterness about the sexual relationship of his parents.

In the rustic lodge, we were all seated on the floor, wearing country clothes. As Gordon described it in a letter:

> The marathon was a day and a half old and I had been somewhat out of things. I was somewhat depressed and withdrawn. Elizabeth was working with Ann, whom I like, and I was watching them intensively. Then I noticed Elizabeth's red underpants and red bra under the sheer blouse which she was wearing. I associated the red undergarments with a whore and it was as if something snapped in my head. I became very agitated. Oh, yes, I realized the next day that my mother's name is also Ann. When Ann finished working out her thing, I could hardly wait. I began

---

[8] Robert did not wish to be unfaithful to his wife, hence his relationship with Alice did not continue after the marathon. As observed elsewhere, inappropriate sexual relationships rarely develop as a result of marathon intimacy.

talking. I can't recall exactly what I said in the beginning but after a short time I began screaming, crying, and vomiting. It was a strange experience in that I could hear myself shouting and fully comprehend what I was saying and was also more or less aware of my surroundings. . . .

It was a strange experience for me too. Gordon was a warm but overintellectual man who tended to be overly self-controlled. I had observed his restlessness and agitation before his outbreak but did not expect his abrupt, anguished shout:

"Elizabeth is a whore! ELIZABETH IS A WHORE!"

He shouted this repeatedly. Someone offered him a pillow, and he began banging on it, shouting "Whore, whore, whore!" After a few minutes he began to cry and shout "Mother, mother, whore, mother, mother!" He left the room, vomited, and returned somewhat shaken but able to discuss the episode coherently. As always happens when irrational transferential rage is fully expressed, his attitude toward me again became rational and friendly. We all recognized that Gordon had been expressing unconscious feelings toward his mother. During the rest of the marathon, Gordon related to me without tension or embarrassment, and in our individual sessions subsequently we were able to explore his Oedipal feelings more fully.

Gordon's account concludes:

The really strange part of this experience was that I did not will the words that came out — I knew it was me but I felt no control over what I said. After it was over I felt that I had been through almost a mystical experience. Until that time I had seen other people go through similar things but I sort of felt it was at least partly theatrical. I now know better. That explosion was something I was ready for. I was at a point where my confusion/dichotomy of mother, whore, therapist, lover, mother, feelings for Elizabeth were all ready to surface. That incident moved me toward being able to understand my mixed feelings about my mother and also about women in general.

The unconscious determinants of this episode were all the clearer because, on a conscious level, Gordon had never perceived either me or his mother, who was actually a conventional Jewish housewife, as a whore, nor did he select sexual partners who might reasonably have been perceived in this way. Gordon's distressing symptom of thinking "little whore" during sexual intercourse disappeared soon afterward.

From these contrasting episodes, in one of which I was perceived as a forbidding mother and in the other as a whore, it seems clear that even when the therapist makes no effort to be a blank screen, unconscious determinants of transference reactions can emerge and be worked through with therapeutic profit.

In keeping with my increasing conviction that therapeutic progress is not stimulated but hampered by the therapist's impersonality, I soon began to abandon the traditional taboo against any bodily contact between therapist and patient. This ban, so sweeping and so absolute as to be properly termed a taboo, was occasionally transgressed even by classical psychoanalysts but, when reported in the literature, was usually presented as a noteworthy exception. An authoritative statement (Menninger, 1958, p. 40) is that "transgressions of the rule against physical contact constitute . . . evidence of the incompetence or criminal ruthlessness of the analyst."

One of the first physical contacts in my practice was with a young woman who had spent several periods of her life working as a prostitute, and who suffered intense masochistic shame when she spoke of it. It became my habit, when she spoke of these episodes, to lay my hand lightly on her shoulder or put my arm around her when she left the office. The gesture seemed completely right and natural to me, and it still seems to me that without this reassurance she might well have left treatment. Yet, when I discussed her case at a small seminar with colleagues, several of them told me gently that if I had said to her "I feel like hugging you to reassure you," without actually doing so, the same purpose could have been served without violation of a taboo.

Other colleagues, especially in discussing possible physical contact between a male therapist and a female patient, feared that any violation of the taboo would inevitably lead to complete sexual gratification—an anxiety which bespeaks extraordinarily little respect for the therapist's wisdom or self-control.[9] Then, as now, it seemed to me that under some circumstances touch is actually essential: as symbolic mothering (which can be offered by either a man or a woman) when the patient is overwhelmed by infantile feelings and is unable to speak; to restore awareness of the external world when this awareness is threatened; and to convey acceptance when the patient is tormented by self-loathing, as with the young woman who had been a prostitute. Since conducting marathons, I have also become comfortable with touch as a natural means of communication; and occasionally my individual patient and I may express our mutual satisfaction with an especially worthwhile session, or share our mutual sadness if a session has dealt with basic human griefs, with a farewell embrace.

In general, however, it still seems to me that far more therapeutic

---

[9] It has sometimes been openly recommended that therapist and patient engage in full sexual intimacy if it is deemed advisable by the therapist (McCartney, 1966). It is well known that surreptitious sexual episodes do occur. Since the patient is paying a fee for a relationship dedicated to his welfare, and since healthy sexuality requires a fully mutual relationship, these episodes seem to involve a basic ethical contradiction (Mintz, 1969).

use can be made of physical contact in marathons than in an individual session. In a marathon, I may sit for a long time in embrace with a patient who longs for mothering, or scuffle physically with a patient who needs to express competitiveness or to find out that his mother-symbol is not easily destroyed. Both the participant and myself are protected by the presence of the group against our conscious or unconscious fears of violence, inappropriate sexuality, or infantile dependency. As in any situation, I offer affection only when I feel it. Insincerity would be sensed intuitively by most patients and would in many instances resemble childhood experiences of feeling bewildered as to whether or not parental affection was genuine.[10]

Group therapy, which I began to offer my patients as an adjunct treatment in the late 1950s, was of course an important precursor of the encounter marathon of today. In those years, the clinical approach to individual psychotherapy was carried over to group therapy almost intact, and there was considerable preoccupation with such questions as the appropriateness of group treatment for patients of various diagnostic categories; what types of people according to their diagnostic categories would work well together in a group; whether combined group and individual treatment interfered with the development of transference; and whether group therapy could or could not be considered psychoanalysis (Wolf & Schwartz, 1962). In many groups, the traditional aloofness of the psychoanalyst was also carried over; some group therapists sat behind their desks and maintained the "blank screen" attitude; others forbade any physical touching in the group, however casual, as "acting out"; still others forbade patients to have any personal contact whatever outside the group situation.[11] Groups customarily followed the pattern of meeting once a week for a session lasting 1½ hours, but Wolf and Schwartz (1962), Asya Kadis at the Postgraduate Institute in New York, and others developed the principle of the "alternate session," in which the group members met alternately without their therapist. Since the principal value of the alternate session was thought to be the increased freedom with which group members could express themselves without the presence of the therapist, the alternate session probably came into being essentially through recognition of the need to move away from the formal and constrained atmosphere of the traditional psychoanalytic group.

Meanwhile, various experimenters and theoreticians were making

---

[10] Chapter 9 discusses more fully the relationships between personal self-expression and responsible marathon leadership. Chapters 3 through 8 offer many examples of meaningful physical contact among group participants.

[11] Personal communications from several colleagues describe a contemporary group therapist in New York as placing a total ban on any communication outside the group. Social conversations in the elevator leaving his office are forbidden. There was an injunction against visits to the hospital to see a group member who became ill.

contributions which, even for practitioners who did not have direct contact with these men, affected in some way everyone who was involved in group therapy. J. J. Moreno, who first became interested in studying group dynamics while working with prostitutes in Vienna during World War I (Durkin, p. 324), developed the technique of psychodrama, in which role-playing by group members is used to facilitate insight and catharsis for the individual and empathic identification for the other members of the group. Moreno's method is well assimilated today by most eclectic group therapists and is taught formally in several institutions,[12] but when it was first introduced many analytic group therapists, among them Slavson, questioned whether it could properly be regarded as psychotherapy at all (Durkin, p. 325).

Among my special interests as a group therapist was an approach which has been found well suited to marathons: leadership by a male-female co-therapist team. This approach was opposed by some group therapists, who, in the classical psychoanalytic tradition, were concerned about the possibility that the development of a pure transference would be contaminated, split, or diluted by the presence of two therapists (Slavson, 1960). In view of the fact that human beings are usually reared by two parents, a situation which is symbolically repeated by the presence of a man and a woman therapist, this objection seems to disregard the usefulness of the opportunity to work out problems originating in a two-parent family and seems to imply that the development of a pure transference is an end in itself.

My specification of a male-famale co-therapist team was sometimes regarded as unnecessary, on the grounds that in a group with two male therapists, participants would consciously or unconsciously respond to one of them as a mother-figure, or would conversely choose one of two female therapists to take the male transference-role. To me, this position seems equivalent to ignoring the reality of gender altogether and may even reinforce the confusion of gender identity from which many people already suffer. In group therapy, the male-female leadership evokes fantasies about male authority and female authority, provides an opportunity to test the family stereotypes against real people in a quasi-family situation, and provides models for the acceptance of gender-role (Mintz, 1965).

In the encounter marathon, these same advantages obtain. In addition, co-leadership gives each therapist a sense of support from the other if the marathon proves especially arduous or challenging. It is especially useful in the rare event that one participant should become so disturbed as to require special attention, in which case one of the therapists can meet this need while the other therapist continues with the group.

Two other major forces leading to the development of today's en-

[12] For example, in Beacon Hill, New York.

counter groups were the work of Frederick Perls, who developed Gestalt therapy; and of the group dynamicists, who included Bion, Ezriel, Foulkes, and the originators of the T-group movement of the National Training Laboratories.

It seems fascinating to me that the same theoretical work was antecedent to both these developments, originating in different parts of the world and with very different emotional as well as geographical climates. The intellectual ancestors of both Perls and the T-group movement were the Gestalt psychologists, Max Wertheimer, Wolfgang Kohler, and Kurt Koffka. A summary of their contribution is offered by Hall and Lindzey, who write (1957, p. 206):

> The chief tenet of Gestalt psychology is that the way in which an object is perceived is determined by the total context or configuration in which it is embedded. Relationships among components of a perceptual field rather than the fixed characteristics of the individual components determine perception.

This is essentially a way of looking at data, rather than a body of accumulated knowledge, though it gave rise to an extraordinarily interesting series of experiments (Koffka, 1935), including the famous figure-ground reversals of Wertheimer, in which, for example, a picture can be perceived as showing either two dark profiles or a white goblet, depending on what the viewer chooses or expects to see. Probably the far-reaching influence of the Gestalt psychologists lay in the fact that they were able to use the data and concepts of field theory in physics and chemistry, whereas Freud, for all his unique genius, was to some extent limited by the mechanistic, rational way of observing data which was characteristic of the basic science of his time.

Group therapists influenced primarily by psychoanalytic doctrine saw individual behavior in the group as determined primarily by intrapsychic components. In contrast, drawing upon the work and thinking of the Gestalt psychologists, several group therapists who had originally been psychoanalytically oriented began to see the group not only as a collection of individuals, but also as a network of interpersonal forces in which each individual affects every other individual at all times, and in which the interplay of forces is constantly changing.

Kurt Lewin, who was associated with the three original Gestalt psychologists, was a pioneer thinker in applying these concepts to group dynamics.[13] His principles were utilized by Foulkes (1957) in the United

---

[13] In this book, I have emphasized the application of psychoanalytic theory and of psychodramatic and Gestalt techniques to marathon encounters because my orientation and my practical approach have been influenced by them primarily, and therefore I am able to make a contribution from personal experience. Lewin's work, however, seems at least equally important in understanding group processes. For a

States, and by Bion (1955) and Ezriel (1950) in England. These therapists, whose work is best described as group-analytic psychotherapy, addressed their attention to the group as a whole, rather than to individuals. Such comments might be made as, "The group is now feeling anxious because one of its members is absent," or, "Part of the group is withdrawing its attention because this topic is threatening, and part of it is showing irritation to resist the threat." Unexpectedly, there are two similarities between this approach and the approach of the "mass turn-ons" of the structured marathon encounter group, although the atmosphere is vastly different. In group analytic psychotherapy there seems to be an impersonal, intellectual atmosphere in which the leader remains as emotionally detached as the most conservative Freudian analyst, and in which considerable conscious anxiety may be generated by this impersonality.[14] The dramatic procedures of the structured Esalen type of experiential group, in sharp contrast, are directed toward evoking and expressing intense emotions in the group. Yet two similarities are undeniable. In both approaches there is an exclusive focus on the here-and-now (a concept which goes directly back to Lewin) and an attempt to deal with the group as a whole, rather than focussing on individuals.

Lewin was directly involved in the beginnings of the National Training Laboratories (described more fully in Bradford, Gibb, & Benne, 1964). In 1964 a conference was held, under the auspices of the Connecticut Interracial Commission, to develop local leaders who could help communities understand and comply with the Fair Employment Practices Act. Three ten-member groups, mainly teachers and social workers, met with the intention of dealing with specific community problems brought in by the members. Group discussion was the chosen approach. It was not planned to analyze the behavior and interaction of the members toward one another.

Under the guidance of Lewin, each group had its own research observers, who in separate evening sessions reported on the patterns of interaction they had seen. Unexpectedly, some of the participants asked to attend these research meetings and were accepted. Benne (1964, p. 82) reports:

> The open discussion of their own behavior and its observed consequences had an electric effect both on the participants and on the training leaders.

thorough discussion of Lewin's contribution, see Hall and Lindzey (1927, Ch. 6) and Marrow (1970).

[14] This comment is based primarily on the writer's experience, in the summer of 1966, at a two-week workshop in group dynamics, sponsored jointly by the Tavistock Conference of England, Yale University, and the Washington School of Psychiatry. Although the leader, known as a "consultant," consistently directed his comments to the total group, this group experience produced the least warmth and involvement of any I have known. Perhaps this experience was not typical.

. . . Participants began to join observers and leaders in trying to analyze and interpret behavior events . . . and reported that they were deriving important understandings of their own behavior and of the behavior of their groups. . . . A potentially powerful medium . . . of re-education had been, somewhat inadvertently, hit upon.

Shortly afterward, the National Training Laboratories were formed to exploit this method of learning group dynamics by simultaneously participating in a group and observing it. Its extended program (see Chapter 11) now comprises the application of this method to industrial management, community-conflict problems, educational advancement, and personal growth.

The NTL time format is typically an extended workshop, ranging from three days to several weeks, in which sessions of two hours each are conducted several times a day. Indirectly, the time format of the marathon springs from the extension of the NTL format to sensitivity-training groups throughout the country. In 1963, Frederick Stoller attended an intensive weekend sensitivity-training laboratory at the University of California at Los Angeles. Impressed by this experience, Stoller began utilizing the extended time format in psychotherapy with institutionalized adolescents and adults (Stoller, 1966). Meanwhile, George Bach had been experimenting with various patterns of extended time in conducting group therapy. In 1966, Bach and Stoller as co-therapists began a long series of marathons, which at present have developed into Bach's specialty of "fight training" for couples (Bach, 1969) and Stoller's family therapy (1967).

The principles of marathon group therapy, as formulated by Stoller (1968), are almost identical with the aims of the broader movement of humanistic psychology. These formulations, which would probably be accepted by nearly all encounter group leaders, include: emphasis on the here-and-now, as distinct from emphasis on reconstructing events in the individual's past; abandonment of the mental illness model; emphasis upon the responsibility of the individual for his own fate; and concentration on the future and on potential for self-realization rather than on conflicts and difficulties.[15]

In 1965, a year of exhilarating professional growth, I came into direct personal contact with several vital aspects of the humanist movement. I attended my first marathon and thereafter began at once to conduct marathons; I attended an NTL workshop in Bethel, Maine; and I had the

[15] Twenty years ago, when I was studying the Rorschach technique, my instructor remarked with surprise that heretofore she had rarely seen a student who routinely tried to evaluate the patient's assets, instead of looking only for conflicts and limitations. Today I believe that most Rorschach teachers would train students to search the protocols for indications of actual and potential effectiveness as well as for pathology.

first of a series of experiences with Frederick Perls as a patient and student. Because I thus met directly some of the most potent forces and personalities involved in the development of the marathon encounter group, and because in many respects my individual experience typifies the experiences of many people, it seems worthwhile to recount these adventures in some detail.

In the winter of 1965, Bach and Stoller invited participants in the annual conference of the American Group Psychotherapy Association in California to attend a marathon. The idea of a marathon was entirely new to me and caused some apprehension. I registered for the group and then began trying to prove to myself that I could not possibly attend and fly back to New York from California in time to meet my professional obligations. It was quite disconcerting when I realized that, unconsciously, I was playing a trick on myself; I was frightened and was trying to avoid the unknown situation. This apprehensiveness is so characteristic of participants, especially in their first marathon, that it seems to me every marathon leader should begin as a participant.

I was frightened. Of what? Simply that I would be in intimate contact with strangers for a weekend, and they might reject me. Perhaps I was unworthily concerned because these people, a continent away from my home and office, would know nothing about my achievements. This challenge of meeting strangers without the protection of an already established identity has deliberately been built into some NTL workshops, where participants are required to take assumed names and conceal their professions (Schutz, 1967). Also, I was in a slight but persistent depression. There was serious illness in my family; the dearest friend of my childhood had just died under tragic circumstances; and I was adjusting with great difficulty to the departure from home of my two grown children.

Having recognized that I was trying to avoid the marathon, I could no longer make excuses. I would attend. Further, I resolved that I would not disguise or conceal my feelings, my emotional problems, or the difficulties of my life situation.

The group, meeting for two days with a short break for sleep, reached an intensity which I had never seen before in any group, though since then I have seen it often. Not only my initial apprehensiveness, but my total marathon experience, was a prototype of the experiences of most participants. When I left early to catch my plane, the group surrounded me with embraces, well-wishing, and even tears. It was a glorious, unforgettable moment for which I would use exactly the same naïve phrase which I have heard innumerable times after the marathons—"I was myself, and they all liked me!" [16]

---

[16] After this marathon my depression vanished. On an emotional level, I would tend to ascribe this to the warmth and acceptance which I received; but here I be-

As soon as possible after returning to New York, I began to plan for my first marathon. In the east, except for the encounter groups for drug addicts at Synanon and Daytop, marathons were almost unheard-of. Colleagues were apprehensive. A friend called long distance to warn of the danger of psychosis under such a stressful situation. With eggshell caution, I selected from my practice people who, I was confident, could tolerate the pressures of a marathon. And the marathon was effective. Almost from the beginning, the participants began to interact with an intensity and spontaneity that I had never seen in my ongoing groups. As the group ended, we all experienced the sense of closeness and communion which I had felt in the Bach-Stoller marathon, and which for me still occurs in most marathons, although seldom in other groups.

In the summer of this same year, I attended a two-week sensitivity-training group given by NTL in Bethel, Maine. By chance my trainer was William Schutz, who at that time was beginning the experiments in nonverbal communication which he later continued at Esalen Institute. Although for years I had been using touch under the circumstances described above, both in group and individual practice, I was unfamiliar with arm-wrestling and other techniques for expressing competitiveness and aggression. In Schutz's laboratory, I found myself engaged in the limited form of wrestling known as the "press" with a muscular young giant and gained considerable confidence in the subsequent use of these techniques by finding the experience exhilarating, nondamaging, and essentially friendly.[17]

Toward the end of this same year, I entered the first of a series of workshops with Frederick (Fritz) Perls,[18] several of which were conducted with his colleague, James Simkin. Fritz's place in the encounter group movement is a paradox. He himself did not make use of group

---

lieve that I would be making the same error as many marathon participants and some leaders, who explain the effects of the marathon as entirely due to immediate emotional experience. As a psychologist, I believe it was important that I could accept and assimilate some of the comments made to me about my situation, and that the atmosphere of affection was important in bringing about a readiness to hear these comments.

[17] My experience, which was actually the first time Schutz had tried the experiment with a woman participant, is described in *Joy*.

[18] It is really impossible to write of Fritz without paying tribute to his spectacular charisma, his humor, his capacity to be disagreeable and disappointing, his warmth, and his general humanness. On his seventy-fifth birthday, in San Francisco, he danced for two hundred of his friends, wearing a white-and-silver tunic, his white hair and beard floating around his head; not one movement was inappropriate or awkward. In his house above the ocean at Esalen, he sat in a room full of his own extraordinary paintings, sharing skill and wisdom with his students, ostentatiously dozing when they bored him, and summarily dismissing them when displeased—although they were accepted back. His autobiography (Perls, 1969c), published shortly before his death, conveys this personality. Movies of Fritz are available and are recommended to anyone who wishes to study his work, which involved so much physical interaction that it cannot be conveyed in writing (Mediasync, Del Mar, California).

interaction. He conducted individual therapy in groups. Indeed, the official position of most Gestalt therapists in groups is that "if a group member insists on 'breaking in' and being helpful, he may be put down gently or asked to explore his own projections" (Beisser, 1970). This is far from the spontaneous interplay among group members which is sought by most leaders of an unstructured group. Fritz sat at the head of the room with two empty chairs beside him. One was the "hot seat," for anyone who wished to work; the other was vacant so that the patient who was working might have the opportunity to play out his own projections, or the alienated parts of himself, by physically changing from one position to the other. He rarely sought to draw out a silent or withdrawn group member. His invitation was, "Who wants to work? I am available." He expressed his own feelings with great freedom, making no pretense of aloofness, but certainly his workshops were dominated by his personality and did not have the democratic atmosphere which usually develops in an encounter group.

Nevertheless, Fritz's techniques can be better integrated with free group interaction than any other approach to individual psychotherapy with which I am familiar. Full discussion of these techniques and of their underlying theory can be found elsewhere (Perls, 1951, 1969a & b; Fagan & Shepherd, 1969). Here it is necessary to describe only the particular features of his approach which render it uniquely valuable in providing intense vicarious experiences for participants who are not working on the "hot seat," and uniquely adaptable for the facilitation of lively and meaningful group interaction.

The empathy and identification which many participants in Fritz's workshops have reported in watching the therapeutic experience of another individual [19] was due to two of his technical principles: the constant insistence on bringing every experience into the here-and-now, and his use of the group as an instrument by which to help the individual. At the same time, without necessarily making a specific identification with another patient, the group members were exposed to the continual challenging and stimulating emphasis on two theoretical or philosophical principles: that each individual is responsible for his own feelings and behavior, and that true aliveness is achieved only by a full acceptance of whatever one is at the moment.

These four points require elaboration.

Fritz's insistence on the here-and-now is sometimes misunderstood. It does not mean that the past is regarded as irrelevant, or that interac-

---

[19] Many participants in my encounter marathons report the same intensity of vicarious experience (see Chapter 5), but only when a problem has been brought into the here-and-now through Gestalt techniques, psychodrama, or nonverbal encounters. I do not believe that a verbal discussion, or an interpretation from the leader, would bring about this effect.

tion is confined to whatever is realistically going on between therapist and patient. His approach, which is analogous to the principle of working with the toxic introject by its externalization (see Chapter 8), assumes that childhood experiences have led to conscious or unconscious [20] alienation of the self from one of its components. The dissociated component must be brought into the immediate here-and-now situation. Talking about the past or about external matters is termed "gossip." Instead, through whatever method seems appropriate for the specific situation and the individual patient, the past is brought emotionally into the present. For example, a girl who speaks of a childhood experience with her father is requested to play it out, taking both roles alternately. Breakthroughs of feeling, which Fritz terms "explosions," often result.

Fritz's use of the group usually involves the technique of going-around,[21] flexibly used for such purposes as getting the patient to experience directly some attitude or feeling which he has been discussing; acting out the suppressed opposite of some habitual mode of behavior; or putting into action some newly discovered way of relating to others. Group members may respond or not, as they choose. This of all the Gestalt techniques is probably the most useful in an encounter marathon and repeatedly creates highly significant interaction in the group.

The principle that each individual is responsible for his own behavior underlies all Gestalt work. It is not implemented by theoretical discussion, but by specific techniques (Levitsky & Perls, 1970). For example, the expression "I can't" is usually more accurate if changed to "I won't." The individual is never asked to change his feelings, but to become aware that he himself is producing them. Here is an example which shows the method of continually asking the patient to accept responsibility for himself, and which also indicates the use of close observation of nuances of behavior which characterizes Gestalt therapy:

> Therapist: I notice your hand is touching your throat.
> Patient: Yes . . . .
> Therapist: What does your throat experience?
> Patient: It's choking.
> Therapist: There is no *it*. Can you say "*I* am choking?"
> Patient: I am choking.
> Therapist: Now can you say "I am choking myself?"

Here the use of the word "it" is dealt with as a method of avoiding self-awareness and maintaining alienation from some aspect of the per-

---

[20] Fritz did not accept the Freudian term "unconscious." For this concept he substitutes "those aspects of behavior that are unavailable or potential rather than actual" (Fagan & Shepherd, 1970, p. 4).

[21] Most of the examples of going-around offered in this book are similar to the way in which this technique is used in Gestalt therapy.

sonality. Through such devices, the patient begins to see himself as active and responsible rather than as the passive target of internal and external forces.

Even more important in Gestalt psychology is the cardinal principle that "change occurs when one becomes what he is, not when he tries to become what he is not" (Beisser, 1970, p. 77). At first this seems a paradox; but the recognition and acceptance of immediate feelings as part of the self is central in various ways to most types of psychotherapy. This self-acceptance bears an analogy to Freud's dictum "Where id was, there shall ego be," which briefly describes the process by which repressed, guilt-laden impulses become conscious and, though not necessarily acted upon, are integrated into awareness. Clinically, this principle is immensely useful. For example, when it is necessary to alleviate the depression of a patient as quickly as possible, one of the best methods is to request him to express his depression in an exaggerated form, rather than try to cheer him up; this approach not only seems to bring the mood to some extent under conscious control but frequently elicits underlying feelings of rage or helplessness. The recognition and expression of immediate feeling is identical to what the experientialists term "authenticity." It is precisely the same phenomenon as the movement from social pretense to genuineness in an encounter marathon, expressed in the metaphor of the removal of masks.

In Fritz's workshops, the experiences of the patient on the "hot seat," who usually manifested an increased sense of responsibility for himself and an increased ability to be alive in that moment of time, were frequently so intense that other group members absorbed and assimilated the change vicariously. Fritz, however, was an individual therapist of such unique skill that perhaps, with him, the one-to-one therapist-patient relationship within the group was worth the sacrifice of group interaction. My own conviction is that the pure Gestalt technique, in which the leader works successively with a number of individual members, has disadvantages which are obviated if these techniques are combined with the encouragement of free interaction in the group. If the leader-patient relationship is primary, and if the patient relates to the group exclusively in a way specifically prescribed by the leader (as in going-around), it is impossible to avoid some reinforcement of the syndrome of irrational respect for authority of which the prototype is the parent-child relationship. Even more important, if free interaction is prohibited, the members of the group are deprived of their opportunity to offer meaningful and spontaneous help to one another, not through advice, but by showing genuine concern and understanding. This mutual helpfulness, which typically occurs in the last phase of a marathon, is in my opinion both a cause and a consequence of the movement toward self-actualization which occurs in a marathon encounter group.

REFERENCES

Bach, G. R. The marathon group: Intensive practice of intimate interaction. *Psychological Reports*, 1966, *18*, 995–1005.

Bach, G. R., & Wyden, P. *The intimate enemy.* New York: William Morrow, 1968.

Beisser, A. The paradoxical theory of change. In J. Fagan & I. L. Shepherd (Eds.), *Gestalt therapy now.* Palo Alto: Science & Behavior Books, 1970.

Berne, E. *Principles of group treatment.* New York: Oxford University Press, 1966.

Bion, W. R. Group dynamics. In M. Klein (Ed.), *New directions in psychoanalysis.* New York: Basic Books, 1955.

Bradford, L. P., Gibb, J. R., & Benne, K. D. (Eds.) *T-group theory and laboratory method.* New York: Wiley, 1964.

Cohn, R. C. Therapy in groups. In J. Fagan & I. L. Shepherd (Eds.), *Gestalt therapy now.* Palo Alto: Science & Behavior Books, 1970.

Durkin, H. *The group in depth.* New York: International Universities Press, 1964.

Ezriel, H. A psychoanalytic approach to group treatment. *British Journal of Medicine and Psychology*, 1950, *23*, 59–74.

Fagan, J., & Shepherd, I. L. (Eds.) *Gestalt therapy now.* Palo Alto: Science & Behavior Books, 1970.

Fairbairn, W. R. D. *An objection-relations theory of the personality.* New York: Basic Books, 1952.

Fenichel, O. *The psychoanalytic theory of neurosis.* New York: W. W. Norton, 1945.

Foulkes, S. H., & Anthony, E. J. *Group psychotherapy.* New York: Penguin, 1957.

Freud, S. *The problem of lay analysis.* New York: Brentano, 1927.

Guntrip, H. *Personality structure and human interaction.* New York: International Universities Press, 1961.

Hall, C. S., & Lindzey, G. *Theories of personality.* New York: Wiley, 1957.

Jourard, S. *The transparent self.* Princeton: Van Nostrand, 1964.

Koffka, K. *Principles of gestalt psychology.* New York: Harcourt Brace, 1935.

Laing, R. D. *The politics of experience.* New York: Pantheon, 1967.

Levitsky, A., & Perls, F. S. Rules and games of gestalt therapy. In J. Fagan & I. L. Shepherd (Eds.), *Gestalt therapy now.* Palo Alto: Science & Behavior Books, 1970.

Marrow, A. J. *The practical theorist.* New York: Basic Books, 1970.

McCartney, J. Overt transference. *Journal of Sex Research*, 1966, *2*.

Menninger, K. *Theory of psychoanalytic technique.* New York: Basic Books, 1940.

Mintz, E. E. Touch and the psychoanalytic tradition. *Psychoanalytic Review*, 1969, *56*(3).

Mintz, E. E. Male-female co-therapists. *American Journal of Psychotherapy*, April 1965, *19*(2).

Perls, F. S. *Ego, hunger and aggression.* New York: Random House, 1969. (a)

Perls, F. S. *Gestalt therapy verbatim.* Lafayette, Calif.: Real People Press, 1969. (b)

Perls, F. S. *In and out of the garbage pail.* Lafayette, Calif.: Real People Press, 1969. (c)

Perls, F. S., Hefferline, R. F., & Goodman, P. *Gestalt therapy.* New York: Dell, 1951.

Racker, H. *Transference and counter-transference.* New York: International Universities Press, 1968.

Rogers, C. R. *Client-centered therapy.* Boston: Houghton Mifflin, 1951.

Schutz, W. C. *FIRO: A three-dimensional theory of interpersonal behavior.* New York: Rinehart, 1959.

Schutz, W. C. *Joy.* New York: Grove Press, 1967.

Slavson, S. R. Discussion. *International Journal of Group Psychotherapy*, 1960, *10*.

Stoller, F. H. Accelerated interaction. *International Journal of Group Psychotherapy*, 1968, *18*(2).

Stoller, F. H. The long weekend. *Psychology Today*, December 1967.

Szasz, T. *The myth of mental illness*. New York: Hoeber-Harper, 1961.

Whittaker, C. A., & Malone, T. P. *The roots of psychotherapy*. New York: Blakiston, 1953.

Wolf, A., & Schwartz, E. K. *Psychoanalysis in groups*. New York: Grune & Stratton, 1962.

3 ENCOUNTERING THE SELF AND OTHERS

Many hundreds of encounter games have been developed for various purposes: to enhance awareness of individual feelings; to become more conscious of one's effect on others; to encourage the expression of emotion; to facilitate the development of trust and intimacy within the group; to heighten self-understanding and self-acceptance; to increase the ability to understand and accept others. Some games are rituals in which the entire group participates simultaneously in accordance with the instructions of the leader; others can be adapted to suit various circumstances; and innumerable games may be invented at the moment, either by participants or by the leader, to meet the specific needs of individuals.

The games are immensely varied. In degree of intimacy, they range from paper-and-pencil tasks to exercises involving the contact of nude bodies in a swimming pool. In level of intensity, they range from children's party games introduced as ice-breakers at the beginning of a group, to therapeutic stratagems which can elicit feelings of violent intensity which may heretofore have been unconscious. They can both evoke and resolve anxiety. They can release feelings of joy, grief, and rage. In the marathon encounter group, the games can become richly meaningful symbols through which participants come much closer to themselves and others.

Some of the games to be described are so powerful that they should never be used routinely, but only in a situation in which close attention can be paid to individual psychodynamics. Others are routine procedures of relatively limited value. Games of limited value, and even a few which to me seem potentially deleterious rather than helpful, will be described to offer a representative sample of these procedures.[1] Since many games serve several purposes at once, classification is arbitrary and is used primarily for convenience.

[1] Some games have been invented by the writer, others borrowed or adapted from colleagues. Since it is sometimes difficult to identify the original creator of a game, and since sometimes the same game may be developed by several workers, specific credit is not given, but my particular indebtedness to Perls, Schutz, Moreno, Finney, Malamud, and Machover, as enumerated in the references, is warmly and gratefully acknowledged.

PRELIMINARY GAMES

In an unstructured marathon encounter group, my preference is not to introduce warm-up exercises, but rather to wait until it is possible to suggest games in accordance with the emerging character and needs of the group. However, if the group is too large for this approach to be practicable, or if its stated purpose is training in interpersonal under-standing or some other goal which emphasizes the cognitive aspects of personal growth, preliminary exercises are useful during the period when an atmosphere of spontaneity and frankness has yet to develop. They may be thought of as focussed on either self-exploration or on the facilitation of group contact, though these two aims are achieved simul-taneously if the group members are able to speak openly to one another about their reactions to the procedures.

The following are some examples of tasks designed to facilitate self-exploration.

Self-Description

Give each participant an identical slip of paper. Ask them to write down three self-descriptive adjectives. Scramble the slips of paper, then let each participant draw one, read it aloud, and speculate about what kind of person is described. The group joins in the speculations. Each participant recognizes his own three self-descriptive adjectives and com-pares his self-image with the conjectures of the group but is not required to reveal his identity unless he chooses. In actual fact, most participants do not find this exercise threatening and usually make the voluntary deci-sion to reveal themselves and to share their impressions about the other group members.

Assumed Identities

Before the group members tell their real names, at the very begin-ning they are asked to assume pseudonyms, perhaps taking names which they would prefer to their real ones. If the group appears ready for role-playing and introspection, they may also be asked to select and play-act a type of personality which they would prefer to their own. A serious woman might choose to behave frivolously, or a retiring man to be self-assertive. The masquerade continues for some time, and subsequently there is discussion about what the assumed names and personalities sig-nified to the participants. Concealed wishes emerge, and an opportunity is provided to explore facets of the personality which have heretofore been repressed or ignored. For some participants this experience leads toward the integration of some formerly unaccepted part of the personality. For others, it yields a sense of contentment with the present personality, a feeling that the real name and the accustomed behavior are actually quite comfortable.

Secrets

All group members are asked to think of the most shameful and embarrassing secret they possess. They are asked not to speak, but to sit in mutual silence, imagining what the reaction of the group would be if the secret were disclosed. Typically the participants begin by fantasying reactions of shock, disgust, and contempt. As the silent fantasies continue, they become less disturbing. Frequently several participants will laugh aloud as they realize that the "terrible secret" would not really be met with such melodramatic reactions. Group members are not asked to reveal the secrets, even indirectly, since this would be a betrayal of the leader's implied promise, but often some members actually insist on sharing the secret and speak with amusement and relief about their former anxiety.

One group member, as his ghastly secret, revealed that his parents had not married until several years after his birth. He was "a bastard." The group was warmly sympathetic toward his pain but almost ridiculed what they perceived to be a trivial cause for the suffering. He was busy in a worthwhile profession, with a pleasant and stable family life—how could he continue to agonize over something which would seem so unimportant to anyone whom he respected? The wisdom of the group prevailed; the "secret" lost most of its shame.

A Trip Within the Body

This stratagem is slightly more threatening to most participants than the preceding tasks and hence is best introduced after the group has been in session for a few hours, when it usually has the effect of bringing about a deeper level of intimacy. Participants are asked to sit or recline comfortably, place their hands over their ears, and shut their eyes, thus partially blocking out environmental stimuli. They are asked to imagine entering their own bodies through any orifice and taking a voyage of discovery through the body's inside. When the voyage is completed, they are to sit up and open their eyes.

At first the idea seems strange, but most participants find the imaginary voyage easier than anticipated. Afterward each member is free to choose whether or not to share the imagined experiences with the group, and most members do so. Visits to emotionally significant parts of the body, such as brain, heart, and genitals, often elicit important feelings about the self-image and sometimes may even modify such feelings in the direction of increased self-esteem. For example, a woman told the group that she had always felt slightly ashamed of the natural odor of her genitalia, and that in fantasy she had visited her uterus and vagina and remained there until she came to accept the odor as normal and wholesome. This type of self-revelation is usually made only in a fairly sophisticated group which is already developing trust and intimacy. The only necessary precaution even in a relatively inexperienced group is to make it clear that fantasies will be shared entirely on a voluntary basis, without any pressure, to avoid any possible embarrassment until the group participants are ready for greater intimacy.

This same stratagem may also be used for intensive self-exploration in response to the needs of an individual. In an unstructured marathon, a woman spoke sadly of her feelings about being emotionally unresponsive, using the metaphor "I have a cold heart." The metaphor was picked up and used literally, in accordance with the principle of translating abstractions into physical terms whenever possible, and she was asked to take a trip through her body and enter her heart. She did so, eyes closed, speaking aloud to the group as she progressed down her throat, through her arteries, and into the left ventricle, where she sat in fantasy for a long time. Then it seemed to her that one spot in her heart was warm. She began to cry, and relived in memory a childhood episode in which she had felt warm and loving, but had been rebuked. The group reenacted this episode with her, playing various family roles with a sympathy she had not experienced in childhood. She wept unrestrainedly. During the remaining hours of the group, she expressed her feelings more freely and related more affectionately to other group members.

GAMES TO FACILITATE
INTERPERSONAL CONTACT

Introducing Your Neighbor

At the very beginning of the group, the participants are divided into pairs. They are asked to talk informally to their partners for a stated period, perhaps five to ten minutes. Each participant is then asked to introduce his partner to the group, giving the first name, offering whatever information he regards as pertinent, and to tell his own impressions of the other. This is a nonthreatening way to initiate group interaction, although it has the disadvantage of temporarily accepting or even encouraging the retention of stereotyped social roles. It is useful principally in groups of people who may be reluctant to abandon conventional behavior.

The method of dividing group members into pairs can be important, especially at the beginning of the group, and especially with participants who are insecure in the group situation. If they are asked to choose partners, or wait to be chosen, there can be marked anxiety, stemming, in general, from the agonizing doubts about popularity and social acceptability which characterize the latency and adolescent periods, and which are exacerbated by the custom of "choosing sides" in competitive games at school and in neighborhood play. It is not in the interest of the group or of individual participants to mobilize this anxiety unless there is opportunity to deal with it.

The easiest way of choosing partners is to ask the group to count around the circle, in one's and two's. Each one-two pair becomes a partnership. When the next partner game is played, like numbers can partner one another, so that the group does not congeal into dyads.

Feedback

Fairly early in the group, each participant is asked to select three people whom he likes and three people of whom he feels critical (a formulation which gives less of a feeling of rejection than the term "dislike"). Reasons for these feelings are given and interaction with feedback is allowed to develop. Participants are encouraged to explore the extent to which their feelings are determined by distorted perceptions coming from past experiences, accidental resemblances, or prejudice. On the following day, when group members know one another better and when their behavior has become more open, they are asked to share any changes in their initial reactions. Typically, although a sense of liking is usually enhanced by further acquaintance, initial critical feelings become milder and turn into approval. It can be pointed out to the group that this change is in part because many people do appear more likeable upon a closer view, and in part because the gradual relinquishing of social defences tends to evoke warmth rather than the anticipated condemnation.

Opening the Fist

Partners are chosen, and the partner on the right of each couple is asked to extend his firmly closed fist. The other partner now has the task of opening the fist by any means he chooses, verbal or physical, while the first partner has the option of whether to resist or to comply. Most people resist obstinately when physical force is chosen but comply readily to persuasion or cajolery. After the game, partners discuss what happened in terms of what it may show about their personal styles of dealing with others. This game is valuable not only in personal-growth encounter groups, but in groups designed to deal with community tensions, since it affords a very graphic demonstration of the efficacy of tact as opposed to forcefulness.

Spin-the-Bottle

This is a children's game which has several times been suggested spontaneously by an imaginative participant in order to dispel the dullness and defensiveness which often mark the beginning of an unstructured marathon group. In proposing this game, the leader may expect to evoke opposition and even ridicule and may find it necessary to raise questions about the prevalent cultural tendency to associate maturity with solemnity.

The group forms a circle. Someone sits in the middle on the floor with a soda bottle, and says "The one whom this bottle points to must . . .", naming a task. The bottle is spun, comes to rest, and points to a member of the circle, who performs the task and then names another task and spins the bottle in turn. Tasks may range from such absurdities as turning a somersault or balancing a plate on the head to such self-revealing assignments as "tell the group why you are here" or "tell us your chief life problem."

Playful assignments have their own value. The human need for active playfulness, as opposed to vicarious participation as a spectator of play, is half-starved in our society. A playful atmosphere not only nourishes the participants but is in itself conducive to trust and intimacy as long as it is not exploited defensively to minimize emotional difficulties. A marathon group which develops a spirit of fun is likely to undertake serious work later.

Eye Contact

All group members are asked to stand and to move slowly around the room until they make eye contact with another member. People who wear glasses should remove them. They are to gaze steadily into one another's eyes until one of them feels like breaking the contact, upon which both of them move away and make contact with someone else. No speech is permitted. Physical contact should be either explicitly permitted or explicitly discouraged. If it is permitted, most eye contacts end with a handshake or embrace. If the leader evaluates the group as being composed of very withdrawn or fragile people, as might be the case with certain psychiatric populations, participants may enter into the group more easily during its initial phases if physical contact is not encouraged until they feel comparatively secure.

This exercise rarely fails to elicit surprise and delight at the richness of an interpersonal experience which comes about through eye contact alone. The beauty and variety of color in the human iris is remarked with wonder. The variety of attitudes which can be expressed in the eyes is noted as participants speak of their experiences, for which adequate time must be allowed in order to make this game meaningful.

Blind-Touch Contact

Participants are asked to close their eyes and move about the room at random. When they brush up against one another, they are to touch one another's hair, faces, and bodies, and try to develop a feeling for one another through physical contact alone.

Objections have been raised to this game on the grounds that it is merely a thinly disguised way of obtaining partial sexual gratification, an objection which perhaps can be balanced by the possibility that the group permissiveness may lead to the diminution of sexual anxieties and help to free the individual for a more satisfying personal life. To me a more cogent objection to this game is that physical contact is substituted for genuine intimacy. It is difficult to see how touching can express or foster true emotional contact when it is the only modality of communication between strangers who do not even look at one another.

The question is sometimes raised as to whether or not the leader should take part in the preliminary games. My observation is that the group more readily becomes a cohesive working unit, and more readily develops confidence in the leader, if he takes part as a peer in group games such as Spin-the-Bottle and Eye Contact. Whether he chooses to take part in games of self-exploration such as Secrets and the Trip Within the Body depends in part on his willingness to reveal himself and in part on his judgment as to the extent to which self-revelation will be useful to the group. If he decides upon self-revelation, it must be done honestly, since the group will detect and resent any insincerity. Probably he should avoid games which would require him to make preliminary evaluations of others, such as Feedback, unless it is his intention to follow the policy of participating fully as a peer for the duration of the group.

His evaluations of the participants, whether favorable or disparaging, are likely to carry special weight and therefore require special consideration before being communicated.

CONFLICT GAMES

As the group moves away from conventional social behavior toward increasingly genuine self-expression, games can be introduced which tap feelings on a deeper level. Such games are less effective if they are presented as exercises to be gone through by everyone simultaneously, instead of in terms of their immediate meaningfulness to an individual.[2] If a group member becomes truly involved in working through an emotional conflict, his feelings are shared with intense empathy by the others, who often report that they also have been able to work through similar conflicts through vicarious participation and identification. This vicarious participation occurs only after the group has already developed a sense of intimacy and contributes in turn to the further heightening of intimacy. Thus a circuit is set up through which genuine self-expression, vicarious participation, and group intimacy continually recharge one another. This circuit, admittedly oversimplified in its description here, is the model of marathon interaction in its middle phase.

The increase of intimacy by no means implies that interaction is necessarily all loving at this stage of the encounter marathon. Hostility, already noted as among the first authentic feelings expressed in many groups, is often strong. If the hostility seems fully conscious, can be adequately expressed, and does not seem associated with anxiety or guilt, the group leader can allow the hostile encounter to take place naturally and need not resort to the use of games. More often, an angry group member seems to find words inadequate, or appears blocked, or does not understand the source of his own feelings. A phrase often used at this time is "I need help getting out my anger." Surprisingly often, there is a complaint about a headache of unknown origin, which upon careful inquiry proves to have begun at a time when the sufferer felt angry about something in the group and did not speak about it because of guilt or insecurity. Disguised fears of hostility are often present when participants speak of difficulty in competing. To meet these needs, it is useful for the leader to have a repertory of games through which hostility can be fully experienced, can be expressed safely through physical channels, and in many instances can enhance self-understanding and self-acceptance in this area.

---

[2] At this stage, a group which includes over twenty people is apt to be unwieldy. Some leaders prefer to divide the participants into smaller subgroups.

Unless the leader intends to limit drastically the intensity of involvement in hostility games, an attitude which is antipathetic to the achievement of fuller self-expression, physical precautions are essential. Heavy cushions or an upholstered couch are needed for the release of feeling by pounding. Gymnasium mats on the floor are ideal for the prevention of accidental injuries. Wristwatches and jewelry should be removed, especially women's earrings worn in pierced ears. The probability of opponents being swept away by rage to the point of injuring one another is actually very remote; the probability of self-injury on a basis of unconscious self-destructiveness is somewhat greater.[3]

Thumb-Wrestling

Participants clasp hands, thumbs upright, and each participant tries to capture and pin down the thumb of the other. This is the mildest of all conflict games, and is appropriate for anyone who would be dangerously threatened by the physical closeness and potential violence of more strenuous procedures.

Arm-Wrestling

Opponents lie on the floor,[4] head to head, right arms resting on their elbows, hands clasped. At the count of three, each attempts to push down the other's arm. If the opponents are a man and a woman, their strength can be approximately equalized if the woman clasps the man's hand with both of hers. The encounter becomes more meaningful if the opponents are asked to look into one another's eyes, and it is sometimes suggested that they also release feelings by making whatever sounds they wish.

Because of the intense physical intimacy, and because opponents can put forth their maximum physical strength without risking injury to themselves or the other, these combats can become extraordinarily meaningful. Men whose boyhood is far behind, and who have spent years in occupations which offer no opportunity for full physical exertion, often experience great delight at the opportunity for direct, primitive conflict.

[3] Arm-wrestling, pushing, and similar techniques have been used by the writer in well over 150 marathon groups. To date only one injury has occurred, which in the opinion of all the participants (including four colleagues) was unconsciously determined by a masochistic need to suffer, which had become clear during the course of the marathon. The injury was caused by the participant's slipping and falling under circumstances which would ordinarily be regarded as entirely safe. This episode, however, led me to adopt the routine use of gymnasium mats or mattresses.

[4] This procedure is sometimes used with elbows resting on a table, which is unwise, because in this position there is some possibility of a dislocated shoulder.

Almost invariably, opponents enjoy the struggle but do not resent defeat, and the combat usually ends in a comradely embrace. Women, for whom physical conflict is still not traditionally acceptable, often welcome an opportunity to express this side of their natures in a noncritical setting. The final result of the arm-wrestling, almost always, is that hostility is released and dissipated, and opponents return to their seats with a sense of exhilaration. The following letter, from an advertising executive, is representative of the arm-wrestling experience.

> The hand-wrestling . . . ended in a stalemate, but for me it was a great victory. I can remember screaming at the top of my lungs, hearing my piercing, primitive shriek. The screaming was almost completely liberating and un-self-conscious. However, I can still remember a faint restraining fear that I would blow down the walls of the office, or that my screaming would offend a neighbor and bring the police. This seems to me the essence of my conflict—how far should I go? The hand-wrestle helped me go a little bit further, but there's still a good part of me that's very afraid of winning. . . . The whole experience left me with a very pleasant exhaustion and a very good feeling toward Syd [his opponent]. I can remember feeling proud of my performance . . . and also a bit ashamed that I hadn't gone all the way and pinned Syd's arm. . . . It was very fitting that the contest ended without a winner. I liked Syd and didn't want to subject him to a defeat and likewise didn't want to be defeated either.

For this participant, wrestling brought greater awareness of what he considered a central problem, his difficulty in becoming totally involved with anything and in making a full commitment. At the same time, he was able to enjoy his own mature willingness to accept the outcome of a tie.

Profound characterological conflicts can come to light after arm-wrestling. Men who have always regarded themselves as highly competitive, dreading defeat, may discover that they are handicapped by an unconscious fear of succeeding. One such man wrote:

> I thought I wanted to win and thought I was winning, then suddenly I was down. My God, I was surprised. Then it occurred to me that I do the same thing at tennis. Set point in my favor, then I start losing.

This man, who believed himself to be wholeheartedly dedicated to his own success in business, had entered individual psychotherapy because of psychosomatic symptoms related to emotional tensions. After his experience with arm-wrestling he became aware that in business situations, as well as tennis, he often lost out unexpectedly when he seemed on the verge of winning. He participated in several more marathons as adjunct treatment to his individual therapy and gradually recognized his fear that if he achieved victory over other men, they would resent him and perhaps retaliate. This conflict could be traced back to a childhood during which his father had resented any effort on his son's part to match him in capability, thus bringing about an especially oppressive Oedipal situation.

An analogous conflict came to light when in a marathon a young woman complained that it was always difficult for her to express her ideas clearly to her female employer. The older woman was not particularly domineering, yet the girl could not assert herself. In the hope that we could explore her feelings about self-assertion with older women, I invited the girl to arm-wrestle with me. Although she was unquestionably stronger than myself, she capitulated at once, "like a cream puff," as she herself expressed it. We then explored her feelings of submissiveness and helplessness toward her mother, after which she went around the group and spoke self-assertively to all the women. Some weeks later, she wrote me saying that she felt much more at ease with her boss and had been able to make several suggestions about the improvement of office routines, which were accepted and had put her in line for a promotion.

In another marathon a homosexual man, Ned, told the group that although he had developed a fine muscular physique through regular workouts in a gymnasium, he had always regarded himself as inferior in physical strength to other men. A heterosexual man, Sam, who also was powerfully built, offered him a friendly challenge to arm wrestle. The ensuing match was a battle of the giants, which held the group spellbound, and which exhilarated the combatants so much that victory, which Sam achieved with difficulty, did not seem important. Thereafter Ned acknowledged that never in his life had he been able to take part in physical competition on an equal basis with any man, and that he had never before believed in his own strength. He told the group that although he did not think this experience would lead him to relinquish his homosexuality, which he had accepted for some years as his chosen way of life, he believed that his image of himself as a man would be permanently enriched.

Arm-Squeezing, Hand-Slapping, and Hand-Pressing

Arm-wrestling engages two people in such a way as to elicit their latent feelings or change their actual feelings toward one another. These three exercises, in comparison, are useful primarily to evoke and release pent-up feelings from the past and bring them into the immediate experiential situation. They can be used in a variety of ways, but I have found them most dramatically effective in offering myself as a mother-symbol and bringing out feelings of rage which have been choked back since childhood.

In arm-squeezing, the group member with whom I am working, usually though not necessarily a man, clasps both hands around the fleshy part of my forearm and squeezes as hard as possible. In hand-slapping, my hand rests lightly on a rug or some other resilient surface, back upward, and the group member is permitted to slap it with full strength, not with the fist but with the open palm. In hand-pressing, most meaningful and dramatic of the three techniques, I offer my hands clasped together, rings removed, finger- and thumb-nails protected within the hands, and permit them to be pressed together as hard as possible from the sides.[5]

It is important to inform the group member that the leader will not allow herself to be hurt, and that if she feels any pain, he will be asked to desist at once. This is partly to help him feel free to use his full strength, and partly to set up a readiness for him to let go immediately upon request, thus protecting the leader in the unlikely event that actual discomfort is experienced. Under these circumstances, most participants are at first reluctant to squeeze tightly or slap hard but become able to do so when they find that at most only a slight discomfort is experienced by the leader.

Because of the immense power these techniques can have, it would be highly inappropriate to introduce them arbitrarily. They are used only after a climate of security has been established, and only when a participant has indicated that he feels out of touch, or felt out of touch in the past, with a significant member of his family. The selection of technique depends primarily on the degree of physical contact which seems appropriate to establish. Hand-slapping offers the least intense contact, hand-pressing the most.

In hand-pressing, the participant is asked to close his eyes and keep them shut. When physical contact is established, he is asked what his mother used to call him as a boy, and what he used to call her. We then speak to one another, using the childhood names. I try to recapture the pronunciation and intonation as given to me, as exactly as possible. Then usually I say, "Now say to your mother whatever it was you always wanted to say and never did."

The results of this technique at times can be extraordinary. Most often, the participant becomes angry, reproaching and cursing the mother

---

[5] None of these techniques should be attempted without preliminary rehearsals in a neutral situation. If the leader is not secure with them, the insecurity will be communicated and the techniques will fail. Hand-pressing is somewhat difficult technically, since the hands must be placed in the right position or there is some possibility of discomfort or even pain. A few women with very slender hands are unable to sustain pressure in this position; almost any man can sustain it quite easily.

of his most unhappy childhood memories, pressing or squeezing with vigor, yet almost never uncontrollably. The rage lasts for a while, then usually he opens his eyes and embraces me, often with tears. The following letter, received three weeks after the marathon, exemplifies the experience:

> My mother has been dead for years, and yet somehow it was as if I never let her go. I thought of her with a mixture of anger and sadness. When you asked me to press your hands and speak to her, it seemed like nonsense, then suddenly I was carried away. It was like a mystical experience. I didn't think of anything except how angry and sad I felt. Then I thought maybe I had killed you, or her, so I opened my eyes and you were looking at me with a friendly face. I hugged you, or her, or both of you together, and I felt so good. Now it's like something is over that should have been over when she died. I can remember the good times and the bad times but they're over, the way they should be.

Another group participant, a capable middle-aged professional man, had almost complete amnesia for a fearful childhood in a Nazi-dominated country, in which a language other than English had been spoken. I repeated his childhood name, pronouncing it as accurately as I could, while he spoke to me in his native language, and finally he began to cry. He told me that this was the first time in many years that he had been able to regain any feeling of continuity with his childhood, with the mother of the childhood years, and with his native language as he had used it then.

Why this approach should so often be so remarkably powerful is difficult to understand completely. Certainly it has something to do with tapping buried feelings through intimate physical contact, which enables the participant to experience and release his repressed rage in a situation in which he is clearly stronger than his mother-symbol, thus undoing the primitive childish sense of helplessness. Perhaps my willingness to run the risk of being hurt, although in reality this risk is minimal indeed, may contribute to a sense of being cared for in which it seems possible to deal with long-buried feelings.

If hot anger or resentment are fully expressed, there is in my experience *always* a sense of great affection and appreciation as the episode closes, usually expressed in a warm hug. It is striking, also, that these episodes seem to have no transference aftermath, provided the anger and the ensuing affection are expressed and, when necessary, discussed briefly. Through the arm-squeezing technique, I was once able to help a contemporary, whom I knew both socially and professionally, to express feelings toward his mother which he had never been able to reach before. Although in general he was a highly defended man, he was carried away into a genuine rage in which he actually roared with fury. When the episode was over, his first thought was to reassure himself that he had not hurt me, and there was a feeling of mutual affection. There has not been any sense of discomfort in our personal or professional relationship hereafter. This episode, along with many similar incidents, leads me to speculate whether symbolic nonverbal communication, along with subsequent clarification of the episode, cannot perhaps not only elicit but also resolve transference more quickly and more thoroughly, at least with some patients and some types of problems, than in longer classical forms of psychotherapy.

If the buried rage and its underlying affection is felt toward a father figure, either the male marathon leader or a fellow participant is selected as the transference target. Usually it seems more effective if the father figure holds up a heavy pillow to be punched, rather than offering his arm or hands. Perhaps it seems natural to use more vigorous and extreme gestures in attacking a father substitute, and more intense and intimate gestures with a symbolic mother. In both cases, the common denominators seem to be the eliciting of choked-back rage; the discovery that this rage can be physically expressed without injuring or offending the parent substitute; and finally a deep, basic awareness that the expression of rage does not destroy affection in either "parent" or "child." It must be emphasized that the potency of this technique depends in part on the appropriate selection of a participant who acknowledges that he has blocked feelings and is ready to explore them; that sufficient time must be given for the feelings to develop and be fully expressed; and that certainly no leader should undertake this particular game, with its physical intimacy and its strong demand on the parent substitute's self-control, if he has reason to suspect ambivalence in his own feelings toward the group member with whom he will be working.

For the exceptional occasions when primitive rage is elicited to an extent which cannot be safely expressed by the technique just described, it is wise to encourage the group member to exhaust his feelings by pounding on a heavy cushion or a sturdy upholstered couch, a suggestion which usually is readily and gladly accepted. Primitive rage in a marathon can ordinarily be brought under control by a deliberate effort, but in this case there are likely to be rather unpleasant aftereffects, such as mild psychosomatic symptoms of nausea or headache, or slight depression, which do not seem to occur if the anger is fully expressed on a physical level.

DIALOGUE GAMES

Communication between two people goes far beyond the simple acknowledgment of what each is trying to say to the other. Genuine communication, in the sense of Buber's I-and-Thou dialogue, implies an acceptance and respect for the total personality of the other, even though the other may not be fully understood on a conscious level. This kind of mutual acceptance tends to be obliterated by wordiness and explanation. Paradoxically, there are times when a playful attitude toward dialogue seems to create more spontaneous self-expression, and more true willingness to allow the other person to express himself, than a serious striving to be understood on a purely intellectual level.

Communication which involves the body instead of verbalization alone can often add a dimension to dialogue. If verbalization is used, it can sometimes become more meaningful if stripped to its essentials. When two people in a marathon group have difficulty in making contact with one another, particularly if one or both of them tend to be over-rational at the expense of emotionality and playfulness, dialogue games are useful. The two interlocutors do not form a temporary subgroup but carry on their dialogue game within the circle, the members of which experience themselves as vicarious participants rather than as onlookers.

Hand Dialogue

Partners sit crosslegged on the floor, facing each other, and improvise a dance with their hands. It is left to their choice whether the follower stays close to the leader, with perhaps an inch of space between their respective hands, or whether the gestures are wide and sweeping. After a while, leader and follower change positions.

Minimally, this strategem loosens the rigidity which may exist between two people who are still bound by conventional modes of behavior. Beyond this, the participants and the onlookers often are able to perceive subtleties of self-expression which might not have appeared in ordinary verbal exchanges. Thus, a young woman who presented an appearance of great docility and conformity in the group, and who stated that her major characterological problem was "being too nice," appeared totally unable to take any cues from her partner when she was in the position of follower. When the entire group pointed this out to her, she was forced to consider the possibility that her "too nice" attitude was a defensive posture and not a genuine personality trait.

Expressive dancing which involves spontaneous movements of the entire body would be an ideal method to accomplish the same purpose. However, few people who have not had special training are able to shed their physical self-consciousness within a few hours to an extent which would enable them to communicate authentically. Social dancing entails the use of ritualized, prescribed steps and, despite its value in other respects, does not lend itself well to creative dialogue.

Foot Dialogue

Partners remove shoes and socks and sit on the floor facing one another, legs outstretched so that feet barely touch. They are instructed to carry on a conversation with their feet. Most participants, even overserious people, are amused by this challenge and find the foot dialogue easier than they had expected. Seductiveness, affection, irritation, and competitiveness can be expressed by the two pairs of feet with surprising accuracy. The unconventionality of this mode of communication, its absence of routinized forms, seems to bring about a childlike gleefulness and a direct experiencing of one another in the two partners.

Nonverbal Relating

A group member who has difficulty in relating to others may be asked to go around the circle and express his feelings toward each of the participants, including the leader, without language. Gestures, physical contact, and even noises or gibberish are permitted. This task is difficult for most people at first, but usually after the first few encounters, it becomes easy to express hostility, affection, indifference or ambivalence, and the participant is likely to feel more a part of the group afterward. People who have trouble in expressing themselves verbally, or who on the contrary use language so glibly that it loses real meaning, can profit by this game.

A variation of this exercise, which can be used for all participants simultaneously, is to ask the group as a whole to relate to one another without words for a stated period of time, such as fifteen minutes. This is effective only if there are several group members who are capable of spontaneity and physical self-expression and can take the initiative; otherwise the game is likely to be blocked by embarrassment and self-conciousness.

Name Game

Here a dialogue is reduced to its very simplest verbal form. The interlocutors face each other, and carry on a conversation consisting entirely of their two names, each to be used in any preferred order and any number of times. Until this stratagem has been observed it is difficult to imagine how meaningful it can be. Not only is it possible for the partners to communicate many varied responses toward one another in the interaction, but also they reveal, to themselves and the surrounding group, nuances and depths of feelings about their own identities. The name is a symbol of the self. Some people find it difficult to utter their own names clearly and positively. In the name game such people usually repeat the name of the partner submissively many times and often experience a real sense of exhilaration when they are finally able to affirm their own identity by a forceful utterance of their own names.

Yes-No Game

Here the only words in the language are "yes" and "no," either of which may be uttered by either participant any number of times and in any order. The device is useful when there is a deadlock of wills, for instance in a difficult marriage, or a community conflict, or even a simple temperamental clash. If an underlying struggle for power is masquerading as a difference of opinion, it may be exposed by this strategem.

Role-Playing

Of all group procedures, role-playing is perhaps the most useful and the most adaptable to a wide range of circumstances. It may involve interaction between two people actually present in the group; or interaction between a group member and another participant who assumes the role of someone not present; or interaction between two conflicting aspects of the personality of a group member. Variations include:

Role-Reversal, which is suitable in a situation where the positions of two group members have congealed to the point where they are aware only of their own points of view and oblivious to the feelings and viewpoint of the other. They are first asked to express their feelings toward one another as fully as possible. Then they are requested to change roles and express the attitude of the other person, a task which is facilitated by an actual exchange of physical positions in the circle. This method is useful in dealing with community conflicts, such as black-white antagonism; with marriage difficulties; and with parent-child problems.

Examples: A wife is unaware of the manipulativeness concealed in her insistence that her husband function consistently as the head of the household and make all decisions, relieving her of responsibility. He feels burdened but does not understand why. They are asked to discuss a household decision in front of the group, speaking as they ordinarily would, then to change places and imitate the attitudes of one another. With the help of comments from the group, they gain a better understanding of their relationship.

Susan, a young woman married to Don, a medical student, wishes him to accept her father's help during their financially difficult years. The husband sees this as demeaning. They discuss the problem, reverse roles, then interact with another participant who impersonates the father and expresses feelings of hurt and rejection. After the situation has been played out on a realistic level, several group members volunteer to function as what Moreno has termed the "alter ego," speaking for the secret thoughts and feelings of one of the participants as they guess them to be. The role-playing proceeds:

Susan: Why shouldn't I have a comfortable way to live? Daddy wants to help us and he certainly can afford it.

Susan's alter ego (standing behind her): You're just angry because Daddy is rich and can afford to give me things you can't. Why, I believe you're jealous!

Don: You're my wife and I want to support you. It won't hurt you to live economically for a few years.

Don's alter ego (standing behind him): I feel castrated by you and your father.

Father: It hurts my feelings you won't let me help you.

Father's alter ego: I want to prove I'm a better man than that young fellow who's my son-in-law!

The alter ego technique, as used in this episode, brought into the open what Don and Susan believed to be one another's underlying attitudes and Don's suspicions about the concealed attitude of his father-in-law. It is impossible to foresee the consequences of an alter ego psychodrama. In this case, once Don's anxiety and suspicions had been ventilated, he decided that they were not justified, and a compromise was reached which satisfied both wife and husband.

Exaggerations is another way to use role-playing when there is a clash between two marathon participants. After the group has had an opportunity to observe the interaction of the two members, as for example a married couple, two other participants take the roles of husband and wife, caricaturing or exaggerating their behavior. In this way it is sometimes possible for the couple to recognize their own inappropriate or destructive attitudes toward one another. A young husband whose attitude toward his wife had been caricatured by Len, another group member, wrote some weeks later:

> I left the marathon feeling that I had been very unfairly treated. It didn't seem possible that I was as unreasonable toward Caroline [his wife] as everybody thought. Len's take-off of my possessive and domineering attitude didn't seem to have a thing to do with me, even though everybody else said it sounded just like me. All week I was cross and withdrawn, and angry with you [myself, as the leader] and the group. Then around the end of the week Caroline came home late from having coffee after a

PTA meeting, and I lost my temper and yelled at her and by God, I sounded just like Len did when he imitated me. It was an ugly experience to face myself like that but I told Caroline maybe I really had been unreasonable. She was very sweet about it and we had a good talk and right now the marriage looks better than it's looked for a long time.

Role-playing is especially valuable when the exploitation of family relationships is being dealt with in the marathon. In its simplest form, this involves the impersonation of a family member by another participant. For example, Elly complains that her mother is constantly telephoning her, expects a visit at least once a week, and in general makes demands beyond reason upon Elly's time and affection. Asked to pick a woman who can symbolize her mother, Elly selects Sarah, and complains to her vehemently about feeling that she is being smothered, declaring repeatedly that she is going to cut short the phone calls and reduce the number of her visits. Usually this procedure has slight value except as a catharsis, but occasionally it brings out attitudes of which the protagonist has been unaware. With Elly, it became strikingly clear that although she continually reiterated her wish to be less involved with her mother, she found it difficult to terminate their conversation, saying goodbye constantly but never really cutting short their dialogue. This was pointed out bluntly by the group, and Elly gradually began to see that for her part she was definitely contributing to the mother-daughter symbiosis.

More commonly, unconscious attitudes are not elicited until the roles are shifted. A middle-aged man, Bernie, expressed deep bitterness and resentment toward his father, now dead, from whom he could recall nothing except disapproval. He chose Fred to play his father's role and spoke to him with strong feeling about his childhood unhappiness. Then they were asked to exchange roles, and Bernie played the part of his own father. At first he behaved like a cruel and obtuse man, but gradually he began to explain to his "son" that he had wanted him to grow up to be a good man but did not know how to achieve this aim except through punishment and scolding. As the "game" continued it grew more and more intense, reaching a climax of emotion when, in the role of his own father, Bernie said, "I'm sorry that I treated you so bad. I'm sorry and I wish I had done better." After this Bernie was able to recognize consciously that his father's unkindness sprang more from ignorance and confusion than from a wish to be cruel. His obsessional resentment toward his father, on which he had been expending a great deal of psychic energy, diminished thereafter.

Role-playing a parent, in addition to the possibility that it may lead to insight as in Bernie's case, also offers the protagonist an opportunity to act out and externalize punitive attitudes toward himself which he has unconsciously taken over from the parent.[6] Moreover, many adults still retain the feeling that their parents are not fallible, forgivable human beings, but vague mysterious forces whose edicts still retain an almost magical compulsive power even when they are defied. Humor is often helpful in enabling group members to see their parents as real people. When several group members are expressing similar feelings toward their parents, such as the feeling that they could never live up to family requirements, or the feeling that they were expected to live for the sake of making their parents proud of them rather than for their own goals, the *Mother's Tea Party* is an appropriate game; usually it is played only by women in the group, but men participants enjoy and empathize with the game.

The instructions are, "This is a tea party for mothers—or a cocktail party, depending on the kind of mother you have. You are playing the part of your own mother, and you are talking about your daughter." Most women pick up the game very quickly and imitate or caricature the mannerisms, speech, and attitudes of their mothers. In some tea parties, the "mothers" compete with one another as to whose daughter is prettiest, most successful, and so on. In other parties, the mothers rival one another in complaints about their daughters' unsatisfactory behavior. Usually the tea party evokes waves of laughter from the group, and its comedy is invaluable in helping the participants see their mothers in perspective rather than as powerful, unreasonable, half-legendary figures.

Role-playing can be used with a maximum effectiveness if the group leader can be flexible about reversing or shifting roles, and also about the decision as to whether an opposite or auxiliary role is best played by the protagonist himself, or by another group member. Perls (1969, p. 121) prefers to request the protagonist himself to play the part of the important figure. He writes:

> "I let the patient play all these parts, because only by really playing can you get the full identification, and the identification is the counteraction to the alienation. *Alienation* means 'That's not me, that's something else, something strange, something not belonging to me.' . . . If I let the patient do *all* the roles himself, we get a clearer picture than when we use Moreno's technique of psychodrama . . . because they [group members playing roles of people important to the patient] bring in their *own* fantasies, their *own* interpretations."

Thus, in Perl's approach, the individual plays each part in his own cast of characters. This enables him to impersonate the disowned or dissociated parts of himself (the "alienated" aspects) as they have appeared in fantasies or memories or dreams, so that he can recognize them and once

---

[6] Chapter 7 describes this process in detail.

more assimilate them as part of his personality. If the individual plays all his own roles, there is no possibility that his fantasies or memories will be distorted by the actual traits of someone else who is playing the role, as may well happen in Moreno's psychodramas.

To me it seems that, balancing out this unquestionable advantage, the psychodramatic approach has the value of bringing the patient into contact with the external world instead of encouraging him to act out and deal with only his own fantasies. When someone else plays the role of the cruel father or rejecting mother, the very fact that the role-player's personality somewhat distorts the personality of the parent makes it necessary for the protagonist to make continual implicit comparisons between his memory or fantasy and the role-playing. This seems better calculated to develop the ability of reality-testing, a central attribute of emotional health, than a drama in which the patient plays all his own roles. Moreover, when other group members participate in a psychodrama, they are likely to offer insights and new perspectives which the patient, moving from one aspect of his inner fantasies to another, might not be able to discover by himself. And finally, other participants who engage in role-playing very often find themselves emotionally involved in a way which becomes directly important to them. For example, after the father-son role-reversal played out by Bernie and Fred, *both* men felt that they could understand and accept their fathers with less pain, even though the episode was planned to center around Bernie.

Since each approach has its own advantages and limitations, it is the responsibility of the group leader to discriminate between situations in which it is most useful for the protagonist to play out all the parts of his inner drama, and in which it is most useful for someone else to play the opposite role. When the conflict is clearly within the self, the former approach is presumably better; when the conflict is with an external figure, such as a parent or with an internalized image of the parent, the latter approach may be preferable.

Role-playing can at times lead to dramatically unexpected insights. A young man who was director of a school for emotionally disturbed children brought to the marathon his feelings of guilt and anxiety about an episode in which, as he felt, he had been unnecessarily rough with one of the youngsters. The little boy had leaped upon another boy and assaulted him, and it had been necessary for the director to intervene physically, but he was puzzled by the violent anger which he had experienced and was worried over the possibility of losing his temper again. He was asked to reenact the scene, taking each of the parts himself, since it was quite unclear what personality traits in either of the boys had triggered off his rage. He complied: first he role-played himself, then the boy who had attacked the other boy, and finally the boy who had been the victim. When he role-played the victim, it became apparent at once that he had strongly identified with the helpless youngster. He curled up on the couch, raised his arms as if to fend off a blow, and repeated again and again "I didn't do nothing, I didn't do nothing." Spontaneously he then recalled an episode from his own boyhood, in which he had been punished unreasonably. Thus it became clear that his problem was not one of uncontrolled violence, as he had feared, but rather of a tendency to overidentify with someone perceived as a victim—an insight which was extremely useful and meaningful to him in meeting his professional responsibilities.

GROUP THEMES

As interaction becomes freer and more trustful, participants begin to scrutinize and evaluate their characteristic ways of relating to people, supporting one another as they try increasingly to relinquish their superficial or defensive poses. In the middle phase, some marathons find a common denominator, a problem shared by many members of the group. Often the group shows great wit and creativity in recognizing and working with this common problem. The game of *Clubs* was spontaneously invented by the participants in one marathon group and has proved adaptable to the needs of several other marathons.

Clubs was invented when someone in the group observed that a woman, who actually functioned effectively both as a mother and as a part-time teacher, seemed determined to prove that she was the most unlucky, inept, and ineffectual member of the group, as if she thought this would confer on her kind of negative distinction. She answered, "You're right, I'm the president of the Losers' Club, Incorporated." The group picked up the notion of the Losers' Club and played with it. For the remaining hours, every time anyone showed a tendency to use complaints and self-criticism as a means of gaining sympathy, the group would chorus, "Now *you're* the president of the Losers' Club," or possibly, "The presidency just changed hands again."

In another marathon, a man who would not have been regarded as personally unacceptable in any situation spoke with genuine agony about a feeling, stemming originally from a boyhood in which he had attained the height of full manhood at an exceptionally early age, that he was some kind of monstrous being, not quite human. In this case the group listened with serious concern, as groups invariably do when the pain is real and not a pose. After a long silence, another participant hesitantly expressed a similar feeling. The two self-perceived "monsters" sat down together on the floor, clasping hands and looking at one another, and after a moment were joined by an especially attractive woman, who sat down with them and said "I'm a monster too." At my suggestion, a Monsters'

Club was formed, and two more participants joined the subgroup. The "monsters" looked at one another with tender sympathy, touching hands.

"You seem so confident. You're the last person in the world I would have thought felt like a monster."

"You're so attractive. How can you think of yourself like that?"

"Well, you too, how can *you*?"

In this episode the therapeutic element was not the group's assurance "No, you are not really a monster," but rather the opportunity to see that other people who were in reality acceptable, likeable human beings shared the same deep, irrational self-loathing. Several of the "monsters" reported profound changes in their own self-images thereafter. One wrote:

> At the time we had the Monsters' Club, I can't remember feeling anything except surprise that some other people, including a woman as attractive as Doris, had that kind of terrible feeling about themselves. I had never really talked to anyone about it before and it never entered my head that other people could feel that way too. I couldn't think about anything else all week and I couldn't get over the amazement. Then one morning I looked in the mirror and I said to myself, "Hey, monster, hi there, you look okay today, monster!" I actually started to laugh. I've had kind of a light-hearted feeling ever since, and I seem to be doing all sorts of fun things, and it's been easier to be nice to people. I know I'll slip back but I'm not going back to being a self-styled monster again ever, ever, ever. I don't feel lonely any more, and if you aren't lonely, you can't really feel like a monster.

Another participant in this same group, a man who had not joined the Monsters' Club, and who had observed its formation in silence, found an unexpected benefit for himself, as can often happen to a silent but empathic participant. He wrote:

> As you know, I've been sore at my parents most of my life, especially my mother, mainly for overprotecting me. I've felt much kindlier to her since the Monsters' Club. She loused me up in some ways, but she tried to build me up, and I certainly never thought of myself as a monster. Maybe I owe that to her just like I owe her some of my problems.

In yet another marathon group, there were a number of successful, ambitious, self-assertive men who were unable to tolerate any kind of weakness or failure in themselves. The theme of the marathon became "Why be a Superman?" A Superman's Club was formed, and again the "presidency" changed hands and a new president was acclaimed each time someone showed signs of a compulsive need to excel or of having unrealistically high standards of achievement. The good-natured bantering which can develop in a group like this is a powerful counter-force to the excessive demands set by an oversevere superego; in this case, the group itself becomes another set of parents, more realistic and accepting.

Self-mockery, not painful because shared by others, was a constructive force for a young woman who confided that she was never quite what she wanted to be—never the best-dressed woman in the room, the most admired, the most effective. Her fantasy, as it emerged, was that she wished not only to be superior, but to be surrounded by superior people.

"The InGroup," someone said.

"The beautiful people."

"The jet set."

"Pick out your superior people, Lorry. Pick out the superior people here and get an InGroup going."

Lorry began to laugh. She saw that her fantasy had a comic quality, yet it was still appealing. She selected three or four people whom she regarded as especially attractive or impressive, and they sat in a sub-circle, playing her game.

"How wonderful to be a Beautiful People!"

"I always *knew* I'd be better than anybody else someday."

They were facetious, yet at the same time they were expressing the familiar adolescent fantasies of being a princess incognito, a great man, a royal prince stolen from his cradle and adopted by commoners, Superman or Wonder Woman disguised as an ordinary mortal. The remainder of the group exchanged glances then quietly went into the other room and drank coffee, talking in low voices. Alone, the InGroup grew bored, formed a delegation, and asked them to return. The entire episode had a light-hearted, almost juvenile quality—yet it evoked and even to some extent dissipated a neurotic fantasy shared by several participants. Lorry wrote:

> I hadn't realized how much I was still haunted by that little-girl idea of growing up to be a Movie Star, or something equally improbable. It almost surprised me when it came out in the marathon, but there it was. I'd have been more embarrassed except that other people seemed to have the same nutty problem. I'm working at it. . . .

SYMBOLIC ENCOUNTERS

In accordance with the principle of translating abstractions into immediate physical terms, it is appropriate in this phase of the group to introduce various encounter techniques which permit the expression of characterological attitudes or personality problems through symbolic actions.

Breaking out of the Circle and *Breaking into the Circle* are exercises which appear superficial and indeed are relatively meaningless if they are introduced merely for the sake of playing a game, but which can be significant if appropriately used. It is fairly common for group members, once the group is at the level of genuine self-expression, to speak of a sense of being fettered by circumstances, of being in a deadlock in which they cannot move toward greater self-actualization, because of the pressures of work or family responsibility or other limitations. The sense of being able to control their own lives is missing. If the group forms a circle, and if the participant is placed in the middle and given the task of breaking out, he usually understands at once that this is a symbolic challenge to find ways of breaking out of his emotional prison. He is instructed to break out any way he chooses, except that he may not bite or scratch, or attack the genitalia of the members of the circle. A determined "prisoner" can almost always break out of the circle without harming either himself or anyone in the circle, although this game also is best used in a setting where there are mattresses on the floor in case of a fall. Unconsciously, the members of the circle presumably enter into collusion to allow the prisoner to break out, identifying with him, and wanting him to gain freedom. A sense of exhilaration invariably follows a successful breakthrough, and the ex-prisoner usually understands the symbolic meaning of the experience with little or no interpretation. One of them wrote:

> These games of yours are crazy as hell. I can't believe what that circle thing did. It sounded wild but I tried it. Believe it or not, I went back to the office on Monday and told the boss I wanted that transfer. You remember, I told the group I'd been stewing about it for months but hadn't worked up the optimism to try to get it. Well, it turned out I just had to try. They had been thinking of me and one other guy for the new job but when I took the initiative and asked for it, that clinched it. So I broke out of my circle. How about that?

Breaking *into* the circle is useful when a participant expresses the feeling that he is somehow shut out from what he wants, or that he is excluded from a world which he perceives as inhabited by luckier, happier people. In this case he stands outside the circle, with the task of breaking in. There is also a special instance in which this game is appropriate: it is well suited to community-conflict groups. A member of a privileged class, such as a white participant in a black-white encounter group, is shut out and faced with the task of trying to break in to the "privileged" circle. Here the physical symbolism helps to develop an empathic under-standing of the feelings of a minority-group member who regards himself as barred from equal participation and feels that he must fight to get in.

Attitudes toward trust and dependency can be tapped at a very deep, intense level by the use of the *Fall-Catch Game, Passing-Around,* and *Lifting and Rocking.* In the Fall-Catch Game, two partners stand a few feet apart, facing in the same direction. The person in front falls backward, feet motionless and body stiff, and is caught under the arms and supported by the person standing behind. If the catcher is lighter and shorter than his partner, the two must stand closer together, but if this precaution is taken, it is possible to catch a very heavy person without any risk. Even if the weight cannot be supported, the fall of a very heavy person can be easily broken, and the partners sink down to-gether without injury if there are cushions or mats on the floor.

This simple procedure can elicit a near-panic reaction in some par-ticipants. The moment of falling is frightening, since it involves placing physical trust in someone who at that moment cannot be seen. It is often helpful, if someone is afraid to trust another person to catch him, to ask the frightened participant to begin by being the active partner and catching someone else. Alternatively, I sometimes begin with a demon-stration in which I myself catch the heaviest person in the room or allow myself to be caught by someone smaller than myself. This game is pre-scribed when a group member wishes to work with his difficulty in trusting other people. Sometimes it takes a quarter-hour or more before the participant is able to let himself fall, and often there is such a sense of triumph when the anxiety is finally overcome that the participant insists on being caught by everyone in the group. As with most of these games, there are bonus benefits for those who are indirectly involved. The catcher may profit also. In a postscript to a long letter, one partici-pant wrote:

> Oh, I almost forgot—the catch game. When I was able to catch big fat Sam, I had the most glorious feeling of being a strong, responsible person. It's great to be able to do something you didn't think you could.

Overcoming anxiety, even on a simple physical level, is a strength-ening experience in itself. The repetition of the Fall-Catch Game until it is possible to fall without anxiety can be viewed as a desensitization procedure according to the learning-theory approach to psychotherapy, and in many instances there seems to be considerable generalization to other situations. One woman wrote:

> As I told you at the beginning of the group, I have always had consider-able difficulty in trusting men. It's really too soon to tell yet, but after I

permitted myself to be caught by several of the men in the group, including one man whom I had instinctively distrusted, I felt that it would be easier from now on to have confidence in them in real life.

In the game of *Passing-Around,* a participant stands in the middle of a circle of other participants standing very close together, relaxes, and is tossed back and forth within the circle. It is important in this game for each woman to stand between two men, since few women can single-handedly support the weight of another person. Typically, the group member who is being passed around is stiff, tense and frightened at first but becomes gradually relaxed and eventually takes pleasure in the experience of trusting.

Lifting and Rocking is also an experience in which the dependency needs of the central participant are symbolically gratified, but this procedure places no demands whatsoever on the person who is being rocked and is therefore an even more potent symbol of being cared for. The participant lies on his back on the floor and is lifted by other members of the group, with their hands under his body and one of them supporting his head. Regardless of the weight of the central figure, this is usually done very easily, and no more than seven people are needed to do the lifting. He is rocked gently back and forth in the air, and someone usually begins to hum or sing, the song being taken up naturally by the group. He is then lowered gently and imperceptibly to the floor and in most groups several other members spontaneously stroke his hair, hold his hand, or pat his body. He is asked to lie quietly with closed eyes for as long as he wishes. It is rare indeed for anyone to have this experience without a deeply gratifying sense of being loved and cherished. People who are lifted and rocked almost always feel much closer to the group afterward, and they become extremely receptive to the affection and concern shown within the group in its later phases.

Despite the infantile dependency which this procedure implies, it is rarely refused by anyone who has even the slightest awareness that he is reaching out for a feeling of being cared for. It is my strong conviction that this technique is among those which should not be used as a routine procedure; not because it is potentially risky, but rather because the experience can be so deeply moving that it should be done only under circumstances which can elicit its most powerful therapeutic effects. It is usually most valuable as a first experience. In one marathon, a burly, successful executive in his forties admitted to the group his feeling that, even though he could function adequately in society on a superficial level, nobody had ever really cared for him and he had never been able to reach out to anyone. He was asked if he would accept the lifting and rocking, agreed, and was picked up and rocked for a long time. When he was finally put down gently, he remained still for a long time, then reached out a hand, with his eyes still closed, into the empty space above him. Someone clasped his hand. He continued to remain silent and wept a very little. When he sat up finally and rejoined the group, he still said almost nothing, but he was for the first time a group member, sharing their warmth.

Two weeks later, he wrote:

> It is a long way back to humanity. I don't know when I left it, almost my lifetime ago, and I'm not back there yet, but now I can feel that somewhere there is light. The moment came when I reached out my hand . . . for the first time.

If this man had gone through the lifting and rocking as a routine procedure in which the group had picked up one member after another, it is unlikely that he would have been able to abandon his lifelong defenses against accepting his basic human need to be nourished and supported. There is an element of surprise in recognizing that *I*, an adult fully grown, can be lifted and rocked like a baby and can feel safe and warm. The surprise can occur only once. The experience derives its value in part from the surprise and in part from the immensely potent physical symbolism, but it can be only a routine exercise unless it is suggested at a time when it is appropriate for the individual. The central figure in this exercise must indicate, however hesitantly, that he is ready to accept the experience of being cared for, and there must be an opportunity thereafter for him to assimilate and share with the group what has happened to him.

RESISTANCE GAMES

As the group develops, there are usually one or two participants who find it more difficult than the others to reveal themselves and to participate. They may be naturally withdrawn and shy; they may be unaware of their effect on others and withdraw because they are puzzled by the feedback from the group; or they may be out of touch with their own inner feelings. There are several techniques which are especially useful here.

Three Wishes is reminiscent of old-fashioned parties for shy adolescents; it is efficacious in bringing out the withdrawn group member and has the concomitant value of acquainting him with his own fantasies. It is also appropriate for the occasional participant who is genuinely concerned with helping others but has difficulty in making requests for his own sake. The instructions are: "You are given three wishes which can be gratified here and now, in this room, by these people." If the group is not yet familiar with encounter games, the leader may be more specific. "You may choose to relate to any of us, or all of us, in any way you wish—affection, hostility, play-acting. You may hug, arm-wrestle, direct a play, or ask questions."

This game elicits a wide range of responses, sometimes unexpected, sometimes humorous, often emotionally moving. An extremely shy man, who had difficulty approaching girls, wished to hug every woman in the room; when he sat down, red-faced and smiling, he was spontaneously applauded. A dignified middle-aged professor, who had been criticized for his pedantic and formal manners, wished to do the silliest thing possible and hit upon a mock bullfight with himself as toreador, which was riotously enacted. A young woman wished to reenact a childhood Christmas experience which had been disappointing and chose members of the group to represent a more loving and giving family. A man who felt antagonistic and competitive toward another man in the group devised a scenario in which he, as a Boy Scout leader, would examine the other man in the role of a Scout being evaluated for a merit badge. More often, the beneficiary of the three wishes makes use of encounter games which have already been introduced and elects to be lifted and rocked, or to wrestle or engage in the fall-catch procedure with someone whose partnership will be especially meaningful for him.

Four Corners is also a resistance game which, because of its playful and childlike quality, will sometimes draw into the group a participant who needs a less challenging situation than the Three Wishes game provides. The protagonist leaves the room, and in his absence four other participants who would like to have some kind of encounter with him each select a corner to represent them. (The corner device has no special significance; the volunteers could as well be represented by colors or numbers.) Upon returning to the room, the protagonist, without knowing which member of the group will respond to his call, makes a wish which can be gratified by one of the "corners." He might say, "I would like to arm-wrestle with that corner"—next, "I would like to embrace that corner"—next, "I would like that corner to tell me what he thinks of my behavior here." The game is admittedly juvenile, and because of this very juvenility, can sometimes induce a withdrawn group member to feel sufficiently at home so that, later on, he will reveal himself in more significant ways. Its primary advantage is that it enables the protagonist to ask for a relationship without naming a partner, thus sidestepping the feeling of shyness which some schizoid patients experience in choosing someone for an encounter.

Mirroring is also a game which can be adapted to a variety of purposes, but it is most useful for a group member who needs to increase his understanding of how he is perceived by others. The partners sit on the floor, face to face. The first partner is asked to speak freely about himself, or perhaps about a topic selected for its relevance. The other partner mimics his sitting posture, arm and leg movements, and facial expressions. At the same time, he echoes every sentence, trying to imitate the precise tone of voice, a task which is less difficult than it seems.

A woman who was unaware of her general ambivalence, and of her tendency to make a halfway gesture of friendliness and then withdraw, was mirrored by another group member. Half-smiles, gestures which combined approach and avoidance, and cut-off sentences were mirrored and echoed. It was a painful experience, but more significant than any verbal description could have been; because of the slight exaggeration of the human mirror, it was probably more efficacious than feedback by means of videotape. She wrote:

> I hated the mirroring and hated what I saw, but now I'm more aware of how many double messages I keep sending—mainly on the job but also with family and friends. Thank you for a lousy experience. Hey, now I'm doing it again. Okay, just thank you. . . .

A special application of the mirroring technique can be used when a participant asks for help in making a crucial decision—marriage, divorce, momentous change of job. He is given two mirrors, representing the two sides of the conflict. He turns from one mirror to the other, expressing his feelings pro and con, and they reflect him accordingly. This is a variation of the Gestalt device of allowing left and right hands to "talk to each other" and represent both sides of an inner conflict. It has the special advantage of providing immediate feedback. This double-mirror strategem ·can be strikingly useful in helping people reach a difficult decision; it is a means by which they can give advice to themselves.

The most spectacularly appropriate use of mirroring in my experience was with two group members, men in their early thirties, both of whom were complaining vigorously about feelings of inadequacy and depression. Genuine grief invariably elicits sympathy and support in a group, but both these men seemed to be enjoying their self-pity and trying to make others suffer along with them. Neither could understand why the group remained hardhearted before their misery. They were asked to sit together and talk about their suffering: first Joe talked about his troubles, and Tom mimicked his whining, complaining voice; then Tom talked, and Joe imitated his voice of theatrical gloom. The group began to laugh, and after the task of mirroring had been shifted back and forth several times, the two men began to laugh at themselves also. The depression, of course, was not miraculously relieved in either man, but after the element of histrionic self-pity was partly dissolved through insight, it was possible to begin to work with the real underlying causes of their feelings.

Induced Fantasy is a method by which a single individual can explore himself, sometimes calling up memories and feelings which have heretofore been repressed. The trip into fantasy is shared by the group, and in my experience no group member has expressed boredom or impatience at being asked to listen to the fantasy, even though it may occupy from ten minutes to half an hour. It is appropriate when a participant speaks of feelings "that I can't get at," or says something like "I just don't know what's bugging me." The group is asked to be silent, and the protagonist is asked to visualize a TV screen or a movie screen, whichever is easier, with his eyes closed. Sometimes, if there is marked anxiety, I sit close beside the participant; sometimes I ask him to select from the group a man and a woman whom he particularly trusts and sit between them, which povides a primitive feeling of security going back to the triangle of mother-father-child.[7] Most participants are capable of seeing visual images, or of fantasying a scenario so vividly that they are able to describe it as if they were watching a play. One woman saw a battle between a little red toy automobile and a huge threatening truck; this was an almost forgotten symbolism from her childhood about the way she had felt in contact with her powerful, dominating mother. A man recalled a scene in which he had felt homosexually threatened by an older boy, and relived the shame, fascination, and terror which he had experienced.

One especially meaningful use of the screen technique occurred with a young woman who had made a decision to divorce her husband. She was apparently quite sure that she had made the right decision and had no doubts about it but was irrationally afraid of living alone. The fear was irrational because she had friends and a benign environment and did not perceive herself as a timid person. Since she could not comprehend the source of her feelings, she was asked to look at the screen behind her closed eyelids. After some time, she was able to describe a scenario of an adolescent memory in which her father, separated from her mother, had visited the house and then left again. She then went still further back into childhood and visualized a scene of her father's leaving the house at the time of the initial separation, when she was five years old. She recalled the grief and pain of the separation, was able to weep, and for the first time comprehended that in separating from her husband she was reexperiencing the anxiety originally felt at separating from her father.

---

[7] Since I "invented" this approach, I have found that it has also been invented by several other psychotherapists (Hammer, 1967; Finney, 1968).

It is characteristic of this technique that it elicits memories, images, and sometimes hitherto forgotten fantasies from the far-off past, rather than from the recent past or present. This phenomenon recalls Freud's description of one aspect of regression as the "transformation of thoughts into images" (1914, p. 544) which tends to move backward in time toward earlier experiences. The TV screen technique appears to facilitate a regression in which experiences can be revived from a time before the clear establishment of verbal and conceptual ability. Since the protagonist is asked to describe whatever images appear on the screen and to discuss them afterward with the group, this process can be viewed as a means of integrating early experiences, with which the childhood ego was not sufficiently strong to cope, with the present-day, more mature self.

It is important, also, not to permit parts of the unconscious or preconscious fantasy to remain hidden either from the protagonist or the group; and it is even more important to help the fantasy-traveler bring out elements of the fantasy of which he is conscious, but which may be embarrassing. Once regressive feelings and images are mobilized, they may reawaken the anxiety which originally led to their repression unless they are expressed and worked through. One method of helping the protagonist explore his own fantasy is by inquiring about any image of something which is not fully visible. For example, the fantasy-traveler comes to a closed door. It might be appropriate to say quietly, "Here is a key. There is a key in your hand. Can you feel it? Now open the door. . . ." Or the traveler may be standing at the entrance to a cave. "Go into the cave, now, go on in. Is it light enough to see? What do you see in the cave?" If the traveler cannot see, he might be offered an imaginary torch or flashlight. A closed box should always be opened in fantasy; a ladder should be climbed; a stream must be crossed. Sometimes, when this aspect of the fantasy has been repressed, the traveler is genuinely surprised at what he finds beyond the barrier. Other travelers conceal a part of their inner experience out of embarrassment and may use such symbols as the box or the door to help them share guilt-laden material with the group. For instance, the man who wished to speak of his boyhood homosexual experience was able to do so only when he saw a closed door on the television screen, opened it, and then entered the room in which the episode had taken place.

IMPROVISED GAMES

In the middle and later phases of a marathon, it is often possible to invent games or scenarios to meet the special needs of someone in the group. Usually these scenarios are more effective than the prescribed games. They may be devised by the leader or by a fellow participant, who, in turn, is enriched by the self-fulfilling experience of using his creativity and good will for the welfare of another.

A delightful example of spontaneous helpfulness occurred in a marathon in which Lowell, a man in his late twenties, showed a withdrawal so alarming that I recalled dire warnings from conservative colleagues who feared that a marathon might precipitate psychotic breaks. Lowell looked not potentially, but actually psychotic. He sat in a corner, knees drawn up and head hunched into his shoulders, expressionless and pallid. Occasionally there was a slight, convulsive shudder, which might be either a tic or shiver of fear.

Lowell had been referred to me by a psychiatrist who was treating him privately, and who was familiar with marathons,[8] therefore I had not screened him. He told us nothing, except for a brief description of an isolated life devoid of pleasure or achievement. He did not react to any other participant, except to express displeasure at the aging appearance of another man—a supercilious, inhuman reaction. My attempts to draw Lowell out were rebuffed, presumably because as the group leader I was too strong a symbol of feminine authority.

His misery was beginning to infect the group when a young woman, not professionally trained but with an intuitive feeling for reaching out to others, spoke to him from across the room. She asked him, "Will you play with me?" He hesitated for a time, then nodded jerkily. Sally crossed the room, knelt before him, and began the old children's game of Pease-Porridge-Hot, in which there is a rhythmical, repeated pattern of hand-clapping. He remained aloof and gloomy for a few minutes, then slowly joined the game. It was almost possible to hear his joints creaking. They played for a while, and when they finished, Lowell's face had some color and his eyes were no longer glazed. He never became a full participant in the group, but for the remainder of the marathon he seemed interested in what was happening, and no longer seemed in danger of a psychotic episode.

A difficult and basic life decision sometimes provides dramatic material for a scenario which can help the protagonist face his conflict. Leonard, a successful eye surgeon, had for some years felt smothered and immobilized in a marriage with a wife whom he perceived as dependent, demanding, and withdrawn. For several years he had been entirely impotent with her, a symptom which was particularly painful to him because he came from a background in which physical virility was highly valued. Within the last year, however, he had begun a relationship with another woman with whom he found himself potent. Now he was

---

[8] Subsequently it transpired that Lowell's psychiatrist had written me inquiring whether or not I would wish to work with so disturbed a patient; his letter had gone astray.

considering a separation from his wife but could not carry it out, in part because he feared this might result in her suicide. He was at an impasse, in which he could neither leave the other woman, and commit himself to remaining in the marriage, nor separate from his wife. Because Leonard placed great value on personal honesty, he was particularly tormented by his deception of his wife.

A three-act drama was devised for Leonard. Act I: He would tell his wife that he intended to leave her. Act II: He would walk in the woods around his house, musing aloud, as was his habit when troubled. Act III: He would return to his house and find his wife dead by suicide. The purpose of this drama was to give Leonard an opportunity to express and explore not only his feelings but his fantasies about his wife's possible suicide.

The drama was carried out. A woman in the group played Leonard's wife, pleading and threatening and clinging. He remained firm in a decision to leave and broke away. For the next act he paced around the room, so deeply immersed in his soliloquy that it was almost possible to see the imagined forest as he dealt with his feelings of anger and guilt. For the third act, he returned home and discovered his wife's dead body, still role-played by the woman participant, who lay motionless on the couch. Leonard knelt beside her, stroking her hair, and speaking about the early days of their marriage. The scene was moving, yet it had a ring of artifice, and several participants questioned the validity of Leonard's feelings.

We discussed the situation with Leonard, who said at last, "Well, I don't really *want* to leave my wife."

"Because she might kill herself?"

Slowly Leonard acknowledged that his wife's threat of suicide was not the only deterrent to leaving her. There were other values in the marriage. He was confused and miserable by a situation which went counter to his basic values of honesty and straightforwardness. Also, he could not make up his mind either to leave his wife or to give up the other woman. As a justification for remaining immobilized, he had perhaps exaggerated the possibility of his wife's suicide.

Rarely indeed do the members of a marathon attempt to impose their own value systems on another participant. In Leonard's group, there were some participants who saw the preservation of his marriage as an ethically preferable decision, and other participants who believed that it was masochistic of him not to leave her. Yet only one participant made any effort to persuade Leonard directly, and the group quickly silenced him, pointing out that it was necessary for Leonard to find his own answer.

The episode of Eugene, a young Catholic priest, also exemplifies the willingness of a marathon group to accept values other than their own. Eugene was intensely dedicated to his vocation and satisfied with its social and spiritual rewards. But late at night, he expressed the conflict which had drawn him to attend the marathon: he was deeply regretful that he would never be able to father a child.[9]

Eugene was offered a pillow and asked to pretend that it was the baby he would never have. Accepting the symbolic baby, he held it gently, rocked it, and spoke quietly, beginning "Baby I will never have . . ." As if the "baby" could understand, Eugene spoke about the significance of the priesthood for him and the meaning of his relationship to his parish and his deity. At the end he put the "baby" aside and said goodbye, half-sobbing.

In the morning, when the group reconvened, Eugene was radiant. He told the group that he had dedicated himself anew to his vocation. There were participants in the marathon who were personally opposed to Eugene's religious philosophy, yet there could be no doubt that he had faced a major conflict within himself and had resolved it in a way which strengthened his identification with his chosen values and reinforced his commitment to his work. Because his decision was genuine, the group received it with joyous congratulations.

Because of the intimacy which develops in a successful marathon, participants often show a concern for one another which is comparable to what is ordinarily offered to close friends and relatives. The concern is temporary, because the group members do not undertake long-term responsibility for maintaining their relationships, but it is intense and genuine.

Terry, a burly businessman in his forties, evoked the group's liking because of his direct and friendly personality and their alarmed concern by his fantastically heavy smoking, admittedly at least three packs a day. For Terry, this was more than a bad habit. It was suicide. He had suffered two heart attacks and had been told by his physician that he was jeopardizing his life with each fresh pack. He never was without a cigarette.

His life history made Terry's danger all the more dramatic. He had won financial success and prestige only in recent years after considerable struggle. His first marriage had been unhappy, and he had recently remarried an attractive and congenial woman. He had everything to live for. But he was, apparently, a victim of his own self-destructiveness, presumably because of deep-seated, unconscious feelings of guilt. Terry

[9] This episode occurred before the contemporary debate over the necessity of celibacy for the Catholic clergy. In any case, Eugene would probably have been reluctant to make a personal choice not officially endorsed by his church.

consistently refused to enter psychotherapy and had come to the marathon only because of the pleading of his wife, who hoped that somehow, miraculously, the group would help him stop smoking.

Because of their affection for Terry, the group worked very hard with him. They reasoned with him, implored him, and screamed at him. Terry agreed with everything and went on smoking. At last someone said, "Let's have a funeral." Rather disdainfully, Terry agreed. He lay down on the couch, closed his eyes, and folded his hands, and all the group filed by to pay their last respects.

Many participants were facetious, perhaps out of exasperation at Terry's obduracy, perhaps because it seemed to them that Terry's self-destructiveness represented an indirect method of winning attention and pity. Someone placed a pack of cigarettes in his hands to represent a prayer book. Someone else said, "Let's have a party, I wish he could be there." But their concern came through, and the last in line of the "mourners" sank to his knees and wept, not histrionically, but because he recognized that Terry could in cold reality be destroying himself.

At this Terry could endure it no longer. He sat up abruptly. "Enough already," he said sharply, "It's stupid to be dead." He did not light another cigarette for the remainder of the marathon. It was, he told us, the longest period of time he had been able to refrain from smoking for a great many years, and he hoped as he left the group that he could abstain.

A frequent theme of improvised scenarios involves regression to a primitive emotional level, followed by the return to emotional maturity. Jenny, in her mid-twenties, told the group that she had difficulty in controlling her impulsiveness. "The feelings just spill out," she said, "I can't control them." She went on to tell us that as a child she had been given to temper tantrums, which her parents had handled by going away, closing the door, and letting her "cry it out." She wished now that instead they had helped her control herself, since she remembered crying harder and harder in the hope that they would return, stopping only from exhaustion.

"What would you have liked them to do?"

"I would have liked Mother to hold me tight and make me stop."

"Would you like to try that now, Jenny? Can you have a temper tantrum now?"

Jenny was outgoing and lively, a personality type whom most clinicians would diagnose as hysteric, with emotions close to the surface. It was easy for her to have a temper tantrum. She lay down, kicked, screamed, and pounded the floor. As a mother-symbol, I went to her and held her tightly. She struggled, but it was apparent that she welcomed the feeling of being restrained. When she was quiet, I signalled another participant to bring a cup of milk from the adjacent coffee room.

I held it to her lips. She sipped and gave it back. I handed it to her again, saying, "Now you must hold it." She held the cup, sipped, and tried to give it back again. I refused, saying "No, you must put it down yourself." She sipped again, put the cup on a table, and opened her eyes.

The symbolism of regression and growing up again was beautifully clear through the use of the cup of milk; the episode culminated in Jenny's taking responsibility for feeding herself, which paralleled her wish to be able to take responsibility for controlling her emotions. By controlling her and then by feeding her, I had functioned as the mother who must perform actions which the young child cannot yet perform, teaching the child and serving as a model for identification, in preparation for the time when the child will be mature enough to meet its own needs.

Most of the scenarios, it is evident, resemble individualized treatment in that they are tailored to meet individual needs, just as in classical psychoanalytically oriented psychotherapy an interpretation is offered only after due consideration of the patient's individual psychodynamics, his readiness to accept the interpretation at that time, and the immediate effect which it will have on the progress of therapy. Rarely does a scenario result in the instantaneous dramatic resolution of a conflict, or the immediate disappearance of a symptom, just as the most skillfully conducted session of individual psychotherapy rarely has such immediate results. Follow-up material on the five patients whose individual scenarios have just been described is representative of the effects which may occur:

Lowell, the withdrawn young man, had been referred to me by a psychiatrist who was treating him individually. Knowing that Lowell might be regarded as too disturbed for a marathon, the psychiatrist had written me about his condition, but the letter had gone astray. When Lowell returned to individual treatment, his psychiatrist reported to me that communication was now easier and that a deadlock of silence between patient and therapist seemed to have been broken by the marathon.

Leonard informed me, several months after this marathon, that he had gone home to his wife when the group was over and had informed her about his affair with the other woman. They talked frankly for the first time in many years, after which Leonard suddenly and dramatically regained his potency with her. Psychologically sophisticated, Leonard ascribed this to his release of anger toward her through the scenario, and also to the opportunity to express his guilt feelings. His marriage was improving, but he had not yet been able to make any decision as to whether or not to break off with the other woman.

Eugene made the choice which he really wanted to make. He had never been seriously impelled to leave the priesthood, and the marathon episode helped him accept a decision which had already been made.

Terry went home, smoked more lightly for a few days, then resumed his three-pack-a-day habit. His physician tried to persuade him to enter ongoing psychotherapeutic treatment, but he refused. Two years later he suffered a coronary attack, survived, and was able to cut down on smoking thereafter. Perhaps if the marathon experience had been followed immediately by individual psychotherapy Terry could have sustained his abstinence.

Jenny's marathon attendance was part of an ongoing experience with a psychotherapist who had suggested the marathon. She had been dealing with her need to develop self-control. Her therapist corroborated Jenny's enthusiastic belief that the marathon episode was helpful in accelerating her progress, but its effect could not be separated from her general movement toward maturity.

Scenarios, like the encounter games in general, are most likely to be effective in helping people move along a path they have already chosen. Some participants enter a marathon to be in more intimate contact with others than their social milieu encourages, to express themselves more spontaneously, to widen their horizons of experience; for them, more-or-less standard encounter games, if sensitively presented, may provide the nourishment they seek. Other participants are struggling with problems of grief or guilt or fear or indecision, and for them the technique of the individualized scenario can be spectacularly effective; but it is most likely to be effective when an opportunity for its fuller integration and understanding is provided by subsequent individual psychotherapy.

Most of these procedures, it should be noted, were devised primarily to help overcontrolled, overrational people learn to express themselves and to communicate more freely. Games which serve as channels for the expression of hostility on a physical level, as for example arm-wrestling, are particularly valuable for participants who are overfearful of their own aggressiveness. With people from a different socioeconomic level, where physical assaultiveness is taken for granted, games of this particular type would not only be of limited value but might involve a risk of precipitating actual violence. Acting-out personalities and people who have never learned to control their impulses need to learn to express themselves verbally, and for them it would seem wise to place greater emphasis on procedures which help them direct their feelings into verbal channels.

The use of fantasy in groups is also particularly appropriate for people whose educational level is such that they have already learned to use their imaginations, to some degree at least. For them, the value of scenarios and other fantasy games is that the secret, hidden fantasies become more explicit and can be shared with others. People who have been educationally deprived would usually require a different approach.

It may be hoped that, as the encounter movement develops, group procedures will be worked out to meet the special needs of people from deprived backgrounds, who require practice in recognizing and controlling their impulses, rather than practice in expressing their feelings more fully.

REFERENCES

Corsini, R. J. *Roleplaying in psychotherapy.* Chicago: Aldine, 1966.

Finney, B. *The eagle trip.* Mimeograph. San Jose, Calif.: 1968.

Freud, S. *The interpretation of dreams.* (3rd ed.) London: Hogarth, 1914.

Hammer, M. The directed daydream technique. *Psychotherapy,* November 1967.

Malamud, D. L., & Machover, S. *Toward self-understanding.* Springfield, Ill.: Charles C Thomas, 1965.

Moreno, J. L. *Psychodrama.* New York: Beacon House, 1946.

Perls, F. S. *Gestalt therapy verbatim.* Lafayette, Calif.: Real People Press, 1969.

Schutz, W. *Joy.* New York: Grove Press, 1967.

4 THE HEALING
OF THE PAST

For contemporary psychotherapists, even those who are identified with the mainstream of classical psychoanalytic tradition, psychotherapeutic success is no longer regarded as depending primarily on the reconstruction of forgotten childhood traumata for the purpose of leading to self-understanding. Even among therapists who regard the acquisition of insight as indispensable to effective treatment, emphasis is increasingly placed on the personal relationship between therapist and patient, on therapy as a reparative emotional experience, and on the release of repressed feelings from the past.

The achievement of these aims, through individual treatment or through ongoing group therapy, has traditionally been expected to require a substantial period of time, with one to three years typically regarded as the mode. Yet even in contributions as widely accepted as Alexander and French's twenty-five-year-old classic (1946), examples are offered of patients who made striking and lasting improvement as a result of two or three interviews, or even one. These authors consider that such successes depend on two conditions: that the therapist should "be able to produce a replica of the traumatic situation with sufficient vividness to make it realistic," and that "the ego can stand this reactivation" (p. 163). Even more vividly, they specify that "re-experiencing the old unsettled conflicts *but with a new ending* is the secret of every penetrating therapeutic result" (p. 338).

The case histories offered in this chapter leave scant doubt that the circumstances of an unstructured marathon encounter group, conducted with an awareness that each participant is unique both in his momentary needs and in his personal psychodynamic structure, are particularly well suited to the occurrence of these dramatically reparative experiences. These reports do not include the euphoric expressions of gratitude frequently offered immediately after a marathon, for which later follow-up information may or may not be available. They have been selected, from approximately fifty similar detailed documents written or tape-recorded by marathon participants, on the basis of my personal knowledge of the participant's stability and veracity; on statements made at least a month later that the effects of the experience were sustained to a subjectively noticeable degree; and on diagnostic impressions which excluded psychopathy, immature personality, strong manic tendencies, marked hysteria, or any other syndrome which might presumably be conducive toward overimaginative accounts of the experience.

It is easier to offer a description of the dramatically corrective emotional experience than to understand and explain its underlying dynamics. Such experiences are described in fiction by the old-fashioned expression "change of heart," as in Alexander and French's example of Jean Valjean from Hugo's *Les Misérables*. It is tempting to speculate that there may be an analogy between this reparative experience and such phenomena as the miraculous cures of Lourdes or the relinquishing of a destructive way of life after a religious conversion. Certainly there are resemblances between some reports of how participants feel after a marathon and reports of the experience of religious conversion (James, 1902). The cures of Lourdes and the religious conversions, however, are usually regarded as related primarily to the preexistence of strong religious faith reaching deep into the unconscious. There are no special grounds to believe that any of these marathon participants possessed a comparably strong faith in either the leader or the group, although it may reasonably be supposed that the realistic confidence built up through extended time may well have helped them be open to new experiences. Nor, in most of these episodes, does the alleviation of guilt through the group's affectionate acceptance seem to be of central importance, although in traditional psychotherapy the alleviation of superego severity is generally regarded as a basic curative factor.

If there is a common denominator in these marathon experiences, it seems to be a regression to childlike ways of feeling and a repetition of a traumatic childhood experience in an atmosphere of warmth and safety, followed by a reintegration of the childhood trauma on a mature level—all of which is possible because of the marathon's extension of time. In line with Alexander and French's second condition, "that the ego can stand this reactivation," it is worth noting not only that all these cases were people whose life histories gave evidence of considerable ego strength, but also that they had all previously undergone individual psychotherapy, even though they reported it as only partially effective in comparison to the marathon breakthrough.

Saul, a psychologist in his early forties, with a stable marriage and two children, said little about his purpose in attending the marathon until late in its first day. Then he told the group that perhaps "when time permits, if no one else has anything more urgent," he would like to work on a childhood episode which still disturbed him. The undemanding tone of this request was characteristic of Saul, whose principal characterological defense was overcontrol, and he was asked at once to tell the group about this episode.

At the age of six, Saul told us, in the days before antibiotics, he had developed an extremely serious bilateral mastoid infection, requiring an operation to remove diseased tissue and scrape the bones. Although he began his account of the experience rather quietly, his voice soon cracked and he began to cry. His written account, several weeks after the marathon, gives a picture of the horror of the experience, for which he could not be given ether because of renal dysfunction and high blood pressure. As ether was at that time the only reliable major anesthetic, the terrified small boy had to remain conscious during an operation generally regarded as among the most painful of all surgical procedures.

> My head and body were strapped down and I could not move. . . . I felt them stick a needle in. I screamed and kicked my legs. . . . Two male attendants ran over and strapped my legs down too. I was now completely immobilized. They repeatedly stuck needles into the same area in a circular pattern. Then they stuck me again and again with other sharp instruments. I stopped answering the nurse's questions and just yelled . . . naked animal yells. The pain that they inflicted on me was excruciating, was unbearable. . . . It was like the whole world had turned on me with a savage, barbaric, torturing wrath and I was completely and helplessly trapped in its steel grip. At last when I tried to scream only voiceless breath came forth. . . . When they apparently finished with my left mastoid they picked me up. I was a limp rag. They turned me around and then worked on the right mastoid. Years later, in adulthood, my mother told me that I had been up in the operating room for two and a half hours. Just before the operation she and my father asked the surgeon how I was. . . . According to her, he said, "Mrs. Solomon, you're fortunate because you have two other children. . . ."

For Saul, although his parents nursed him tenderly during the prolonged and painful convalescence, the terror and the physical pain were exacerbated because, undoubtedly with good intentions, his family joined in a pretense that although he had been sick, nothing else had really happened.

> There appeared to be a strange conspiracy of silence. Nobody, even the nurses and physicians in the hospital, ever acknowledged the pain I had suffered. Apparently the surgeons did not tell my parents about it. Probably they looked at my parents as uneducated immigrants and thought that telling them would only upset them.

Consequently, Saul repressed the entire memory. Not until he was 23 years old, undergoing psychotherapy for the relief of chronic tension and obsessive-compulsive symptoms, did he regain the memory. Thereafter Saul experienced considerable relief of his neurotic symptoms but remained phobic about any accidental brushing against the mastoid area.

In later life, when he himself had become a qualified professional psychotherapist, he reentered psychotherapy. He considered his treatment extremely helpful but realized that he had never completely worked through his reactions to the mastoid operation. It was for this reason that he entered the marathon, feeling that he was limited both personally and professionally by the effects of the early trauma, which still haunted him.

> I have been eager to become a group therapist. However, I have been painfully aware that in almost every group situation, I almost always clam up completely and become totally passive. . . . It occurred to me that perhaps the mastoid operation as an overwhelmingly traumatic early group experience was related to my failure to function adequately in current group situations. . . . Perhaps this negative effect could be undone if I could more thoroughly work through the mastoid operation in a group situation. . . . The night before the marathon, I could not sleep at all. I kept thinking about reenacting the operation in the marathon. These thoughts saddened and frightened me. . . . I feared the possibility of a psychotic break or losing control and becoming violent.

This fear of losing control is fairly common among marathon participants who approach the reenactment of an early trauma. My observation is that this fear tends to be most acute among participants who are characterologically overcontrolled and who in reality would be most unlikely to "become violent." The fear is a manifestation of an exaggerated taboo against free self-expression, imposed by the environment in childhood and incorporated into the personality structure. Never have I seen this extreme fear of losing control occur in a patient who was realistically likely to do so. Saul's self-diagnosis seemed accurate:

> I must admit that I am the obsessive-schizoid type. Full or direct emotional expression is rather rare for me. I keep my emotions under tight control generally and often cannot even contact them.

This was Saul's position when he brought up the mastoid operation in the marathon. Asked how he wished to approach it, he said uncertainly "Perhaps we could go through a scene. . . . I could pretend that I was going through the operation, work it out that way. . . ." This procedure of directly reenacting a trauma, which Saul had already observed in the marathon, is often useful. In this instance it did not seem appropriate, because Saul was already conscious of the helpless terror which he had experienced. Instead, I decided to try to offer Saul the sense of safety and comfort in his environment which had been so spectacularly absent in the hospital. Therefore, I asked Saul to go around the circle and request each member to stroke and touch his mastoid areas very gently. In order to enhance Saul's feeling of being in charge of the situation, and partially to undo his former helplessness, they were to do this only *after* his request. Conceptually, this approach can be viewed as an application of Freud's familiar recommendation that psychoanalysts, at an appropriate point in treatment, should require phobic patients to confront the phobia; in terms of learning theory, it can be viewed as a desensitization procedure.

It was difficult at first for Saul to comply. He wrote:

> I told of my apprehension lest I have a psychotic episode. . . . You [addressed to myself] said that you were willing to take that risk with me. I said that I was also willing. I said that if I did reenact it and someone starting poking his finger at the site of the mastoid operation, I feared that I would lose control and . . . kill him. You said you were sure no one there would stick his finger into my mastoid region.

My confidence in the group proved wholly justified. Saul went around the room, kneeling before each of us in turn, and asking us to touch the mastoid area.

> With the first few people it was quite uncomfortable and unpleasant, but not unbearable. . . . It became easier as I forced myself to go along. Perhaps the deep feeling reactions that I sensed from most of the others made it easier. I saw love and warmth and tenderness in their eyes. . . .

As he saw the affectionate compassion in each face, Saul began to respond with gestures of affection. Toward the completion of the circle, as his anxiety diminished, he suggested that they could press somewhat harder. He completed the circle.

"Saul, was there anybody in the circle who made you afraid that he might not touch you gently, maybe even that he'd try to hurt you?"

"Yes, *him*." Saul indicated another man, Rod, whose hostility had already become apparent during the marathon. Rather shamefacedly, Rod admitted that indeed he had been aware of a fantasy of poking Saul unexpectedly, although he had not actually come close to doing so. Thus Rod became a symbol of Saul's fear of being helpless and injured—and he became the natural antagonist for Saul in the next act of this scenario.

In accordance with the psychoanalytic formulation that the helpless child first fears the aggressor, then introjects him, and thereafter persecutes himself as the aggressor has once persecuted him, Saul was not asked to play the role of himself as a small, helpless boy. Instead, he was asked to take the role of the surgeon, whom inevitably he had perceived as a monster of cruelty and power. He was also given the choice of who would play the nurse, the attendants, and his parents. The man whom Saul feared, Rod, was to be the helpless little patient.

Rod, as the patient, lay down on the floor. The lights were lowered.

The parents said farewell and left the room, the attendants held Rod down, and as the surgeon, Saul approached his patient.

"Will you hurt me, doctor?"

"No," said Saul, repeating the lie with which, in Saul's probably correct memory, the surgeon had tried to reassure him. Then he began to "operate." There was no hint of levity. The group was totally intent. Saul's face looked grim and earnest. He poked his finger repeatedly at Rod's mastoid area, as if digging in a scalpel. Then there was an unexpected development. Saul looked at me. Hesitantly, he said, "I have a fantasy. . . ."

"Go ahead with it, Saul."

Saul went ahead. Poking his finger-scalpel at Rod's mastoid, he began to scream, over and over, with increasing intensity, "I'll kill you! *I'll kill you!* I'LL KILL YOU!"

In my opinion, this was the crucial point of the whole episode. Certainly the surgeon had never threatened to kill the terrified child, nor did Saul have a conscious memory of any such threat. But unquestionably, in his bewilderment and panic, he had felt as if he were about to be destroyed. And it seemed equally certain, according to talion law, that he had reciprocated with a violent longing to destroy the torturer.

Saul shouted more and more violently, still jabbing with his finger, yet on some level still in complete control, so that it never occurred to anyone that Rod might actually be injured. Perspiring and trembling, at last he seemed exhausted. As quietly as possible, I asked him to change places with the patient and to lie down where Rod was lying. Since he had now expressed his pent-up rage, and since the operation was over, I wished him to experience being loved and cherished.

Saul lay down in Rod's place. I asked the group to lift him up, hold and rock him, and then place him on the couch. They did so wordlessly, moving in complete harmony with one another, caught up in their empathy for Saul.

Saul lay on the couch relaxed and limp. His "parents" came to his bedside and bent over him solicitously. Saul cried, "It was too much, it was too much!" and burst into uncontrollable tears.

When he had quieted down, someone suggested that we should now go through the motions of the blood transfusion which Saul's parents had actually given him after the operation, and which had been nearly as painful and bewildering as the operation itself. It seemed to me that it was now important for Saul to make his own decisions and I asked him whether this was what he wanted, or whether there was something else. Saul answered that he wished to kill the surgeons.

You then asked whether there was anyone else who felt angry at doctors who would join me. Helen [a group member who had her own reasons for feeling resentful toward surgeons] volunteered to do so. She and I both knelt down and pounded the couch. I pounded as hard as I could, screaming, and kept it up until I was exhausted. . . . I was just too tired to undertake anything more.

The purpose of offering Saul a companion was to give him the feeling that he was not alone in his rage, as he had been given the feeling that he was not alone in his reenacted pain, when he was lifted by the group. Now it was over. Saul said, "That's it," and gradually regained composure. We spoke briefly about the episode, gave Saul time to recover, and then went on to someone else.

Here is Saul's account of the results:

The principal effect that followed immediately and lasted well into the next day was the overwhelming feeling of inner peace, completion, and total serenity. I was filled with the fullness of myself. I was free of any desire or need to say anything or even to move. I did not need or want the presence of the group any more but neither did I want to go away. I could have been anywhere. It was enough for me just to sit and just to breathe. Such an experience of pure being, I believe may come once or twice in a lifetime. . . .

Among the therapeutic elements in Saul's experience, as he himself recognized, was the fact that his family's ignoring the horror of his experience had at times made him wonder whether the whole episode had really occurred, although hospital records, which his analyst had obtained, later confirmed it. Therefore the recognition of the group that he had really undergone this appalling trauma was especially important.

I needed that corrective emotional experience within a group setting. . . . After the operation there had been the solid wall of silence. . . . Did it really happen or was it a psychotic hallucination? . . . I needed witnesses, I needed a group of people to bear witness and affirm that it actually happened. . . . The response of the group reinforced my belief in my own senses.

Saul's final report was written about two months later.

In the first few weeks after the marathon, I was intensely aware of my changes because they were very dramatic and in sharp contrast to how I had been before the marathon. Now it is almost two months, yet in large part, the changes have remained intact. . . . Since the marathon I feel clear as a bell. I feel unblocked, cleansed. . . . Before, whenever I said or did anything to move toward people, to express feeling, to be assertive, there was a powerful inner resistance. . . . The result was great tension, extreme strain, and deep anxiety. Now this resistance is gone and the strain and anxiety as well. . . . The barricade doesn't exist any more. . . . I sleep much better than ever before. I used to sleep fitfully. After a night's sleep I would feel tired. Now I feel fully rested when I arise. . . . After the marathon, I found that my orgasms became more deeply enjoyable. My wife tells me that she experiences me as more aggressive in love-making. I more frequently and easily express my anger . . . and am also more free and spontaneous in expressing positive feelings toward her. I relate more openly to my daughters. . . . I am more open and spontaneous as a therapist. . . . I feel freer to participate in group situations. . . . The marathon was the single most powerful therapeutic experience of my whole life. This within the context of some excellent and rewarding experiences in psychotherapy.

Like the other experiences related here, Saul's breakthrough depended on an unusual combination of circumstances. As his life history shows, he possessed considerable basic ego strength. He had a history of consistently struggling toward self-fulfillment, as shown by his professional effectiveness and also by his seeking and persisting in psychotherapy. His recognition of the gains that he had made in therapy, and his positive attitude toward the two therapists with whom he had worked, indicated that his drive toward self-fulfillment was essentially stronger than his resistance.

At the same time, the traditional therapeutic dyad obviously could not offer Saul an adequate re-creation of an experience which not only had been traumatic in itself but had become the focal point and symbol of all his childhood feelings of helplessness, bewilderment, and futile rage. As he himself recognized, the presence of the understanding, empathizing, compassionate group was of central importance. The time extension of the marathon allowed leeway for the experience to gather momentum and be fully worked through, as could not have been done in a conventional ninety-minute ongoing group. Finally, I believe that my ability to suggest a scenario designed in accordance with the psychodynamic principles laid down by analytic theory led to a far more profound and intense experience than could have taken place if Saul had simply discussed his experience, or even reenacted it directly.

The technique of reducing a phobia by placing the phobic patient in control of the feared situation, in the reassuring setting of the marathon, is nearly always effective, though not always so spectacular in its results as in Saul's case. Felicia, a wife and mother and a part-time high-school teacher, could function well in many areas but was the victim of severe claustrophobia. She felt hemmed in by crowds, to the point where she sometimes had to leave a supermarket or department store. Elevators and subways were almost intolerable. Like Saul, she had undergone individual psychotherapy and had profited, but felt that the phobia was still relatively untouched.

Felicia was sitting next to me as she told the group about her phobia. I could feel her trembling, and when I took her hand it was ice cold. My comment on how terrified she seemed, which to me seemed matter-of-fact, appeared to have a special meaning for Felicia, analogous to the importance of having the group "witness" his suffering in the case of Saul.

"Thank you . . ." she said. "People don't realize . . ." Then she told the group about a previous marathon in which the leader had asked her to enter a dark closet and then had instructed the group to hold the door forcibly shut. Since this experience had merely repeated and reinforced her original sense of being shut in helpless in a small, dark space, the phobia had been exacerbated, and now Felicia was afraid that we would repeat the same procedure.

After promising Felicia that nothing would be done without her knowledge and consent, I asked the group to pick her up and rock her in their arms, in order to give her a feeling of safety. She accepted this with some difficulty, but after she had been swayed gently back and forth for a few moments, she relaxed and was able to enjoy the sense of being cared for. She was put down, rested for a while, and then was asked to enter an adjoining closet, shut the door, and remain alone in the dark until her fear subsided, or until she felt she could no longer tolerate the fear. Nobody would try to hold the door. She herself would make the decision when to come out.

Felicia complied, remained in the closet for a surprisingly long time, and came out looking radiant. She told us that at first she had been frightened but had then reminded herself that she was a free agent and could open the door whenever she chose. She was delighted with her own achievement, for she had remained alone in the dark until she was no longer frightened. Two months later, she wrote:

> At the marathon I was really afraid that I would have to go into the closet and be held in just because I know this does get me in touch with the fear. When you and the group responded so positively and sensitively to the fear, that was a help in itself. The extent of the fear had not been appreciated before. Combining with this, the rocking and realizing that the group was with me . . . did indeed help. It has however required more work. . . .

Felicia wrote later that she had attended another marathon, had worked further on the phobia, and found that it was now almost eradicated, a report which is in accordance with my belief that the value of a series of marathons does not necessarily depend on a sustained relationship with one marathon therapist, provided that the leadership is effective.

I went beyond the fear at last . . . and got in touch with the desire for survival. After it was over I felt very brave both now and as a child. . . . This made me feel marvelous and ready for anything.

The expression "brave now and as a child" suggests that with Felicia, as with Saul, a corrective emotional experience not only diminished the phobic anxiety of the present, but also seemed to drain away part of the sense of helplessness from the childhood memory itself. The experience of being lifted and rocked, which appeared crucially important for both Saul and Felicia, was offered to Saul *after* he had relived his childhood in order to provide him with a different, happier ending (as quoted above, "re-experiencing the old, unsettled conflicts but with a new ending"); it was offered to Felicia *before* she confronted the phobia because she needed reassurance before she could summon up the determination to take the initiative in handling her fears.

Although personalized scenarios and group interaction are in themselves powerful agents for fostering emotional growth, they are at least equally important in creating a climate of warmth and intimacy in which the participants can reach inward to their own feelings, as well as outward to the other members, in search of whatever nourishment they need. For certain people, the group seems less meaningful as a stage for meaningful scenarios than as an encircling support.

Ben was a dark, rugged-looking man who came from an economically and emotionally deprived background and had gone through great struggles to earn an education which had culminated in a doctorate. An early marriage had been bitterly unhappy. Now, with an associate professorship and a good second marriage, he still found it difficult to believe that life could be rewarding, or that he was entitled to enjoyment.

Reserved and taciturn by nature, Ben did not present an artificial front in the beginning of the marathon but found it difficult to be spontaneous. That night he discussed the marathon with his wife Miriam, who was attending with him, and spoke of his feeling that he "had a number of impulses to do things with other people, helpful things, but had held all of them back." The next day, his dissatisfaction with himself increased when he had an impulse to express the feeling that another group member was evading her real problem but was unable to do so until the group leader, as Ben put it, tacitly "gave him permission" to do so by expressing a similar feeling. After a brief inner battle, Ben decided to expose his feelings to the group. In a tape which he dictated to a machine the next day, and which was afterward transcribed, Ben said:

Somebody else wanted to talk next but I asked very strongly that I be allowed a turn. And I told the group about my feeling of not being able to really openly be myself and allow my impulses . . . free play. And I

talked about my feeling of not really making much of an impact on anybody, of being alone. And of being cut off because nobody was interested
in me. The night before Miriam had told me this was ridiculous, that I
did make an impact on people but when this happened I usually cut
them off, and she told this to the group. And then I remembered and told
about an experience when I was in college, about a girl who looked at me
one day when I had taken my glasses off and she said, "Gee, Ben, you
have pretty eyes." And I answered quite bitterly "A hell of a lot of good
it does me" and literally turned my back on her.

Ben's brief anecdote presented the group very vividly with a picture
of the solitary, angry, hurt young man whom he had been, and they
listened in quiet sympathy. Someone remarked softly on how great his
pain had been. In the center of the circle, Ben sat hunched up, reliving
the pain which had never altogether left him. One of the men sought to
comfort him, but Ben motioned him away. He needed solitude within the
circle of the group's concern, and the group offered it.

I sat there with my eyes closed, trying to reach the pain, to feel it. . . .
Gradually it became quite enough and I got collected enough so that I
began to feel inside me the terrible pain and loneliness that I'd felt so
many times before in my life. And as I sat there, feeling this, I began to
rub my hands together and someone . . . told me to keep on with
what I was doing with my hands and let it go. And I became slowly
aware that what I was doing was caressing myself, and someone told me
to be gentle with myself. And then not only did I feel a tenderness for
myself, but I felt myself in a literal sense, more sensitively and acutely
than I had ever before. I was experiencing a feeling of tenderness for
myself that I had never felt before in my life and then an acceptance of
that tenderness which I had never felt before in my life. And this same
woman in the group urged me to keep on feeling myself in this way. And
my hands went over my hands and my arms and on an impulse and with
relatively little embarrassment I kissed the palm of my hand. And someone said, "Rub your hand over your forehead that way." And I did,
gently. And I was feeling myself as I never had before in my life,
tenderly, concernedly. And suddenly I had a thought, simple and crystal
clear. I thought, Ben, I love you. And the struggle to say it aloud was so
great that several people said things trying to be helpful but I told them
all to stop. And I think I said out loud, "This is the hardest thing I have
to do but I have to do it." And I finally said out loud, "Ben, I love you."
And I began to cry. I cannot recall ever having cried like that before.
I've shed tears, but almost always quietly. And this time I cried from the
bottom of my gut. And I felt terrible but I felt good, so very good. And
while I was crying I became aware that someone else was crying too.
. . . I thought, I'm not the only one. Somebody else feels more or less
the way I do.

When Ben lifted his head, several people in the group were weeping with him. His wife, who had awaited the right moment, came and embraced him. Ben, who all his life had found it difficult to speak of love, said to her, "Oh, my darling, I can really love you now." They were alone together and also with the group.

> And then several people got up and spontaneously came over to me and I went around the room and embraced everybody there. And for the first time in my life I believed all the way down to the bottom of my gut that they meant the things they were saying, the remarks about me and my strength and my guts were true, their smiles were really warm and really accepting. It was certainly one of the most important and moving experiences of my whole life. And that's not hyperbole, that's true.

For the remainder of the marathon session, Ben related fully to the group. According to the almost invariable pattern by which a new level of maturity is achieved after a regression has been fully experienced, he became active and skillful in helping others, especially in offering a kindly, insightful humor which enabled several participants to obtain a better perspective on their difficulties without feeling wounded.

> I felt freer and more open and more of one piece that I had perhaps any time in very few times in my life [sic]. I was a very active, useful, strong, meaningful part of what was gong on. . . .

Later in the marathon, several participants dealt with pent-up grief and regret about their fathers, both for actual losses through death and for the feeling of having been deprived of a fulfilling relationship in childhood. Ben mourned his father also.

> And I think in part it was through my father mourning the part of me that had—that had been dead for so long, neglected for so long. There was practically no intellectual reasoning about what had happened or thinking about it. . . . I could formulate now a great many ideas in verbal terms but many of the things I could formulate I've always known as intellectual ideas. I've always known that I didn't truly love myself, that I didn't truly care for myself, that somehow there was a little piece of me that always made Miriam's love for me and particularly the physical caressing tender side of her love a kind of—a kind of idiosyncrasy of hers. Like she was physically fond of me in spite of what I was like rather than because of it. . . .

Ben's statement that his breakthrough involved "things he had always known as intellectual ideas" has been made by many marathon participants, especially those who have achieved cognitive self-under-

standing through introspection or through traditional forms of psychotherapy, but who have not been able to achieve corresponding emotional
release. Yet, paradoxically, a breakthrough such as Ben's seems more
likely to occur when some intellectual self-understanding has already
been gained, most often through traditional psychotherapy. Perhaps there
is less resistance to the full, and often painful, emotional impact of self-
knowledge if there already exists an intellectual willingness to accept it.

It seems apparent that Ben's experience involved a return to an
extremely primitive level of experience, on which a child would ideally
develop feelings of healthy self-love and self-acceptance through a
nurturant environment, in this instance symbolized by the affectionate
acceptance of the group. Although during the experience he did not express or feel any specific oral cravings, such as would developmentally
accompany this period of early life if there were actual or symbolic oral
deprivation, it is noteworthy that shortly after his regression he "wanted
to drink something . . . wanted milk and couldn't find it . . . and made
a simple decision that it wasn't worth the trouble to ask for it. I made do
with a cup of tea. . . ." Having regressed and returned again to maturity, Ben's wish for the symbolic drink of milk was not sufficiently compelling for him to run the risk of interrupting the group.

Among the aftereffects of Ben's experience, however, was a striking
change in his attitude toward food and drink.

> There have been some very noticeable aftereffects that . . . may last a
> long, long time or maybe even forever. For the first time in my life, after
> the marathon was over we [Miriam and he] were in a bar having a drink,
> and I drank two drinks and I drank them slowly but without any feeling
> of holding back. I have always eaten and drunk rapidly. Sometimes I
> deliberately slow myself up. This was the first time I ever drank slowly
> without that conscious awareness. When I went home it was a very con-
> spicuous difference about the way I ate. I tasted what I ate more clearly
> than I usually do but I didn't eat fast, I didn't devour my food, and when
> I had eaten enough I stopped . . . without the—the kind of ambivalent
> reluctant feeling that has been so typical for me all my life.

Having been a deprived child, Ben had always eaten as fast and as
much as he could, still affected by the infantile fear that the food would
never be enough or that it might even disappear. The change in his attitude toward food is particularly significant because during the marathon
there was no reference to food and its individual meaning for him. On
the symbolic primary-process level of experience, the food which Ben
could now savor in safety, and the loving acceptance which he took from
the group, were identical. His final metaphor, in the closing sentences of
his taped description, is an expression of feeling more closely in touch
with life.

I feel as if gloves have been taken off my hands somehow. They're more sensitive. They touch in a way that they never did before.

The impact of the experiences undergone by these three participants can perhaps be better understood in the light of a recent discussion of regression by Balint (1968). Although the setting in which they occurred is vastly different from the traditional psychoanalytic dyad on which Balint bases his observations, these episodes fit remarkably closely into his conception of what is needed by the regressed patient. He warns convincingly against the analyst's making an effort to dissolve the patient's regressed needs through interpretation, as the classical psychoanalytic approach would require, or attempting to satisfy them, as in Ferenczi's pioneer experiments (1955). Either approach, he points out, may intensify the dependency to the point of malignancy by making the analyst appear omnipotent.

Regression in the presence of the group, it seems to me, bypasses this danger. The group symbolizes a supporting, loving mother, yet since it consists of approximately a dozen people, all of whom have been revealing their human needs and fallibility, the group can hardly evoke a malignant transference reaction to an omnipotent object. Nor can it arouse irrational expectations that dependent needs will continue to be gratified for an indefinite period of time. Simultaneously, because of the objective feedback which continually accompanies the interchange of symbolic gratifications of dependency needs, the group also represents reality. In marathon groups, I do not hesitate to offer myself as a mother symbol, sometimes providing prolonged comfort by holding a regressed participant in my arms for a long time, which I would usually regard as unwise in individual psychotherapy (Mintz, 1969). Thus far, no participant has ever sought a prolongation of such a relationship or remained in the clinging, infantile position. After the experience of being held, the group member almost invariably moves away of his own volition and becomes constructively active in his interaction with the other members. No marathon participant has ever decided to leave individual treatment with another psychotherapist and enter treatment with me, or requested individual treatment with me as a result of the marathon experience, except individuals who were already considering doing so.

What Balint recommends is a simple acceptance and awareness of the patient's condition, which may at times include the "relaxed need for physical contact" (1968, p. 146). He refers to this acceptance as a "harmonious interpenetrating mix-up" similar to the relationship of an organism to the air it breathes or the earth it treads. He draws a distinction between "regression aimed at gratification," in which there is an implicit or imperious demand for direct libidinal satisfaction, and "regression aimed at recognition," in which only this deep and simple acceptance is required. For Saul, Felicia, and Ben, the recognition of the group appeared crucial. Saul speaks of the need for "a group of people to bear witness"; Felicia writes "when you responded so positively and sensitively to the fear, that was a help in itself"; and Ben seemed to need only the warm, silent presence of the group to explore his inner desolation.

Technically, it seems highly relevant that these participants either initiated their own regression voluntarily or were given a clear choice whether or not to undertake the journey into the past. To me it seems without value, and even potentially harmful, to ask anyone to undertake an exercise designed to initiate regression without this clear consent.

A group technique has been described to me by a colleague [1] in which each member is asked to sit on the lap of the member next to him, cuddle close, shut his eyes, and imagine that he is being nursed by his mother—irrespective of the age or sex of the purported "mother." A similar exercise sometimes used as a group procedure involves reaching arms out into the empty air and repeatedly calling "Mother" or "Father" in the expectation that feelings of need and dependency will emerge. It seems possible that the psychotic or suicidal reactions which are occasionally anticipated as a consequence of encounter groups might indeed occur if a disturbed participant were subjected to such exercises, designed to stimulate regression, without adequate safeguards. Three conditions appear necessary: that the participant undertake the experience of his own volition; that there be a nurturant object—another member, the leader, or the group itself—ready to provide support in an appropriate symbolic relationship; and that circumstances permit individual attention until the experience is worked through. Regression is among the most powerful of all therapeutic agents; it has even been regarded as the central process in psychoanalysis (Menninger, 1958) and so potent a force should not be thoughtlessly evoked. [2]

Reparative emotional experiences can, apparently, take place not only through the reliving of a childhood trauma with a different ending, but through the acceptance of a nourishing experience which was absent

---

[1] Personal communication, Natalie Mann, who observed the group but did not participate. This particular technique, in its total disregard of the basic realities of age and gender, is an invitation to discard reality-testing altogether, hence would be highly unsafe for anyone predisposed to psychotic episodes.

[2] Techniques deliberately invoked to elicit regression seem even more hazardous in individual treatment. A well-authenticated though unpublished example is that of a woman in her early forties, who consulted a psychotherapist because of a reactive depression provoked by disappointing life circumstances. He attempted to offer a reparative relationship and tried to encourage regression by such techniques as reaching out the arms, described above. When this approach mobilized dependent feelings, she was instructed to suck her thumb and was then embraced by the therapist. A strong ambivalent transference resulted, the dependent needs being countered by the patient's resentment at "being made to act like a child"; the word "made" appears crucial. The young therapist, frightened by the intensity of her feelings, broke off treatment, thus exacerbating the depression considerably.

in childhood. This may occur through a role-played relationship with a parent substitute.

Annette was about to be married. She had lived with her fiancé for more than a year and was certain of her decision but was nevertheless wistful and sad about her mother's detachment over the marriage, which Annette regarded as a total commitment to a lifelong relationship and to bearing and raising children. Apparently the mother was a well-meaning, conscientious person who, presumably because of an undeveloped or conflicted feminine identification, had never taken any special interest in feminine matters. She liked her prospective son-in-law but took no interest in the furnishing of Annette's apartment or in her choice of what to wear for the marriage ceremony.

"I asked her whether she thought I ought to wear a beautiful white dress or just get a good expensive suit, and she just said, 'Whatever you like, dear.'" Annette's deprivation was trivial only on the surface. This young woman had a deep need for her mother's emotional support, symbolized by a concern with furniture and clothing, at the time of her own commitment to the full responsibilities of womanhood.

Annette went on to describe her girlhood. Her mother had never taken her shopping. Practical clothing had been ordered from a catalogue. She had been taught to wash her hair regularly, but until a small girl friend had instructed her, she actually did not know that social conventions required a girl to arrange her hair becomingly. Even now, although she was naturally pretty, she had a quality of drabness.

"Annette, let's go shopping together. Right now, I mean. Here." After a marathon group becomes accustomed to the use of fantasy and symbolism, such an invitation is readily comprehended. "What store shall we go to?"

"Well . . . Franklin's was the best store in our neighborhood."

"Let's go to Franklin's then. How old are you?"

"I'm . . . eleven." Intuitively, Annette had picked the age at which, as the latency period ends, a female child begins to think of herself primarily as a girl, rather than primarily as a child.

"What shall we buy?"

"I want to buy party dress . . . and shoes."

Annette and I went shopping. With another group member acting as a salesgirl, we discussed various styles and colors, tried on our favorite choices, decided finally on that paradigm color of feminity: of course, *pink*. We had a little difficulty with the shoes, since for my generation the purchase of the first pair of high heels would have marked the inauguration into girlish sophistication, but finally we purchased the flat-heeled sandals which would have been the dream of Annette at eleven. We also bought a necklace.

The effects of this scenario were out of proportion to its apparent superficiality. Annette said, almost two years later, "At that marathon. I learned a great deal about being a woman." Of course, she already had known a great deal about "being a woman," as was evidenced by her ability to commit herself to family life; but the shopping trip, frivolous as it seemed, represented to Annette the encouragement of a mother figure in enjoying and enhancing her own physical attractiveness.

With Cynthia, the childhood deprivation went deeper. Her father traveled a great deal and was rarely home; when he was home, he seemed both detached and strict. Cynthia's parents were divorced when she was eleven, and after that she saw her father only occasionally.

Like most other marathon participants whose ego strength is sufficient so that regression can not only be tolerated but used as a constructive growth experience, Cynthia was an effective person both socially and professionally. She was a psychiatric social worker, highly efficient, and had fairly enjoyable relationships with several men friends. However, as she herself recognized, there were difficulties. She often found herself acquiescing resentfully in whatever men requested from her out of a panic that she might displease them. She was reluctant to marry and tended to avoid marriageable men. A more subtle problem, described in Cynthia's written words, was that she "managed to keep [herself] fairly isolated from being *fully* aware of other people's caring for me."

In individual psychotherapy which, like Saul and Ben, she evaluated as having been helpful although incomplete, Cynthia had explored relationships between these problems and her childhood deprivation. Her first allusion to her father in the marathon came when she spoke of her reluctance to cry; her father, said Cynthia, regarded crying as a contemptible weakness, which was forbidden and even punished. Bitterly, she added that even though she had tried hard to please him by stifling her tears, he still had never seemed to care for her. Her present feeling for him, Cynthia said, was rage, and only rage.

In accordance with the Gestalt principle of figure-ground reversal, by which patients are asked to treat the environment (in this instance, the group) as they were once treated by destructive childhood figures (Perls, 1969), Cynthia was asked, as a beginning, to go around the room and tell each member of the circle not to cry. This was not a difficult task, and she was readily able to make contact with the members and to vary her message appropriately.

"I saw you crying earlier, shame on you." "Don't cry, it's weak." "Don't cry, it's silly." "You're strong, you'd never cry." "You ought to be ashamed, even for feeling like crying." And so on.

As she continued speaking of her father, Cynthia sounded resentful but not hurt. She felt that he had rejected her almost entirely. His only interest in her had been disciplinarian. When he had finally left his family altogether, his physical absence seemed only a slight change from his emotional absence when he had been in the house. Again, in accordance with the principle of reversal, Cynthia was asked to go around the room and reject everyone as her father would have done, and again she complied easily.

"Go away." "I don't care for you." "You don't matter." "I'm going away." Cynthia's words to one member of the group, a professional man in his late forties, seemed especially virulent. She stared at him for a long time, then said malevolently "And you—drop dead!"

These were preliminary tasks, designed in the hope of assisting Cynthia to achieve a somewhat greater degree of emotional distance from her hated and rejected father. By the slight degree of caricature which naturally accompanied her imitation of him, she could increase her awareness of what he had been like. Hence she might obtain a better perspective, which would help her separate out the attitudes carried over from her relationship with him from the attitudes now appropriate toward herself and the people around her. And to the extent which she separated herself from the inward image of a rejecting father, she might be able to accept a different image of a loving father.

"Cynthia, who is there here in the group whom you could possibly imagine as your father."

"The way he really was, or how I would have liked him?"

"Either. Just a father."

Cynthia could either use her father surrogate as an object for a full, cathartic expression of rage, or she could use him as a different and more loving father. This should be her decision, not mine. I had confidence in her will toward growth. In any case, if she were to use the father-daughter role-playing in a defensive way, it would probably be possible to suggest a second and more relevant psychodrama.

Cynthia, without hesitation, indicated Gene, the gray-mustached, fatherly looking man to whom she had said "Drop dead." He was not surprised. In his own subsequent written account of the experience from his point of view, he said:

> When she chose me, I was not particularly pleased although not surprised. . . . Suddenly this girl pointed at me and I knew when I sat down with her that something would happen. For one thing I had felt her presence in a special way, and when she had stared at me earlier and finally muttered "Drop dead," I felt it as a sort of love-hate benediction and cry.

Cynthia's choice of Gene was an example of the uncanny appropriateness with which, time and time again, I have seen marathon participants pick out partners or opponents for psychodramatic scenarios. Gene had told us little about himself. In fact, he had entered the group in part from professional curiosity (he was a psychologist) and did not really plan to reveal himself. He wrote, "It was getting close to the end of the group and I felt that I had survived the whole thing when suddenly she picked me out."

As it later appeared, Gene had his own reasons for becoming deeply involved with Cynthia. When she selected him, he crossed the room and sat down close to her, without touching. He spoke to her softly, gently, pleadingly, in the tone which might have been used to a six-year-old girl. His words perhaps seem sentimental on the printed page, but there was nothing sentimental about the intensity with which they were spoken.

"Cynny. My Cynthia. My little daughter Cynny?"

"Fuck off." During the first part of this encounter, Cynthia remained obdurate. Her unvarying reply was monotonous and harsh. Gene never turned his gaze away from her, but she did not look back.

"Cynny, I love you. I really love you, Cynny."

"Fuck off."

"Cynny, I want to talk to you. I want to be with you. I want you to be with me."

"Fuck off."

This went on for some time, Gene cajoling and Cynthia reiterating her toneless curse. Gene wrote:

> When I sat across from Cynthia and said "Cynny" and she kept shooting back—and when she continued in this impenetrable way to maintain the barrier between us—I started to find my consciousness of the group receding—and for this part of the encounter I found myself striking against a wall—I felt awkward—tense—proving stymied. But one thing kept going through my mind, I could not be the one to leave this time. I could not quit no matter where the game led.

To his poignant regret, Gene felt that twenty years ago he had "been the one to leave" a little daughter when she was only six years old. Because of the peculiar circumstances of his marriage, he had taken most of the care of her when she was an infant, but after separating from her mother, he did not see her again until she was eighteen. Thus he had been deprived of his fatherhood in the years when she was growing up. Gene had not told the group a word of this, nor did I know of it until he wrote me subsequently. Yet his involvement with Cynthia was so intense that everybody in the group could recognize that something extraordinary was happening.

Cynthia varied her "fuck off" only once, and this was when she felt that Gene was about to reach out for her physically. She said, "I'll strike you if you touch me. I'll strike you for real, too." But Gene did not yet try to touch her.

> I felt the empty sense—where do I go—what magic? . . . I don't know if it took five minutes or almost an hour. I felt almost hypnotized by Cynthia's barrage of "fuck offs." Something then happened inside and I felt I wanted to ask her to help me—I resisted this for a short while—but then began to be carried away on this current—and spoke to her about needing her—wanting her—asking her if she would help me—talking to her of her early years with me, mixing her up with Debbie [his daughter] and yet I knew somehow that I was really talking to this girl whom I was starting to love with a strong pain in my chest. . . .

Speaking to Cynthia of his memories of his own years with his tiny daughter, Gene was the prototype of every father who has loved a child, and who regrets the loss of a tender father-child relationship.

"Do you remember how I read to you? How I read you a storybook every night? Do you remember how I used to sing to you? How hard you used to hug me? I used to call you 'hard-hugger.'"

Cynthia's "fuck off" had grown almost inaudible, and now she was answering Gene's questions with a murmured, frightened "No." Her voice had a different quality. Now she was in contact with Gene, and also in contact with something else in her own feelings.

> When she responded for the first time with a word other than "fuck off," I had this feeling of euphoria and sudden calm—because now I was climbing on a precipice—and I waited and waited at that time—for the words to come to me—and I think the real words must have come. I decided to ask her to do something for me—and I said—I remember the words but I am not quite sure. . . .

Gene said, firmly and gently, "Now, Cynny, I am going to ask you to do something and I am going to ask you only one time and I will never ask you again, do you understand me?"

> And she said "Yes." And I said "Will you come to me and hug me and put your arms around me?" and this beautiful girl said "Yes but I must keep my eyes closed"—and she came to me—and redeemed me—and then I held my lost baby in my arms—and held this girl who smelled so good and fresh—and I whispered to her—and she whispered to me—and she felt soft and warm and loving—and I was flooded with love for her.

They sat together for a long time. Cynthia asked very softly, like a puzzled small girl, as she remembered her real father's disappearance, "Why did you go away?"

"Not that I didn't love you, Cynny. But I was in a prison and I had to escape."

"Prison?" said Cynthia.

"It was a prison. I felt that I would die if I couldn't leave." Cynthia was speaking to him as if he were her real father. Gene was answering as if his own daughter had asked why he had left her.

> She tried to say "Come home" and her voice cracked and she couldn't speak—and she said "Will you sit with me?" and I said "Yes" and we went back to the couch and sat there—and I felt emptied of a pain—and warmed by the girl at my side—and with a need to tell about Debbie but felt it would be wrong at that time because this was for Cynthia and I had already gotten so much. While we were sitting on the couch together—I still had the sense of Cynthia so soft and firm and warm and healthy in my arms—and I retained this feel and smell of her for days— and while we were there she said softly once "Don't let this get sexy" and I said "Fathers don't get that sexy with their daughters, they send them out into the world to find another man"—and she settled back and that's how it was until the end of the group. The impact of that encounter is still with me. What I experienced that evening carried over with my patients and my friends . . . in good ways—I have been more warm and loving and more open and more tolerant of criticism and even readier to reveal how I am, so thank you for a very special thing.

Cynthia's letter, although she described very positive aftereffects to her experience with Gene, focussed far more on the results and less on the experience in itself. Perhaps a happy child takes the loving care of its parents for granted, in contrast to a loving parent, for whom the individual personality of the child is of paramount importance; and perhaps this accounts for the disparity in Gene's emphasis on the experience and Cynthia's emphasis on its consequences. It is noteworthy that Cynthia actually was uncertain of Gene's name, although her appearance of competence made it impossible to see her as having a generally poor memory. She may have been unconsciously unwilling to perceive him as an individual, with a name of his own other than "Daddy," instead of as her father substitute.

> . . . I would like to discuss my "good father experience" with Gene— I'm not sure of his name but I think that was it. What I got out of that mostly I think, was, first, really being in contact with my feelings of having been rejected by my father. The anger at him has always been easy for me. The sense of loss and being rejected I had understood intellectually but was never willing to experience the hurt before. Then I also understood that it was not really something that was wrong with me personally that caused my father to stay away, both literally and emotionally, but related to other things going on inside him. Again, in my

individual therapy I understood this intellectually . . . but never as vividly.

In the closeness of her psychodramatic father-daughter contact with Gene, Cynthia could ask him why he went away and understand his answer that he felt imprisoned, which had been true of Gene himself when he broke off his first marriage and unwillingly surrendered his daughter to her mother. And, in replying in terms of his own life experience, Gene had gotten through to Cynthia the unquestionable truth that her father had left her because of his own needs and probably also his own limitations, but not because of any fault or lack in his small daughter.

The changes which Cynthia described in herself are in perfect accordance with the general assumption that the relationship of a boy or girl with the parent of the opposite sex forms a transition to the heterosexual relationships of later life. As Gene said, in a good relationship, "fathers don't get that sexy with their daughters, they send them out into the world to find another man." And Cynthia wrote:

> I felt more whole and more willingness to be feminine. . . . One behavioral concomitant has been an increased ability to say "No" to men— or rather an ability to say yes only if I really want to go somewhere or do something, and not to say yes out of an anxiety about being unattractive and unable to hold a man. . . . I think the marathon experience helped also in strengthening my desire to get married and have children. . . . And I have not only the sense of being more real and feeling more joy than I have ever before, but also outside confirmation from other people about the way I have been acting. . . .

Neither Cynthia nor Gene, despite the beauty and value of their transitory psychodramatic relationship, expressed the slightest interest in meeting again. Without exception, at least in my own experience, marathon participants have not sought continued relationships to other members with whom they have shared experiences primarily on a psychodramatic or symbolic or fantasy level, regardless of the meaning and intensity of the experience.

Friendships sometimes begin in a marathon, and so do sexual relationships, which seem to have about the same general probability of being ephemeral, long lasting, or permanent as would be the case if the same two people met under any other circumstances, such as a cruise or an especially successful social gathering, which would have made it easy for them to get to know one another quickly. Relationships which are emotionally real but not objectively real, such as Cynthia's and Gene's, have to my knowledge never resulted in a longing for continuation. Gene made no effort to turn Cynthia into an ongoing substitute for his grown daughter, or to engage in a flirtation with her under the unconscious pre-text of fatherliness. Cynthia made no effort to use Gene as a substitute for the father who was lacking. This observation fits in precisely with my other observation, noted above, that marathon participants do not seek to continue with me in individual psychotherapy unless they have entered the marathon with a realistic expectation, about which both of us have agreed in advance, that if we both felt an appropriate rapport, we would undertake long-term individual treatment.

In view of the typical importance of regression in these reparative emotional experiences, and the genuine concern of many clinicians about the possibility of a marathon participant's pursuing continuation of re-gressive satisfactions, these findings appear highly significant. The value of the time-extended marathon situation appears here once again, in that it permits adequate time for experiencing a full regression, for dealing with it afterward on a cognitive level, and for reintegrating the feelings on a more mature level.

Even without regression, psychodramatic encounters in a marathon setting occasionally lead to the recovery of positive memories from early childhood which have been repressed. Effective psychotherapy is gener-ally seen as including the release of repressed anger, especially toward parents, but perhaps insufficient emphasis has been placed upon the recovery of loving and happy memories. Such memories, presumably, were repressed because the child had too often been disappointed when the happy experiences came seldom, and the repression continued into adulthood. When such memories are recovered, the participant usually experiences a surge of joy and often reports gratifying aftereffects. Since, to a certain extent, identification is inevitable even with a parent who is hated, feared, or despised, the recovery of positive feelings almost in-evitably modifies the self-image in a positive direction.

Paul, in two marathons, had expressed bitterness toward his mother. Even now, in his thirties and with his own family, Paul remembered feel-ings of embarrassment and desolation when, day after day, he would come home from school to find his mother drinking. Hardly a day passed when she was not drunk. He spoke of her with a mixture of shame, anger, and heartbreak. Perhaps because he spoke of her so frequently, or per-haps because of some quality in his voice, it seemed to me that there were other feelings than what he expressed.

"Paul, let me represent your mother, talk to me."

Readily Paul picked up the invitation, looking as if he relished the opportunity. He sat down opposite me, folded his arms, and almost glared.

"You—drunken—bitch!"

"I'm sorry, Paul."

"Why didn't you ever have dinner ready when you should? Why didn't you keep the place picked up? Why were you always soused?

Don't you know that's why my daddy always went off on those long trips? He couldn't stand it, that's why he went off on those long trips. I didn't have a mommy, and I didn't have a daddy."

"I'm sorry, Paul." It is not always possible to account rationally for whatever determines the decision as to how to interpret a psychodramatic role. In retrospect, my reasons for choosing to play a loving and regretful mother probably had to do with an intuitive feeling that underneath Paul's anger was affection and the need for affection.

"I just don't think you even loved me. If you loved me, how come you hit the bottle all the time?"

"I loved you, Paul."

"If you loved me, how come you were always drunk? If you loved me, how come you loved the bottle more? If you loved me, how come you didn't take care of me?"

My answer came, it seems to me, from an intuitive response to Paul's need rather than from a reconstruction of the actual circumstances of his childhood. I said, as gently as I could, "I took good care of you when you were little, Paul."

He stared at me. We paused for several moments. Then he said slowly, "Why, yes, that is true. You took good care of me when I was little." There was another pause, and then, even more slowly, he said to himself, "She took good care of me when I was little."

The memory, or at least the feeling-tone of a period of comparative happiness and safety in the first few years of life, had been recovered. Gradually Paul began to smile. He reached out toward me and hugged me.

"Thanks, Elizabeth." He did not say "Thanks, mother." When the psychodramatic encounter is over, if regardless of its brevity the feelings have been adequately expressed, the protagonist usually moves easily and of his own accord back to reality from fantasy. Paul said:

> You gave me back my mother—or anyhow a part of her that I had forgotten. She did take care of me when I was little. I remembered more about it later and felt good about remembering.

It is difficult to evaluate the relative importance of the warm, trusting marathon atmosphere in comparison to the appropriate use of specialized encounter techniques. These factors appear to complement one another. Major emotional breakthroughs do occur in a marathon which failed to occur in ongoing psychotherapy, but this may come about through a verbal interchange alone.

Leon was an ambitious, hard-driving businessman, married, with three children. He was personnel director for a huge corporation and had entered his first marathon some years ago primarily to enlarge his professional knowledge. Rather unexpectedly, he found the marathon gratifying, as a situation in which he could stop striving and worrying about appearances. He continued to take part in marathons approximately every half-year, to "recharge his batteries." Although he was not undergoing concurrent individual treatment, he became discernably warmer and more relaxed after perhaps a half-a-dozen marathons.

Leon had a keen sense of the ridiculous and a gift for absurd puns. As he himself readily acknowledged, this was in part a maneuver to keep people at a distance and to "keep himself from showing," but it was impossible not to enjoy his wit, which was never malicious. The group laughed at Leon's wisecracks, saw past them, and tried to work with him on his present problem, which was the compulsion to overwork to the point where he had little time for anything else.

> I began to speak of my dissatisfaction of my fully realizing my role as a husband and as a father—namely, that I withhold my time and relatedness. Characteristically, my approach grew intellectual, diffuse, and unconvincing. . . . However, my fellow participants appreciated that there was an ache behind the fast footwork and were willing to work hard at getting me to work harder.

Because Leon was focussing on his family life, he was asked about his own father and responded with great bitterness that his childhood had been totally barren. Of his father, all memories were of curtness and indifference, except for one small glimpse of a newspaper which his father brought him nightly in the pocket of his jacket, so that the little boy could pull it out. This was his sole memory of affection. He spoke of this memory again now, although somehow, he wrote, it seemed "more personal." The group stayed with Leon, clustered closely around his chair, not arguing or forcing him, but saying softly again and again, "And that's all? Can you see his face? Did he *always* look cross? . . ." Sometimes it seems to me that, even without any kind of training, groups appear to know what clinicians spend many hours to learn: that if a patient claims a perfectly happy childhood, with a single painful or frightening episode, he is repressing; and if a patient claims that there was nothing positive or happy, but only fear and pain, he is again repressing. At any rate, Leon's face flushed suddenly, and a new memory broke through:

> Then I recalled playing pinochle with my father and my older brother and sister. . . . I had never been able to touch my affection for my father and his for me. Suddenly it struck me as a wonderful thing for my father to play pinochle with me, a ten-year-old kid, or eleven. That was affection and love. I could visualize a score of games. He actually loved me! I felt moved. The group was pushing me to express feelings about my father. I remember alternating between denying any feeling

for him except contempt and tentatively expressing a longing. . . . Then I murmured, "I want my father."

Because there are times when the simple reiteration of a meaningful phrase, over and over, can tap the feelings with which it is associated on a deeply primitive level, Leon was asked to keep saying, "I want my father." He was able to do this. At last this competent, well-defended, wisecracking man began to sob, not painfully but with relief. Two weeks later he wrote:

All I can say is that I still feel gripped by the experience. When I returned from the marathon, I experienced (and still am) a surge of affection for my three children and my wife, expressed some of it, and they have been responding enthusiastically.

Here once again is the pattern of a reparative emotional experience (in this instance the simple recovery of a memory of being loved) accompanied by regression (in this instance, Leon's sobbing and his call for his father), followed by the return to maturity with increased ability to love and be loved on an adult level.

These phenomena occur. They are deeply moving at the time both for the protagonist and for the group, some members of which may report that the intense empathy which they experienced made them feel that they, too, were changing and growing. The follow-up reports show that these regressive, reparative episodes can bring about long-lasting changes.

Some theoreticians would consider that the primary curative element in these experiences is the reliving of a trauma with a happier ending (Alexander & French, 1946; Balint, 1968). This different ending may consist of dependency satisfactions offered in symbolic, temporary forms by such media as lifting and rocking; or by providing the protagonist with an opportunity to control his environment, as in Saul's case; or by the group's mere understanding and acceptance, as with Leon and Ben; or by any combination of these elements. Spokesmen for the traditional psychoanalytic viewpoint would emphasize the value of catharsis, not so much because it usually provides temporary relief, as in Kris's classical contribution about the value of regression "in the service of the ego" (1936), but because it facilitates the development of insight (Greenson, 1967, p. 48). Spokesmen for the contemporary experiential position (i.e., Gendlin, 1964), would emphasize the immediate, continual flow of feeling between client and therapist as the primary therapeutic factor.

There is no doubt but that analogous major curative experiences occur in widely varied types of psychotherapy or growth experiences. It seems probable that any major therapeutic breakthrough, or growth-enhancing peak experience, depends upon a constellation of favorable circumstances which may well differ among different individuals. As already suggested, the marathon format is especially valuable in that it provides ample time for regressing and then growing up again, without reality demands being interspersed by an interruption of the group. Moreover, the group, as already suggested, cannot be regarded in transference by the regressed participant as the ultimate, long-yearned-for answer to dependent longings, since it consists of a dozen people who are able and willing to offer sensitive, warm gratification to the protagonist's dependency needs for an appropriate period of time, but who will shortly wish to reveal and gratify their own legitimate needs.

An additional value of the marathon encounter group for the facilitation and working-through of regression is that this function, which in a marathon is usually experienced as a privilege rather than a burden, is shared by a group and a trained leader. A leader alone, without the support and sharing of the group, may find a regressed patient too demanding, or even threatening, and perhaps this is why so many therapists react to regression with more-or-less subtle rejection.[3] A group alone cannot be expected to possess the theoretical and technical knowledge to respond adequately. In these regressive experiences, when the marathon is functioning effectively, it is the group-leader unit which serves as the therapist, the parent, the supportive environment, the symbolic womb, the representative of reality, the significant other, and all of these together.

REFERENCES

Alexander, F., & French, T. M. *Psychoanalytic therapy.* New York: Ronald Press, 1946.

Balint, M. *The basic fault.* London: Tavistock Publications, 1968.

Ferenczi, S. *Notes and fragments.* New York: Basic Books, 1952.

Gendlin, E. T. A theory of personality change. In P. Worchel & D. Bryne (Eds.), *Personality change.* New York: Wiley, 1964.

Greenson, R. *Technique and practice of psychoanalysis.* New York: International Universities Press, 1967.

James, W. *Varieties of religious experience.* New York: Longmans, Green, 1902.

Kris, E. *Psychoanalytic explorations in art.* New York: International Universities Press, 1936.

Menninger, K. *Theory of psychoanalytic technique.* New York: Basic Books, 1958.

Mintz, E. E. Touch and the psychoanalytic tradition. *Psychoanalytic Review,* 1969, 64(3).

Perls, F. S. *Gestalt therapy verbatim.* Lafayette, Calif.: Real People Press, 1969.

[3] Cynthia, whose experience with her father-surrogate is given above, wrote: "I remember in my first analysis, and my first analyst was excellent, but I think he was wrong about this one thing, that my analyst would accept these child feelings but never actively encourage, or when they came up would gently remind me that I was in reality twenty-odd years old and it could never be as I wanted it. But part of me was three or seven."

5 THE GROUP AS THERAPIST

In later phases of the typical marathon, interaction between group members is usually of as much therapeutic value as interaction between the leader and the group, and sometimes more. Indeed, the function of the leader has been conceptualized, at least insofar as T-groups are concerned, as "that of consultant to a group which is seeking to become an effective learning environment for all of its members" (Bradford, Gibb, & Benne, 1964, p. 30). At the opposite end of the leadership-activity continuum is that of the therapist (for example, Bindrim, 1969) who offers his groups carefully structured experiences usually directed toward the development of sensory awareness, peak experiences, and emotional breakthroughs. Although both approaches are valid, depending on the basic purpose of the group, my personal conviction is that one of the primary functions of the leader, and possibly the most important function, is not only to create an atmosphere in which it becomes possible for the group members to relate meaningfully to one another, but also to introduce techniques by which they can be mutually helpful, techniques usually directed toward the intensification of immediate experience, and followed by the clarification of its meaning.

The therapeutic functions of the group, and the activity of the leader, can be viewed as going through a series of stages which are directly related to the phases through which the group as a whole, and most of its individual members, progress.

In the first phase, which I have described metaphorically as the phase in which social masks are worn, group members usually make an effort to be helpful to one another, but these attempts typically are lacking in empathy. The participants ask questions, seeking factual information rather than feelings. They give advice. Sometimes this particular phase of interaction seems to spring from a wish to appear intelligent and helpful, or from a wish to avoid self-revelation, rather than from genuine concern. This is the period which often brings about boredom or anxiety both in the group and in the leader, and in which it is sometimes a temptation to introduce warm-up techniques. My choice is usually to remain passive in this difficult beginning period rather than to insist upon games which may further the appearance of intimacy rather than its reality.[1]

---

[1] In Chapter 1 the rationale for this initial passivity is discussed more fully. Other group therapists have also observed that premature directiveness or structuring

The second phase of a marathon, in which participants experiment with revealing their genuine feelings about themselves and one another, may begin in any number of ways—indeed, it is different with every marathon. Sometimes it is a gradual, undramatic movement from socially stereotyped behavior toward authenticity. Sometimes a participant breaks through the preliminary get-acquainted chitchat and shares a real problem or true feeling, either from the pressure of anxiety or from a wish for emotional contact with other participants. Quite often, the initial breakthrough of feeling (as discussed in preceding chapters) is anger either toward the leader or toward another participant. When the anger is directed toward another participant, it is frequently triggered off by a nonempathetic attempt to be helpful.

It would be inaccurate and unfair to regard any individual group member as nothing more than a stereotype. Nevertheless, two stereotyped roles of pseudohelpfulness can often be identified at this time: the Red Cross Nurse and the Assistant Therapist. If the leader of the group can deal with this pseudohelpfulness appropriately, it facilitates the emergence of a deeper and more sincere helpfulness within the group. Fortunately, most groups in any case tend toward the development of more and more genuine helpfulness as time goes on; yet it is useful for the leader to be aware that if pseudohelpfulness is accepted as valid, this may hinder the group's movement toward more intense interaction.

The motto of the "Red Cross Nurse" [2] is, "Cheer up, things are not really so bad," or even, "If you don't pay attention to the problem, it'll go away." The implication is that painful feelings or difficult problems can best be handled by being ignored.

For example, a woman in the group is in anguish because she has recently learned that her two-year-old son is showing unmistakable signs of infantile autism. Prolonged treatment has been urgently recommended by a well-qualified specialist. Another member reassures her, "The doctors don't know everything. Kids grow out of these things." This is an extreme example of Red Cross Nursing. It may support the mother's natural wish to deceive herself about her child's illness, cause her to delay treatment, and deprive her of the opportunity to work through her own pain and confusion.

In this particular group, the Red Cross Nurse was overborne by genuine helpfulness from the group members. Another woman shared her own feelings of guilt and responsibility for the difficulties of her teenage

---

may actually limit interaction rather than furthering spontaneity. For example, War-kentin (1970, p. 165) points out that "if the therapist prohibits personal indifference between group members, this is just as much a hindrance as if he were to prohibit expressions of hatred or some other particular feelings experience."

[2] For this phrase we are indebted to Bach (1969). The phrase itself is highly unfair to the Red Cross.

daughter, which made the first young mother feel less isolated. The group as a whole then helped her accept the necessity for her child's treatment. Intervention by the leader was not necessary and would have been less effective than the action of the group.

However, if the group had not been able to assume this responsibility, intervention by the leader would have been required. Fairly often, one of the first tasks of a marathon leader is to help the group recognize that Red Cross Nursing is essentially destructive, as opposed to sympathy, which carries the message, "I'm sorry you feel bad," or empathy, which implies, "I think I understand the way you feel." Moreover, with minimal intervention by the leader and sometimes with no intervention, even an inexperienced group seems to understand quickly that affection, however genuine, is not useful if offered when someone is just beginning to confront a painful inner feeling but is useful only as support after the pain has been fully experienced.

Despite the destructive effect of Red Cross Nursing, it seems to me equally destructive if the leader sets an example of attacking the "Nurse" by sarcasm. A Red Cross Nurse is someone who cannot face his own inner agonies, and who therefore cannot bear to face the pain of others. These people use denial and rationalization to smooth over their own difficulties. Nevertheless, their aspirin-and-bandaid approach nearly always has an admixture of a genuine, though mistaken, wish to be helpful. Red Cross Nurses can easily become the scapegoat for groups and leaders who equate confrontation with slashing abuse. If the marathon leader can convey a recognition of the helpful intention, along with a brief and simple formulation of the nonhelpfulness of Red Cross Nursing, the group itself quickly takes over the responsibility of avoiding meaningless reassurance and false comfort to its members.

The Assistant Therapist is usually someone who invokes intellectual understanding as the panacea for human grief. In a fairly sophisticated group, psychoanalytic interpretations are likely to be offered by Assistant Therapists, and even though they may be accurate, they are almost never useful. Aside from his obvious wish to exhibit his intelligence, which is almost invariably picked up by the group, the Assistant Therapist is motivated by a need to defend against his own problems by intellectualization.

For example, Sheldon is speaking of the impending death of his father, who is expected to die within the next few months. His grief is real. His father was sometimes harsh, but he was also loving, and now Sheldon wishes that they had been able to spend more time together. Sheldon is anticipating a phone call which he knows he will receive soon, announcing the death itself or its immediacy, and he is going through the fantasy of what he will say to his mother, and how he can help her through the crisis.

Another group member, probably because of his own family conflicts, cannot bear the intensity of feeling. He blurts out abruptly, "Maybe you really hate your father, maybe you'd really like him dead?" [3]

Sheldon is sure enough of his feelings, as it happens, so that he simply gives the Assistant Therapist a contemptuous glance and a brief curse and continues speaking. If Sheldon had been frightened by a strong unconscious death wish, severe anxiety and repressed guilt could have been precipitated. The group, however, was with Sheldon.

"You jerk, can't you see the guy really cares about his father?"

"So the old man was rough on him sometimes. Shel likes him anyhow. My old man was God-awful sometimes, but when he died I mourned for him. I really did."

In this particular marathon, several hours followed in which the group dealt meaningfully with ambivalent feelings toward their fathers; the Assistant Therapist, although his comment was inappropriate, had opened up an important area of exploration. It was unnecessary for the leader to intervene to protect Sheldon. It was, however, necessary for the leader to protect the Assistant Therapist, who rapidly was placed in another stereotyped role which is often assigned to a member during the marathon's second stage—the role of Scapegoat. He was attacked by the group for his clumsiness, his lack of feeling, and his "Freudian shit." It was pointed out that the group was making use of their Scapegoat to avoid confronting their own feelings. Eventually the man who had first been the Assistant Therapist and then the Scapegoat was able to deal with his ambivalence toward his own father and to express his hostility more directly within the group.

The leader, of course, is most likely to be Scapegoat if the first breakthrough of real feeling in the marathon's second phase is anger. The leader is too directive, too domineering, does not permit events to take their natural course; equally often, the leader is too passive, does not offer help.[4] When a participant is selected as Scapegoat, this is usually because his behavior tends to sabotage the essential purpose for which the group is meeting—the purpose of direct, frank, open confrontation. Intellectualization is criticized. Pompousness is attacked. Anyone who assumes an air of superiority is vehemently assaulted.

Here the group itself acts as a confronting therapist. Under its barrage, some participants give up their defenses and acknowledge,

---

[3] Freud has called our attention to the existence of unconscious death wishes toward our parents. Because of the long, frustrating period of infantile helplessness, there is undoubtedly some validity to the Freudian death wish even in a predominantly loving parent-child relationship. The wish, however, can certainly coexist unconsciously with genuine feelings of love and concern, which were the predominant feelings of Sheldon.

[4] Either criticism may be valid, or partly valid. See Chapters 2 and 9 for further discussion of the role of the marathon therapist.

sometimes in words and sometimes in their behavior, that the intellectualization or pompousness is merely a mask.

Bertha, a woman of forty, had been referred to the marathon because her individual therapist felt, in the therapist's own words, that nothing except verbal "shock treatment" could ever pierce her cold, haughty, self-righteous aloofness. She had resisted two years of individual treatment, and I had accepted her for the marathon only upon the therapist's pledge to see her daily during the next week if necessary. It seemed clear to both her therapist and to me that behind the haughty facade was an insecurity so deep that there was the possibility of a psychotic breakdown. Bertha claimed consistently that she had no emotional problems, and that she was in treatment only because she had been told that her nine-year-old daughter, who suffered from a severe school phobia, could improve only if the mother-daughter relationship improved. Bertha's need to maintain a righteous self-image kept her in treatment, since treatment had been recommended to her, but she had never acknowledged that her behavior toward her daughter was anything but perfect.

In the group, she showed precisely the same attitude. Her comments were sparse and caustic, and every effort to make contact with her was superciliously dismissed as "sentimental" or "stupid." She was embarrassed by warm emotional contacts among other group members, viewing them as "fake." The group tried for a while to reach her, some of them with affection and some of them with hostility, but she remained obdurate, sitting apart with a contemptuous smile. When I tried to draw her into the group, she remarked, "Well, you work for your fee, don't you?"

All of us, including myself, were beginning to feel that Bertha would never become a member of the group, when suddenly there was an outburst, an explosion, from a younger woman. Because this outburst was not taped, it cannot be exactly reproduced, but it went something like:

"Be human! Why can't you be human like the rest of us? You have a heart, don't you, don't you have feelings? Don't you know your daughter loves you? Don't you know that's why she's acting crazy? She can't get to you any other way, that's why she's acting crazy. She loves you and she wants you to love her. You bitch, cold-hearted bitch, why don't you come down off that pedestal and love your daughter?"

The tirade went on and on. The younger woman was almost in tears. Her intensity was so great that several other members of the group began to weep. Bertha remained stone-faced—then, suddenly, she put her head into her hands and began sobbing.

At once, although until then everyone had disliked her, several members of the group went to her and put their arms around her. Bertha sobbed bitterly and finally choked out that she did want to love her daughter, perhaps she actually did love her, but somehow she couldn't show it. She cried for some time, accepting the physical affection she was shown by the group. At last, when she stopped crying, her face looked softer, and she was able to talk a little about how she had suffered from the coldness of her own mother and how difficult it was for her to accept and give affection. During the remainder of the marathon, she was accepted by the group, showed concern for several of the members, and exchanged embraces with them when the group ended.[5]

Except for the vehement, pleading attack of the younger woman, it seems unlikely that Bertha could ever have been reached. She entered the marathon in order to prove that she was doing everything possible for her daughter, rather than in search of personal growth. She entered for the purpose of maintaining a false self-image, and it was only by chance that she evoked such therapeutic passion in another member of the group. My efforts, and the usual interaction of the group, would probably never have touched her.

In general the group from its second phase onwards performs a function analogous to that of the classical psychoanalyst. He interprets defenses; the group attacks defenses. Masks are ripped off, as Bertha's was ripped off. This is done with forcefulness and sometimes with hostility, which might be inappropriate and possibly even risky in a one-to-one therapeutic relationship. If a group member is deeply hurt or frightened by an attack on his defenses, there are always other participants who let him know that they can share his feelings and that he is not alone.

In general, insincerity and aloofness are the primary targets for attack. As yet, I have not seen a member of the group attacked merely because he is different from the others. For example, in many marathons there have been one or two homosexual participants who anticipated rejection and disapproval from the group. In every marathon thus far, the group tried to work with the homosexuality as a problem only if the homosexual participant was dissatisfied with his adjustment and wished to change; if the homosexual participant accepted his adjustment and wished to work with other problems, the group has accepted this attitude also. On a very few occasions, when an individual participant has attacked homosexuality as a vice or a disease, the group has defended the right of the homosexual man or woman to choose his own way of life.[6]

[5] Long-standing, deep-seated pathology such as Bertha's cannot be instantly alleviated by an emotional breakthrough. Her therapist reported that after the marathon Bertha was somewhat more related and responsive in treatment, and that there were slight signs of improvement in the family relationship.

[6] It has been pointed out, by Warkentin (1970) and many others, that the attitudes of the leader may be indirectly conveyed to the group even without deliberate efforts to do so. My marathon groups may intuitively pick up my conviction that homosexuality, except in the rare instances when it takes a form that is destructive to others, should be regarded as a therapeutic problem only if and when the individual homosexual is dissatisfied with the homosexual adjustment.

When a marathon participant considers that his experience has not been useful to him, it is usually because he has not been able to accompany the group in its movement from the defensive phase into the phase of direct intimate interaction. Although written feedback comes mostly from participants who have positive feelings about their experience, there are a few letters which express this attitude:

> Everyone was so close together. But I didn't think they were really close together. I thought the whole thing was a great big phony acting-out. I don't think they really gave a damn about each other. When they cried, I didn't believe it. Fake when they hugged each other too.

> I made a resolution that I would hold back and not let the group know where I really was. I kept that resolution. That's the only thing I got out of your God-damned marathon.

> They tried to reach me and I think they meant it. But I stayed alone and like a big cold polar bear on top of my iceberg. After the marathon I realized how cold I was.[7]

In this second phase of a marathon, which consists principally of a preliminary expression of authentic feeling, I am likely to be more active and even directive than in any other phase, in contrast to my choice to be passive rather than to introduce warm-up techniques in the beginning. In this period I seek for fuller expression of rage, grief, fear, and love by emphasizing the basic rule of honesty and the here-and-now approach. In this period, also, various techniques to make the here-and-now approach more meaningful can be introduced, such as the use of scenarios and physical encounter games.

During this second phase, one of the therapeutic values of the group situation is that the self-disclosure of each member makes it easier for other members to engage in self-disclosure also.[8] Other aspects of the group's therapeutic function at this stage include: increasingly frank feedback as to how the participants react to one another; a growing

[7] No further feedback is available from the writers of the first two letters, but the writer of the "polar bear" letter eventually went into individual therapy, accepted other group experiences, and found them valuable.

[8] The value of offering patients an opportunity to imitate the open, problem-sharing behavior of other patients has recently been discussed, with reference to experimental data (Goldstein, Heller, & Sechrest, 1966). Also, the use of "modeling procedures" has been specifically applied to sensitivity-training groups by beginning a group with filmed and taped examples of the interaction in other sensitivity-training groups (Whalen, 1969; Heller, 1969). Such techniques can be helpful if the participants are not familiar with the idea that interpersonal openness may be constructive. However, in groups conducted at growth centers or in private practice, most participants are initially familiar with this approach and do not need to become acquainted with the new idea by watching other groups on film. In groups of this type, participants who are relatively willing to reveal themselves serve as natural models for those who have more reluctance.

mutual concern which accompanies and transcends the sharp personal criticisms often characteristic of this phase; and a developing awareness that self-disclosure does not necessarily provoke attack, and that in any case the attacks are not unbearable. In some groups, individual members decide at this time to reveal data which is regarded as intensely shameful, and which in some instances has never before been shared with anyone. Every group, in my experience, deals with such revelations by working to diminish the guilt, provided that it is exaggerated or unfounded.[9] If the guilt is associated with a genuine problem, as in the case of a man who was tortured by a constant temptation to make sexual advances to preadolescent girls, the group attempts to understand and work with the problem but does not seek to intensify the guilt which is already present.

Written evaluations having to do with this phase of the marathon group include such statements as:

> Seeing other people with problems, including some people who came on very strong at the beginning and made me feel kind of small and weak by comparison with them, makes you feel you're not alone after all.

> Personal insights: My domineering tendencies. Being less nice than I had supposed, possibly less well-intentioned, rather selfish. But being much stronger in the light of criticism than I had in my faintest dreams imagined.

> The experience of revealing yourself and finding out how others see you, revealing what you feel to be your defect, it really doesn't seem so bad when exposed to the group. I myself after three marathons have none of my former paranoid concern about revealing myself.

> Most people though strangers can feel with one another and be so willing to help and comfort one another as though they were brother and sister.

> It is the exposure of others' troubles and heartaches that encourages me to believe that mine are valid and I may also open up and hope for love and compassion and help.

> The awareness that others were not afraid to be vulnerable in exposing their feelings made a fantastic impression on me. Why does one have to

---

[9] An example was described in Chapter 3 from a marathon in which with great embarrassment one participant revealed his illegitimate birth. Other revelations included the disclosure that, as an adolescent boy, a member had been impressed by the pageantry of the initial phases of Nazism and had fantasied himself as a Storm Trooper, although subsequently he had recognized the actual nature of Nazism. One participant christened this kind of self-disclosure the "Silver Spoon Game" after a marathon in which I had shared with the group the exaggerated guilt and shame which I had felt for years over my own theft of an ornate silver spoon as a small child, my purpose being to demonstrate the absurdity of suffering over long-past episodes.

feel either vulnerable or protected? It seemed to be a ridiculous waste of energy going around continually protecting myself against attacks that in reality were never there. Especially one man had a profound effect on me. He had a magnificent body, strong features, very masculine in appearance, a seeming rock. In my mind he could have no real problems. . . . He was everything I would like to give the appearance of being. He then worked on his problems, exposing his vulnerability and allowing me to reach him as a person. It let me see the rigid false set of external values that I was using in judging myself. I could accept more humanly my problems then as well as his.

Along with the developing concern for one another which characterizes this second phase of the marathon, participants spontaneously begin to use physical contact in expressing their feelings toward one another. The most cogent reason why I refrain from introducing prescribed encounter games of touching and feeling at the beginning of the group is that bodily contact is more meaningful when it is used spontaneously. No explicit permission or encouragement from the leader is necessary. If bodily contact is not expressly prohibited, it occurs naturally.

As the group enters the third phase of deeper self-exploration and mutual acceptance, the activity of the leader can usually become minimal, unless anxiety slows down the interaction or unless a participant is working in depth on a problem for which special therapeutic help is required. In general, the group itself now truly becomes the therapist. Repeatedly I am delighted and impressed by the wisdom and resourcefulness shown even by participants who have had no previous group experience. Frequently they invent scenarios or devise encounter games which are as appropriate, and sometimes even more imaginative, than anything that could have been proposed by myself. In a marathon people discover within themselves a genuine wish to be helpful and a real capacity for helpfulness.

Inez, a woman in her early forties, was a former Catholic nun. She had belonged to an active order which, because of her capability, had entrusted her with the task of traveling around the country to handle a specific executive responsibility in various convents. About a year before the marathon, she left the order as a result of growing doubts about her vocation. Her efficiency and experience enabled her to handle her life easily in practical matters; she had a good job and an apartment, and she made an impression of confidence and poise. However, she felt detached from life. Accustomed to the prescribed activities of her order, she had difficulty in making spontaneous contact with others. She was attractive, but there was something in her manner that seemed forbidding, though in fact she was merely shy. Inez was lonely. She described her life as "a dark forest." In an effort to bring Inez into relationship with the group, I asked her to show us what it felt like in the forest by wandering around the room as if among the trees. She complied, and from that moment the group itself took over.

Inez was moving hesitantly around the room, making no contact with anyone. Slowly and gently, one of the men rose and approached her, touching her hands lightly, and began walking beside her. Then on her other side another man joined them. Somehow, without any deliberate suggestion from anybody, their steps began to turn into a dance movement, and the group began to hum a waltz. Almost tenderly, with an awareness that Inez was not a skillful dancer, one man after another took Inez as his partner, danced with her for a few moments, and then relinquished her to the next man.

The group sat without interfering. Nobody spoke. No woman made the slightest effort to join in the dance. Every woman there realized that this was Inez's drama. The dancing had a slow and almost dreamy quality, and it went on for a long time, and then Inez began to cry.

I do not know whether or not I gave the signal for what happened next, or whether the group undertook spontaneously to lift Inez and rock her, a procedure with which they were already familiar because it had been used earlier in the marathon. We swayed Inez slowly back and forth for a long time. Her body relaxed. She stopped crying. Then she was wafted gently to the floor.

Here is part of Inez' letter, written two weeks later:

> The meaning of what happened will become clear only in time. . . . I woke next morning with new insights about the forest. . . . I have only been in the dark forest and need to grow familiar with the light. . . .
>
> I feel whole, with a readiness to grow. The marathon provided the possibility for me to force my fears outside myself where they could be seen for what they are worth. There is not so much to fear any more. Deepest of these was my own fear of myself. A fear that if I looked too closely I would find nothing. I looked and I found something—"me"—and I liked what I found.
>
> At the conclusion of my "dramatic episode" while I lay there quietly just feeling, my right hand turned palm upward. This gesture summed up so much of what I was feeling—my vulnerability, my desire to receive, my willingness to trust myself and others. Then from deep inside came the realization which finally found words—I am not alone.

Physical contact is always an important aspect of the affection and concern which a group shows for its members. In letter after letter, participants speak of the meaningfulness of physical demonstrations of affection. Typical is the letter of a man who wrote, "It was so good to find that there was something else besides a handshake on the one hand, and the idea that touching somebody means hopping into bed." Men, in particular, express their deep gratification over the experience of being able to embrace other men without an implied threat of homosexuality and being able to embrace women without the implication of a sexual advance. Often the experience of physical contact has an extremely deep, specific meaning.

Nicholas was a serious, hard-working lawyer in his early forties, married, with four children. Although he recalled his parents as warm and supportive with him in his childhood, his early years had been extremely difficult because of a severe attack of poliomyelitis at the age of two and a half. His hospitalization had been lonely and terrifying, he had suffered intense pain for months, and during most of his boyhood he had worn a heavy brace. He was now a fairly active man, and his sexual functioning was unimpaired, but the leg was still partly shrivelled, and he could not walk rapidly without a cane. Nevertheless, Nicholas was a determined man and had lately been experimenting with learning to dance. Although these attempts embarrassed him, he was physically capable of dancing if he did not try to cover the dance floor with long steps or to move rapidly.

In the second day of the marathon, when trust and intimacy had already developed, Nicholas told the group awkwardly that he would like to come to terms with his half-shrivelled leg. Sitting in the middle of the room, with the bad leg clumsily thrust forward, he told the group that he did not really think of this leg as part of himself. Sometimes he even fantasied that it would be best to have it amputated and replaced with an artificial limb. Without two good legs he was incomplete, not really a man. He hated the bad leg, and yet he wanted to accept it.

Without words, half-a-dozen members of the group surrounded Nicholas, sat on the floor with him, and drew the shoe and sock from his bad leg. Half-weeping, half-protesting, Nicholas allowed it. As he began to speak directly to the alien leg, many pairs of hands moved gently on the partly-atrophied muscles and somewhat undersized foot, caressing and stroking.

"I hate you, . . . you're a bad part of me, . . . yet you're part of me. I've taken care of you, you've taken care of me. Sometimes I want to cut you off and have a wooden leg, but I don't want to do that either. . . ."

Nicholas at first winced under the caresses and tried to draw away. But gradually he relaxed. Someone stroked his forehead, someone else patted his shoulder, and he continued in a breaking voice.

"You're part of me. . . . I don't like you and yet I have to like you if I like myself. Why couldn't you be good and strong like other legs?"

Nicholas began to cry. Nobody spoke, but the hands continued their reassurance. It all lasted for perhaps a quarter of an hour. Then, perhaps without even being aware of his gesture, Nicholas reached down, patted the bad leg, then suddenly he lifted up his head and laughed.

"It's time to dance!" he said. He stood up, and the group began to hum and clap. Nicholas picked a partner, did a few steps, then another partner. He moved with enjoyment and only a slight awkwardness. Later, he told the group that his leg now seemed a part of him, and occasionally he reached down to touch it.

Written feedback in this instance came from Nicholas's wife, whose appreciative letter told me that after the marathon he had been able to discuss his childhood illness with her more freely than ever before and with less bitterness, and that their relationship was closer than it had been for some time. As often happens in marathons, the episode of Nicholas also had a powerful impact on other participants, perhaps because his attitude toward his crippled leg was an especially intense manifestation of the feeling many people have, to a greater or lesser degree, that there is something wrong or imperfect about them physically.[10]

Lillian, a forty-year-old woman who had participated in this marathon, described its effects:

> As you remember, one of the participants who was crippled in early childhood by polio addressed his deformed leg, . . . hated his leg and addressed it as if it were a thing apart from him. . . . And though I had disliked him earlier, I now found myself vibrating along with him in the most intense, grief-stricken way. But I was addressing myself to my vagina, to my being a woman. My pain was so sharp that I imagined jumping from a window. My rational self knew that I was reliving an old grief but I could find more support in the thought that the room was full of strong, loving men who would not let me hurt myself. Then you, Elizabeth, began to recite to Nicholas all the good things his leg had been to him, and I felt a sweet, tender, tearful release thinking about how my vagina had been the passageway for the birth of my two daughters, my flowers, and how it has given pleasure to me and warmth and receptiveness to my husband. Yet I was faced with really not being able to accept myself as a woman. I felt during this experience something that all my years in therapy had never been able to reach, the part of me that feels like a castrated male. It was one of the most powerful experiences that I have ever gone through.[11]

[10] As a psychotherapist, I note this attitude repeatedly, even among people who are not actually handicapped in any way. My conjecture is that, quite aside from specific traumatic childhood episodes, two aspects of our culture may contribute to such feelings: first, our extreme emphasis on the social desirability of having an attractive appearance; and second, the lack of social encouragement for the enjoyment by adults of natural, simple, physical activities such as walking, dancing, or swimming, the absence of which tends to make us feel alienated from our bodies.

[11] Lillian's sudden awareness of "part of me that feels like a castrated male" can be viewed either as a symbolic expression for a sense of feminine inferiority based on specific life experience, or as a manifestation of biologically determined penis envy,

For Mac, also, the experience of Nicholas was personally significant. Mac was a minister, a solidly built man in his mid-fifties, married, with three children. He wrote:

> For me the marathon was a real breakthrough, which came about mostly through the games. From early childhood I had a kind of phobia about touching, in any affectionate way, another person except my mother and grandparents. I was an only son. I wouldn't show physical affection even for my two younger sisters. If another person, even family or friends, put their arms around me I was embarrassed and uneasy and would draw away. . . .
>
> The game that affected me most was when Nicholas was asked to affirm his deformed leg as a part of him even if unsightly because of the paralysis. He was asked to sit in the center of the room without his shoe and sock and let us all see it. His deep resentment of this as a shame was about to preclude him from continuing when, almost as one, the group went to him to give him their love and encouragement. At this point I sat behind him and when somebody first touched his foot, he fell back almost in agony into my arms. He was encouraged to speak words of acceptance to his leg as they finally bared it and laid their hands on it and caressed it. After a while I laid his head in the lap of one of the women and continued to stroke his shoulder as others in the group used physical touch to affirm their support of him and their loving acceptance. I had never expressed love in a physical way to a man before this day. I myself, in a certain sense also "crippled" by my phobia against physical contact, was freed to experience its rightness and genuine human warmth. My "homo hang-up" disappeared as a result of this experience. It was the imvolvement of the entire group that made it possible for me to act and feel as I did.

The use of physical contact in encounter groups is often criticized as merely providing indirect sexual satisfaction and as lacking any genuine therapeutic meaning. For Mac its effects were lasting. His letter continued in detail to describe various episodes in which bodily contact was important, especially after he had confided his touching-phobia to the group, which responded by repeatedly offering him friendly physical gestures.

> I was given every opportunity by everyone present to face my phobia. All were aware of my need. . . . All of them together succeeded in helping me break through a phobia which had lasted forty-five years. As we

---

depending on one's theoretical preference. The significant element in her experience was that identification and empathy made possible the emergence of repressed feelings which to some extent had hindered her enjoyment of her feminity.

were leaving the marathon my new freedom was realized. I was able to give affectionate hugs to both men and women and feel natural about it.

I had the opportunity to experience my new freedom again a week after the marathon. One of the members in my church died suddenly of a heart attack. His elderly widow was asking for me. When I arrived at her home, I immediately held her in my arms for a moment while I expressed my words of sympathy and comfort. After the embrace she thanked me and we continued talking. I had never done this in thirty years as a pastor but I then realized that here was an important way of expressing Christian love and affection that words alone could not. . . . Since then I am also able to hug my two grown sons and also my son-in-law for the first time. It has added a new warmth to our family get-togethers.

The group experience for me was a community support of great depth. I was able to throw my hang-ups into the pot with the others and there was a kind of team spirit. We were honest with each other and we were also kind.

It is worth noting that Mac's conquest of his touching-phobia occurred in his second marathon and probably could not have occurred without the preliminary experience of his first. When Mac initially telephoned to inquire about marathons, he had expressed concern lest the group should be inhibited by his being a minister and had even considered the possibility of concealing his occupation. My original conjecture was that Mac might be suffering from doubts regarding his religion and wished to avoid the possibility of ideological challenges from the group. My conjecture proved unfounded. In his first marathon, it became evident that Mac required himself to be reassuring, comforting, and inspiring in all his personal contacts, since this was what his parishioners sought and he wished to meet their expectations. In the marathon, he wanted to work as a peer without this responsibility. His first marathon, as another group member expressed it, was "a vacation from his vocation" and he was relieved to find that nobody in the group expected him to be free from human conflicts or anticipated that he would be morally judgmental. This first marathon constituted a preliminary experience, of being himself and being accepted by the group, which provided a foundation for the emotional involvement which, in the second marathon, resulted in his conquest of his touching-phobia.

Concern is sometimes expressed lest the prolonged intimacy of the marathon, along with an atmosphere which encourages the physical expression of affection, might lead some participants into sexual involvements which they would not have chosen under ordinary circumstances, and which might not only elicit subsequent feelings of guilt but possibly in some instances result in the disturbance of family ties. The question has also been raised as to whether the permissiveness of the marathon, with its implicit challenge to reexamine social conventions and stereo-types, may not constitute a threat to the religious or ethical values of the individual. Possibly these risks exist but can be minimized if the leader's attitude is one of respect for whatever values are genuinely held by an individual participant, and if furthermore the leader is aware of the possibility that an occasional participant may be threatened by the group's permissiveness. It has never been necessary for me to intervene in order to protect a participant against such threats, although it is certainly possible that such intervention may at times become necessary. Groups thus far have invariably respected individual values. For example, many groups have included people with strong religious commitments, such as priests or ministers, along with irreligious or even strongly antireligious individuals, and no difficulties in communication have arisen. Clashes would, however, unquestionably occur if either point of view were assaulted, and it is my prediction that in this case the group would attack whatever participant showed an inability to respect the viewpoint of others. Mac, for example, was never challenged about the validity of his religious beliefs, nor did he attempt in any way to alter the beliefs of others.

The wisdom of the group is also shown in offering exactly the degree of new experiences which an individual participant is able to accept. In a series of four marathons during the course of the year, with concomitant individual psychotherapy by a psychiatrist, Georgia was able to overcome a deeply rooted fear of sex and men which she had been taught in childhood.

Georgia was a slim, dainty woman with a childlike manner which made her appear far younger than her forty years. There was a wistful, quaint, old-fashioned air about her which, since it was not an affectation, was extremely appealing. Her life story, which she told in her first marathon in response to gentle coaxing, left the group aghast. She had grown up in a tiny, sequestered community as a member of a small religious sect in which virtue was equated with self-deprivation and pleasure was equated with sin. The atmosphere was nineteenth-century puritanism; there was considerable preoccupation with such matters as card-playing and the modesty of women's dress. Georgia until her early thirties had devoted herself to caring for her parents and to volunteer work for her church. Her total inexperience of life was astounding. When her parents died, Georgia went into psychosis, was hospitalized for several months, and received shock treatment. My impression, corroborated by her psychiatrist, was that the psychosis represented a desperate, unconscious effort to break out of the internal prison of her self-denial.

By the time she arrived at the marathon, Georgia was decidedly not psychotic. After being discharged from the hospital, she came to New York, entered psychotherapeutic treatment, and developed her secretarial skills sufficiently to find a job with a religious organization which, unlike her small church back home, was very much in contact with the community and emphasized positive religious values rather than self-deprivation. Her psychiatrist worked carefully and slowly to help Georgia get into touch with life and with her feelings. Nonetheless, by the time of the marathon, Georgia was still extremely afraid of anger and even more frightened of men. She had never had a single date—not one in her entire life, despite her prettiness. She wished to date, said Georgia timorously, but she simply did not know how to be with men or talk to them.

Someone suggested gently that perhaps Georgia, here and now, could go around the circle and be flirtatious with the men. She need not touch them; she could merely say something flirtatious. Georgia responded with a little scream of terror.

"Even the *married* men?"

Georgia went around the room, giggling and flushing in a way which would have seemed self-consciously coy or cute if it had not been genuine. Nobody showed amusement. Her compliments to the men were like those of a flirtatious little girl and not a woman. Yet when she sat down, pink and sparkling, there was a light, affectionate patter of applause. When the marathon broke up, and the participants as usual embraced each other in farewell, the men were particularly aware of Georgia's anxiety, touching her gently in such a way that she would not be frightened.

Despite her naïvete, Georgia was by no means unintelligent. She wrote:

> A wall inside me has been cracked and someday it's going to come tumbling down! At last I know that feelings can be in people and can be expressed. . . . I saw first hand that anger doesn't have to destroy. It can help build a meaningful relationship. It seemed impossible to believe my eyes and ears that two people could be so very angry at each other and end up hugging.

> I wonder now to what degree I was really afraid of men. Perhaps it is more true that I was just afraid of sex and couldn't separate the two. I think what happened in the group made the separation clear. Men as human beings with feelings come first, and sex is secondary. . . . I'm sure the fear of sex will disappear as I learn more about the feelings of men.

Georgia's psychiatrist also reported on the results of her experience. He wrote that she had purchased her first pair of slacks after the marathon, and that an almost constant psychosomatic headache had diminished. He wrote also, "She seemed to have been able, for the first time, to conceive of herself as a woman, apparently because she responded to the warm feelings of the various men in the group."

A few months later, Georgia went into her second marathon. Here she told the group that she was no longer quite so afraid of men, and that she would like to be able to be close to a man, although she was uncertain whether or not he would represent her father. A friendly man responded, crossing the room to sit with Georgia, and put his arms around her. Georgia was tense and ill at ease at first, then cuddled close and sighed, "You do make a nice daddy!" It appeared that, in the marathon, she was allowing herself an experience which she had been denied in childhood, the experience of physical affection with her father which normally prepares a little girl to grow into a sexually responsive woman.

The changes within Georgia went beyond the gradual development of an ability to accept men as people and a diminution of her sexual phobias. She wrote:

> I have stopped hitting myself against the wall about the love denied to me in childhood that my parents were unable to give me. I think it finally hit home that I must look elsewhere for love and affection. Somehow I felt this childhood gap had to be filled before I could get well. But even if they weren't dead it couldn't be done and besides it isn't even necessary. . . . Also, I know now that it is necessary to be able to accept affection and love before I can give and return. I don't HAVE to give. I can take. This sure takes the pressure off.

In this same letter, Georgia also expressed a temporary reaction which is not uncommon after a marathon; when the initial exhilaration vanished, she felt depressed because there was, at that time, nobody in her life who could share and respond to her growing ability to be spontaneous and warm.

> The deep depression came just about a week later . . . but after a few days the pieces came together and now I've levelled off . . . and I must now get myself some "practice" with dates.

By the time Georgia came into her third marathon, her appearance was changing. Her clothing was more sophisticated. She no longer seemed so fluttery and little-girlish. In this marathon, for the first time, she was able to offer affection to others. A young man in the group had been through a catharsis of agonizing feelings of loneliness and deprivation left over from his childhood. As he lay sobbing on the floor, Georgia, to everyone's amazement, went up to him without hesitation, lay down beside him, and embraced him. It was the first time in her life she had ever embraced a man as a woman and not as a child.

> In the last marathon when the other man held me, most of my feelings were that this was how I would have liked my father to hug me. This time I wasn't even thinking about my father. I wasn't just taking, I was giving something too. Now I must learn to think of my dates as just men to have fun with and get acquainted with. It would be such fun to see a man as a PERSON!

The phobia about men and sex was almost gone. Georgia decided, on the basis of a genuine system of personal values which had now replaced the puritanism she had been taught, that she would date, but that she would not accept intercourse merely for the experience, but only if there were strong mutual feelings of affection. She came into her next marathon, however, with a somewhat different problem. In her childhood, said Georgia, she had never had an opportunity to wrestle with a boy. She had never fought with a man. She wanted to fight with a man, in a half-aware recognition that she could not be completely at home with a man until she could stop fearing his strength and her anger. Asked to pick a wrestling partner, Georgia—who weighed only a few pounds over a hundred—selected an athletic six-footer and challenged him.

The resulting match was rather like a fight between a Great Dane and a kitten, and it was both absurd and touching. Once so demure and inhibited, Georgia launched herself repeatedly at her wrestling partner, arms flailing. He fended her off gently from time to time but accepted the harmless blows, then finally picked her up and spun around with her in his arms. Finally he put her down. The episode was Georgia's proof that a man's strength need not be hurtful, and that it was not necessary for her to be in control at every moment.

At the end of this marathon, Georgia thanked all of us warmly and told me that she did not think that she would be returning, at least not for a while. She was ready for life. If further blocks arose in her living, she would be back for other marathons. Her final letter was:

> I have come a long, long way but the worst part of it is over. There is still work to be done, but it will be worth the effort as life will be fun. I was overwhelmed by the strength that a man has, but now instead of fearing it, it has to be taken with faith—that it will be used to protect you and not harm you.

In presenting the description of what occurs in marathons, it is natural to select episodes which involve physical interaction and dramatic expressions of feeling. Actually, the simple, accepting, affectionate concern among the members of the marathon's later stages may be even more important than dramatic catharsis.

Trudy, a woman in her late fifties, brought to the marathon the history of an exceptionally tragic life. Her childhood and girlhood in Germany had been bloodied by the Nazi persecution of the Jews. She had lost a beloved twin sister, who had died only a few years ago. She had undergone a series of illnesses, which had left her physically and emotionally depleted. Despite all this, she was able to function in a profession which required considerable dedication—and then, about a year before she entered the marathon, she was the victim of an automobile accident. She walked with a brace and crutches, suffered considerable pain, and had been told that probably there was no prospect that her injured leg would ever improve. She was a cripple. She had resumed work and was fighting hard against self-pity, but as the marathon continued, she told the group that she was struggling with thoughts of suicide.

They took a particular form. She had been given a sharp, powerful electric knife for cutting meats and frozen foods. Every time she entered her kitchen, Trudy had the fantasy of taking this knife, plugging it in, and sawing through her wrist. It seemed meaningful to her that, since she had substantially lost the use of her legs, she had fantasies of destroying herself by means of her arms.

In this group, there were several participants who already knew Trudy both socially and professionally and who respected her greatly. Yet perhaps the most meaningful contact for Trudy was with Leonora, who had not met Trudy before, and who had entered the marathon struggling with a depression of her own.

Leonora had been subject to rather severe depressions as a girl and as a young woman, but a prolonged period of individual psychotherapy had alleviated them to a considerable degree. However, the depression—though less severe than in former years—had been reawakened by the recent death of her father and the impending death of her mother. Leonora entered the marathon, as she expressed it, "in a web of apathy, . . . a doleful mood, which I felt too exhausted and helpless to struggle through because the circumstances were supported by reality. . . . It was the first time in many years that I had felt submerged in emptiness."

When Leonora first met Trudy, she was shocked because the older woman seemed so strongly to resemble her mother in this period of her terminal illness. She wrote:

> When I first became aware of Trudy's presence, I was frightened. Here sat today's mother in appearance, emaciated and lifeless, a woman stricken, . . . incapacitated and hopeless. . . . She actually looked like my mother, it was uncanny, every anguished line in her face was familiar to

me. . . . But there was a difference. I liked her immediately and felt all her vast warmth beneath the pain. . . . Yet she seemed so enmeshed in torment that I felt she had already given up, and I felt so totally helpless that I fell back into my old aloneness.

As the group reached a phase when intimacy was possible, Leonora approached Trudy and spoke to her, so privately that what she said was not heard by the group. The interchange (reported to me later) was quite simple.

"Don't die, Trudy. Please don't die."

"All right, don't worry, I won't die."

The words, for these particular two people, carried a great deal of meaning. Leonora's mother, as Leonora described her, was not a fighter, but a "skilled and accomplished martyr" who exploited her illness to wring from her family as much guilt and suffering as she could. Moreover, Leonora had always felt that, no matter what she did and how hard she tried, she could never either help her mother or succeed in pleasing her. With Trudy, who quickly sensed her meaningfulness to Leonora and who responded with appreciation, it was different. Leonora wrote:

> Her immediate response to me assured me that . . . I did not have to do anything or perform anything for her to be pleased that I was there. . . . My deprivation in my early years was never feeling loved just for being born, for being there. . . . What I received from Trudy gave me a rebirth with someone who would welcome me and care about me only for my presence. . . . We recognized almost from the beginning that we were on the same wave-lengths. . . . Perhaps after all I was finally ready to pardon my mother.

Except for their brief conversation, not much happened between Leonora and Trudy, except that they sat clasping hands for many hours. The group worked hard with Trudy's death wish, not only by offering her warmth and reassurance, but also by pointing out to her certain personal difficulties which made her life unnecessarily difficult, such as an unyielding pride which kept her from accepting help and appreciation even when it was offered gladly. Trudy wrote:

> I experienced acute hurt when someone spoke of "my pride which humiliates others." . . . It will require much self-investigation. . . . But I welcome this present confusion which will permit honest work. It's that kind of remark which can best be made in a marathon. . . . While there were surely many gratifying episodes in this marathon, its overall effect was to begin the process of a reevaluation of myself. It does give me food for thought . . . but the atmosphere was such as to leave an impact, but not injury.

This letter of Trudy's expresses an observation which can be made repeatedly in every successful marathon: that, after an atmosphere of mutual warmth and concern is established, confrontations can occur which might be painful and even injurious under other circumstances.

For Trudy, the effect of the experience was clear. Her letter ended:

Since then I have not "seen" the knife nor has there been any suicidal intention or even thoughts of death.

For Leonora, her contact with Trudy had a rather unexpected result. She became playful. Leonora's natural personality was reserved and quiet, and the childlike playfulness which was also a part of her had been totally repressed until near the end of her psychotherapy. Although her playfulness was expressed more in her voice and face than overtly, she showed a delight in being alive which was apparent to everyone, and which she still remembered some months later:

Little did I realize how much I had wished for the child within me to emerge and be carefree and romp. . . . Now I see that the child is more available than I had realized. That kid is still slightly cautious but I am still able to play. . . . It is such fun!

As Leonora's former individual psychotherapist, it is possible for me to evaluate the dynamics of her experience with Trudy. Unlike Leonora's mother, Trudy was a fighter rather than a martyr. At the beginning of the marathon, she was nearly overborne by the real grimness of her life situation, yet she wanted to live as fully as she possibly could. With Trudy, the younger woman went through a healing experience. Trudy's gallantry, in contrast to the self-pity of Leonora's mother, released Leonora from some of the guilt feelings which had possessed her almost constantly until the concluding phase of her treatment with me, and which had recently been reawakened by her mother's illness. Also, Trudy could accept Leonora's help and return her affection to a degree of which her mother had never been capable. After the marathon, Leonora was able to accept her mother's illness with sympathy and with practical help, but without the apathetic, guilt-ridden depression from which she had been suffering.

Although episodes as poignant and meaningful as this cannot be expected to occur in every marathon, they are by no means infrequent. Part of the value of the marathon situation is that the participants not only are able to share their conflicts and limitations, but to profit by sharing their strengths and their helpfulness.

REFERENCES

Bach, G. The marathon group. In H. R. Ruitenbeek (Ed.), *Group therapy today.* New York: Atherton, 1969.

Bindrim, P. Facilitating peak experience. In H. Otto & G. Mann. (Eds.), *Ways of growth.* New York: Grossman, 1969.

Bradford, L. P., Gibb, J. R., & Benne, K. D. *T-group theory and laboratory method.* New York: Wiley, 1964.

Goldstein, A. P., Heller, K., & Sechrest, L. G. *Psychotherapy and the psychology of behavior change.* New York: Wiley, 1966.

Heller, K. Effects of modeling procedures in helping relationships. *Journal of Consulting and Clinical Psychology,* October 1969, 33(5), 522–531.

Warkentin, J. Intensity in group encounter. In A. Burton (Ed.), *Encounter.* San Francisco: Jossey-Bass, 1970.

Whalen, C. Effects of a model and instructions on group verbal behavior. *Journal of Consulting and Clinical Psychology,* October 1969, 33(5), 509–521.

6 LET THE BODY SPEAK

Examples have been given, in preceding chapters, of the use of physical contact as a natural expression of affection or of hostility; as a way of conveying the acceptance of regressive feelings and subsequently gratifying regressive needs; as a means of providing emotional security; and as a method of helping undo outworn childhood taboos against the appropriate expression of such feelings as sexuality and anger. All these approaches are essentially ways of communicating on an interpersonal level, using the language of the body as well as the language of the voice. They are ways of overcoming the separation between people.

There is another kind of separation, an intrapersonal separation, between the physical aspect of the self and its conscious aspect. A striking paradox of our society is that, although immense industries exist to meet the demand for products to improve the body's appearance, there is a schism between the body and the feelings in many individuals, not only those who are clinically ill but also in "normal" individuals. Alienation from the physical self, in terms of inability to be joyful and spontaneous in using and appreciating the body, is as common as alienation from others. Gross signs of this alienation include the finding that an impressive proportion of our population are physically unfit; the high incidence of psychosomatic illness; and the extraordinary preference of the average person for passive recreation, such as television or attendance at sports events, as compared to active enjoyment. In a reaction against this alienation, an integral part of the humanistic movement consists of an effort to reunite man with his body (Gunther, 1968; Schutz, 1967).[1]

The orthodox psychoanalytic tradition, when it is inflexibly followed, has tended to perpetuate this body-mind alienation (Mintz, 1969). Patients may be asked to report bodily sensations as part of the free-association process, but physical activity is generally discouraged in the belief that it dissipates energy which should be used for the furtherance of the

[1] Philosophical considerations about the ultimate nature of reality are involved here in the choice of language. For convenience in communication, it is easiest to speak as if mind and body were separate entities which may become disassociated and must be reunited. However, it should be noted that many philosophers, and many clinicians, view the body as constituting the whole reality of the human being, while others view mind and body as different aspects of the same reality. Luckily, it is possible to deal with clinical material without adopting any specific metaphysical viewpoint.

analysis. Patients are requested not to rise from the couch, not to turn around to look at the analyst, and—with some practitioners—even to avoid shifting their physical position. If therapeutically valuable physical activity does occur in a psychoanalytic session, it is likely to be regarded as an exceptional and noteworthy occurrence.[2] A converse technical approach is used by the bioenergeticists (Reich, 1949; Lowen, 1969), who assume an identity between patterns of muscular tensions and patterns of emotional pathology. These therapists may instruct the patient to go through highly specialized physical movements or may exert direct physical pressure in order to dissolve chronic muscular rigidity, which is seen as "character armor." Thus physical pain might be deliberately inflicted in order to overcome pathologically rigid defenses against experiencing grief or fear. At their respective extremes, the former approach tends to overemphasize the cognitive aspect of psychotherapy; the latter approach tends toward the mechanical use of physical routines; and both approaches (again, at their extremes) thus deprive the patient of a flexible, human-to-human relationship with his therapist.

The marathon encounter group is ideally suited to the sharpening and heightening of bodily awareness. In a structured marathon, this may be done by sensory-awareness exercises (Gunther, 1968; Schutz, 1967) in which the entire group participates. In an unstructured marathon, in which activity arises out of the unique needs of the group, awareness of the physical dimension of human experience can help in the recognition, the exploration, and even in the resolution of deep-seated characterological problems.

The values of the marathon time format in this area are analogous to its value in the area of interpersonal encounter. If we assume that "every chronic muscular tension inhibits an impulse" (Lowen, 1969, p. 284), then clearly a sustained period of time is required for the individual to become aware of his tension, to investigate its personal meaning, and to experiment with expressing the impulse, relinquishing the tension, or with both together.

The physical climate of the marathon is in itself conducive to relaxation and spontaneity. Marathon participants, after the initial self-consciousness, easily move away from the taut, upright posture learned in the long years of classroom conformity. They lounge, sprawl, and stretch. With almost no encouragement from the leader, they begin to feel at home with physical self-expression—a casual hug, a playful blow with a pillow, an unembarrassed yawn. They eat and drink freely according to their individual needs, as an infant is fed on demand, rather than waiting for the group sanction of a scheduled coffee break. Only a

_____

[2] As with Balint's example of the analysand who spontaneously turned a somersault as a graphic representation of her increased ability to tolerate emotional mobility (1968, p. 131).

few unfortunate people have been so immobilized by their training that they do not respond by feeling increasingly at ease with their bodies.

Most participants also respond very readily to leadership which takes into account several dimensions of human experience—awareness of bodily feelings, awareness and release of emotion, and cognitive integration. If the group leader does not tacitly exclude any of these dimensions from recognition (as ultratraditional psychoanalytic group therapists once interdicted any physical contact, and as some contemporary encounter group leaders forbid cognitive activity as "intellectualization"), the group will also include these dimensions, both in self-exploration and in working with one another.

Certain specialized techniques for the elicitation of strong physical responses, or for the correction of deep-seated psychosomatic pathology,[3] should clearly be practiced only by therapists with special training in physiology as well as in psychodynamics and should not be suggested for routine group use. However, there are several methods of enhancing bodily awareness which can be introduced in a marathon and are usually picked up by sensitive participants, and which in the setting of a responsibly conducted marathon are no more risky than a verbal interchange. These methods include: work with breathing; massage or gentle physical pressure; and recognition of disparities between an emotion which is being described and an emotion which is being expressed by the face or the body.

In psychotherapy, it is often possible to observe a patient inhibit his breathing when he wishes to avoid feelings which are unacceptable to him, such as rage or fear or guilt-laden sexuality. People who continually repress their feelings are likely to breathe shallowly most of the time. Sometimes these feelings will emerge if the patient is asked to attend to his breathing, particularly to the full and gentle expiration of breath (Proskauer, 1968), after which the incoming breath deepens without hyperventilation. In the reassuring presence of the group, a participant who is fighting back his awareness of feeling is often willing to deepen his breathing when requested. This is merely an incidental procedure but occasionally has unexpectedly far-reaching effects. One woman, after an episode in which she had been asked to breathe more fully in order to help her face a phobic reaction more directly, reported:

> In the marathon we didn't talk about my sex life, in fact I didn't even mention it, because although it's not the greatest, I never really thought

[3] Such as the work of Ida P. Rolf at Esalen Institute on the structural realignment of the body through manual pressures which are often painful and which require great skill by the practitioner; or the bioenergetic techniques for inducing involuntary muscular vibration through certain physical postures (Lowen, 1969) or attempting to stimulate breathing by pressing the hands outward against the jaws from inside the mouth.

it was a problem. But that night in bed with Jack [her husband] I suddenly remembered when I found out about my breathing and for the
first time I noticed that in sex I kind of hold back on my breathing. So
I tried the business of breathing out very deeply and gently and I realized
that I hold my breath just before the climax. I tried not to and I've been
trying not to and it seems as if this helps me enjoy sex a lot more. It's a
little bit frightening, but I like it.

Probably the breathing exercise in itself could not be regarded as
solely responsible for this woman's enhanced sexual enjoyment, but her
willingness to breathe more naturally apparently contributed.

Massage has a variety of uses. Its value in conveying affection and
acceptance has already been described. It is also useful in working with
muscular tensions which are associated with emotional conflicts. A group
member walked and sat with a marked stoop, giving the impression of
carrying a heavy weight, which was an exact translation in bodily terms
of his exaggerated need to accept and carry responsibility. He lay down
on his face and was gently rubbed, kneaded and pummelled by several
group members. After this he expressed a sense of relief and refresh-
ment and showed a more relaxed attitude in discussing his workload. Untrained people should certainly not attempt corrective massage for any
kind of orthopedic problem, but most group members are entirely
capable of perceiving and alleviating ordinary muscular tensions.

Most group members are also well able to perceive discrepancies
between feelings which are expressed verbally and feelings which are
expressed by the face and the body, and their comments are often pithy.

"You claim you're angry, but you come on with that blah expression."

"Every time somebody criticizes you or gets sore at you, there is a
kind of smile on your face. Is that the way you keep it from getting to
you? Or do you get a kick out of provoking people?"

Such incongruities denote a resistance to experiencing or revealing
the actual, inner feelings. When they are pointed out, the mask is sometimes abandoned and the real feelings come through.

There is a continual effort to translate feeling into bodily expression and to interpret bodily expression in terms of feeling. Emotional
breakthroughs may occur as a consequence of appropriate physical activity, as in the following episodes of Norman and Peter. Postural oddities
may provide a clue to repressed feelings, as with Irving. Physical action
may symbolically help toward a resolution of profound conflicts, as with
Lynne and Jeffrey. Full expression of feeling in physical terms, as with
Curt and Serena, can provide at least a partial relief of tensions which
may have existed for most of a lifetime.

Encounter games involving the use of the body, many of which were
previously described (Chapter 3), are used as they become appropriate.

Among the most useful is couch-pounding, for two purposes: to permit the full expression on a physical level of primitive anger which has already been evoked; and to tap and drain off a part of the basic reservoir of rage.

This basic rage reservoir probably exists in most civilized humans. It can be thought of as an ongoing tendency toward anger, analogous to the "free-floating anxiety" described in psychoanalytic theory. It derives from childhood experiences in which the expression of anger, or in some environments even its existence, was disapproved, thus establishing in the child an unconscious tendency to counteract angry impulses by muscular contractions which in time become automatic and unconscious. In some people, the impulse toward anger may persist on a somatic level even at times when there is no specific outside stimulus to evoke it. If such people go through physical movements which express anger, there may be a breakthrough of feeling accompanied by a physical and emotional relief of tension.

Couch-pounding is an exercise by which the protagonist can put forth his (or her) full strength without risk, using the biologically natural gesture, which can be observed in infants, of clenching the fist and bringing the arm downwards vigorously from the shoulders with the elbow slightly bent. This natural gesture is usually adopted spontaneously when couch-pounding is suggested. The protagonist kneels before the couch and uses one fist, both fists at once, or both fists alternatively, depending on his natural pattern of movement, which sometimes alters during the course of the exercise. He is told that if he wishes he may shout, scream, or curse, and many protagonists begin to shout "Damn you!" or "Drop dead!" or "Take that!" in a rhythm which accords naturally with the rhythm of the body movement.[4]

If rage is deeply inhibited, it is literally impossible for a man or woman to clench his fist and strike hard, even once, against any surface, either in individual treatment or in a group. Several people with whom I have worked, people capable of adequate social functioning and in good physical health, were totally unable initially to clench their fists and strike hard, even once, against any surface. This inhibition can usually be worked through in psychotherapy, or in a series of marathons.

To me it does not seem appropriate, either for therapy or for the stimulation of personal growth, to use this pounding procedure routinely in order to investigate or release feelings of anger. Its effectiveness usually depends on its being suggested at a time when a participant is already searching for an outlet for his anger, or expresses a wish to get

---

[4] The couch must be sufficiently well built to withstand the blows and sufficiently well upholstered not to bruise the knuckles. It is desirable to provide an environment in which the protagonist need not be requested to control his shouting, which may become astonishingly loud.

in touch with his own rage. When a connection is made between the physical motions and the pent-up feelings, the protagonist sometimes experiences a sense of being swept away on a tide of feeling, of moving vigorously and yet without deliberate effort, described thus by one participant:

> It's hard to believe what happened. I never experienced that kind of loss of control before. Just wanton physical expression, releasing of energy, murder rage. I felt . . . like striking back for years of something and maybe it didn't matter.

If this experience is to end in genuine emotional closure, someone should be available for support to the protagonist when it is over, and frequently after the energy is spent I suggest, "Ask for the person you want."

> I was feeling extremely exhausted. Elizabeth asked me to call for somebody to be with me and I called for Sandy who came and sat with me and how good it was that she was there, and that pretty much ended it except for my amazement. . . . It was an expression of the feeling that I didn't ever remember, an intensity and depth of feeling and experience that I don't remember ever having. And it was joy even though it was agony and it was life.

If a protagonist who wishes to pound the couch seems embarrassed, I may ask him to choose a "brother" to pound along beside him. In one such episode, it was the "brother," Norman, who had an unexpected emotional breakthrough. He wrote:

> When I was chosen as a "brother" I felt exceedingly self-conscious. . . . I tried to pace him, since he had chosen me . . . to help him pound the couch and achieve some kind of breakthrough. I was trying to get him to pace his momentum more and more quickly. . . . And I said a couple of things to get him involved, "Kill 'em," and that sort of thing. . . . As we went on I began to get involved. I can't say that I enjoyed it but I got involved in just the sheer physical motion, doing it with all my might, and I had the realization that there must be a father involved. . . . I began to think about my father and some rather unpleasant experiences with him. . . . As the moment built up I was no longer aware of the group's presence, I just got involved in the actual pounding to the point where I almost hallucinated my father's head as I hit the couch. . . . The rage and fury just welled up in me, . . . at that point I finally broke down.

Norman, a coolly self-contained young man, surprised the group when he began to cry violently. He hid his face and turned away from the group, as if he had always cried alone and did not hope for comfort. With my arm around his shoulders, I sat near him saying repeatedly, "You don't have to cry alone any more."

> I felt acutely ashamed of myself for having broken down. I felt that I had to go to some corner. I felt exposed, as if some secret part of my soul lay bare. . . . When you said something about other people being with me and my not having to cry alone, I really couldn't believe it. I felt that I would get the same kind of disdain and contempt that my parents gave when I cried. . . . Afterward I had difficulty looking at any of the other members of the group.

Here, once again, was the repetition of a traumatic experience with a new outcome. Norman expected to be contemptuously ignored. Instead, several group members offered affection and reassurance. His report was written a month afterward:

> The breakthrough was really shattering, so that afterward when I thought back, I could feel the tears again. These were feelings which apparently I had stifled. . . . They kept coming up. . . . Tears came up for me for a few days every time I thought of the experience. However, there was an interesting sequel, . . . namely, that I felt more open that night and the next few days to my own feelings and also to other people. I'm much more responsive to their feelings. . . . I had always felt very much inhibited. Now since that point I am easier about permitting feelings to come up and accept the feelings of others, whatever those feelings might happen to be.

Couch-pounding, effective as it is at times, fails of its purpose when the protagonist unconsciously or consciously holds back from becoming involved. However, since the extent of the involvement is left entirely up to the protagonist, the possibility of a dangerously uncontrollable breakthrough of rage seems practically nonexistent. On the other hand, holding-down, which is another of the physical encounter techniques, may elicit such violent rage that it is among the few procedures which, to me, does seem to entail some risk.[5] It should be used only with emotionally stable participants, and then with due regard to possible dangers on a physical level.

The subject lies face up on the floor, which should be softly covered. He is held down by his arms, legs, and head so firmly that he is completely immobilized. For this, a surprisingly large number of people are

---

[5] Until I recognized that this technique was being publicized in the lay press, I was reluctant to demonstrate it except before qualified professional groups. As it is now becoming well known, it seems wise to familiarize group leaders with the risk which accompanies its potency.

required, since some participants (women as well as men) mobilize an astounding degree of strength in this position. Participants must be directed not to press on vulnerable parts of the body, such as stomach, throat, and genitals, and not to twist the skin. It is essential for the subject to be able to speak, shout, and especially to breathe with complete freedom.[6]

The purpose is to tap feelings of primitive helplessness which, with most subjects, turn to primitive rage. However, reactions other than rage may occur, which usually represent a characterological attitude toward being helpless.

Reuben, who was waging an inward struggle against deep-seated feelings of inadequacy, expressed a humorous fantasy that he was compelling the group to hold him—"Look how powerful I am! I'm making you all pay attention to me!"

Leon, a hard-working business man (whose recovery of a childhood memory was described in Chapter 4), let himself go limp and said happily, "How wonderful! I can't do anything!" expressing a passive wish for which his hyperactivity seemed to be in part a compensation.

Ian struggled with spectacular energy until he was exhausted, and a few minutes after his release he terrified the group (and myself) by smashing a heavy piece of furniture against the floor. He was with difficulty induced to expend his energy by pounding the couch. The episode ended constructively in his expressing and discussing his fury toward a malevolent childhood authority-figure. For him, the aftereffects were expressed in his statement, "I got rid of something, I feel great." For me, the aftereffects were an increased caution in the use of this technique.

Gig struggled vigorously, decided he had enough, and quietly asked the group to release him. At once they did so. Later, in a poem, he expressed the insightful comment that "oppressive shackles" are only imaginary bonds left over from childhood, and that the real struggle is "against nether images of the past."

An exercise so powerfully suited to enabling the participant to make contact with his reservoir of primitive rage should be used judiciously, with adequate indications for its use, adequate preparation, and sufficient follow-up. A responsible psychoanalyst would never make a deep interpretation having to do with the Oedipal conflict on the basis of a statement by a beginning patient such as "I used to get sore at my father";

---

[6] If there is any reason whatsoever to doubt that the group member is in good health, or even if there are such reasons as middle-age, overweight, or heavy smoking to suspect that there might be a predisposition to a heart attack, it is prudent to ask the subject in advance if he is in good physical condition. Probably this is an overcautious attitude, since the actual physical exertion of being held down is of rather brief duration.

similarly, a responsible marathon leader would never propose the holding-down technique without a sense of comprehending the dynamics of the individual and without taking time for preparation and closure.[7] Curt's episode may illustrate such a procedure.

Curt was a husky man in his early fifties who occupied a challenging, responsible career job in the state government. In his own phrase, he "was a family man, and liked it." He was with us primarily to explore the usefulness of encounter groups but participated sincerely. He was friendly and did not seem irritable. Yet he somehow conveyed the impression of an underlying basic rage, and it was not a surprise when he volunteered "I'd like to do a little work on anger."

As a preliminary exploration of his feelings, Curt was asked to go around the circle and express anger. His reaction showed the hesitance and control which had already appeared in the phrase "a *little* work on anger." He made such statements as, "I'm angry for the way you underestimate yourself." "I'm angry you don't let yourself have fun." There was no anger, only disguised advice. Another member—Lynne, a sculptress in her early forties,—reacted to his evasiveness with strong personal involvement. She wrote:

> As Curt was telling each one he was angry, he became my father-boss, who treated us as though we were children and he was the only one who knew what to do. When no one responded to him, I could not stand it.

Lynne, as Curt approached her, rose unexpectedly to her feet and launched herself at him in a tackle. If the floor is softly covered, such a fight between adults is seldom any more dangerous than a fight between youngsters in a schoolyard. As expected, Curt easily withstood Lynne's onslaught and took control of the situation without hurting her. But this was of no value to Curt, who needed a situation in which his anger could get past his iron self-control, and anyone with Curt's sense of social responsibility could do this only in a situation where he knew nobody could be harmed. In the hope of mobilizing Curt's underlying rage, which had not come through in the least when he went around the circle, I suggested the holding-down technique.

At once Curt acquiesced. The group, which numbered over a dozen, had to exert itself to hold him, for his struggles were gargantuan. Since Curt was both strong and stubborn, the group could not keep him

---

[7] In these seemingly disparate situations, the two risks would be identical; first, that the psychoanalyst's premature interpretation would merely strengthen the resistance and fail to elicit any significant response from the analysand, while the marathon group participant would merely go through the exercise mechanically; and second, that there would be a painful and possibly harmful rush of anxiety.

immobile, and there appeared some possibility of a strained ligament or dislocated limb, a possibility for which the leader must always be alert during this exercise.

The group was asked to release him. Curt arose, red, panting, and apparently bewildered by his own feelings. Immediately it was suggested that he pound the mattress on the floor. There was an extraordinary display of physical rage. Curt flailed the mattress with endless vigor, roaring like a lion. It seemed a long time before he finally collapsed, panting, began to breath more gently, finally began to smile, and at last was surrounded by group members offering affection and handshakes.

Exhilaration usually follows such exertion, but exhilaration in itself is not the goal. Any full physical expression of feeling diminishes, though perhaps only to an infinitesimal extent, some of the chronic, automatic muscular tension by which the feeling has been continually held back.

It is of therapeutic value also that the group does not reject the manifestation of a feeling which was penalized in childhood but instead receives it with the appreciative respect always elicited by genuineness in an encounter group. Finally, a character trait can often be so vividly demonstrated to the participant by his own physical involvement that he can see it in sharper perspective.

When Curt returned to his chair, he was told that this was one of the few occasions when I had interrupted the holding-down procedure for fear the subject might damage himself by the vigor of his struggles. Curt acknowledged that he had been determined to escape, impossible or not, regardless of the cost to his own body. He understood that it was his sense of helplessness, which he had been unable to tolerate, which had mobilized his fury; and in a few thoughtful words he was able to make a connection between this experience and a general unwillingness to compromise, even when it would be appropriate to do so.

As frequently happens, one meaningful episode in the marathon led directly to another. Lynne was tense and miserable the day after her brief wrestling match with Curt. Her experience had been incomplete, since she had no chance to put forth her full strength. In such a situation victory or defeat is often irrelevant, but if there is no opportunity for maximum physical exertion, there is usually an aftermath of frustration, sometimes accompanied by such minor physical discomforts as headache, slight indigestion, or muscular tension.

Lynne told us about her feeling that there was a lifelong clash between her temperament, which was naturally assertive, and her early training toward conforming to the social stereotype of the submissive, yielding woman. Lynne's work as a sculptress required her to handle such materials as wood and marble, and she was physically vigorous. Her strength embarrassed her. She feared that it might be seen as unfeminine.

"Lynne, a man whose affection is worth having isn't frightened by a woman's strength."

Across the room Curt nodded emphatically, and so did several others. But we needed a game by which Lynne could put forth her full strength against a man, with a chance to defeat him, and find that she was still appreciated as a woman. Therefore a variation of arm-wrestling was proposed to equalize the biological disparity of strength between man and woman. Lynne and Curt were to wrestle in the usual prone position, head to head, but Lynne was allowed to use both hands. Moreover, Curt began in the position of defeat, with his right arm already on the floor. Thus it was her task to keep his forearm down with both hands, while it was his task to overcome her pressure, lift his forearm, then bear her two arms to the floor in the opposite direction.

The handicap worked beautifully. The match was even, and the opponents were magnificently competitive. Lynne gasped, Curt grunted, and both perspired and vibrated with their efforts. In a great surge of strength Curt finally managed to lift his forearm, but Lynne called upon her full resources and put him down. This happened several times, then both collapsed in laughter. Symbolically, Lynne had won.

As I had expected, Curt was sure enough of his own masculinity so that the defeat did not distress him. They embraced, laughing like children. When they stood up, Curt picked up Lynne and swung her around. Other group members came up, hugged Lynne, and told her she looked wonderful. She was glowing. She had been given a chance to use her full energy, had defeated a strong man, and instead of being rebuked and rejected, she was appreciated as a woman.

The symbolic meaning of this encounter was expressed by Lynne, in a letter written two months afterward:

> The changes are still taking place within me. The strength and love are coming together in ways that have never been possible before, and I am very excited about being alive.

The episode of Serena is an example of how a deep-lying conflict, in this case an Oedipal situation, may be resolved primarily through the release of feeling on a physical level; it is of special interest also in that Serena, at the beginning, was aware of a physical symptom but did not know what area of conflict it represented.

Serena was a dark-haired, quiet woman in her twenties, who said almost nothing until the marathon's second day. She was attending the group with Phil, her husband, apparently not to work on any marital problem but rather to share the experience. It did not come out until much later that they were in conflict over the question of whether or not to pay a visit to Serena's parents in another part of the country. He

seemed reserved too, and although they appeared glad to be there together, the underlying intensity of their relationship did not emerge until
later.

Serena had a headache. She suffered for several hours before a lull
in the group's activities encouraged her to speak. It was like a tight band
around her head, said Serena, and she suspected that somehow it might
be related to "a worry, or a problem," though she had no notion what this
might be.

Although it would seem rash to maintain that a headache *always* has
an emotional component, it is impressive how frequently the pain can be
cleared up in a marathon group after an emotional conflict is revealed
and worked through.[8] But with Serena, the usual preliminary questions
("When did you first notice the headache?" "Do you get headaches usually
on any special kind of occasion?") offered no clue.

When no signpost can be found indicating the origin of an anxiety,
the device of the "television screen" is useful. The room is darkened, the
group is requested to remain silent, and if there is reason to assume that
the unconscious conflict may be frightening, I sit close to the protagonist
or else ask him to select a companion whom he trusts. My instructions,
which are usually repeated several times, may induce a condition similar
to light hypnosis, but this is not their purpose. "Close your eyes. Keep
your eyes closed, please. Now visualize a television screen with your
closed eyes. Can you see it? Keep looking and you'll see it. . . . Good.
Now watch the television screen and you will see a picture. Don't hurry,
just watch and you will see a picture. Keep your eyes closed, keep watching, tell us what you see."

Instead of offering specific instructions, representing my guess as to
what might be behind the anxiety, I prefer to trust the participant's drive
toward self-understanding to allow the spontaneous emergence of a visual
image related to the conflict. The process is somewhat analogous to the
psychoanalytic process of free-association in that the participant is expected to suspend his rational judgment, describing whatever he sees,
very much as an analysand verbalizes his thoughts. Suggestions as to the
possible development of the television "scenario" are offered only when
the drama is under way but appears to be blocked, an intervention which
is somewhat similar to resistance analysis. Interpretations of what is happening on the screen are offered only when they seem completely justified. Thus far, every participant who has been willing to become
seriously involved in watching the "screen" has visualized an image leading to a meaningful association, or sometimes to the reliving of an
important childhood experience.

---

[8] My policy is to discourage aspirin until the sufferer has been offered an opportunity to explore any possible underlying conflict.

Serena was easily able to see the screen, but for some minutes it remained blank. She decided to leave her chair and instead to recline on the floor. Almost at once she then visualized a face, which at first seemed to be a well-known political personality often regarded as a father-figure. Then the face became clearer.

"It's my father," said Serena. Lying on the floor, she began to move around restlessly, turning her head from side to side, with an occasional slight moan.

"What do you see on the screen, Serena?"

"The same thing, just my father's face." Serena twisted on the floor more violently, and there were tears on her cheeks. Her voice was like that of a little girl.

"How old are you, Serena?"

"I don't know—five, six, maybe younger."

"And where are you, Serena? Is it dark or light?"

"It's dark."

"And is it warm or cold where you are?"

"Warm."

"And is it hard or soft?"

"It's soft."

"Maybe you are a little girl in bed, Serena. Maybe you are in your crib." Serena cried harder. Her movements seemed feverish. She was reaching out her arms as if for an embrace.

"Let your body go, Serena. Let it do whatever it likes." Someone handed her a small pillow, and she began to hug it, moaning softly. Through the soft moans and sobs, words became clear.

"Don't go away, Daddy. Stay with me, Daddy. Please stay, Daddy." It was a child's soft, plaintive voice. Here is Serena's written report, sent to me about ten days after the marathon:

> When you asked me to picture the TV screen I almost immediately saw a man's face, . . . the presence of my father. . . . I was sure it was my father. What I was feeling in my body was like muscle spasms, . . . not large but very small ones all over, like my body was going to break into large movements but couldn't. . . . I was aware of being concerned that what was happening would be very hard for Phil to see because I know how hard it is for him to see me in pain. . . .

My impression at the time, which was supported by Serena's letter, was that she was acting out the role of a small girl in bed, longing for her father, and that on an unconscious level this longing was sexually charged and was expressed in unconsciously sexual movements.

> While I was crying and shaking I was not in pain. I never cried so freely. Usually when I cry my throat is choked . . . but this crying was just the

> opposite, my throat felt so open, so free. . . . I was trying very hard to picture him [her father] as he is now, his grey hair. Finally I remembered a picture I have of him and I could keep that image. . . .

Efforts to recapture childhood memories are often confused because the image of the aging parents of the present time obliterates or blurs the image of the younger parents of childhood. Serena was preoccupied with the father of her childhood, not the grey-haired man of the present.

> Then you said to let my body go and . . . I just was my body. It was just restless movements, the spasms leaving me as I let my body be itself. Somewhere in there I put out my arms for my father but he did not come. . . . Someone put a pillow in there and I talked as if it were him but it wasn't like having him. I still could not see him, just sense his presence going away. . . .

Now Serena was almost thrashing about on the mattress. Her voice was so choked that her words were not understandable. Increasingly sure that she was reliving a childhood scene, I said to her softly, "You're in the crib, Serena, what is happening in the crib?" This seemed helpful, perhaps simply because it was an acceptance of the fantasy.

> You said "You're in the crib" and then I stopped trying to see him as he is now and then the image became real and my father as he must have been when I was very young was there. He was not in my arms or I in his, but he was there . . . and I was calm that he was there now. . . . He seemed like he was going away and was waiting for me to say something, and I thought of saying goodbye to him. It wasn't a sad goodbye— just something he was waiting to hear before he left.

In the group Serena's small girl voice had continued moaning "Daddy, don't go away," as she convulsively embraced the pillow. The moaning and the feverish movements continued and continued but finally began to diminish in their intensity. Then I said softly, "Maybe he *has* to go away."

Serena relaxed. As she seemed to be emerging from the fantasy, I gestured toward Phil, who had been watching intently without interrupting. At precisely the same moment, Serena reached her hand out toward him. Instantly he was with her on the floor, embracing her.

> Then I heard Phil calling to me so I reached out to him . . . and he said some things . . . and then he said "Don't say goodbye to me, Serena" and at this point I was already saying goodbye to my father and I said to Phil "You aren't my father" and it felt very very good to have him in my arms. Then he told me he loved me and we didn't need anyone

but each other. . . . I just wanted to say goodbye to my father, but he had to be there to say goodbye to. Through that experience he was there and I said goodbye to him.

In her husband's arms, the frantic quality of Serena's motions changed. Their embrace was tender, as if they had both been fulfilled. In Serena's letter the phrase "I felt like I do after intercourse" was deeply meaningful.

> Then I wanted Phil on top of me, not because I wanted to have inter-course, but because I felt like I do after intercourse, and I love to have him stay on top of me after, when we're both so completely peaceful, and loving, and happy and free and relaxed and everything. And he did and that is what it was like. The whole thing wasn't painful even when I was crying.

Serena appeared to have a satisfying sense of closure. During the remaining hours of the marathon, she and her husband seemed very affectionate and contented. The headache disappeared. Later, she and her husband reached an amicable decision to postpone their visit to Serena's parents. The final paragraph of her letter also expressed a sense of closure.

> The marathon was a very good experience for me. . . . I don't think anything else could have reached what was causing my pain. Phil asked me if I was curious about what had actually happened that I was reliving, and strangely, I was not. It is good to have said goodbye. The pain is gone.

In several respects this episode resembles the "somatic language" of conversion hysteria (Fenichel, 1945, Ch. XII). Similarities include the involuntary nature of Serena's movements, her unawareness of their sexual quality, and the central importance of her relationship to the opposite-sexed parent. The question arises whether the resolution of the Oedipal conflict which first manifested itself in Serena's headache (probably also a conversion symptom) was really as complete as it appeared, and as Serena's letter indicated, without her conscious recognition of the sexual component in her feelings toward her father.

If Serena had still seemed in distress at the conclusion of the epi-sode, or if her embrace had not expressed a total physical and emotional acceptance of her husband, an effort would have been made to explore this aspect of the father-husband conflict. However, though she seemed unaware of the specifically sexual element in her reliving of the child-hood longing, she certainly accepted the sexual element in her embrace with her husband. She also seemed entirely aware that it was necessary for her to say goodbye to her father, in the sense of breaking the child-hood tie, before she could function completely as a wife.

The therapeutic factors in this episode are identifiable. Serena sensed that her headache was a sign of some emotional problem and chose voluntarily to deal with whatever problem it might be. The television screen device permitted her unconscious preoccupation with her father to emerge of its own accord, rather than as the result of an outside suggestion. She remained in control of the situation. She chose to recline on the floor. She permitted herself to be carried along by her own feelings and body movements. She signalled to her husband when she was ready to return to reality from fantasy. The environment was maximally supportive; she was in the presence of a devoted husband, of an accepting mother-figure, and of a sympathetic group. It was a para-digm example of "re-experiencing the old unsettled conflict but with a new ending" (Alexander & French, 1946, p. 338).

The principle of interpreting bodily attitudes in terms of feeling, and of translating feeling into bodily actions whenever possible, is especially useful with participants who find it easier to talk about their emotions than to experience them. Diagnostically, many such people could be described as obsessional character types, and frequently they have great difficulty in making decisions, spending a great deal of their energy on inner debates.

Jeffrey, twenty-two, appeared considerably older, in part because of badly stooped shoulders. He was earning his living as an accountant. However, he was uncertain whether he wished to remain in this occupa-tion or to enter graduate school and become an engineer. He was also uncertain whether or not he wished to get married, and if so, whether his present girl friend would be right for him. As he told the group about his situation, he played incessantly with his hands, gesturing first with the right and then with the left, locking them and separating them, twist-ing and stroking. He was asked what his hands were debating.

"Everything," said Jeffrey. "My job. My girl. My life. I do that all the time."

Jeffrey was asked to speak for each hand in turn, right and left, let-ting each hand represent one side of the debated questions. My hope was to make his debate less abstract, less intellectual, by establishing a con-nection between his body and his words. He complied readily, choosing to debate with himself about his marriage but went mechanically through the motions of following my instructions and continued to sound as emo-tionally detached as before.

In an effort to demonstrate to Jeffrey how he separated his ideas from his feelings, he was next asked to play the "mirror game" in which his posture, gestures, words, and intonations would be imitated as closely as possible by another participant (see Chapter 3). It was hoped that by seeing himself in a "mirror," Jeffrey would recognize how detached he was and might begin to consider whether he really wished and needed to remain detached.

As his mirror, Jeffrey chose Don, another participant, a dignified-looking psychologist twice Jeffrey's age. The choice seemed surprising, since usually a mirror is chosen on the basis of similarity of age and appearance. As it turned out, Jeffrey had selected his mirror on the basis of an uncanny intuition as to which group member might best meet his own deep needs, an intuition which is not unusual in marathon encounters.

Sitting face-to-face on the floor with Don, Jeffrey described his confusion and unhappiness, and Don mirrored him. A letter describing the marathon which Jeffrey wrote his girl friend, of which he sent me a carbon, recounts the experience:

> Don was an absolutely fantastic mirror. He was able to capture both my physical movements and my emotional movements. His eyes watered when my eyes watered and when I began to know that I was hurting, he was hurting too.

Instead of merely offering him a picture of his own behavior, the mirroring game did something far more valuable for Jeffrey. It gave him a sense of sympathetic understanding from a father figure. He began "to know that he was hurting," and when he felt his inner pain, he cried. But he suppressed the tears. Moving away from his father-mirror, he sat bent over, in the hunched-up attitude which was characteristic of him. Don, myself, and another group member who liked Jeffrey moved near him and began to rub his back. Someone asked why he always looked hunched-up.

> They started to ask me about the hump on my back and I said it was just poor posture and they said no, it could not just be poor posture. . . . I did not want to discuss it but I am aware of the association I then made. I associated the hump with both of my parents and they were always saying I should stand straight and if I did not, I would have a hump when I grew up. And their saying that if I did not they would take me to a doctor and then I would have to wear a brace. And I could never get myself to tell them that I wished they really would take me to a doctor because I wanted to be able to stand straight. I blame them very much for the fact my posture is so bad I have to walk hunchbacked.

In his letter, Jeffrey also described the unhappy feeling that he had always been misunderstood by his parents. His attitude toward them was a mixture of extreme resentment and a wish to please. The sense of being misunderstood seemed to explain why he had been so deeply touched by Don's sensitivity to his feelings. Apparently, also, he felt that the burden which, as he viewed it, his parents had placed on his back, was far more than a habit of bad posture. As he described it:

> While I was thinking about this and blaming them for my hump my hands started fighting each other very strongly . . . very hard and very heavy. . . .

It is a cardinal rule that a group member is never permitted to hurt himself physically but instead is asked to turn his destructive energy outward. Jeffrey was actually tearing at his own hands, an extreme intensification of the earlier debate, and was given a pillow to maul instead. Half-sobbing, he twisted and beat the pillow, shouting "No! No! No!" He did not, however, achieve the kind of complete physical expression which Curt had experienced, nor did he at that time share with the group what was going on in his mind. The same indecision which tormented him inwardly, and the same rigidity which produced his hunched-up shoulders, made it difficult for him to let himself go more fully. Neither insight nor full bodily release was present; there was no closure; and on the second day of the marathon, Jeffrey felt miserable. He wrote his girl friend:

> It was a feeling that no one loves me, no one wants me. I did not feel man enough to cope with life. I felt depressed and hopeless and wanted the attention of the group.

True to his characterological indecisiveness, Jeffrey did not appeal directly to the group to help him but found an indirect way to get attention. I had gone out of the room for ten minutes, and Jeffrey rebuked me. I was in charge, I was responsible for the group, and something might have happened in my absence. In reality, Jeffrey understood his feelings better than his words indicated.

> Actually I felt deserted by Elizabeth's absence. I must have been reacting to the time when my parents went off and deserted me. She was the authority figure and she left.

In criticizing me, Jeffrey was simultaneously expressing his dependency on "the authority figure" and striving to attain adulthood by attacking it. Everything fitted together: the dependency, the rebelliousness, the indecisiveness, the lack of self-esteem. Jeffrey needed an authority because he had no sense of an authority within himself.

"Jeffrey, you seem to think I'm a pretty poor authority. Suppose you be the authority for a while. Go around the room and find all of us guilty of something and give us penalties."

Jeffrey cheered up. Afflicted as he was with mingled feelings of resentment and submissiveness toward authority, it probably seemed like an agreeable change to act as the authority himself.[9] As he went around the circle, he began to exert his authority in a spirit of play.

A woman whom he perceived as indifferent to others was sentenced to attend a marathon each weekend until she learned to feel. A young man and girl who were obviously enjoying a flirtation were sentenced to sit on opposite sides of the room. An older man with whom Jeffrey had engaged in a heated argument at dinner, and whom he perceived as dogmatic and reactionary, was thus sentenced:

"You are to listen to my views on communal marriage and the SDS for two hours without saying anything."

The group roared with laughter. I was sentenced:

"You are to lead this marathon straight through all night until tomorrow night without any rest and without leaving the room."

"Can't I go to the bathroom?"

"You may raise your hand and ask."

This was not merely facetiousness, nor merely a change of mood. Jeffrey was using his sense of humor to gain perspective on his difficulties with authority. Yet, as he finished the circle, Jeffrey's good humor faded. In spite of his resentment, he said gloomily, he still yearned for the approval of anyone he saw as an authority.

"Jeffrey, you need to be an authority over yourself. How about going around the room and saying to each of us 'I am my own authority.'"

"I can't." Jeffrey's shoulders hunched further up despondently.

"Try."

"I can't." He banged once on the mattress, weakly.

"Jeffrey, who is the chief authority in this room?"

"You are."

"Okay, and is there another chief authority?"

"Yes. Him." Jeffrey indicated Don, the paternal-looking psychologist.

"What if the two authorities don't agree?"

Jeffrey grinned very slightly. "That would be pretty awful," he admitted. At once Don and I, with Jeffrey between us, began firing a rapid salvo of contradictory orders.

"Stand up!"

"No, sit down!"

"Keep still!"

"Say something!"

"Turn a somersault."

"Look here!"

[9] The psychodynamics of the zestful response often elicited by role-playing are discussed more fully in Chapter 7.

"No, look at me!"

In the center of the room, Jeffrey joined our game. In mimicked panic and confusion, he spun around, thrashing his arms and legs frantically in a pretended attempt to please us both. It was a caricature. Physically, he was acting out simultaneously his contempt for authority and his subservience to authority.

When he paused exhausted, the group was roaring with laughter. But more than humor was involved. By a physical expression of both sides of his conflict, Jeffrey had perhaps found a different, freer way of releasing the physical energy which he had been using to immobilize himself. And perhaps he had obtained a better perspective on his conflict. After the room stopped laughing, once again Jeffrey was asked to go around the circle and say "I am my own authority."

Rather hesitantly, Jeffrey arose, now accepting the task, but without confidence. As he began to go around the circle, his voice was faint. But it grew stronger as he proceeded. When he spoke to Don and myself, his two principal authority symbols, he pointed toward us and shouted gleefully.

"I AM MY OWN AUTHORITY!"

Here is his own description, again quoted from his letter to his girl:

> I don't know what got me to say it but finally I could meekly say "I am my own authority." I am my own boss. I. I was not convinced at first. Also I did not think that I had the energy to convince others and I knew that I would have to do so but I did. I am my own authority. I did it. I did it. I I I I I I I I I I I!
>
> Not only did I say it but I also believed it. I shouted with all my might and all my force. I went around and told everybody that I am my own boss, and felt it.

In the earlier part of his letter, ostensibly to type faster, Jeffrey had written without capitals, not even capitalizing the pronoun *I*. After describing this final episode, *I* was capitalized. In the last part of his letter to his girl, Jeffrey wrote:

> After this I had a natural desire to walk straight. And I have been walking tall naturally all day. Of course I am aware of it. It is a totally different feeling. It requires different breathing and thinking but I am doing it. . . . So the time has come to put the cards on the table and call the game. And the game is me. It is time for me to live my own life. . . . I think I am beginning to control my own life.

The expression "different breathing and thinking" expresses Jeffrey's new awareness of his body. Instead of regarding his stoop as a misfortune about which nothing could be done, since his parents had not forced him to correct it, he could now see it as something over which he himself had control, along with the feeling that he had control of his life in general.

Two months later, Jeffrey was asked for a follow-up report on his posture. His response showed that, although the stoop had not miraculously and permanently disappeared, he had retained a sense of contact with his body and a feeling that he was in charge of his own behavior.

> Concerning my standing up taller and walking straighter, the results have continued to some extent. It is very dependent on my feelings and evaluations of myself as to just when I stand up tall. I would say that I probably do it about 50 percent of the time. It appears to be necessary for me to concentrate on it. . . .

Hand-pressing [10] is among the most effective methods by which repressed emotions can be tapped through a physical experience. If the protagonist is able to put forth his full strength in exerting pressure on the clasped hands of his partner (for example, myself as a mother symbol) there is almost invariably a breakthrough of feeling. If he is asked to speak, the sentences are always simple, like those of a child, expressing feelings pent up since childhood. Even though the protagonist is physically in control, the feelings expressed are often helpless, such as "Let me go! Let me go! Stop bothering me!" or "Don't do that, stop, I hate you!" Less frequently, the first reaction will be a plea for love. "Oh, ma, I love you, please ma, love me back," usually followed by anger.

As with other bodily techniques intended to release pent-up feelings, hand-pressing can have multiple values: it provides catharsis; it offers a reparative emotional experience when anger is accepted instead of punished; and it may lead to insight, since the experience is discussed afterward. Usually the other members of the group become empathically involved in a hand-pressing experience, since everyone has been required to repress or at least control negative feelings toward a parent in childhood, and often the onlookers declare that they felt as if the experience were happening to them simultaneously.

Unless the protagonist is able to exert his maximum strength, there is no release of feeling. In this case, as with people who are unable to pound the couch forcefully, there is a deep and often unconscious fear of their own hostility. A man who cannot press hard is often afraid that if he uses his strength against a mother figure, he will damage her seriously, or perhaps even be carried away to the point of destroying her. A full discussion of these fantasies sometimes lifts the physical inhibition.

Although the emotions evoked by this procedure may be intense to the point of violence, it is my experience that a contact with reality is always maintained, analogous to the familiar psychoanalytic concept of

[10] See Chapter 3 for a detailed account of this procedure.

"a split in the patient's ego between a reasonable, observing, analyzing ego, and an experiencing, subjective, irrational ego" (Greenson, 1967, p. 47). The episode of Pete, in many ways a typical example of the use of the hand-pressing game, shows this split dramatically.

Pete was a college teacher, with a gentle, humorous manner and a soft, drawling voice. As various marathon participants were recalling childhood clashes with their parents, Pete remarked, "There wasn't anything like that at home with me. We kids were told 'Do that!' and we just did it. No arguing, especially with mother."

"Never?"

"Nope. I just never, never said 'I won't.' "

Some sentences are uttered with a special resonance, a quality which to an alert ear suggests a special meaning or importance, even though the speaker may not consciously have meant to emphasize the statement. Pete's "I won't" had this resonance.

"You never said 'I won't?' But all the children say 'I won't' at times."

"Nope, I don't think I ever did. I was a good, good, goody-goody boy."

"Well, would you like to try saying it now?"

Pete grinned, half-intrigued and half-skeptical. "Why, su-ure," he said, and we sat facing one another on the floor. I explained the procedure and demonstrated the position of the hands, but before we began, I asked "What did your mother call you, Pete, when you were little?"

"Oh, Lord, she used to call me Petey-boy."

"And what kind of thing did she tell you to do, the times you never thought of answering 'I won't?' "

"Oh, little things. Like take the garbage out, put on your rubbers, do your homework, stuff like that."

"Shut your eyes, Pete, press hard. If you hurt me, I'll say stop. I promise if you hurt me, I'll say stop." At the time of the episode with Pete, it had never become necessary for me to interrupt the pressure, and I intended this promise merely to give him the freedom to put forth his full strength. After this episode, I realized that the instructions were simultaneously a protection for myself, in that they established in my partner a readiness to let go immediately at my request.

Pete began to press my hands. Despite his gentle manner, it became apparent at once that he was not unduly inhibited by fear of his own hostility, for his pressure was very firm. Waiting until I felt we were in complete contact, I began to try to reach the repressed part of him which, as a little boy, had wanted to say "No."

"Take out the garbage, Petey-boy!" I tried to imitate the cadence he had used when quoting his mother. "Put on your rubbers, now!"

The pressure grew stronger. Pete's face became deeply flushed, and the veins stood out on his forehead. This was the hardest pressure I had ever experienced in perhaps twenty such episodes. Pete, who was by no means clinically psychotic, was reaching the deep level of primitive rage which usually is reached only in psychosis, and therefore his grip was undoubtedly far beyond his ordinary strength.

My hands were beginning to hurt, and Pete was pressing still harder. One of the other men in the marathon moved close to me, understanding my eye signal that I might need help. "Stop, Pete," I said, as softly as I could.

Pete's eyes had been closed. The minute I spoke, he opened them, nodded, and released my hands. The man beside me replaced my hands with his, and Pete closed his eyes again and gripped the hands of my substitute. Instantly Pete's face assumed the same expression which had been there when he was dealing with his witch-mother, now represented by a man, whose hands could tolerate the grip.

"Now do your homework, Petey-boy."

Pete's teeth were clenched, his arms and hands were vibrating with the force of his pressure, he muttered something—almost growling. At last the words emerged.

"I won't."

"What?"

"I won't."

"What did you say?"

"I won't."

"Put on your rubbers! Do your homework! Put out the garbage!" Pete was in a grim, genuine rage. The sturdy man who had taken my place was withstanding Pete's pressure with some difficulty.

"I WON'T! I WON'T! I WON'T!" Pete swayed back and forth, pressing with extreme intensity, shouting furiously. Such exertion could not be long continued, and in a few minutes he was exhausted. He remained gripping the hands of the man, with his eyes still closed, for a few minutes longer.

Then he opened his eyes and looked at the man whose hands he had been pressing. The situation, which had been deeply serious, abruptly became funny. Pete and his male mother-substitute grinned at each other, scuffled in a comradely embrace, and then Pete reached out to hug me.

"How do you feel, Pete?"

"I feel like ten men. Wow! Hey, Mom, you're a real bitch. Thanks a lot."

"I'm not Mom any more. I'm Elizabeth now." This type of closing comment represents an effort (at first intuitive, then deliberate, and by now usually spontaneous) to facilitate the movement away from the reliving of a childhood fantasy and back to reality. It has some similarity to the analysis of transference; it reminds the participant that he has just been bringing feelings from his childhood into the present, but that in reality he is now an adult. Such a reminder could well be experienced as criticism, or even rebuke, if made for the purpose of discouraging the participant from expressing childhood feelings. But if made as part of the closure of a regressive episode in which childhood feelings have been expressed and accepted, it is almost always received as a friendly and respectful acknowledgment of the return to maturity.

For the same reason, it is my custom to discuss with the participant any aspect of a meaningful episode, especially if it has involved regression, which may not be clear to him on a cognitive level. Therefore I reminded Pete that I had asked him to release my hands and inquired how he had felt about that. It turned out that he had been so caught up in his emotions that he barely recalled the substitution of the man's hands for mine. His initial reaction was apologetic, concerned, and rather embarrassed. With the backing of the group, he was assured that though he had been intensely immersed in the childhood fantasy, he had responded instantaneously to my request, and he was congratulated on his ability to move back into appropriate contact with reality and then allow himself to return once more to the reliving of his childhood feelings. If this aspect of the episode had not been explored, Pete would probably have been left with a half-conscious remembrance that he had been asked to cease his pressure, and with a suspicion that it had been necessary for me to protect myself against his dangerous hostility. Instead, he was left with a well-justified feeling that he could depend upon himself, and others could depend upon him, to control his hostility. This type of discussion, which with Pete lasted possibly five minutes, appears to me essential for the ego-integration of the regressive and cathartic experience. If Pete had been left with vague doubts about what had happened when he was asked to release my hands, the experience would have been less strengthening and perhaps even confusing to him.[11]

Dissociation between the body and the emotions can often be ameliorated by asking the participant to continue concentrating his attention on his physical position (by using such simple expressions as "stay with your hands, what are they doing") until the feeling breaks through, often with dramatic suddenness. This is a technique developed principally in Gestalt psychotherapy (Perls, 1969).

Irving was an energetic fifty-year-old business executive who prided himself on his physical strength, his competitive tennis, and his general disregard for the ordinary daily cautiousness of most people. He had undergone several years of classical psychoanalysis, primarily for a

---

[11] In preparing the reports offered in this book, my original hope was to include no episode of which the effects could not be corroborated by taped or written feedback from participants. This proved only partly practical. The difficulty of research about the effects of psychotherapy is notorious. Pete never wrote; but in ensuing months, he referred two friends for marathons.

tendency to depression but considered the treatment only partially effective. My impression was that Irving was so accustomed to experiencing and expressing his emotions in a physical way that for him the psychoanalytic confinement to verbal self-expression had not been an optimum approach to therapy.

Irving's dangerous symptom might not have come to light in a marathon held under the usual circumstances, since he did not consider it a problem and might not have called attention to it. He was participating in a five-day group in which participants and leaders lived together in a woodland setting,[12] where it was necessary to use automobiles to reach the dining hall. Irving's driving was reckless. When we expostulated, he said with bravado, "Yeah, I know I'll get killed that way," and, "If I ever have an accident, it'll be fatal."

The unconscious self-destructive impulse seemed glaringly apparent. However, by chance, because of the residential setting, it was possible to assess Irving's degree of conscious control over his driving, and also to assess the destructiveness toward himself as central, rather than destructiveness toward others. After an especially narrow escape, his passsengers pointed out emphatically that he might be entitled to kill himself, but not to kill them. After that his driving, when he had passengers, improved noticeably.

Irving's wild driving was brought up in our next working session, not by him, but by myself. He agreed to work on it, and his first association was the death of his father some fifteen years ago in a collision at a railroad crossing. His voice was choked. He did not sound as if he had completed the necessary work of mourning for his father. Also, it seemed possible that an identification with his father was a factor in his dangerous driving. By far the quickest and most effective way of exploring a possible identifiction is through role-playing. Irving was requested to reenact the scene of his father's death, with himself taking the role of his father at the wheel of the car.[13]

In a scenario, it is often helpful to use props, even on a naïvely unrealistic level. An automobile was constructed from pillows and chairs, and Irving went through the fatal collision with the railroad train. The extent to which he became involved in it was impressive. From a tape recording, here are his words:

> That train is coming. It's coming. I don't want to get hit. God, I don't want to get hit. I'm coming downhill now. I can't stop the car. I don't want to get hit. I'm really so frightened. . . .

[12] Observation of the everyday behavior of group participants is among the opportunities given by the contemporary trend toward conducting workshops or marathons in a residential setting.

[13] In this episode, most of the therapeutic interventions were made by my co-therapist in this group, Dr. Frank Rubenfeld.

The panicky, heartbroken screaming on the tape cannot be conveyed on the page. It did not seem histrionic, but rather like the full emergence of an unconscious fantasy about what his father must have experienced. At the moment when he imagined the train striking him, Irving allowed himself to fall off the chair which represented the driver's seat and began to sob, "Dad, I'm so sorry you're hit." And then, moving toward the present, "Dad, I felt terrible when you died."

When he recovered, we talked with Irving about the factual circumstances of his father's death; he had been at his desk when the news arrived, had flown home at once, and had gone down alone to the grade-crossing where the accident had occurred, and had spent perhaps an hour thinking of his father. This may well have been the time when he engaged in the identification fantasy which he enacted in the marathon. Because Irving still seemed agitated, and there was no feeling of completion, we asked him whether there had been any other occasions when he had felt the same panic which he had just shown us.

"Yes," Irving said. When he was a small boy, he had walked in his sleep. One night he had awakened standing on top of the bureau, and he remembered being very frightened, without knowing why. Again, he was asked to reenact the scene, with impromptu props. A tabletop represented the bureau, and Irving climbed to the top of it, still agitated and shaking.

His hands were clasped in a peculiar position behind his neck, elbows bent forward, pulling his head down. It appeared uncomfortable and unnatural. Irving was asked what he was doing with his hands. He replied, with consciously sincere but clearly defensive rationalization, "Just holding them naturally." According to the Gestalt principle of requesting a patient to continue with a meaningful physical gesture and exaggerate it, Irving was asked to continue pulling his head forward, and complied.

The tapescript gives the dialogue:

> Therapist: Keeping doing that with your hands. Keep doing that. What are your hands saying? (*Pause*)
> Irving: (*Screaming*) I'm drowning! I'm drowning! My God, I'm drowning!
> Therapist: What are your hands doing?
> Irving: They're hurting Irv's neck and back! I'm drowning! I'm drowning! I'm not going to die! I don't want to die! I don't want to die!

Such violent episodes of apparent terror and pain, in my experience, need not be interrupted and *should* not be interrupted. Usually the protagonist reports afterward that his agony was less intense than it may have appeared to the group (recalling the famous *belle indifference* of hysterics [Fenichel, 1945, p. 234]), probably because the tensions are to some extent present at all times in the form of latent readiness to respond, and there is considerable relief in the physical discharge alone. Even more important, any interruption would be essentially destructive, robbing the protagonist of an opportunity for healing which, on some level, he himself has chosen to seek, regardless of the emotional pain involved in the experience. Irving sobbed and screamed until the pent-up terror of his childhood had expended himself. Then he relaxed, accepted the affectionate gestures which a group invariably offers in such a situation, and we could now talk about the meaning of the episode.

The memory which had risen to the surface was of an incident at the ocean when he had been about eight.[14] Swept out by an undertow, he had almost drowned before being rescued by an older brother. After that, Irving told us, he was already afraid of being "yellow" As a boy, he had repeatedly dared dangerous adventures to prove his courage. He had successfully concealed his terror, and to some extent had apparently succeeded in not even feeling it. The sleepwalking, which occurred soon after the near-drowning, seemed related to this dissociation of the panic. To this day Irving's personality had been counter-phobic. Both in sports and in business, he accepted nearly every challenge.

His reckless driving now appeared as overdetermined. In part it was an identification with his father, for an identification with an admired figure can include identification with less admirable traits, such as absent-minded driving. In part it seemed to be counter-phobic, an insistence on disregarding danger, which was related to the near-drowning.

After the reliving of these two episodes, with the concomitant release of feelings, Irving's driving changed radically and consistently. He himself, and some of his associates a year later, reported that he no longer took risks, kept his mind on the road, and had no more narrow escapes.

Another approach which is often useful in dealing with a pathological schism between the body and the feelings is direct physical pressure, although (like any other active therapeutic technique, verbal or nonverbal) it is best used only by a group leader with special training, and only if there is a positive rapport which would prevent the subject from experiencing the physical contact as an invasion of privacy, or even as an infliction of pain which might incur resentment or provide masochistic pleasure.

Steve,[15] for example, was deeply inhibited both physically and emotionally. In a marathon group which, for him, was one of a series during all of which he had sat silent and rigid, he seemed to be more tense than ever, especially through his neck and back. He told the group that he

[14] This memory had remained under repression during several years of intensive highly orthodox psychoanalysis.

[15] The final example of this chapter, the case of Steve, was generously provided by the therapist, Mrs. Ilana Rubenfeld, who combines the muscle relaxation methods of M. Alexander (1969) with Gestalt techniques.

lacked feeling (an accurate description, subjectively speaking, since he did indeed lack contact with what he felt).

Although his face remained rigid, there were tears in Steve's eyes. Since he could not be induced to speak, the therapist tried physical contact. She touched his back and shoulders, which to her hands felt like iron. He was asked to lie down, and the therapist began to press the tight, knotted hard muscles along his shoulders and back. Steve was asked to breathe deeply and make whatever sounds he wished, and he started to groan softly with clenched teeth. As she continued pressing the tight muscles, he breathed more deeply and began to yell "It hurts, it hurts."

He was asked to change his wording to "I hurt," in accordance with the Gestalt concept of requiring the patient to take full responsibility for whatever he experiences, rather than allowing him to view pain as something which happens to him. When Steve complied, he began to sob, and there was color in his face. Released from pressure by the therapist, he continued to say "I hurt" in a voice which sounded more alive.

When the therapist again touched the hard area on his back, it felt softer. She began the pressure on areas which still felt hard and tense, and he began to scream, "You're killing me!" He was again asked to change his wording, this time to the expression "I'm killing myself" (which was true metaphorically, but also in the sense that the pressure on his back was painful only because of the muscular tension which to some extent was now under conscious control).

Suddenly Steve's face lit up, and he said deeply and excitedly, "I am killing myself. I am killing myself by not feeling my own hurt." The therapist ceased her pressure and asked him to sit up slowly. His face was flushed, he was crying, and he described the experience of increased sensory awareness for which the Zen term *satori* is sometimes used. He said (quoted by his therapist), "People in the group look clearer and closer to me; colors are so bright! I never noticed the colors of that poster. They're beautiful. My shoulders and back feel good. . . ."

He went back over his experience. "When I screamed more, the pain became less. I've been giving myself a lot of pain without knowing it." In line with the observation of marathon therapists in general about participants who have undergone an intense cathartic experience which has ended with relaxation and with regained maturity (shown in Seve's case by his ability to accept responsibility for his own pain), Steve displayed a greatly heightened ability to relate helpfully and effectively to other group members. Some weeks later, he reported that he continued to feel more alive and more open to both joyous and painful feelings.

Such people as Steve tighten their bodily muscles constantly in order to deaden their self-perceptions and thus prevent themselves from experiencing their own suffering. To a greater or lesser extent, such people succeed in turning themselves physically and emotionally into zombies. A situation in which physical relaxation and spontaneity develop naturally, such as a marathon, provides an atmosphere in which these chronic physical tensions and their relationship to chronic emotional conflicts can be explored at leisure and with minimal threat. Wherever emotional problems exist, there is alienation both from other people and from the body. If defensive physical tensions are relieved and feelings can be experienced more freely and naturally, then rewarding relationships with other people become easier.

REFERENCES

Alexander, F., & French, T. M. *Psychoanalytic therapy.* New York: Ronald Press, 1946.

Alexander, M. S. Selections. In E. Masel (Ed.), *Resurrection of the body.* New Hyde Park, N.Y.: University Books, 1969.

Balint, M. *The basic fault.* London: Tavistock Publications, 1968.

Fenichel, O. *Psychoanalytic theory of neurosis.* New York: W. W. Norton, 1945.

Greenson, R. *Technique and practice of psychoanalysis.* New York: International Universities Press, 1967.

Gunther, B. Sensory awakening and relaxation. In H. Otto & J. Mann (Eds.), *Ways of growth.* New York: Grossman, 1968.

Lowen, A. Bio-energetic group therapy. In H. M. Ruitenbeek (Ed.), *Group therapy today.* New York: Atherton, 1969.

Mintz, E. E. Touch and the psychoanalytic tradition. *Psychoanalytic Review,* 1969, 56(3).

Perls, F. S. *Gestalt therapy verbatim.* Lafayette, Calif.: Real People Press, 1969.

Proskauer, M. Breathing therapy. In H. Otto & J. Mann (Eds.), *Ways of growth.* New York: Grossman, 1968.

Reich, W. *Character analysis.* New York: Orgone Institute Press, 1949.

Schutz, W. *Joy.* New York: Grove Press, 1967.

7 THE EXORCISM OF
THE ENEMY WITHIN

Lisa was young, pretty, and apparently almost lifeless. Her personality was without color, her expression without sparkle. She responded to questions politely and appropriately, with no sign of spontaneity. We learned, by asking questions, that Lisa was the daughter of wealthy parents; that she worked occasionally and received a generous allowance; that she had gone through a brief marriage and divorce and was not greatly interested in any man at present. Lisa did not, in fact, seem interested in herself, in the marathon, or in life.

The marathon went well. When the members of a marathon become involved with one another, they are reluctant to let anyone remain outside the circle. Toward the middle of the second day, the group began an unplanned, undirected effort to find something which would strike a spark from Lisa. Probably by sheer chance, someone noticed that when Lisa talked about her mother, whom she described as a glamorous and very successful business woman, she became more vivacious.

"Do you admire your mother, Lisa? Would you like to be like her?"

"God, no!" But Lisa's voice was more alive.

"Tell us about your mother, Lisa."

"Well, to begin with, she is absolutely perfect—ask her!"

"No, wait, Lisa. Don't tell us, be her. Imitate her. Come into the room, walk like her, talk like her, say what she would say to us. . . ."

Lisa arose, left the room, and reentered. Her manner was more energetic, her voice stronger, her face alight. She said, "Good morning, you peasants!" in a condescending tone. For perhaps ten minutes she delivered a monologue in which she presented a caricature of a narcissistic, exhibitionistic, and self-consciously charming woman with an inner feeling of contempt for others. It was such a bravura performance that when she finished, the group applauded.

There ensued a discussion of Lisa's childhood. She had undergone no overt deprivation or rejection but always felt completely crushed by her mother's egocentricity. Lisa talked freely now, but the change in her manner was far more striking than what she said. She looked and sounded alive and maintained her animation throughout the remaining hours of the marathon. It was an impressive demonstration of how a toxic introject can almost entirely stifle vitality and spontaneity, and how under favorable circumstances this pathology, at least temporarily, can be undone.

The concept of introjection is probably among the most fruitful of psychoanalytic formulations in furthering our understanding of personality development and is also among the most useful in clinical application. In marathons, its utilization is of particular value therapeutically, because there is time to identify the introject; to try various methods of helping the marathon participant gain perspective on the introject and hence begin to separate from it, at least in part; and finally to stabilize these gains through group discussion and interaction.

Introjection in itself is simply an instinctual process which contributes to ego development. The infant and later the growing child takes into itself the significant aspects of its environment. This begins with its relationship to the nursing breast which, under reasonably good circumstances, leads ideally to a capacity for self-nurturance in later life through the deep, unconscious, taken-for-granted conviction that there is a good breast within the self.[1]

It is considered probable that even under auspicious circumstances, the infant also fantasizes that there are two breasts, one good, one bad and denying, but subsequently forms an integrated, realistic picture which combines both aspects. But if the feeding period is very unsatisfactory, if the mother-baby relationship is very unsatisfying, or if the situation is very traumatizing in other ways, the denying or inadequate breast becomes part of the unconscious self. The breast within is not giving, but denying. The denying breast is the prototype of the toxic introject. It brings about a chronic emotional hunger which is often associated with such oral cravings as excessive smoking, drinking, and eating, or excessive dependent demands on others, or in some cases (though by no means necessarily) with schizophrenic symptomatology.

Empirical data is lacking as to whether the marathon encounter group can be useful to this type of personality, but it is my personal guess that patients of this type would probably profit by marathon experiences only after prolonged individual psychotherapy. Even in individual psychotherapy, it seems likely that the deep emotional hunger cannot be alleviated solely by insight or by verbal interpretations (Balint, 1969). It may require the long-term conveying of a primitive sense of physical and emotional security, as for example by appropriate emotional contact with a parent figure, so that the primitive unconscious image of the denying breast may be at least in part replaced by a more benevolent introject.

---

[1] Readers who seek a less cursory discussion of this topic are referred to Fairbairn (1952, 1963) and to Segal (1964), who offers a summary of the complex contributions of Melanie Klein.

It is generally easier to work therapeutically with toxic introjects (superego introjects) which are formed during later years, when the child's sense of "right" and "wrong" and the resultant self-approval or self-reproach are developing. The behavioral standards of the parents become a harmonious part of the child's personality if they are not excessively severe and if they are conveyed to the child with adequate love-rewards.

But if the parents are perceived as overstrict or unloving, the child cannot or will not meet their standards. Such a child may rebel. If he feels too helpless to rebel, he may unconsciously resort to introjection as a defense, swallowing the parental attitudes and visiting upon himself the rage once felt toward the parents. He may be angry at himself as he once felt his parents to be angry toward him. He may be angry at himself as he once felt angry toward his parents. He may introject aspects of his parents which are essentially opposed to self-actualization and happiness. He may develop, as part of himself, attitudes of guilt or self-deprivation or self-destruction. These also are toxic introjects.

If the swallowed introject is fully assimilated and becomes ego-syntonic, in the sense of being experienced as a natural, integral part of the personality, there is little or no conscious conflict. Even when it is toxic in that it hinders the pursuit of happiness, there may be little or no conscious conflict, as in personality types where the "anti-libidinal ego" (in Fairbairn's phrase) is completely dominant. Such a personality structure can usually be modified only by prolonged individual psychotherapy, or extremely fortunate life-experiences, or both.

However, if the toxic introject is perceived as a destructive and alien aspect of the self, and especially if it is contrary to the values which are consciously accepted by the individual, then he can seek freedom from the enemy within. Then it is less difficult, although not easy, to defeat the inner enemy, to detach the parasite, to exorcise the demon.

In this exorcism, the most useful technique is frequently role-playing. There are two basic approaches, which may be used separately or successively.

First, the toxic introject may be role-played by another person, in order to increase the patient's awareness that he is actually facing neither himself nor another individual in the external world, but an inner representation of a destructive authority figure from childhood.[2] This approach also, when successful, mobilizes the patient's energies to combat the inner enemy, through focussing them on the enemy's symbolic representative.

Sometimes this mobilization of energy takes a physical form. Occasionally the outburst of energy is spectacular. Several times, in role-

---

[2] This can be done through various applications of Moreno's psychodramatic approach (1946) or through the therapist's more-or-less serious impersonation of a pathological aspect of the patient's personality.

playing the malevolent aspect of the patient's real mother, I have been physically attacked in earnest, though there was always a rational, controlled part of the patient's personality which kept me from being in any actual danger. Even though striking successes may occur with the use of this technique in individual psychotherapy (Nelson, Nelson, Sherman, & Strean, 1968), the group situation in my opinion provides a setting in which the patient feels freer to allow his hostility to the original malevolent figure to express itself toward whoever is playing the role. The rational and observant part of himself is always aware that the group is present to serve as a shock absorber and to prevent any physically injurious rage explosion.

Second, the patient himself may be asked to play the role of the toxic introject, as in the example of Lisa. It is astounding how frequently, as with Lisa's case, this procedure is followed by a release of energy. Although the exact dynamics of how this occurs would be difficult to ascertain precisely and would probably raise many complex metapsychological questions, we may speculate that considerable psychic energy gets bound up in the toxic introject itself and also in the patient's unconscious efforts to overcome the introject in the search for self-fulfillment.

After the first of these role-playing procedures, it is often desirable to encourage the patient to express in the group a more positive aspect of himself; metaphorically, we could express this procedure as a filling of the inner vacuum left by dismissal of the introject; psychodynamically, we could conjecture that by this method the energies hitherto bound up in the introject are while still mobile channelled in such a way that they can henceforth be available to the healthy, rational ego.

After the second of these role-playing procedures, it is often desirable for the patient to accept a benevolent replacement for the banished introject. The patient frequently takes the initiative in these procedures, as with Max, whose story follows.

The example of Max recalls the classical psychoanalytic dictum that introjection, typically introjection of the malevolent aspect of the mother as seen in early childhood, may in fantasy be performed by way of the mouth (Fenichel, 1945, p. 63). In adult life, under appropriate circumstances, this fantasy may become conscious.

Max, a clothing salesman, was almost certainly unfamiliar with psychoanalytic theory; yet after a highly dramatic dialogue in which I had played out the hostile aspect of his mother, which by association with a childhood fairytale he called the pig-mother, Max said spontaneously "I want to get rid of you; I'm going to vomit you up," went into an adjoining bathroom and vomited, returning with an expression of exhilaration and relief, but trembling at the same time. He sat beside me and clasped my hand for a long time, while the group worked on without him. Probably he needed to reassure himself that by vomiting up the pig-mother aspect of his mother, he had not also destroyed the good aspect. Since in the marathon I represented to him both of these aspects, he presumably needed not only to make certain that he had not destroyed me, but more realistically that I was not responding to his anger with hostility. Thus I became a benevolent replacement for the malevolent pig-mother.

Other marathon participants as well have sometimes expressed the wish to vomit up a part of themselves which they perceive as alien, and this wish is accepted, sometimes even to the point of providing a bucket in case the participant should wish to use it. This convenience is very seldom exploited, but its provision offers symbolic encouragement for the symbolic ejection of the introjected person. However, I do not myself suggest the possibility of symbolic vomiting, preferring to leave the patient free to select this symbol if it is appropriate, particularly since it is believed that introjection may occur symbolically not only by swallowing but also by breathing, smelling, or hearing (Fenichel, Ch. V).

It is not difficult for group members to understand the concept of the introject, if it is discussed in imagery and metaphor rather than in the language of theory. Participants are often familiar with the term *dybbuk* from Meyer-anski's play "The Dybbuk," in which the spirit of a girl's dead lover takes possession of her body—a brilliant presentation of what psychoanalytic theory would explain as a regression from object-relations to identification with a lost love-object. Expressions such as "It's as if you have your mother still inside you" or "You attack yourself the way your father used to do it" are easily understood. Often the participant will spontaneously choose such terms as "witch" or "evil spirit," not superstitiously but as a poetic metaphor, and in this case the term "exorcism" becomes understandable and appropriate. Very often, the expression "part of myself" as opposed to "myself" is used, indicating that the introject is perceived as an alien body within the personality.

There are various procedures by which the exorcism may take place. After the source of the introject (mother, father, other significant person) is identified, sometimes as a surprise to the participant, another group member may play the role of the bad object, giving the participant an opportunity to vent the rage and resentment which as a child he had to swallow. Alternatively, the participant himself may take the role of the bad object, thus externalizing the introject and hopefully gaining distance from it. Symbolic action may be taken through which the participant replaces the toxic introject by expressing in the group a more positive aspect of himself or by accepting someone else as a benevolent replacement (as when Max held my hand after vomiting).

The example of Marnie illustrates how an introject may be discovered. She had studied acting intensively and had been fairly successful as a serious dramatic actress, then had given up the stage to rear children. With her children grown, and with her husband's acquiescence, she wished to return to the stage but became frightened whenever she took an active step, such as telephoning a theatrical booking agency. The anxiety seemed partly a consequence of her uncertainty as to whether she could repeat her earlier success but was often accompanied by an unclear inner voice with a warning or discouraging tone, which began with the words, in Yiddish, "A Jewish girl" or "A good Jewish girl." Marnie had not been fully aware of the voice until she told the group about it and recognized its origin unmistakably only when she was questioned.

"It's my grandmother's voice."

Her grandmother had been dead for years, but Marnie could well remember how the old matriarch had reacted when the girl was first drawn to the theater. It was unheard-of for nice, good Jewish girls. Only whores were interested in the stage.

"How did she say it, Marnie? What did she actually say? In Yiddish."

Marnie spoke in Yiddish, then translated for us. "A good Jewish girl . . . doesn't show her body to men. Doesn't prance around on the stage."

"Where do you see your grandmother when she says all this?"

"In the kitchen. Making blintzes, terrible blintzes, the worst blintzes in the world."

"Who here speaks Yiddish?" When memorable words have been spoken to a child, the childhood scene can be recreated most effectively if the words are repeated in the original language. If nobody is present in a marathon who can speak the language, myself or someone else may attempt to catch the correct pronunciation of "Little boy," or "Bad girl" or "Don't do that," or whatever simple phrase has become significant, in hope of evoking whatever feelings were connected with the original process of introjection.

Only Archie spoke Yiddish, a bearded biology teacher who did not resemble a grandmother but who agreed to play the role. He busied himself about an imaginary kitchen, making imaginary blintzes, speaking in a low voice. Later he told us that he had spoken simply about the duties of a Jewish girl, and about his (her) certainty that the stage was only for whores. The scene might have been amusing but was not, for Marnie turned pale and burst into tears. In vain she tried to talk back to the grandmother figure but could not do so convincingly. She had not realized that the old taboo was still so effective. The role-playing merged into a discussion of how the grandmother now spoke to Marnie from within herself as once she had spoken from the kitchen; and how the original taboo which forbade a young girl to show herself on the stage had now fused with the idea, which influenced Marnie emotionally even though neither she nor her husband accepted it on a rational basis, that it was equally improper for the mother of children to seek a theatrical career. We spoke also of how Marnie had not only resented her grandmother but had also loved her. This ambivalence is typical of childhood relationships ultimately perpetuated as ego-dystonic introjects. Affection makes it difficult for the child to defy the authority, while resentment makes it impossible to assimilate the partly beloved figure as a harmonious part of the child's personality.

To be therapeutically useful, a scenario which brings the protagonist into symbolic confrontation with the introject need not always be carried to a dramatically impressive conclusion. With Marnie, and also with Dorie, whose case follows, the use of a scenario in which there is a symbolic presentation of the introject did not reach a closure, nor did it fully resolve the basic problem. Indeed, there is no reason to expect that the dissolution of a long-present toxic introject could be achieved in an hour or two of a marathon scenario. Such a scenario, however, often brings very sharply to the attention of the protagonist the existence of the introject and its malevolent effects, hence constitutes an important step toward its mastery and dissipation. It may also happen that a scenario built around the effort to dispel an introject will lead to unexpected insights. For instance, the protagonist may find himself unable to behave in the way that the scenario originally called for, or in the way that he intended or expected to behave. Consequently, he must recognize the existence of feelings which hitherto were repressed and actually unconscious, or which were experienced only in an indefinite, anxious, foggy kind of way.

Dorie, in her early thirties, attended a marathon with her husband, Lloyd, for the purpose of working through some difficulties in a vital but stormy marriage. They opened the marathon with a vigorous argument, each seeking to enlist sympathy and arouse indignation rather than to face their problems. They were asked to refrain from speaking about the marriage for a few hours and to pretend they were there as separate individuals, in the hope that they would respond to the self-disclosure of other participants by becoming less defensive about themselves. This appeared to occur. Next day both approached their relationship less argumentatively. Lloyd told Dorie that she seemed still to belong to her family rather than to him and their children, not so much in terms of the actual time spent with them but by her continuing emotional preoccupation with her parents and brother. He expressed it graphically. "It's like they fill up your vagina so I can't get in."

Dorie agreed that she would try to get rid of the ghosts of people who were actually still living but who nevertheless haunted her. She asked Frances, whose age was appropriate, to role-play her mother. The exorcism went according to plan. After a dialogue in which Frances assumed the mother's personality according to Dorie's instructions, and after Dorie had announced firmly that she no longer needed a mother, Dorie (who was athletic) bodily picked up Frances (who was slight) and carried her from the room, returning exuberantly to announce that she was now ready to get rid of her brother.

Dorie's older brother, she told us, had engaged in sadomasochistic sex play with her when they were small. She knew that her fear of her brother still extended to other men and sometimes prevented a full sexual response to Lloyd. He, in turn, reacted as if his brother-in-law were an actual sexual competitor, a reaction which proved to be essentially justified. To play her brother, Dorie chose a good-looking man a few years older and made a rather unconvincing effort to push him from the room. Her behavior, however, was so seductive that he refused to go, responding instead to her sexual provocativeness, half scuffling with her and half embracing. The group's reaction to this situation, though in different words, proffered precisely the same interpretation which would have been given by a competent psychoanalyst interpreting the obvious incestuous tie between Dorie and her brother. "This is a *brother*?" "This is a sister?" "No wonder Lloyd can't stand the thought of him."

Dorie seemed literally unable to let go of her "brother" or to terminate the sexual, aggressive teasing. In the group, her brother-symbol was evoking behavior which probably had been present only in its latent form with her actual brother, but the intensity of its manifestation here was showing how strong was her sex-hate ambivalence. It seemed to me that to insist on a symbolic resolution of this conflict would be artificial. Dorie was so bound up in her own ambivalence that a pseudo-solution could be found only if the marathon leader deliberately weighted the scales in favor of one choice or the other. Therefore I was satisfied to hear Dorie acknowledge that her difficulties in breaking off emotionally with her brother were stronger than she had anticipated, and that she could now better understand and accept her husband's resentment of this relationship.

A similar, though less painful insight, was achieved when, as the third part of her task, Dorie tried to get rid of the ghost of her father, who seemed a passive but kindly man. To impersonate him, she selected a gentle-mannered man of appropriate age, embraced him affectionately, and tried to tell him to leave. Then Dorie's decision faltered. He didn't have to leave altogether. He could go into the next room and be comfortable with television and slippers and a glass of tea, and she could visit him there whenever she wished. Dorie could not at this moment give up either her inward dependence on her father, or the stimulating sex-hate feelings toward her brother; but she was now more fully aware of the part she herself played in perpetuating these inward relationships. She recognized that essentially she was involved with her own internal images rather than with the actual people.

Going-around, in which a participant circles the group and relates to each member in turn, is probably the most useful single strategem in group therapy and is especially valuable for the purpose of exorcising a toxic introject and trying to replace it by a more benevolent introject. Since going-around involves the self-expression of the protagonist toward a number of people, and since these people also represent various aspects of external reality, this technique beautifully creates a situation in which inner and outer reality can be experienced simultaneously, and this is probably why movement around the circle is almost invariably marked by a movement from pathology toward health.

For example, Sam, a middle-aged business man, told the group about a recurrent nightmare in which he faced a horrifying monster with a sense of total, helpless panic. He was asked to go around the circle and play the monster, letting the monster's behavior change as his own feelings and impulses changed. Sam began by behaving as a King Kong creature, hands upraised, face distorted, snarling and growling. Yet there was something slightly comical about the impersonation, as if the monster might be playful. The group members responded accordingly. Some recoiled in mock terror, others retaliated with pretended counter-threats, but all of them responded in an essentially friendly way.

As Sam went around the circle, the monster became milder. Toward the end, he was close to being a lovable clown, and the young woman who was the last member of the circle responded accordingly. "Poor monster, I don't think you really want raw flesh; sit down with me and have an apple." Sam sat down smiling, put his arm around her, and remarked in a matter-of-fact way that probably the dream would not frighten him any more. Some months later, he wrote that the dream had recurred and was still an unpleasant dream, but that the intense nightmare panic was gone.

My request that Sam play the monster role was based on the assumption that each symbol in a dream represents part of the self (Perls, 1969) and if the symbol is fearsome, it represents an aspect of the self which, consciously or unconsciously, arouses anxiety. If the dreamer is able to accept the task of pretending to become the frightening creature, it can actually be predicted that the fearsome symbol—snake, spider, dragon, ghost, witch, devil—will become increasingly less horrible. It retains its terrible, uncanny quality only when dissociated from the self.

These frightful symbols usually go back to childhood. Destructive rage is evoked in the child by his surroundings, or introjected when he perceives someone important as being destructive and enraged toward him. Unable to tolerate his anger because of the resultant guilt and also because of its shattering intensity, the child projects it on to an unconsciously selected symbol, and becomes the victim of phobic terrors or appalling nightmares; perhaps there is no greater terror than what a child suffers from a nightmare.

If the fearsome symbol is once more connected to the conscious self, the horror is dissipated. Anna Freud (1936, p. 119) exemplifies this exquisitely in her anecdote of the little girl who was afraid of a ghost when crossing a dark hallway, until she hit upon the device of making peculiar magical gestures, and explained to her brother, "There's no need to be afraid in the hall, . . . you just have to pretend you're the ghost who might meet you." Anna Freud also recognized the general efficacy of role-playing the frightening thing, adding, "there are many children's games in which, through the metamorphosis of the subject into a dreaded object, anxiety is converted into pleasurable security."

Clinical observation (A. Freud, 1936; Corsini, 1966; Perls, 1969) leaves no doubt but that role-playing an unacceptable part of the self may diminish or even dispel anxiety, release tension, and contribute toward the integration of guilt-provoking feelings or impulses with the total personality. It is easier to observe and describe this process than to explain it. With Sam, the dream monster seemed related to childhood experiences (as he told the group) with an uncle who was half-teasing and half-frightening and who scared the child. Quite probably, the small boy sensed an element of sadism in the teasing, although the rest of the family viewed this uncle as a lovable clown. Confused and angry, Sam became afraid of his own feelings toward the uncle and tried to imitate him because he found no other means to cope with his behavior. Thus the uncle became a toxic introject, later transformed into the evil dream symbol, which the adult Sam did not connect consciously at all with his early experiences.

It would be a tempting but unjustified oversimplification to assume that Sam's evil dream symbol simply represented a childhood figure who had frightened him, that unconsciously he had remained frightened of his uncle and that the fear was dispelled when he realized that as an adult he need no longer fear the memory. However, insight *followed* the role-playing and did not precede it. Consciously Sam did not realize that he was offering the group a performance of his ogre-clown uncle. It seems more likely that Sam had introjected some of his uncle's sadistic mockery, which was alien to his conscious values and which he therefore could neither accept nor express, but which became less repellent to him when he acted it out and found that the group responded with amusement and friendliness.

Certainly there can be no doubt, after the observation of many episodes such as Lisa's and Sam's, that energy is somehow bound up in the toxic introject and may be released by exaggerated role-playing. Since the introject is typically alien to conscious goals and values, perhaps it must be kept encapsulated by a sustained unconscious effort, according to the well-established psychoanalytic finding that psychic energy must be continually expended in the maintenance of defenses. Lisa, for instance, did not like her mother and certainly would have disowned any part of herself that she recognized as copied from her mother; yet the identification was there or else she could not have role-played her mother with such gusto. Perhaps her enhanced vitality after the role-playing was due to the release of energy hitherto bound up in keeping her self-image separated from the introject of her mother. Perhaps, also, the group's congratulatory and amused applause enabled her to see the introjected mother as less overpowering.

Humor at times, as with Sam, is of immense importance in the rites of exorcism, since it helps the patient to achieve both intellectual and emotional awareness that the terrifying figure was, after all, only a human being and in any case is now far away in the past. Janet, thirty years old, had gone through the kind of childhood which often causes us to regard with amazed respect the resiliency of some human beings. She had been placed in a girls' orphanage at five, and although her physical needs were met and she was not actually abused, she had been subjected to an upbringing which can only be described as sustained mental torture. There were punitive enemas, as well as a variety of other imaginative and humiliating punishments, and apparently an all-out effort to mold Janet and the other little girls into obedient automata. Moreover, there was little doubt that the head of the orphanage, Rose, was either a latent or overt Lesbian who exploited her position for gratifications which stopped short only of actual sexual contact with the children. For example, when their breasts began to form in early adolescence, she insisted that they pose naked for her and kept an album of photographs of the breasts of all the young girls in her charge. She disliked men and advised the girls to avoid them. She also requested them to caress her feet when she was tired. Since she was the most significant figure in Janet's childhood except for an affectionate but inadequate mother who visited the little girl but did not care for her, it was inevitable that she would influence Janet in many ways.

At thirty, Janet was functioning very effectively as a physiotherapist in a hospital setting. She did not seem to have an especially strong homosexual component, perhaps because homosexuality had been presented to her in an unattractive guise when she was little. However, though she was objectively attractive, she could not see herself as desirable. She had difficulty in relating to men, driving them away by a bristly shyness and oversensitivity.

It may be of importance that the marathon in which we worked with Janet's toxic introject was a nude marathon.[3] Perhaps it was helpful

---

[3] This marathon did not focus primarily on structured group activities fostering regression and bodily relaxation facilitated by nudity, as in Bindrim's technique (1968). It was conducted in the same manner as my other unstructured marathon encounters. Nudity was optional, though all participants (informed in advance that it

to her feminine self-concept to appear nude, especially since several other participants commented on the attractiveness of her body.

Early in the marathon, someone commented critically on Janet's self-negating voice. In her follow-up letter, Janet wrote, I think correctly:

> This criticism hurt and infuriated me. . . . Looking back on it, this episode might have set the stage for me to deal with my hostility, something I hadn't really acknowledged as a part of me.

As the marathon continued, Janet became more and more tense and nervous. The group felt that she was ready to explode. She had described to us her early experiences with Rose (Janet had a gift for language and described this woman as a "cigar-smoking, key-swinging, opera-singing Lesbian"), and she was asked now to enact the role of Rose.

In my memory, this role-playing, despite the bitterness and terror which came through, indicated a humorous awareness of the comical aspects of this genuinely malevolent figure. Janet caricatured Rose's movements, her grimaces, her strident voice. She requested the other women in the marathon to pose for an imaginary camera, so that she could add photographs of their breasts to her imaginary album. She requested them to "tickle her toes," which had been Rose's euphemism for semisexual caresses of her feet and legs. The other women complied, taking the parts of terrified, submissive, resentful, helpless little girls. In her follow-up letter, what Janet remembered was her direct hostility, rather than the humor of her caricature.

> I played Rose. I never screamed so loud. I pulled and yanked everyone in the vicinity into line, even though they weren't saying anything, or if they tried to say anything. I really carried on!

Janet felt disgusted by Rose and found herself switching without my direction into the role of her mother. Her description shows a striking intuitive recognition (to my knowledge, not suggested by any sophisticated theoretician) that she felt as if she had a choice between choosing to be like introjected Rose, or choosing to be like her mother.

> When I was through playing Rose, I felt undone. Since all this had come out of me, then it must really be a part of me. I resorted to the role of playing my mother. I knew this because I actually got her physical symptom of a painful, swollen right knee. As mother, I was not evil, only . . . very lonely, very infantile, very unhappy. Having unleashed Rose, and feeling then stuck with being mother, I was in a state of unrest for some days.

---

would be a nude group) accepted it without much difficulty. My personal judgment was that, except for a few participants, nudity made little difference in the developments within the group or in its general effects.

Janet at that time was also in individual treatment with me, on a once-a-week basis, which probably was a key factor in her ability to integrate what happened in the marathon. A second installment of her follow-up letter, written eight months after the marathon, described the subsequent experiences:

> Elizabeth made the interpretation that on some deep level I felt I had to choose between the role of Rose (which I had absolutely rejected all my life) and the role of mother (which I chose with some changes and found unsatisfactory). It made sense. She proposed that there was a third possibility, being myself, which was neither of these women. That made sense. But it was about two weeks before I really felt myself again.

> As I became more integrated with the marathon experience, I found myself confronting a co-worker of considerable prestige whom I had hitherto detested because she reminded me of Rose and whom in the past I had always avoided. I had always cancelled this co-worker out and avoided her. Now I was no longer afraid of her hostility. So she was hostile, but her hostility was no longer an overwhelming and incomprehensible threat. Now I can actually enjoy this woman and recognize what she has to offer in spite of her hostility.

An important realistic event which occurred immediately after the marathon was that, for the first time in many years, Janet was able to behave in an appropriately feminine and seductive way with a man whom she wanted to go out with. He responded by dating her, and they had a pleasant although not permanent relationship. Janet wrote, in her eight-month follow-up letter:

> The effect of this marathon was that I felt more feminine. It was most noticeable in my dress. Inwardly I felt a new sureness and freedom to be creative. I rediscovered beads and necklaces. Whereas previously I had felt silly assuming [sic] to wear a piece of jewelry, I now wore exciting combinations of beads and earrings and bracelets with ease and proudly. I felt neither surprised or anxious when I got complimented. This process began right after the marathon. I changed my polo shirt for a sheer blouse, put a ribbon in my hair, and remembered that I owned contact lenses.

The example of Eva, another young woman who was seen both in individual treatment and in a series of nine marathons, shows how a toxic introject was exorcised principally by the technique of going-around in a series of marathons. Eva was able to describe her experiences with unusual vividness and frankness, and my observations are interspersed with quotations from her written accounts.

Eva was referred for marathons by a male colleague with whom she had been in treatment for some years. She had sought help in her late teens for feelings of confusion and depression and had made good use of treatment. Now she and her psychologist agreed that she should see a woman therapist.

Tall, dark-haired, in her mid-twenties, Eva usually conveyed an impression of warmth and aliveness, but at other times seemed sad, puzzled, and somehow bedraggled. She was struggling valiantly toward self-fulfillment. Her mother, hospitalized several times and diagnosed as a paranoid schizophrenic, had left Eva's father when the child was nine. Since then, as Eva wrote, "She continued living with her parents. She never went out with men or functioned as a woman after that." Mother had also arranged an "unholy allegiance" by which Eva's father was to be regarded as a monster. Eva's brother, five years younger, more deeply disturbed than his sister, had broken completely with the family, including Eva.

Eva's description of herself in her middle and late teens follows:

> I "knew" I could never commit myself to a man, not knowing why, and feeling so apart from everyone, so different, and not being able to get at it. It was just fated and I couldn't break that spell for years and years. Joan Baez's song "Silver Dagger" was with me in those days, during my college years. I identified with it so strongly; its lines would run through my head very very often. I still remember some of the verses. . . .

> I was involved intensely then with Joe in a relationship which lasted almost seven years but I always "knew" I could never marry him. I "knew" I could never be anybody's for I was my mother's. I didn't believe Joe loved me. I didn't believe I loved Joe. I didn't think I was capable of loving or of having any decent relationship with a man.

Eva could neither make satisfactory contact with her mother, nor break off altogether from seeing her, though she was able after graduating from college to support herself as a teacher and maintain her own apartment. She was deeply affected by her mother's psychotic episodes, which were marked by overt schizophrenic symptoms including hallucinations. She perceived her mother as self-righteous and overcontrolled during periods of remission, yet could speak of her as "my poor sad witch mother."

The relationship with Joe continued to be difficult. She wrote "I loved Joe, hated myself for needing him, couldn't get out of this bind. . . . I felt desperate, beseiged by dreams and emotions revolving around my mother, my identity as a woman, sex, helplessness. . . ." These chaotic feelings led Eva into an unconsciously wished-for pregnancy by Joe, which she terminated with an abortion, followed by many months of depression and overeating. She broke off with Joe, and it was shortly thereafter that she appeared for her first marathon.

Although at this time I know little of Eva's history and of her relationship with her mother, an emotional rapport between Eva and myself developed quickly. For her, it was based on a need and readiness for motherly affection; for me, on a response to this need, along with a natural liking evoked by her genuineness and warmth. Early in the marathon Eva wept, and I put my arm around her without realizing how deeply significant this gesture would prove to be. Indeed, if I had embraced her because of a wish to be therapeutically helpful rather than because of a spontaneous impulse, it would perhaps not have been significant at all.

Despite our contact or because of it, Eva was so frightened that on the second day of the marathon she slept through the ringing of the phone and the alarm clock and arrived three hours late. She was nevertheless able to talk to the group, telling us about her discomfort with men, and her inability to feel attractive and feminine with them. Because of Eva's traumatic relationship with her mother, it seemed to me that she needed the permission and support of a mother-substitute to accept and enjoy her womanliness, permission which is normally conveyed in a good mother-daughter relationship, but which Eva had never received. Therefore I suggested that she go around the circle and speak flirtatiously to each of the men. Eva shrank back, and I offered to walk with her, side by side.

She approached each man in turn, trembling violently, so that I put my arm around her shoulders. With the first few men, she made light, somewhat flirtatious comments ("I like your necktie"); then her trembling diminished, and I let go of her shoulder and took her cold hand as she continued. She struck another man playfully, clasped hands with the next one, and at this point as I felt her hand grow warm, I relinquished it and she continued by herself. The last man in the group reached out his arms, and Eva curled up in his lap, remaining there relaxed for several moments.

Here is Eva's account of the experience of first being held by me and thereafter relating to the men, which symbolically recapitulated the normal experience of a little girl who receives warmth and security from being mothered and can then move onward to relate to boys and men. Repeatedly I have seen in marathons this same process, in which men as well as women will accept mothering, from myself or from another woman in the group, and then move on to the experience of symbolically expressed heterosexual mature feelings.

Eva wrote, after this first marathon:

> You say to go around and relate to all the men in the group as a woman.
> O. K. I'll do it. . . . My heart thumps faster than usual. But before you

ask this of me, you give me mothering. You hold me and something so needed and longed for the lacking comes through to me. . . . And then miracle of miracles. You say, go out and be a woman with men. What an extra beautiful thing. So good. So good. Sure I'll do it. I know this is healthy even though I can't take being a woman completely seriously now. . . . Just go and be a woman for my own pleasure and growth. I'm amazed. Can this be possible? . . . You hold my hand to give me support as I begin going around to the men. I feel good now. You've given me so much that I don't need to hold onto you to be a woman. I go around to each of the men, kissing some on the cheek, hitting one who was obnoxious and turned off to himself, holding the strong beautiful hands of one man whose hands gave me some of their strength, and then feeling the sexual aliveness of a woman embraced and held by a man. I was accepted and responded to as a person and a woman by these men. Amazing! . . . I had interchanges with all the men and felt good about them and about me.

Shortly after this marathon, Eva formed a relationship with the first man to whom she had been able to respond since breaking off with Joe after the abortion, toward whom she felt "probably the most loving I've ever been in my life." She also wrote that on at least a few occasions, she could "relate to my mother as a human being with warmth and straight-forwardness."

In a later marathon, it became apparent that Eva's experience with a loving, heterosexually permissive, good mother-symbol had truly been assimilated. Another group member, Arlene, was about the same age as Eva but seemed years younger because of her timid voice and withdrawn manner. Arlene told the group that she was "absolutely petrified" when she went out on dates, to such an extent that she sometimes actually in-vited sexual intimacy because she could not find any other way to relate, and Eva came to Arlene's rescue.

"You need practice in talking to men," said Eva capably. "Come on, we'll go around the room together; I'll go right with you so you won't be scared." Just as Eva and I had gone around the room together, more than a year ago, so now Arlene and Eva went from man to man, Eva's arm around the shoulders of the other girl, encouraging her while she spoke to one after another, and gradually withdrawing to leave her on her own as she gained confidence. Apparently my support of her wom-anly sexuality had been integrated sufficiently so that she could use it not only to nourish herself, but to nourish others. Eva was deeply gratified when the group called her a good mother, and she wrote:

Yes, I am a good mother and it comes naturally now. Maybe a long time ago when I wanted so badly to be of help to my mother in her suffering, maybe then I was also a good mother. Toward my kids at school, too. I love them. I'm a good mother to them. My breasts are bared to them in my dreams. . . . I'm helping, I'm not nothing, dead, impotent. But why is it so confusing to see myself this way? I like it, but it's connected up with something that befuddles me.

Eva now began dealing on a deeper level with the introject of her sick mother, perceived sometimes as evil and sometimes as pathetic. In an extraordinary dream, which she wrote down along with some of the memories which it evoked, she found a vivid image for the sick part of her mother.

> . . . A dream about my family being served a weird clawed creature, neither fish nor fowl, in a plate. . . . I had the image of this little beast in my belly which had to be expelled and anticipated I would do this at the marathon. For I saw her symbolically as this awful creature, as a separate entity bound in me, with power to influence me; an evil matter in me. And I can remember when I was in an even worse position—when she wasn't bound to me but when I was bound to her. When I felt little and powerless, fated to live out a direction that she created. . . . I remember . . . hearing my mother cry in the next room and being overwhelmed with feeling. Dear God, when she suffers, I suffer.

No poet, and certainly no psychologist, could have expressed with more poignant imagery the sensitive person's awareness of an introject as a weird, foreign creature—"a little beast in my belly which has to be expelled"—along with the pity, dependency and resentment which were present in Eva's original relationship with her mother, and which now bound her to the introject. As Eva wrote, she entered her next marathon "feeling that I was plagued by my mother and had to release her. . . . I felt the need for a primitive ritual to be enacted for this purpose."

It was Eva's feeling that she could expel the sick and evil mother within herself, the introject, only if she could succeed in making her mother well. This was not a psychotic delusion, but a poetic image from the creative unconscious, in which she expressed her intuitive awareness that somehow she must not only separate from the internal bad mother but replace her with an internal good mother. On another psychological level, she was probably expressing the feeling that she was not entitled to be healthy and joyous if her mother continued to be miserable. Eva was asked, therefore, to go around the room and say to each of us "I am here to make my mother well," with instructions to allow the words to change if her feelings so dictated.

Once again the process of change from pathology toward health occurred in the going-around. Eva repeated the words automatically several times. Then her voice began to sound angry. She said, "No, I am here to make *me* well!" She said this firmly to many people and then sat down, looking relaxed. After this, she wrote:

I went around the circle, saying "I am here to make my mother well." As I continued along the circle of people saying these words my feelings started changing. . . . I was angry. I was not there to make my mother well. "I am here to make me well—me, me, not my mother, me. I am here to make Eva well." Me—I am Eva, separate from my mother. I cannot make her well and that't not my purpose. This was clarified for me in the marathon in a nonthinking way and without thought my previous plaguing compulsion to expel her subsided.

From her second marathon onward, Eva was increasingly appreciated by the other participants for her ability to give. It was easy for her to offer physical gestures of affection, and she was often called upon for comfort. At times her inner warmth gave her a look of actual physical radiance, but at other times she still was unhappy and confused. Eva and I both felt that these bad phases were in some way tied up with anger, which she had always found difficulty in expressing. She had been reared in an atmosphere of constraint, which she described:

> Letting go by being angry and nasty and just bitchy was never done in my house. My mother could seethe inside but be patient, soft-spoken and quite rational. Her controls functioned to such an enormous degree that she was actually split inside. . . .

Clinically, the intermittent schizophrenic episodes of Eva's mother could be seen as the periodic breaking down of these brittle defenses. It was inevitable that Eva should be afraid of her own anger.

> I was always terribly conscious about just being and expressing myself freely with boys; . . . the clamps were tight . . . and with my girlfriends the bond was typically an unconditionally accepting, sympathetic one with very little negative feelings expressed—the social worker attitude.

In her fifth marathon, more than a year after her first, Eva indicated that she wished to deal with her anger and spoke of her mother's inner violence and outer control. She felt that somehow she resembled her mother in both these aspects, and since she was already acting out the controlled part, she was now asked to act out the hostility. She was requested to go around the circle and relate to everyone as if she were their bad mother—not necessarily in an imitation of her own mother, which might merely have replicated her mother's controls, but rather in an expression of the bad mother within herself. Eva did so, and she wrote:

> It wasn't easy for me to think of bad things to say to everyone . . . only one interchange felt really biting, when I called one woman an "immoral hussy" and she responded "you're a jealous cow." To most of the others

I seemed to give bad advice like "Keep on remaining undecided whether you want to go back to school or not." But . . . I wanted to be a bad mother and I was. I felt as if I could breathe more easily after going around. I felt exhilarated. . . .

Eva described the freeing of the energy which had been bound up with her identification with her mother's overcontrolled anger. Her account once more indicates the way in which psychic energy can be tied up with an introject.

Yes, I'm a mean cruel angry bitch and I love being able to express it. I'm so alive being in touch with this part of me. I tingle with breathing in all of my body. I am not helpless at all. I can fight for myself.

There's usually a split—something I repress down which keeps me quiet and it's not there when I can be angry. Not caring what the hell I look like to anyone else. Yes, I'm the alive me when I let myself be. And it's just too bad if I hurt someone in the process of being me. Just too fuckin' bad. I'm strong. I have to live for me! After this marathon it gave me great pleasure to remember myself as the bad mother. What had felt like my mother inside ceased to plague me. And my life and also my dreams immediately turned on to me as a woman with men.

Yet the struggle with the introject was not over. During all this time, Eva had seen me twice a month for individual appointments and had also seen her male psychotherapist occasionally. She made no inappropriate demands on either of us but saw us frankly as substitutes for her sick mother and rejecting father, and expressed a fantasy (which all of us greatly enjoyed) that we would someday be present as surrogate parents at her wedding. She was aware that she was happier and healthier than ever before, and that she was still growing. Yet there were still the times of depression and apathy. At this time, with Dr. Frank Rubenfeld as co-therapist, I first experimented with a four-day marathon, in a country setting where the leaders and the group could share a rustic lodge. Eva participated. There was swimming and impromptu dancing, which she enjoyed intensely. As usual, she liked and was liked by both men and women. Yet, on the last night of the group, she told us that for some hours she had been feeling uncomfortable and sad and felt "as if I brought my mother with me."

In some marathons, there are episodes which would seem less strange if they could be filmed, but which in description may well seem bizarre; episodes in which rituals are carried out, often suggested by the participants, which resemble the magic ceremonies of primitive peoples or the myths of other civilizations. The toxic introject, as investigated and conceptualized by contemporary personality theory, is undoubtedly what in times past was regarded as demoniacal possession, and perhaps that is why the use of symbols is particularly appropriate and useful here. With Eva, as she spoke of feeling that her mother was with her, there was an actual change in the appearance of her face, visible to everyone, which centuries ago would certainly have been interpreted as a demoniacal presence, and which today recalls studies of split personality (Prince, 1938; Cleckley, 1957). Eva's face became sly, malicious, hypocritical—the very reverse of her usual personality. And it was probably not a coincidence that, this very afternoon, she had suffered a bad burn on her leg by carelessness—a mishap which was in general unlike her. Neither Frank nor I nor Eva herself could withstand the impression that Eva's inner mother, like a medieval demon, was stubbornly refusing to be banished.

"Magic is needed." I do not recall which of the three of us said this, but Frank took over the part of the good magician. Tenderly and dramatically, without facetiousness, he enacted literally the metaphor of the introject as an actual foreign object within the body, pretending to coax the witch from Eva's lips. The group was as intent and serious as if they too took the symbol literally. As the miniature drama reached the point when the "witch" was supposedly emerging, one of the group members brought forth a broom and suggested that, as there was a full moon, the witch-mother should be sent away. The broom was ceremoniously taken outside the door. Eva began to laugh, sounding delighted and relieved. The group laughed and congratulated Eva and crowded around the window, waving, pretending that they could see the witch on her broomstick dimly receding into the night. This was the last episode of the last night of the marathon, and the evening ended in dancing. It seemed as if this use of symbolism, playful and yet serious in its recognition of a core of essential inner reality, had been exactly appropriate.

Not so. In the morning Eva was distraught and depressed. She told us that she had "lost her feelings." She felt nothing; she missed her feelings; she wanted them back. A very early symptom, which had disappeared so long ago that I had never heard it, recurred—a kind of lisping or hissing in her voice at the end of her sentences.

"I think you miss the witch. You miss your mother." But interpretation did not seem adequate for the loss of the introjected mother, who although she was malevolent was still to Eva a necessary part of herself. Frank, myself, and several other members of the group who were especially fond of Eva crowded around her, holding and embracing her. She was unresponsive and remote at first, then gradually seemed to return to us.

"I think you went off on that broomstick too. Come back!" Eva laughed, began to respond to our affection and gradually became herself again. Yet it is probably significant that she did not choose to describe this episode in writing, except to write briefly "I got in touch with my witch-mother and copped out." As she had loved and hated her mother, so Eva now loved and hated the introject. Although her reality relationship with her mother was now far less difficult and painful, and although she could enjoy her womanhood more and more, the inner mother still stood between her and self-fulfillment. In Eva's description of her next two marathons, the most meaningful sentence seems to be, "I needed to forgive her in order to release her from me." The banishment on the broom had represented the rejection and punishment of an introject which after all was part of Eva. The inner mother had to be forgiven.

The motive of forgiveness had first come to Eva's attention in an earlier marathon, in which a young mother had gone around saying to each participant, "I have deprived my children. Do you forgive me?" Eva had been deeply affected by this, and wrote, "I forgave her knowing that I couldn't forgive my own mother."

It is my conviction that, for many people and probably for all of us, self-fulfillment and emotional well-being cannot be achieved without a genuine forgiveness of our parents, regardless of whatever malice or mistakes they have visited upon us. This is not a matter of religion or ethics, but of personality dynamics. For good or ill, the formation of personality depends to an enormous extent on identification with an introjection of the parents, and anyone who maintains resentment toward them must on some level also maintain resentment toward the self. The resentment usually cannot be dissipated until, through effective psychotherapy or through other beneficial life experiences, it becomes conscious and can be felt without guilt or fear; usually it must also be expressed, either directly to the parent or to a symbolic figure, as in marathon groups and other psychotherapeutic situations. But having been experienced and expressed, the resentment must be relinquished, for anyone who cannot deeply and genuinely forgive his parents remains a child.

With her intuitive awareness of psychic realities, Eva seemed to know this. She wrote, after the marathon in which she had forgiven her fellow participant, the young woman who had deprived her children:

> I must look at her [her mother] and die of the pain. I must forgive her her terrible humanness. . . . That clawed little beast is her, that shrivelled animal form that feels itself important but can only be impotent sitting in the plate looking ugly and clawed and small. . . . I must open the door to this weak deformed woman, this endlessly suffering form of humanity, my mother, my sister, my child, me, and see her and cry and cry and cry and die.

Here Eva gives intense poetic expression to her intuitive recognition that she cannot keep the "door," which is presumably a metaphor for admission to full consciousness, closed to her mother but must face the pain of accepting and forgiving her, even though the pain seems great as death.

> I have deprived my children. Do you forgive me? [Eva here imagines her mother speaking to her.] Yes, you have deprived your children. I do not forgive you yet. I am in the process of bringing to a close my hard closed hatred of you. Eventually I will forgive you with the help of people who will be with me and help me while I die in forgiving you. No more to suffer with your racking pain of helplessness, no more to writhe with the anger and hopelessness of your death sentence, your straightjacketed paralyzed life, your persecuted martyred denial of Woman, Sex, Love, Anger, your isolated path of the castrated, wronged, bitter woman, your self-righteous self-victorious brilliant analysis of life leaving you a crying screaming infant alone in a cold dark place, your two-headed big-worded dialogue on life and right and morality, your self-violating destructive self-control, your dutiful execution of your obligations like a zombie, your defensive dissection of humanness . . .

Eva was alone when she wrote this diatribe of hatred and did not show it to me until some months later. Yet, having "given release to my hatred of her on paper," she was ready in her next marathon to work toward forgiving her mother. Eva was asked to conduct a dialogue with her mother, in which she would forgive her. She chose to speak with an imaginary mother, rather than to have someone role-play the part, and she made an effort, but she could get no further than the words "I would like to forgive you." As she describes it:

> We acted out bringing my poor sad witch mother into the room and I conversed with her. I was chilled talking to her. I had no warmth to give her and it became clear that I needed to forgive her in order to release her from me, . . . something I couldn't do this night.

But the next day of the marathon, Eva herself proposed a different method. She wished to role-play her mother, and to go around the circle, saying to everyone, "I have deprived my children. Do you forgive me?" Eva wrote:

> I began the circle feeling as my mother, up-tight and guilty. I was for-given by some, not by others, forgiven from afar but not with emotion by one girl, forgiven with passion and life by you [she is speaking of me, to whom the description is addressed], and with sadness and crying by another girl. One man said "Could you have done otherwise?"—a hard question to answer. And one man who was acting as my brother said, "You don't want my forgiveness." Marilyn said, "I can't answer you. You're Eva, not your mother," which was true because along the circle I

became myself and no longer my mother needing forgiveness. I was me, feeling happy, light, womanly, and ready to go on being a woman!

When a marathon participant goes around the circle, the therapist is always included, and it is my policy to adopt the same attitude which I request of the others—that is, I follow my own impulse whether or not to respond, and with occasional exceptions I voice my personal feelings. When Eva, in the role of her mother, asked my forgiveness, I found myself saying without any conscious foreplanning, "Yes, I know Eva well. I am her therapist and I have worked with her in many marathons. She could not be the way she is unless you had given her good things too, along with the bad. And I forgive you." This was so meaningful to me that my voice broke. A group member suggested that I might be thinking of my own need to forgive my parents, or to be forgiven by my children. This may have been so, but I was aware only that I was expressing one of my strongest convictions: everyone who has the strength to reach toward self-fulfillment, by seeking psychotherapy or by any other means, has sometime been loved enough to develop the capacity for hope. Eva's mother could not possibly have been all witch.

With special clarity, this last episode illuminated the characteristic progression from pathology to health in the procedure of going around the circle, as shown by Eva's words, "Along the circle I became myself."

It is noteworthy also that Eva could not achieve forgiveness of her mother when she attempted to use another group member as a mother-surrogate, but only when she herself took the role of the mother who must be forgiven. Nor did she feel released when the witch-mother was in fantasy sent off on a broomstick, but only when the introjected mother was symbolically invited back and treated with compassion. The toxic introject, even when it is experienced as alien, is to some extent an aspect of the self.

Rather often, patients will say "I must get rid of this part of myself, I must kill it," [4] when they were speaking of an aspect of themselves which they dislike. To me this appears as either an indirect expression of self-destructiveness, or else as a search for an impossibly easy method of getting rid of conflicts. Exorcism is a poetic symbol which aptly describes a therapeutic process but does not explain it.

[4] Therapists who use an active approach and who recognize the value of working with symbols sometimes encourage a patient to vent his rage on a couch or pillow by beating "this part of myself" to death. I have seen this work effectively, but to me the pretense of self-beating gives a misleading impression of the actual dynamics. In my opinion this approach works because the patient feels that he is finally asserting himself against the original traumatogenic childhood figure, not against "part of himself." Rage turned against the self implies depression or masochism, not freedom.

The toxic introject is a paradox. It is alien to self-fulfillment, yet it is also a part of the self. What appears to be an inner demon is actually a system of pseudovalues, insincere or self-defeating behavior, and conflicted or unacceptable feelings. The toxic introject, the inner demon, must be acknowledged as part of the personality, but as part of the personality which can be modified and outgrown. It was not really Eva's mother who kept her from relating to men, but the half-conscious values and standards which her mother had conveyed to her and which Eva could only partially discard.

Role-playing of the introject appears to undo the dissociation by which victims of the toxic introject seek to separate themselves from its influence. The voice which spoke from within to Marnie, and the monster figure of Sam's nightmare, were actually dissociated parts of themselves. Once the dissociation is undone and the toxic introject is acknowledged, the energy expended in maintaining the dissociation is freed. The witch, the demon, the enemy, the monster appears to be exorcised; but what actually happens is that a fixed energy system becomes mobile and is henceforward available to the individual in his search for self-fulfillment.

REFERENCES

Balint, M. *The basic fault.* London: Tavistock Publications, 1968.

Bindrim, P. The nude marathon. *Psychotherapy: Theory, Research and Practice,* September 1968.

Cleckley, H. *Three faces of Eve.* New York: McGraw-Hill, 1957.

Corsini, R. J. *Roleplaying in psychotherapy.* Chicago: Aldine, 1966.

Fairbairn, W. R. D. *An object-relations theory of the personality.* New York: Basic Books, 1952.

Fairbairn, W. R. D. Synopsis of an object-relations theory of the personality. *International Journal of Psycho-Analysis,* 1963, *44.*

Fenichel, O. *Psychoanalytic theory of neurosis.* New York: W. W. Norton, 1945.

Freud, A. *The ego and the mechanisms of defense.* London: Hogarth, 1936.

Moreno, J. L. *Psychodrama.* New York: Beacon House, 1946.

Nelson, M. C., Nelson, B., Sherman, M. H., & Strean, H. S. *Roles and paradigms in psychotherapy.* New York: Grune & Stratton, 1968.

Perls, F. S. *Gestalt therapy verbatim.* Lafayette, Calif.: Real People Press, 1969.

Prince, M. The dissociation of a personality. In A. A. Roback (Ed.), *Clinical and experimental studies in personality.* Cambridge, Mass.: Science-Art Publications, 1938.

Segal, H. *Introduction to the work of Melanie Klein.* London: Heinemann, 1964.

8 MARATHONS FOR ADOLESCENTS

by Barry Sherman

Marathons for special populations (families, couples, business executives, teachers) are reported in the literature, as summarized in Chapter 11. To my knowledge, though adolescents may participate in special marathons such as those conducted for families or for drug users, no account has been given of group processes in a marathon for adolescents who are suffering primarily from the intrinsic difficulties of being adolescent.

Barry Sherman's description of adolescent marathons is especially thoughtful in its discrimination between groups composed of younger teenagers and those for older teenagers, and the difference between them and marathons for adults. The difficulty of working with this age group, and the urgent necessity which many youngsters have for help in finding themselves, make Dr. Sherman's contribution of immediate practical importance.

Readers may be puzzled over the lack of attention to drug usage among adolescents. Dr. Sherman tells me that, although frequently the teenagers will discuss their use of marihuana, he deliberately refrains from raising this as a problem or emphasizing it when it arises. He feels that the development of identity on the one hand, and ability to communicate on the other, are the central problems for adolescents. Hence he directs himself to what he regards as basic issues. Youngsters for whom drug usage has in itself become a primary problem are usually treated in groups which are focussed specifically on this syndrome.

Perhaps I should add that, in my opinion, no one should attempt to lead an adolescent marathon unless, like Dr. Sherman, they have had considerable experience in working with adolescents on an individual basis.

—Elizabeth E. Mintz

The adolescent is an ever changing creature. In the most poetic sense, his developmental task is to emerge. In our culture, this process follows a pattern involving several relatively distinct stages. The adolescent marathon must respect these stages, and to a great extent is shaped by them.

Two kinds of adolescent marathons must be distinguished; that in which the age range is approximately 14–17, with the mean age 15, which will be called the younger adolescent group; and that in which the age range is 17–20, with a mean of 18½, which will be called the older adolescent group. In this discussion they will be compared and contrasted with marathons for adults, in which the age range is variable and usually unplanned.

In adult marathons there are essentially four stages: (1) getting acquainted, establishing relationships and expectations, and at the same time using and displaying individual defenses in a new setting; (2) a reaction to the disappointment that magical expectations have not been met, usually anger, boredom, or depression; (3) a shift in the defensive structure allowing unresolved feelings to surface into awareness, usually experienced as abreaction, catharsis, or insight; and (4) the synthesis, conceptualization of the cathartic experience and a concomitant change in behavior, trying out being with one's self and others in the group in a new way.[1]

As with any treatment situation, the marathon experience begins before the marathon itself. Reasons for coming, fantasies, expectations, and even the first phone contact affect what will happen later. Adults usually come to marathons of their own choice. In contrast, although many of the younger adolescents are already in treatment, they are usually there because their parents sent them or because they have been referred for therapy by the school; similarly, many come to marathons because of the urging of their parents or other authority figures. Another group of young adolescents phone eagerly because their parents have been involved in marathons, and sharing in the mystique of the marathon becomes a symbol of "the grownup thing to do."

Such reasons usually become clear during the first phone contact. A young boy or girl calls up and says something like "Hello, I hear you're having a marathon. I want to come." The name is rarely offered spontaneously. I reply that I am leading a marathon in the near future, and ask how they heard about it and why they want to come. By the time this conversation is finished, I usually have a fairly good idea who the adolescent is and whether he is coming for his own sake or because of pressure. If he and the referral source are totally unknown to me, I

---

[1] These four stages, described in different words and conceptualized differently by different writers, have been noted by nearly all marathon leaders. Dr. Sherman is undoubtedly correct in calling attention to the disappointment over lack of magic which may trigger the first angry outburst, but I would be more inclined to emphasize anger as a defense against the threat of intimacy and of self-revelation.—E. E. M.

ask if he'd like to come in and see me for a few minutes. Then I tell him the fee, ask him to discuss this with his parents and call me back. Surprisingly seldom do the parents ask to speak with me.

Quite a different process and experience will be undergone by the youngster in a marathon, depending on whether he is in a younger or older adolescent group. In the younger group, a participant rarely acknowledges specific problems beforehand. Also, since most of his peers are not in therapy, his contact with therapy may in itself be taken as an affirmation that the internal chaos which is usually experienced at fifteen years old actually does mean that there is something wrong; he is different from his friends. This sense of being different is very strong and must be dealt with during the marathon. The most effective method is for the leaders to talk about their own feelings of anxiety or tension, as openly as possible and as soon as possible. This encourages the adolescents to talk about themselves and, insofar as the leaders and other members acknowledge some similar feelings, this gives each the assurance that what's going on inside him is not unique.

Adolescents in the older group most often come not because they are sent, or because it is "the thing to do," but for reasons of their own. They do not succumb so easily to parental pressure. In comparison to younger adolescents, who are involved in searching through their inner turmoil for aspects of personality which bear some correspondence to outside standards, the older adolescents have usually established a personality style and come looking for its validation. Also, youngsters in this older group are often more able to discriminate and articulate their problems and can be more explicit in identifying problem areas.

The overall tenor of premarathon fantasies of younger adolescents is fearful, as vividly demonstrated by the number of last-minute cancellations. Once we received a telegram just as the marathon was about to start. The wire read, "I'm sorry but I'm just too chicken." Older adolescent fantasies tend to be positive, adventuresome and exciting, while the fantasies of adults are hopeful but heavily laden with anxiety. The younger adolescents want confirmation that their inner sense of chaos is not "crazy." They may also be seeking justification for their feelings of diffuse anger. Older adolescents hope for confirmation of the social personality role which they have chosen and sometimes for a chance to work out specific problems. Adults hope for increased intimacy and better ways of handling anger and its expression.

A major purpose of the marathon experience, as I see it, is confrontation with the maladaptive aspects of the individual's defensive structure. Therefore it is crucial to compare the defensive makeup of the two adolescent age groups and to see how it differs from that of the adult groups.

In the younger adolescent group, individual defenses have not yet crystallized. The major task of this age group is to separate from parents and establish an autonomous identity. The traditional way to do this is to move from the nuclear family into peer group settings and form an identification with the peer group. This provides transitional support on the road to individuation and also allows for psychic borrowing. By this I mean an upsurge of transient imitative behavior, acting like someone in the group because it seems attractive or effective, or acting very much *not* like someone in the group for the same reasons. In becoming an adolescent, the child moves away from his family and into the peer group where he begins actively to question who he is and develop his definition of selfhood. This is an anxiety-provoking time, aggravated by physiological changes during puberty, by the emergence of sexual feelings, and by the reactivation of the Oedipal conflict. The younger adolescent has not developed adequate mechanisms for dealing with all these new feelings and relies on the group to bind his anxiety. He can focus on the group rather than on his own inner turmoil. The group involvement deflects energy which would otherwise be used up in too much isolated introspection, and the group also prohibits one-to-one interactions on a frighteningly deep level. The group itself, and the activity of grouping, become the major defense at this age.[2]

Older adolescents are at a different stage. These older teenagers, by and large, have found a more distinct way of being themselves and no longer depend to the same extent on the peer group for safety and identification. As a rule, their major preoccupation is how to validate the role each has adopted. Stylistically, each tends to exaggerate the statement, "This is who I am." Although this statement will usually undergo changes in the next few years, at this point it is loudly and clearly acclaimed as the definite, ultimate ME. In some ways it is analogous to first love; in some ways it *is* first love. One has found out who one is, and wants to let everyone know. The feeling is vibrant and alive and unlike any previous experience. If it's painful, it's the most painful thing in the world. If it's beautiful, its beauty is of a uniqueness which defies description.

Well-established adult defenses are much more subtle. Adaptive or maladaptive, they are comfortable old friends. On some level, adults usually come to a marathon wanting to be rid of some of their maladaptive defenses. Nonetheless, these defenses are hauled out at the beginning of a marathon as faithful standbys. Whether we want them or not, they're the best we've got, and in a new setting we put what seems to be our best foot forward.[3]

The younger adolescents, however, do not have this option. They have no comfortable individualized set of defenses. Consequently the

---

[2] Blos (1962), speaking of this in a slightly different way, calls this defense "uniformism."

[3] This is another way of describing the phenomenon for which I have used the metaphor of the social mask.—E. E. M.

beginning of their marathon is extremely different from that of the adult groups.

What the younger adolescents do have to help them is their ability to group. This is their major defense, and as soon as they come together with the understanding that they are to spend a considerable length of time together, their automatic and facile response is to group. This begins to happen as soon as the second participant arrives. The two, then others as they arrive, begin at once to chat in a way which seems intimate and comfortable, usually beginning with questions like "I wonder what's going to happen here?" and "Where do you come from?" and then going on to discussions about school, rock groups, and so on. As new members arrive, there is practically no acknowledgment of the new person, but instead there is immediate inclusion of him in the group. Usually the arrival will pick up the conversation at once and behave as if he had been there from the first. There is an *appearance* of sharing, ease, and openness which may superficially resemble the final phase of the adult marathon. Frequently I feel left out during this time. Except for questions such as "How many are coming?" and "When do we start?" I am ignored, and rather than insisting upon my role in the group, it seems to me essential to remain apart and not interfere. Both the grouping behavior and the apparent exclusion of the leader are in sharp contrast to adult marathons. There, if participants do not know each other, there is usually a tense silence or superficial chitchat as well as attempts to establish some contact with the leader.

Manifestly, the younger adolescent group seems in the beginning to resemble the final stage of an adult marathon: open, trusting and sharing. This is not in fact the case. For these teenagers, identity in the adult sense does not yet exist. My feeling is that the best possible goal for each adolescent during the course of the marathon is to move closer to individuation and to be less dependent on peer group identification. Only when an individual has defined himself emotionally is he free to share with others. In other words, my goal for the younger adolescents is to reach the *first* stage of the adult marathon: that of people who know who they are and can relate to others without losing a sense of self.

The older adolescent group is sharply different. These older teenagers are concerned with validating their self-concepts and wish to use the group for comparison and acceptance. As a result, each participant begins the experience as a separate and even isolated individual. A striking example occurred in a marathon which I conducted for college sophomores in a midwestern university. These older adolescents had elected to live together and take classes together, forming a living-learning commune within the campus setting, and thirty-five of them moved into a common domicile. During the first week of their project, they requested a marathon, which was attended by about twenty participants.

I began by asking each of them to speak briefly with their neighbors on either side, then introduce the person on their right to the group. To my surprise, it became apparent that most of the participants did not know facts about or even the names of most the people with whom they had made a year-long commitment to live. They seemed unaware that this was at all strange, exclaiming, "Oh, I'm glad to know your name," or, "I thought I'd seen you around this week." For many of them, the major experience was to display themselves for approval or disapproval. This was manifested in the introductory go-around by one fellow who said "The person on my right is Jim . . . oh, no, that's my name."

These superposes of selfhood in the older group are various. For example, some adolescents are extremely poetic and let everyone know it by being lyrical at every opportunity. Others may be serious, buffoons, overintellectual, or supermen. Each presents his position whenever an opening occurs.

It may well be that one of the goals of responsible maturity is to be intimate with others while taking one's own identity for granted. But the older adolescent isn't there yet, and to force intimacy upon him prematurely is deleterious. It may encourage him to assume a pose, taking an "as if" stance of intimacy, and it robs him of the time he needs to define more securely for himself who he is. Also, the marathon setting is threatening because of its regressive pull back to the grouping defense of the younger adolescent period. Therefore, in the early stages of the marathon I do not interpret these superstatements of Who I Am, nor do I pick up the other members' comments about them.[4]

The first stage of the younger adolescent marathon is, then, characterized by grouping; for the older adolescents by exaggerated statements of self-definition; and for adults by the display of their characteristic defense patterns. For adults, the second stage is usually anger and boredom combined with criticism of one another and of the leader.[5] In the younger adolescent group, the second stage is totally different. Participants are not critical of one another, as adults may be at this point. The younger an individual is, the less likely he is to evaluate behavior as deviant or maladaptive. The notion of "craziness" is acceptable and almost commonplace. The fourteen- or fifteen-year-old is much too concerned with his own way of being in the world to be openly judgmental about others, especially in a setting where he himself feels insecure. Also, a major philosophical tenet of today's youth is "Do your own thing," and this contributes to tolerance for others' behavior. In the second stage of the younger adolescent group, therefore, anger exists, but the youngsters

[4] Technically, there is an exception. When a superpose is too blatantly exaggerated, it is no longer a plea for personality validation but a cry for help and requires therapeutic attention.

[5] As described in Chapter 1.—E. E. M.

are unwilling to express it directly. Also, these younger teenagers are somewhat predisposed to view the leader as a good parent-substitute, and most of them are accustomed to following adult orders because of school indoctrination. Rebelliousness and anger therefore, may, take indirect forms. The following is a good example of this reaction.

Ben was a fifteen-year-old who attended a special school for emotionally disturbed children. During the first few hours of the marathon he talked often, always with a smile, making comments which were almost always disruptive. He could not tolerate attention nor could he endure it if the group concentrated on anyone else. He would, with exquisite sensitivity, sabotage any interaction between participants which promised to be fruitful. He would make jarring comments if anyone tried to share a feeling or idea with the group. After this had been pointed out to him several times, I asked him to try *not* to say whatever came into his mind but instead to withhold it for a count of fifteen, during which time he was to think about whether his intended comment had anything to do with whatever was going on, or whether it was designed to stop whatever was happening. With obvious discomfort and moderate success, Ben went along with my suggestion for about half an hour. An hour or two later, sensing anger toward me from Judy, another participant, I asked her what was going on. Judy replied, "I'm angry because you told Ben to shut up. I thought we could say or do anything we wanted to here!" Without exception, all other participants agreed loudly and adamantly, and all made their anger toward me very clear. I restated my reasons for my suggestion to Ben but admitted that I might have been wrong. Then I asked why, since everyone had been annoyed, no one had mentioned it before. The response was, "Well, you're the leader and we figured that you knew what you were doing and it must be right. But it still wasn't nice."

In an adult marathon this kind of reasoning, though not unheard-of, is less frequent. There are always one or two participants who are willing to attack the leader if they disapprove. Unquestioned belief in leadership fortunately dies an early death for most people.

Another feature of the younger adolescent marathons is underscored by the group's reaction to Ben. His disruptiveness was apparent, but Ben's right to "do his own thing" was considered paramount.

Will, another fifteen-year-old, was amazingly adept at exploring any area of feeling that came up. If anxiety was discussed, Will would immediately talk about his anxiety and work himself into an anxious state. The same held true for fear, loving, intimacy, boredom, or whatever feeling emerged in the group. The hollowness of his experience was appalling. It became clear that Will was working for approval, especially from the leaders. His motto was, "I'm being the very best possible whatever I'm supposed to be." Explicit permission for Will to be angry would have led to sham anger, because he would have felt it was expected. This was an extreme example of the need for adult approbation which still motivates younger adolescents, even though they are in the process of trying to separate from parents and parental ideals. If the youngster is to be given a chance to find his own center and direction, it is crucial to work with this kind of behavior.

With Will, my task was to ignore his efforts to please me or imitate me, and instead to encourage and approve any spontaneous interaction with his peers. He finally became aware of this and said, "You don't like it when I agree with you, do you?" I told him that I did not, that it felt unreal to me and made me feel tight inside. He looked very surprised and said, "It makes me feel tight inside too. But you know, it's just like what I always do with my father. I think he'll like me if I'm the way he is, but it makes me feel tight inside too." He then talked for some time about these feelings, and the group identified and became involved in terms of their own experiences.

When Will finished what seemed to be his first genuine communication (during which time I was as quiet as possible), I asked him how he felt at that moment. He said he felt good. I replied that I, too, felt good when I shared feelings with friends. During the rest of the weekend Will was less involved with winning my approval and more concerned with his peers.

In this second stage of the younger adolescent marathon, the youngsters are usually caught between a need to comply with the implicit demand for honest self-expression and their reluctance to express anger toward one another and the leaders. This conflict brings about anxiety, nervousness, or boredom. Since the group is new and does not have much autonomous strength, the group defense collapses under this increased pressure. Individual contributions begin to characterize the second stage. The underlying theme of these statements always is the question, "Who am I?"

An example of this kind of statement comes from fifteen-year-old Diane. When the tension mounted, Diane made a confession. "A lot of what I said before was just lies. I lie all the time. I lie to get noticed. I lie to get my parents to say No to me so I'll know they love me, and here I just lied because it was a habit. I tell so many stories I don't know who I am most of the time." She also mentioned that she was considering taking LSD and getting pregnant, seemingly in a search for some kind of self-defining experience.

Diane was questioned by the group in a very sympathetic and understanding way, and I encouraged her to examine the feelings behind the lying, telling her that I didn't believe that she had been lying in the group just because it was a habit. She agreed but could not continue. After several exercises, such as asking her to make up a deliberate lie and tell us how she felt as she was doing it, Diane said, "I lie because I'm frightened that there's really nothing there." This was said with great feeling and some weeping. Diane then seemed relieved and was told by the group that they felt she was real even when she was not lying. Then she began spontaneously to talk about the lying as a way of competing with her brother. Another member was then able to tell about a superficial suicide attempt, undertaken ". . . so my parents would notice me and because I was bored." She too was able to arrive at a better articulated understanding of why she had done this. One youngster's personal statement often encourages others, even though the manifest content may be totally unrelated.

My request to Diane that she deliberately tell a lie is an example of the way in which games and exercises can sometimes help a youngster to make a personal, individual statement. Most fourteen- and fifteen-year-olds, when asked about their thoughts and feelings, respond with some variation of "I don't know." This is partly true and partly a defense against the anxiety which accompanies inner exploration. A simple task, such as requesting a member to go around and tell everyone in the group how he feels, or what he likes or dislikes about each one in turn, sometimes helps to speed up the process of self-exploration. Since grouping is in itself a primary defense for these younger teenagers, group games are not used, although they may be useful with the older adolescents.

After the participants have shared their individual statements, the group continues to be very different from adult marathons. There is no coming together as a result of this self-expression. Instead, tension and vague uneasiness pervade the room. This state of malaise leads to the third stage of the marathon: experiencing and expressing anger. The youngsters are disappointed that they do not feel changed and angry at the leaders for not having changed them. At first this anger is expressed rather tentatively. Exploration of its unconscious dynamics is inadvisable. However, it is productive to encourage fuller *expression* of the anger, as for example by throwing a pillow, encouraging someone to pound on a couch, or lie down on it and kick his heels if he feels like it (and even if he doesn't). This releases the physical tension which the younger adolescents often experience and gives explicit permission for them to express their feelings in this setting.

Despite the fact that I don't press for information about the underlying causes for the anger, some of this content comes out spontaneously. The artificial yell becomes real and is put into words. Anger toward parents emerges, and even greater anger toward siblings. Initially I was apprehensive about using exercises to help the expression of anger, fearing that the adolescents would experience the games as either phony or frightening. However, not only is this technique experienced as positive, but frequently one participant after another asks if he can yell and scream also. Feelings of anger and chaos are so close to the surface at this time in life that permission to express them is a liberating experience.

After the ventilation of anger, the tension decreases markedly, and a sense of the group again develops, less defensive than in the first stage. Participants share personal information and ask factual questions. Sometimes they express satisfaction in such phrases as "Boy, do I feel different! . . . Something really special happened . . . I feel like a new person." This fourth stage of the cycle is like a combination of the first and last phases of an adult marathon, in that there is a closeness, a sense of something enriching having happened, and a sharing of biographical information.

The striking and unique feature of these younger adolescent groups is that these four stages occur more rapidly than in other marathons and are repeated several times in the course of the entire marathon experience. The breakthroughs of the second and third stages occur after two or three hours, rather than in the tenth or fifteenth hour, as in the case with adult marathons. What appears to be insight and working-through is actually more a tentative exploration of the possibilities of feeling safe in making a personal statement.

The cycle of the younger adolescent marathon, then, is in some respects opposite to that of the adult groups. These teenagers go through (1) an easy and fluid sense of groupness; (2) individual insight and self-defining statement; (3) expressions of anger; and (4) a less defensive grouping and the sharing of biographical information. All this will happen in four or five hours. It is, in a sense, an experiment in moving toward maturity. This may account for the lack of a sense of authenticity in the enthusiastic "Boy, do I feel different" statements.

The remainder of the marathon is a repetitive cycling of the four stages which have already occurred. Several complete cycles take place during the weekend, with less time spent on the amorphous group of the first phase and on feelings of anger in the third phase. Usually problems which have been identified in the first cycle will continue to be worked on, and adolescents who did not make individual contributions during the first cycle will probably do so in the second. Each time a youngster deals with his problems, they become less frightening. Each time the fourth phase of biographical sharing occurs, it provides an opportunity to try out more comfortable and adaptive defenses. At the very end, there is a feeling of warmth and of having shared an adventure.

These cycles have a natural, almost autonomous rhythm. At the end of each cycle I suggest a rest period of fifteen or twenty minutes. When we reconvene, I am frequently startled by the extent to which we seem to be back at the beginning all over again. There may even be an unwillingness to refer to what has occurred. With each successive cycle I become more directive in encouraging individual statements, and after the first cycle I focus less on the expression of anger if it does not arise spontaneously. With each cycle I feel that the communications have more depth.

With this age group, however, it is essential not to probe. The goal for younger adolescents is *not* to dig down into the unconscious for material which has made behavior go awry or lead to anxiety, fear, or unhappiness. The youngster in the throes of puberty is more in touch with his unconscious than he wants to be. His job is not to tear down maladaptive defenses but to develop adequate defenses. Hence these marathons lack some of the intensity of the adult or the older adolescent groups, and they are more tiring and less immediately rewarding for the leaders, but in my opinion this is what the young teenager needs.

Since it is important to avoid the weakening of defenses by fatigue, I provide frequent breaks and rest periods, and a full eight-hour break for sleep. As many youngsters travel some distance from home to attend the marathon, they are accommodated at a hotel, three in a room. I inform them that I am also staying at the same hotel. In this way, although it is not stated explicitly, they know that I am available in an emergency. Also, though again this is never made explicit, there is a reassurance against the possibility of sexual involvement, which at this age is usually both a threat and a challenge.

Since the external reality of the younger adolescent involves dealing with his parents, co-leadership is especially important for this age group. In general, the leadership of a man and a woman therapist is recommended for most marathons.[6]

As described above, the first stage of the older adolescent marathon is quite different from the amorphous grouping of the younger teenagers. These older adolescents are very much concerned with personality validation. Their major preoccupation is not the question "Who am I?" but rather the statement, "This is who I am . . . damn it!" Except for this major theme, these marathons resemble adult marathons more than they resemble the younger groups. Most importantly, cycling does not occur.

The second stage of the older adolescent group, like that of most adult marathons, is marked by opposition and anger, though with a continuation of self-defining statements. Negative feelings are frequently first directed toward the leaders. A typical example occurred with the marathon for college students which was mentioned above. I suggested that they play a game of breaking into triads, in which each member would get to know the other two. After ten minutes they would decide which of the three would leave the group, that member then moving into another triad. Eventually, though the instructions are given one at a

---

[6] My warm acknowledgement is due to Vivian Guze and Felice Gans, with one of whom most of these marathons have been conducted.

time and the conclusion of the exercise is not known beforehand, each member returns to his original triad. Adult groups often have great difficulty in deciding who is to leave the triad in this exercise, but these difficulties may be even greater with the older adolescents. In one marathon, two of the triads flatly refused to break up. After the exercise was over, those who had not moved were vehement in declaring their "right to do what they wanted," not to be artificial, and not to break up a meaningful discussion. Those who did not participate accused the game, and by implication the leaders, of being stupid and irrelevant. They would not acknowledge the statement that something good had happened which was made by those triads that had gone along with the instructions.

As with adult marathons, the second phase in older adolescent groups is characterized by anger. The anger is usually first released as a way of challenging the leadership or, just as frequently, as a response to someone else's self-defining statements. For example, one superman in a marathon was quick to take his superrole whenever possible. When a young girl mentioned that she was frightened of sex, Marty said at once that although he usually didn't have affairs with girls like this, with the few he had known he was warm, gentle, understanding, and patient but urging, and the girl would always finally come round. When someone else talked about academic concerns, Marty mentioned sympathetically that although he had always been an A student, he could appreciate academic worries. When a very idealistic young girl spoke of feeling guilty because so many poor people had to do dreary work every day, Marty offered the remark that many of the jobs he had had "over the years" were boring and tedious (making me look at him closely to verify that, in fact, he was only eighteen). As was to be expected, the group finally became furious with Marty, to his absolute surprise. By my acting as his alter ego, according to the psychodramatic method of having someone speak for the unverbalized feelings of another group member, his underlying anxiety and need for approval were made clearer. This was helpful both to him and to other group members.

The third phase of intense emotional involvement is similar to that of adult groups except that it is more intense, and frequently the encounters are very dramatic. An example is the story of Michael. My intervention here was a response to an emergency, and not typical of marathon techniques for this age group, but the flavor and intensity of the experience is representative.

Michael's identity stance was different from the average, though by no means unique. He was Tortured And Intense. He drew attention to himself in quiet ways, always looking intense and fidgeting in such a way as to indicate that he had been holding himself back for a long time. His voice was so beautifully mellifluous that it sounded pained. Sometimes he began to speak, then stopped and shook his head and gazed downward. At one point he jumped up and left the room, and when he did not return, I declared a fifteen-minute break and went to look for him.

When I found him pacing a corridor, he told me that he had become extremely anxious and had to get out. He said he knew many people felt they were crazy, but he *knew* he was *really* crazy. After we had talked a little, I told him that we would now be starting the marathon again, and that although he did not have to speak, it sometimes helped people if they did talk. To give Michael an opening, I resumed the marathon by asking for a brief statement of what everybody was feeling, beginning as always with a statement of my own feelings.

At Michael's turn to speak, he said he felt very alienated from the group. Another young man asked what he meant. Michael said he didn't feel a part of what was going on and was not sure he wished to. The questioner became angry, and after a brief quarrel Michael jumped up and hit the other young man with a pillow. Then he looked very troubled and said he did not want to continue. His opponent said that he felt better about Michael now, and we agreed that this was enough for the time being.

Sometime later, when another member asked Michael if something was wrong, Michael said in a dead voice "I think I'm going crazy," in a way that turned the group immediately silent. I went over and sat directly in front of him and asked what was going on inside him. After a long silence, he said that he felt as if he were going to burst or fall apart. I held out my arms and he fell into them and began to sob. After a few minutes he leaned back and said he didn't want to be held. I asked him what he wanted. He said he wanted either to fight or to be cuddled like a baby. I said he could not have both things at the same time and asked him which he wanted now. He said that being held was scary, and he wanted to fight.

I suggested a sensitivity game. Each of us stood up, placed our hands on the other's shoulders, and pushed as hard as we could. I asked the other men in the group to stand behind us and keep us from falling. We began to push each other. I am four inches taller and fifty pounds heavier than Michael, but within seconds I was across the room, the wall of men going with me and Michael pushing without a stop. We finally worked our way back to the middle of the room and after about five minutes we both fell to the floor exhausted. Between gasps I asked Michael how he was feeling, and he said, "Better, I guess, but it isn't enough."

I said, laughing, "Please, I don't have enough breath to fight any more."

He smiled and said he didn't mean that. I asked him what he did mean. There was a long silence. Finally he said in a panicky voice, "I can't see you."

I said, "What do you see?"

There was another long silence, then I said, "We're too far away from each other" and moved closer, directly in front of him, and asked him again what he saw.

He said, "I can't see."

I took his head in my hands and held it so he had to look in my face. After a while, I again asked what he saw. He said, "I see the devil." His pupils began to dilate and constrict rapidly and once or twice his eyes started to roll up until only the whites were showing.

I asked him what he thought I might be feeling, and he said, "You hate me."

Truthfully, I answered that I was feeling close and warm toward him. He said, "My father hates me."

I replied, "I'm not your father and I feel very close to you right now. I don't hate you at all." I asked again what he saw, and finally he said, "I see you."

Michael now began to tell us that he had been in therapy for years, that he always felt as if he were held together by a thin string and he was always afraid he would crack. I told him that I was glad he could see me now, and not his father, and that this made him stronger. I said the more he could see what was really there, the stronger he would be, and that this would happen every time he saw things clearly. He said he felt much better. I looked around the room (suddenly aware that I had tuned out everyone but Michael for the past twenty minutes) and became aware that many of the young men and women were visibly moved.

The importance of this experience for Michael could be seen in his greater ease and participation during the remainder of the marathon. After we finished the weekend, when everyone was leaving, Michael said playfully to me, with a big smile, "So long, Dad!"

The episode of Michael exemplifies some basic points. His pain was very real in the here-and-now, and therefore I stayed with him in the here-and-now, trying to help him feel less paralyzed by his anxiety and more able to organize his immediate perceptual world. Since I knew that he was also in individual treatment, I did not try to give him a more complete understanding of how his feelings toward his father interfered with his present functioning. Had he not been seeing another therapist, I would have spoken with him privately at more length after the marathon.[7]

---

[7] This was a transitory psychotic episode, which can occur in any marathon but is probably more frequent among the adolescent groups. Two serious mistakes could have been made: Michael's theatrical gloom could have been misunderstood as sheer histrionics, rather than as the cry for help which it really was; and depth interpretations could have been made, rather than the wise and skillful decision of Dr. Sherman to reinforce Michael's sense of reality. This is an example of the type of episode which requires an understanding of psychodynamics on the part of the marathon leader.—E. E. M.

This experience also illustrates the need for two therapists as leaders. Michael required intense individual attention to help him with disruptive feelings which to some extent are experienced by most young men. The ambivalence toward his father, expressed in his simultaneous wish to be held by me and to fight with me, evoked strong feelings in most of the other young men, and for many of them this became the dominant theme during the remainder of the marathon. Had another leader not been available, I could not have engaged Michael intensively and exclusively, as he needed. It is also important that the co-leader was a woman. In discussing how she felt about the incident with Michael, my colleague helped the young women get in touch with their own ambivalence toward their parents.

The fourth phase of the older adolescent marathon is, again, similar to adult marathons, although more intense. As with most experiences, the eighteen-year-old is both passionate and defended against his passion. The sense of closeness and sharing is acknowledged with an intensity which is both joyful and awesome.

Experientially the older adolescent marathon is, in many ways, more like the adult group than the younger adolescent group. The goals for each of these three experiences, however, are somewhat different. The goal of the younger adolescent marathon is to help each individual develop appropriate new defenses—or strengthen old ones—for his expanded life situation (i.e., adolescence and subsequent adulthood). The goal for the adult group is to replace maladaptive defenses with adaptive ones or to encourage the individual to use current defenses more adaptively.

The goals for the older adolescent marathon include some aspects of the goals for each of these other two groups. Terminating with the grouping defense of early adolescence, to the extent that that's appropriate for a given individual, implies that some other set of defenses has come to take its place. To the extent that an adolescent may need encouragement and support in this transitional period, the marathon may be a setting where he can find it. To the extent that the new defenses which he is trying out are not working effectively, the individual may want help in reversing or changing some of these trends. To the extent that they are adaptive but still too new to be appropriately flexible, he may want to use the marathon time to explore this and hopefully to become more comfortable with himself.

In evaluating feedback from participants in both the younger and older age group, I find that youngsters who are already in individual therapy seem to gain more understanding of their problems. Therapists who are seeing these youngsters concurrently report that the marathon experience seems to consolidate therapeutic gains. Several adolescents who had previously been resistant to individual treatment were able to accept it after a marathon. One adolescent girl, not in therapy, felt that she did not profit at all, and indeed said, "Not only was it worthless, but I was furious for weeks afterwards. I think it was awful." More representative are the words of another participant, who said, "Man, this is like an LSD trip, only better."

REFERENCES

Blos, P. *On adolescence.* New York: Free Press, 1962.

Keniston, K. *The uncommitted: Alienated youth in American society.* New York: Harcourt Brace, 1965.

Keniston, K. *The young radicals.* New York: Harcourt Brace, 1968.

9 BEING A MARATHON LEADER

Conducting marathon encounter groups places special demands upon the leader, offers great rewards, and involves some special difficulties. I do not see how it could ever become a routine professional task. In this chapter, I shall discuss my personal experiences.

It has been pointed out, correctly, that leaders of encounter groups may choose this occupation out of their own needs (Goldman, 1969; Lakin, 1969). Aside from the legitimacy of seeking an occupation which provides personal gratification, it seems to me that the physical and emotional strain of conducting marathons could not be sustained without considerable personal reward. There are less taxing ways to earn a living.

Marathons in which little or no reliance is placed upon routine encounter games are more demanding for the leader. The demands are not intrinsically greater than those required for conducting individual psychotherapy or ongoing therapy groups, but they are different.

If group and leader come together with the intention of recognizing, expressing, and dealing with deep, primary emotions,[1] then the professional qualifications of the leader are similar to those needed by any group therapist—knowledge of individual psychodynamics, knowledge of group dynamics, and the ability to communicate and to understand the communications of others.[2] For the leadership of a marathon, additional

---

[1] As distinguished from groups which meet primarily to clarify and resolve social conflicts. Appropriate training for the leadership of such groups is offered by such institutions as the National Training Laboratories and the Workshop Institute for Living-Learning. Training for leadership must include the ability to recognize temporary or basic emotional disturbance in the group and deal with it so that the group member is not harmed and the group not disrupted. More specialized training, in my opinion, is required to handle such disturbances therapeutically. However, some writers seem to regard the group, even without professional leadership, as sufficiently powerful to offer therapeutic help (Gibb & Gibb, 1968).

[2] The relevance of formal disciplinary training in psychiatry or clinical psychology as a background is a topic of increasing concern, which has been touched upon in Chapter 2. The American Psychological Association is currently attempting to deal with this problem through the formation of an ad hoc Committee on Professional Training "to review criteria for evaluation of new and innovative programs," such as the California School of Professional Psychology. The use of trained paraprofessionals to meet the mental health needs of the community is also being vigorously recommended. More extensive discussion of these topics can be found in most contemporary professional journals (i.e., *Professional Psychology*, Winter, 1970).

personal qualifications include: adequate physical vitality; the ability to accept prolonged intimacy; and the ability to cope with whatever inner feelings are evoked by the strong, unpredictable, constantly changing stimulation of the marathon.

However, the physical vitality required for marathon leadership is not so extraordinary as is sometimes assumed. What is essential is that the marathon leader should be familiar with the needs of his own body. For example, my own preferred time format gives me a free morning for rest and exercise before the marathon begins and eight hours at night for rest and solitude. More vigorous leaders can work without interruption for twenty-four hours or even longer. For me to attempt this would be unfair both to myself and to the participants. It is also essential for a marathon leader to allow sufficient time for family, friends, rest, and recreation during the week. To conduct a marathon group in addition to an ordinary week's workload would be destructive.

If a marathon leader feels ill or extremely fatigued, to the point at which he cannot function effectively, it is appropriate for him to discuss this with the group rather than to conceal his discomfort. Group and leader can then decide together whether he should retire or remain in the room and function as best he can. Co-leadership, among its other advantages, provides a safeguard here, enabling one leader to take over while the other retires. If this happens (it is surprisingly unusual), both leaders must be prepared for a variety of transferential reactions having to do with dependence upon and resentment toward authority.

"I paid for two leaders. Now I just get one."

"I felt safe with *her*. Now she's conked out. I don't feel safe with *you*."

"*He* would have been able to handle this. I don't think *you* can."

"If you're not husky enough to handle a marathon, why give one?"

"Now I feel bad, I feel you got sick because I got so sore at you a while ago. I feel guilty. Maybe you can't take it?"

As with other situations which arise unexpectedly in a marathon, this event may be used constructively, provided that free expression of feeling is not blocked and is shared by the leaders.

A marathon leader must also be familiar with his own emotional needs. Some excellent therapists, capable of deep and genuine emotional involvement with individual patients, acknowledge that they would find it difficult to accept the sustained intimacy of a two- or three-day marathon. Such therapists may work better in the modified time format of the workshop, meeting for several two-hour sessions each day for several consecutive days, with rest periods in between.

These practical considerations are easily settled. Far more complex is the question of under what circumstances, and to what extent, the group leader should reveal personal feelings.

The encounter group leader, particularly within the experiential school of thought, is sometimes seen as "self-disclosing of his own feelings and reactions toward the group as well as sharing his own conflict areas in his personality" (Rachman, 1969). It is assumed that this openness provides immediate feedback for the participants regarding their effect on others and may help them identify areas in which they tend to assume nongenuine social poses. It is further assumed that the freedom and spontaneity of the leader will serve as a model for the participants, encouraging them to reveal themselves with equal freedom.

My personal conviction is that, since the group has accepted me as a leader and is paying a fee not only for my knowledge but also for my total attentiveness, it should not be used as a means by which I can work out my unresolved emotional problems or obtain support for whatever life stress I may be undergoing. If I find myself burdened with acute personal difficulties during the period preceding a marathon, I request a colleague to speak with me for an hour or two in order to relieve my tensions and free my energies for the marathon.

There are, however, three specific occasions on which I choose to share my own difficulties: first, when I am unable to surmount an emotional problem which is interfering with my effectiveness in the group as a whole; second, when I become aware that something in me is interfering with my relationship to an individual in the group; and third, when a particularly dramatic situation in the group seems to demand that I share personal feelings.[3]

Because the marathon in itself is so exciting to me, it happens rarely indeed that I am preoccupied with an external personal difficulty to the extent that my attentiveness and my relationship with the group are impaired. It has, however, happened, and it is usually possible to recognize the signs. Subjectively, my interventions become rather stereotyped. My attention is indeed focussed upon the group, but it is primarily an intellectual involvement, rather than the spontaneous empathy which I feel when I am psychologically in tune with myself. Some groups are so strong in their movement toward self-disclosure and self-actualization that they can function well even with somewhat marginal leadership. In this case, there is no need for me to speak. Other groups sense that something is being concealed in the room, become vaguely uneasy and begin to behave in a withdrawn way, or return to the superficial social pseudo-relatedness of the first phase.

In this case, I inform the group that, to my regret, I am not fully with them. This has nothing to do with them. It has to do with a personal

---

[3] Marathons are less fatiguing now for me than when I began to conduct them six years ago. I believe this is, in part, because I have developed a flexible but fairly consistent approach to the question of how much self-revelation on my part is optimal for the progress of the group, hence need not approach this as a fresh challenge whenever it arises. It must be stressed, however, that my attitude represents an *approach* to the problem and could not possibly be codified as a set of rules; moreover, what is appropriate to my temperament might not suit other marathon therapists.

difficulty which I am facing at the moment. Usually, this revelation in itself is enough to dispel the blockage of interaction and self-expression, and the group resumes its work at a more meaningful level. On a few occasions, the group pauses and its members gaze at me expectantly, and in this case I describe—frankly, although without going into detail— whatever difficulty I am currently facing.

Whenever this has occurred, the group has become able to move again thereafter. It is not necessary for me to ask the group's help in working through my problem, nor would I regard this as appropriate. Often several members seek to be helpful, and in this case I express my appreciation but inform them that the group is not here to offer me assistance, and that I have shared my troubles simply so that they will understand where I am and what I am feeling. Thus far, this approach has always worked, almost magically, for both the group and myself. My preoccupation with my own problem dissolves temporarily; I feel at one with the group, and we go on together.

It is a different situation when an individual member in the group evokes reactions which make it difficult for me to relate to him. To my recollection, no marathon participant has ever elicited an instant antipathy or rejection in me; if this should occur, I would regard it as my personal problem and would not share it with him or with the group, unless I became convinced that his habitual behavior was such as to elicit this reaction, and moreover that he had sufficient ego strength to cope with my feelings.

On many occasions, however, marathon participants express strong negative feelings toward me, particularly in the second and typically hostile phase of the marathon. Usually I am rather exhilarated by this, do not respond with counter-hostility, and regard it as a challenge to work out whatever transferential elements may be involved. On other occasions, I have been hurt or threatened. These occasions do constitute a problem, both on a technical and on a personal level. Let me offer two examples, one of which I believe worked out reasonably well for both the marathon participant and myself, the other of which remained unresolved.

Because of my own background and my own individual conflicts,[4] I am able to accept hot rage more easily than cold criticism. This insight

---

[4] Only a few years ago, some therapists still maintained that "the therapist who practices his profession in a group setting . . . must be completely and thoroughly rid of his own emotional conflicts. . . . If the therapist carries with him an unresolved conflict, if he has some emotional residue still to be worked out, he is vulnerable" (Locke, 1961, ix). Today I believe that the myth of the perfectly secure therapist has generally been discarded, and that most clinicians would consider an awareness of their own personal vulnerabilities as adequate protection against damaging the group by personal limitations. To me it seems impossible, unnecessary, and perhaps even undesirable to reach the stage of such calm self-esteem that no attack of any kind could possibly distress me.

was underscored for me in my experience with Rita, the wife of a psychiatrist, a woman of my own generation who was attending the marathon at the suggestion of her husband. He had participated in a previous marathon, liked my approach, and thought that perhaps I might be helpful to them with their marital tensions.

Rita arrived with a mixture of preliminary feelings. Consciously and sincerely, she hoped that we could establish rapport because she wanted help with her marriage. On the other hand, she resented her husband's pressure to attend the marathon, which she had not really chosen for herself. Perhaps, unconsciously, she also resented her husband's choice of a therapist whom she had never met as someone who might help them.

By chance, several group members began to deal with major emotional conflicts rather early in the marathon, and my involvement with them prevented my being attentive to Rita. Also, she tended to make comments which were always acute and intelligent but which impressed me as so intellectual that they hindered the expression of feeling. Perhaps because of this, and perhaps also in a counter-transferential reaction to her growing antagonism toward me, I suggested several times that she was blocking the free interchange of feeling.

Rather quickly, Rita began to feel completely rejected by me. She withdrew from contact with me, although she was able to maintain contact with other group members, some of whom tried to point out that I was not really treating her in a rejecting manner. One of the group members suggested that Rita and I should embrace—a suggestion which both of us rightly declined on the grounds that we would be faking. She became more and more critical, not only of my attitude toward her, but of my activity in the group in general. At the same time, she was able to derive some emotional release, especially in the area of her chronically inhibited breathing, through interaction with other group members, and acknowledged this with satisfaction.

With some discomfort, I gradually became aware that Rita was hurting my feelings, not so much by her criticisms as by her withdrawal. After an inner debate, I told the group that although I had not felt rejecting toward Rita at the beginning, I was now indeed beginning to react by withdrawing from her in turn. I acknowledged that, because of my own hang-ups, cold withdrawn hostility was particularly difficult for me to endure.[5] After this, it became possible for Rita and myself to speak to one another with a greater degree of openness and warmth. The

[5] This is an example of the principle, which I try to follow, of sharing my individual problems with the group only insofar as it is judged helpful to them in expressing their own feelings. I did not discuss the aspects of my background which made cold criticism especially painful, but only told the group that this was a special sensitivity which I had never been able to overcome.

impasse was never fully resolved, but when the marathon ended, Rita expressed the feeling that it had been a worthwhile experience.

There have been a few occasions which I refrained from expressing my own emotional reactions although, in retrospect, it seems to me that their expression would have been better for the participant, the group, and myself. An example is that of a young man who had entered the marathon through a contact with my co-therapist, and who produced an elaborate fantasy about me. Although he had heard indirectly that I had a family, he refused to believe this. He remarked woundingly that I "must have been quite pretty when young," and fantasied that at sixteen I had been very much in love, had been rejected, and since then had striven for professional status, hating men and having nothing to do with them. He saw me as a sarcastic, disappointed, dried-up woman with a bitter sense of humor. At the same time, this group member perceived my co-therapist,[6] an exceptionally self-assertive man, as a delicate and wistful personality, who took his greatest pleasure in growing flowers. My co-therapist took the paradigmatic position (Nelson, Nelson, Sherman, & Strean, 1968) [7] and congratulated the young man on having understood us both so well and so completely. Perhaps this ironical position was ultimately advantageous to the patient (who was in concurrent individual treatment) in helping him work through his attitudes toward male and female authority figures.

In retrospect, however, I realized that the wound to my feminine narcissism had paralyzed me and had prevented me from helping him explore his fantasies constructively. If I had been able to admit that I felt wounded, it might have opened up new areas for exploration. Only afterward did I realize that, although nothing of what he imagined had actually occurred in my life history, it was almost exactly like my own adolescent fantasies of the worst fate that could possibly befall me. After this insight, I am less vulnerable to attacks on my femininity in marathons and can deal with them more appropriately.

The third kind of occasion on which it seems appropriate and even necessary for me to share personal feelings is when a situation in the group taps my own emotions so strongly that it would require an unnatural self-control, even amounting to withdrawal, for me to maintain objectivity. This can happen if there is a serious disturbance in the group, or if a participant touches inadvertently upon an area of special meaning in my personal life.

In one marathon, there were two participants who found it difficult, for precisely opposite reasons, to become part of the group. Evan was an

[6] Dr. Leonard Schwartz.
[7] These same authors offer a thorough, logical discussion of the theory and techniques of role-playing, from a viewpoint different from that of Moreno's psychodramatic approach.

extremely constricted, overcontrolled man in his middle years who had been referred by a therapist who hoped that the marathon would stimulate an emotional breakthrough; he was unable to make any emotional contact in the marathon or to express any feeling. Though we all worked to draw him out, he remained aloof. Roxanne, his mirror opposite, was an ebullient young woman who had for many years suffered from an illness which kept her alone and withdrawn, and who was now putting her exceptional vitality into a genuine effort to relate to others—which, however, at times led her to be overdemanding and overresponsive. He sat aside, and she was always in the center. When her excessive needs were not adequately met, she began to see me as the rejecting, indifferent aspect of her mother and developed a full-blown transference hatred.

Without warning, on the second day of the marathon, Evan suddenly said "Goodbye" in a low voice and was out the door and down the hall.[8] At once Roxanne followed suit. She screamed at me, "I don't blame him, you're a bitch!" and also disappeared. The group and myself sat stunned. Together we had to work through the pain of losing two of our members, the sense of failure which we all felt, and the group's perception of me (partly correct) as needing reassurance. We shared our feelings, became a group again, and the marathon turned into a successful and rewarding experience for us all.

In another group, my deepest feelings were evoked at a highly personal level. A man, who was actually too old to be my son and who did not resemble him, brought to the group his distress over his irritability with his wife, and even more with his mother. It was clear that both relationships were essentially loving, but he could not bring himself to admit that he was wrong when he had lost his temper. Especially he wished that he could ask his aging mother to forgive his outbursts of the past. In an attempt to dissolve his block against asking forgiveness, he went around the circle and requested forgiveness from all the women.

As usually happens, the interaction became more intense as he circled the room. He was forgiven with such phrases as "Of course I will," "You can't be perfect, who can," and "I have a bad temper myself, it's easy to forgive you." As he approached me, I found myself close to tears, without quite realizing that the situation had tapped my own grief over the friction which then existed between my adolescent son and myself. As he knelt before me, his words changed, and he said, "Can you love me even when I'm angry?" We embraced, I cried wholeheartedly and told him, "My son is angry at me now and I do love him very much."

---

[8] Only five marathon participants out of approximately 1000 have departed from the group before its scheduled conclusion. There is no follow-up on Evan, who did not respond to my letter. The other four participants were able to explore their anxieties with their individual therapists, and two of them, including Roxanne, returned for subsequent marathons.

Such episodes occur rarely; when they do occur, the interchange becomes especially meaningful for the participant as well as for myself.[9]

Far different as a subjective experience is the type of role-playing which has been described in other chapters. For me there is a clear distinction, understood perfectly in most groups, between role-playing for a therapeutic purpose and a straightforward expression of what I am feeling or thinking. In psychodramatic role-playing, with its many variations, I often take the role of the witch-mother. What is sought is a breakthrough, or a cathartic expression, of feelings which the group member has repressed or overcontrolled in his relationship to the witch aspect of his real mother.

The role of the witch-mother in her various aspects—rejecting, guilt-provoking, seductive, demanding, whining, possessive, self-pitying, domineering, critical—is not only easy for me, but fun. Since all these obnoxious qualities unquestionably exist within me to a greater or lesser degree, I enjoy expressing them in a situation in which they are not merely nontoxic, but helpful.

If the group member is able to release toward me the feelings which he has suppressed toward the witch aspect of his actual mother, there is a breakthrough of violent anger. Once or twice, when I was deliberately goading a participant by an exaggerated imitation of his mother, the situation has seemed to approach actual violence. One young woman upset my chair, and a man (whom I did not know to be a karate expert) stopped a karate chop within two inches of my throat. During these psychodramas, the men in the room, especially my co-therapist, are always alert to intervene if it should be necessary. It has never been necessary. No matter how furious the protagonist becomes, he knows on some level that he is actually working with a marathon leader who is attempting to be useful to him. Once the rage breaks forth, it can be physically dissipated by couch-banging or pillow-pounding.[10] Such psychodramas are never undertaken unless the group member has indicated a wish to explore his feelings in this area. This approach, of course, could not be risked with any participant whose reality-testing might be defective. An ambulatory schizophrenic, for example, might actually

[9] The participant, and probably the entire group, recognized that I was expressing personal feeling. However, in accordance with the principle discussed above, I did not make use of the group to discuss and explore my family situation any further.

[10] If the rage is not physically dissipated, resentment toward me usually continues, in contrast to the affection which is experienced after the rage is fully expressed. Sometimes a marathon participant who cannot fully express this transferential hatred will divert his bitterness into a rationalized disapproval of the marathon approach itself, rather than recognizing that there has been a mutual failure of participant and leader. Other than this, I know of no lasting bad effects from unexpressed transference-hatred.

endanger me and, even more likely, might be endangered himself by an overwhelming rush of anxiety about his own rage. Nor do I ever undertake to role-play the malevolent mother unless my basic feelings for the group member are positive.

After the cathartic experience, the participant can see me realistically. He may be relieved and even amused to see that the uncanny witch-mother is, after all, only a woman.

"Funny, you don't look like my mother any more."

"Elizabeth, you're really not a bad old bag at all."

"You let me yell at you. *She* never let me yell at her."

Sometimes this realistic perception of me is tinged with an idealization of me as the longed-for mother who is completely nurturant and loving. As every therapist knows, it is a temptation to accept such feelings as realistically justified and to regard negative feelings as entirely transferential. Perhaps it would be difficult to work with the intense negative feelings which may be directed toward me in a marathon unless, to some extent, I could support myself by this rationalization.

Here again, the marathon encounter group offers an opportunity for the evocation and release of deeper feeling than can occur in most dyadic therapeutic relationships. The presence of the group allows my symbolic, temporary "child" to live through his deepest fantasies without being overpowered by them. Insight usually follows naturally after such an episode. Interpretations, if necessary, can be brief and simple and are frequently offered by other group members.

"Apparently what really got to you is the times your mother made fun of you."

"You really wanted to love her, didn't you, and she wouldn't let you near her."

"Well, at least now we all know why you can't stand your wife when she gets sick."

Similar psychodramatic episodes may occur when a group participant, usually a young man, needs to assert his strength symbolically by physical conflict with a father figure. Usually the male co-therapist takes this role, which may also be played by an appropriate father-surrogate in the group. Such wrestling matches often become so intense that I must resist the temptation to intervene, relying on the men in the group to draw upon their boyhood knowledge of playground wrestling to discern when the situation might become dangerous. Here, too, intervention has never become necessary.[11] And here, too, once the rage has been physically expended, the episode invariably ends with an expression of mutual warmth and respect between the two men.

[11] Several co-therapists, particularly John Brinley, Frank Rubenfeld, and Daniel Miller have impressed me by their willingness to engage in this kind of real though symbolic combat.

Affection, unlike other feelings, should never involve role-playing. Rejection or contempt or anger can be simulated, but never affection. Pretended affection would inevitably be sensed by a group member and might well repeat a situation in which, as a child, he could not be certain of the genuine love of his parents. For me, also, it would be distasteful to offer a physical gesture of affection which was not sincere. Fortunately, a genuine reaching-out for warmth is almost certain to evoke an appropriate response; a kind of interaction which can, in the broadest sense, be understood as a transference-counter-transference phenomenon, in accordance with the psychoanalytic finding that the therapist's emotional reaction to a patient is determined not only by the patient's real personality and overt behavior, but also by latent or even unconscious elements in the way in which the therapist is perceived by the patient. For me, as for my temporary and symbolic "child," the maternal relationship ends when the marathon is over, and there has been no instance in which either of us has sought to perpetuate it.

My belief is that each of us has a reservoir of love which can be tapped and expressed under appropriate circumstances, just as each of us has a reservoir of the other basic emotions—sexuality, anger, fear, and grief. It is this reservoir of maternal love within me which is tapped when it is genuinely needed. Occasionally, though rarely, my sincerity has been questioned in marathons, but I am profoundly sure that the affection which I express is genuine, although not in the sense that it is expected to form the basis for a lasting relationship. Rather often, men participants who go through such an episode with me have reported, weeks or months later, that there was a significant improvement in the relationship with their wives or mothers, and several women have reported an increased ability to accept the friendship of other women. Presumably such improvements are based in part on the expression of pent-up rage which has distorted the perception of women, and in part on finding that it is a safe experience to receive and give affection. In turn, I am emotionally nourished by the affection which I receive and reciprocate and do not regard this as the fulfillment of a neurotic need.

Nevertheless, it seems important to me that any therapist, perhaps especially a marathon therapist, should be aware of whatever characterological attitudes of his own may be called out by the group interaction. The frequency and intensity with which I am taken as a mother symbol, either malevolent or nurturant, probably has to do with personality factors outside of my function as a female therapist in a marathon, although in my personal life I do not seem to evoke these reactions to any unusual degree. For this reason, I have given particular consideration toward my attitudes about dependency.

Some therapists are repelled by the dependent needs of their patients and tend to respond critically or satirically. My own tendency is to be overresponsive. My belief is that either attitude can be constructively therapeutic, provided the therapist is sufficiently aware of his own bias to be judicious.

If the therapist who rejects dependency is aware of the deep hurt and anger which may be provoked by this rejection and can see the patient through it, then the rejection can strengthen the patient by helping him face the unrealistic sense of helplessness which underlies the dependent needs. If, on the contrary, I gratify dependent needs by accepting the position of a loving mother, or if the group as a whole offers the nurturance, the patient gains strength through this gratification *if*, when the episode concludes, he can reassert his adult status, usually by symbolic means.

Such symbolism may, on the surface, be trivial. For example, after a woman in a marathon had been offered symbolic mothering by being lifted and rocked, she said to me half-jokingly, "Elizabeth, will you make me a sandwich?" I answered cheerfully, "You're grown up now, make it yourself." Repeatedly, after such episodes, the protagonist in the symbolic drama takes an increasingly mature position in the group, with a clearer perspective on his own difficulties and a heightened awareness of the needs of others.

With increasing experience as a marathon leader, I find it more and more easy to express my feelings spontaneously when it is appropriate, and to disregard them if it seems to me that they will not be useful in the group. Experiential therapists have suggested that every authentic expression of feeling on the part of the therapist is helpful if the therapist is himself a fully self-actualized person, who might be termed a Boddhisatva.[12] This concept of the therapist's role makes me feel rather like a tightrope walker with no net beneath. I cannot regard myself as a Boddhisatva. Some of the time I feel enlightened and much of the time I feel loving, but I do not believe that I can rely upon my enlightenment and my lovingness in itself to be helpful to the members of a group. Instead, I place reliance upon a knowledge of psychodynamics which, most of the time, is sufficiently well assimilated so that it comes to me automatically; upon my deliberate decision to share my feelings if and when they seem likely to be helpful; and upon my ability to pay close attention to what is happening within the group.

My attentiveness, of course, wavers at times when I am preoccupied with my own needs. Indeed, it seems to me that the most sensible reason for maintaining that a therapist should be relatively free from personal

[12] The Boddhisatva, according to Zen Buddhism, is "an exemplar of a turned-on life, a revealer and sharer of how *he* has found his way, . . . awakened and liberated . . . but not out of this world" (Jourard, 1969, p. 50).

problems is merely that personal problems may intrude upon the capacity to pay attention. When I am able to pay complete attention to the group, there is a self-forgetfulness which resembles the self-forgetfulness that may occur in being swept away by an extremely beautiful experience with music or nature or personal intimacy. This experience in itself is one of the primary rewards of being a marathon therapist, and at the times when it occurs, my work is at its best.

Another reward of being a marathon leader is the sense of closeness in its concluding hours. At this time, if the marathon is effective and successful, leadership becomes almost unnecessary. The group itself takes care of its own members, working with great skill and honesty to draw out whatever difficulties have been unresolved.

"Frankly, I think you should go into private therapy. You need help."

"The only trouble with you is that you just can't accept that you've made it. You're in good shape, man. For you it's just too good to be true. Believe it!"

"So you're worried about dying. Well, now, who doesn't have to die? You're making such a fuss about it, you can't even live while you're alive."

"Come out of your corner and get hugged."

In the last moments of an effective marathon, the members of the group always find a way to express their sense of human communion. Usually they stand in a circle in a close embrace. In one marathon, everybody in the circle danced, and in a spontaneous similarity to the tradition of regional folk dancing, each member in turn took the center of the circle and danced alone, expressing his individuality at the same time he expressed his delight in being a member of the group. In another marathon, a young man began the humming of the ancient Buddhist syllable *OM*, which for him had mystical connotations not shared by other group members, but which was taken up by the entire group. At such times, I am completely part of the circle. When the group breaks up, I stand slightly aloof, in order not to force my affection upon participants who may be going away with unresolved negative feelings toward me, but most of the participants approach me with warm and appreciative embraces, and my feeling of oneness with the group is often a true peak experience.

And then the marathon is over. And the management of my own feelings after the marathon is sometimes difficult.

There is no question but what I have grown enormously, both personally and professionally, as a consequence of my marathon experiences. Yet it is often hard to face the aftermath of a marathon. I have been intimate for two days with people who have struggled in the group, who suffered, rejoiced, and revealed their essential humanness. Some of them

I will never see again; others I will see in comparatively superficial social or professional situations. Some of them I will never know as well again as I have known them in this marathon. I am in my office, which is a shambles of half-eaten food, empty paper cups, reeking ashtrays, and strewn pillows.

If I am working with a co-therapist, it is easier. We sit down together and unwind slowly, sharing our enthusiasm and our disappointments. But even with a co-therapist, I find that I am likely to be tense, exhausted, and overexcited when the group ends. This is partly because of the demands of professional leadership, but it is also because the intense interaction of the group must inevitably stir up unconscious feelings within me which I must disregard in taking responsibility for the group. After a marathon, I tend to become talkative, self-centered, and childishly demanding, and I need the companionship of someone who can accept this. Through years of experience in conducting marathons, this reaction has become milder, and I have learned that it can be partially managed through such simple devices as walking, swimming, and arranging extra time for sleep and reading. To attend a party after a marathon, except for a small gathering of close friends, is almost painful. Indeed, one of the minor penalties of being a marathon leader, for me at least, is that the ability to enjoy superficial social relationships and cocktail chitchat has diminished almost to the vanishing point. I am uncomfortable wearing a social mask and impatient when those around me appear to be wearing them.

The rewards far outweigh the difficulties and exertion. There is my personal enjoyment of the drama and excitement of each marathon. There is the probability, in most marathons, that most participants will profit, and that some will profit greatly. There is even some possibility that, as our knowledge of group interaction expands, it may foster a kind of honesty and a concern for one another which, as in the vision of human-istic psychology, could become a counter-force against war and hatred and pollution.

Awaiting the arrival of participants for the next marathon, I am always exhilarated. Each group is different. We may disappoint each other. We may be nourished by each other and grow and thrive. It is always an adventure.

REFERENCES

Gibb, J. R., & Gibb, L. M. Emergence therapy. In G. H. Gazda (Ed.), *Innovations to group therapy*. New York: Charles C Thomas, 1968.

Goldman, G. Panel Discussion, Convention of the American Psychological Association, 1969.

Jourard, S. M. The therapist as guru. *Voices,* Summer-Fall 1969.

Lakin, M. Some ethical issues in sensitivity training. *American Psychologist,* October 1969.

Locke, N. *Group psychoanalysis.* New York: New York University Press, 1961.

Nelson, M. C., Nelson, B., Sherman, M. H, & Strean, H. S. *Roles and paradigms in psychotherapy.* New York: Grune & Stratton, 1968.

Rachman, A. W. *Marathon group psychotherapy.* Mimeographed communication, 1969.

10 FEEDBACK AND MEASUREMENTS

by Lorelle Saretsky

> We must be patient and await fresh methods and occasions of research. We must be ready, too, to abandon a path that we have followed for a time if it seems to be leading to no good end.
>
> Freud, *Beyond the Pleasure Principle*

Based on the subjective reports of participants, data regarding the effectiveness of marathons appears convincing to me and to others who offer marathons. Yet, despite the enthusiastic feedback from most of my participants, who either refer friends and relatives or who request another marathon in numbers now considerably higher than was reported in an earlier article (Mintz, 1969), I am sharply aware that probably there are disgruntled and dissatisfied participants from whom I do not hear again. Moreover, with the exception of some marathon groups offered in industrial or institutional settings, my groups have consisted principally of well-educated, well-functioning individuals who, although they have usually had some experience in individual psychotherapy, do not present major psychiatric problems. They are, on the whole, the same clinically normal type of population from which the T-groups of NTL and similar organizations draw their members. Research on this type of population is open to the same kind of objection once made by a sardonic psychologist about most academic research with human beings: that it reveals primarily the psychodynamics of the college sophomore, since Psychology 1 classes are traditionally the source for experimental subjects.

For this reason, it is heartening to note from Lorelle Saretsky's survey that hospitalized psychiatric patients, former drug addicts, and others suffering from severe social or personal difficulties have been included in some investigations. My personal conviction is that the time format of the marathon, with whatever modifications may be appropriate to the composition and goals of the group, has a unique value. My further conviction is that encounter techniques, verbal and nonverbal, can be effectively utilized with appropriate modifications in a wide variety of group situations. Certainly no responsible leader would use the same procedures with a group of well-functioning participants seeking personal growth, a group of institutionalized psychiatric patients, a group of supervisors seeking to iron out their difficulties in an industrial plant, and a group of youthful drug addicts. Nevertheless, it is my hope that in time we will accumulate enough research data so that we can not only identify the modifications of therapeutic techniques and encounter techniques which are appropriate in diverse situations but can also identify fundamental conditions which promote human growth and healing and which may cut across individual human differences.

Research on the outcome of any kind of psychotherapy is notoriously difficult. Not only is it difficult to find appropriate methodology and suitable measurements, but it is at least equally difficult, as Saretsky points out, to isolate specific variables without disregarding an almost infinite number of other variables which are involved in the subtle, complex processes of growth and healing. For example, as this survey indicates, the approach and background of the leader have been relatively disregarded as variables in the effectiveness of marathon groups in comparison to groups with more traditional time formats.

Objective evidence does not yet exist as to the optimal time format for various group populations, the wisest approach and the necessary and sufficient training for the leader, or selection of group members. This evidence will accumulate in time. Meanwhile, although Saretsky's survey deals with data which as yet provides us with few conclusive answers, it does suggest some pathways along which we may move in search of answers.

—Elizabeth E. Mintz

Since it is possible to regard the marathon as a special form of group therapy, it is appropriate to begin our consideration of the research with an overview of research in this field.

In 1962, Rickard surveyed the literature and found only twenty-two studies which met minimal methodological standards. In the ensuing years, there has been a constant increase in the number of published studies on group psychotherapy and some indication of greater rigor and sophistication in the designs of those studies. An updated examination of the currently available literature revealed forty-five outcome studies that have employed, as minimum research standards, the use of a control group, and at least one objective criterion to measure behavior change (Bednar, 1970).

Nevertheless, the overall impression is still disappointing. A central issue in group psychotherapy research is the lack of systematic attempts to formulate sets of principles, postulates, and hypotheses about relationships among the relevant variables, which can then be tested empirically. This need for an explicit statement of theory is necessary to guide research efforts and to provide an interpretive framework for the results. Ex post facto explanations of findings make for broad, general speculations that do little to define operational constructs or enhance objective observation of small units of meaningful data. Closely related to the problem of theory building is the need for more attention to the analysis of the behavior of groups—the interaction of group members— as opposed to the outcome of that behavior. There is also a necessity for improved methods of observing, recording, and analysing group dynamics.

The major focus of this chapter is a review of research data dealing with time-extended, intensive group procedures. Our primary concern is the relatively new and unexplored area of the marathon group; however, a sample of the investigations of T-groups will be presented first' to serve as a frame of reference in terms of content and methodology for subsequent discussions of marathons. (For comprehensive reviews of the T-group literature, the reader is referred to Buchanan, 1965; Campbell & Dunnette, 1968; House, 1967; McGrath & Altman, 1966; Stock, 1964.)

T-GROUPS

Undoubtedly, the T-group method is an outgrowth of the cultural revolution that we are now going through. Many people are interested in the transformation of governing institutions and structures, which hopefully will permit changes in man's relationships, values, and outlook. The T-group approach is providing a format for problem solving in a wide variety of community situations. Used for such diverse purposes as to help diminish racial tensions, train paraprofessionals, help to integrate a school system, ameliorate relationships between the community and the police force, or resolve campus disturbances, the T-group offers a new approach to conflict resolution.

The purpose of T-groups is to increase empathy, sensitivity, ability to communicate, and accuracy of interpersonal perception (Campbell & Dunnette, 1968). Their overall goal is the improvement of social skills, and they have been termed (Benne, 1970) "therapy for normals." Hence the orientation of many research studies is the evaluation of how T-groups affect the degree of accuracy with which a participant is able to perceive the attributes, attitudes, opinions, and reactions of other participants.

The usefulness of T-group procedures is emphasized by Gibb and Gibb (1967) in a series of experiments and field studies designed to evaluate longitudinal processes of change in small groups. They observed groups in natural settings such as social clubs, work groups, and families. Comparisons were made between these natural groups and groups which met for the specific purposes of growth and training, through the use of questionnaires, analysis of taped recordings, individual depth interviews, and coded group observations. Their research indicated that groups differ in (1) the degree of reciprocal trust among members; (2) the validity, depth, and quality of the feedback system; (3) the degree of directionality towards group-determined goals; (4) the degree of real interdependence in the system. The first factor is the variable upon which group growth is dependent. Following the establishment of trust, each succeeding variable is dependent upon the prior dimension in the hierarchy. Group growth variables are hypothesized to be related to parallel factors in personal growth.

Gibb and Gibb conclude that in the natural setting of the usual organizational structure, man reaches only a fraction of his potential growth. In laboratory and therapy group settings, moments of optimal group actualization and of sustained creativity and trust were seen most often: (1) during sensitivity training in semiweekly sessions for eight or nine consecutive months; (2) during marathon sessions for 98–120 hours with little or no sleep; and (3) during twelve-hour daily sessions for twelve or thirteen days.

Interpersonal Studies

Several groups of investigators have tried to measure changes in the individual's orientation toward interpersonal relations as a result of T-group experience. Schutz and Allen (1966) used the FIRO-B, which measures attitudes toward control, affection, power, and close personal relationships, to test this variable. It was administered to both the experimental (E) and control (C) group at the beginning and end of a two-week laboratory, and then six months later. Content analysis revealed significantly more favorable changes in interpersonal behavior following T-group experiences for the E group than for the C group. The large majority of respondents reported a substantial increase in their "intellectual understanding and enhancement of personal relations in terms of lessened tension, more honesty, assertiveness, confidence, self-acceptance, and flexibility" (Schutz & Allen, 1966, pp. 285–286). Four-fifths of reported changes grew over time and one-fifth faded. Negative changes appeared among a few participants, but the authors attributed this to "self-searching" and "emotional growing pains."

Harrison (1966) tried to measure interpersonal orientation changes in a group of 115 men and women from the middle levels of responsibility in government, industry, and educational organizations. An adaptation of Kelly's Role Construct Repertory Test (REP) was administered to each individual. His task was to select a member of a triad in the group, choose a word which would discriminate that member from the other two, then give a word which was its opposite in meaning. The words were then coded by the experimenter along two dimensions: concrete-instrumental (power-powerless; man-woman; competent-incompetent) and inferential-expressive (warm-cold; afraid of people-confident; personal-cold and formal). It was found that people perceived by the group as seeking and using information about feedback regarding themselves tended to move more toward the use of inferential-expressive concepts as opposed to concrete-instrumental concepts. In addition to the REP test, these laboratory participants rated each other on twelve scales, each dealing with the way in which the members responded to information about themselves from others (feedback). Data analysis indicated that a change in the individual's orientation toward the inter- and intrapersonal does occur with training and that these changes increase with time. Changes seem to coincide with the amount of active involvement in the program.

A number of research workers have attempted to study the T-group's effect on the diagnostic ability of participants,[1] with varying findings. Stock (1964) cites a study by Glidewell, who explored the extent to which T-group experience enhanced the ability to see organizational problems in terms of multiple causation rather than single causation, the ability to see their own contribution toward these problems, and the ability to recognize these problems as related to organizational structure rather than as depending primarily upon the adequacy or inadequacy of personnel. Analysis of the data, based on questionnaires administered before and after extensive T-group experience, suggested that the effects of T-group participation were in part related to the initial attitudes of the participants. Attitudinal changes after the T-groups were evaluated separately for individuals showing various identifiable syndromes of approaches toward problem-solving. (1) the term "stepchild syndrome" was used to describe people who worried about the way in which others treated them and hoped that they could be induced to treat them differently. Sixty-seven percent of these individuals moved toward becoming more aware of the importance of skill and awareness in interpersonal relations as determining the way in which organizational problems could be solved. (2) The "innocent bystander" syndrome referred to individuals who tended to see problems as belonging to others. Seventy-one percent of

---

[1] The term "diagnosis," which is frequently used in T-group literature, is not employed in its customary clinical sense but rather implies the ability to understand the feelings and attitudes of others.

these individuals changed in the direction of becoming more concerned with their own improvement in handling interpersonal relationships. (3) The "service" syndrome described people who saw their own ability to give service to others as a crucial factor in problem solving. Sixty-seven percent of these individuals showed positive change in developing greater insight. (4) The "do-it-yourself" individuals were those who saw problems as depending entirely on their own adequacy. Forty-two percent of these people developed a more realistic outlook. (5) "Managers-of-the-year" individuals, who at the beginning of training already exhibited maximum constructiveness in their view of organizational problems, showed little or no change as a result of training. In all, sixty percent of the participants changed in a positive direction.

Another investigation of the effects of T-group experience on the ability to comprehend and deal with organizational problems was conducted by Oshry and Harrison (1966). They administered a questionnaire on problem analysis to forty-six participants before and after a two-week experience in a human relations laboratory. Changes in the viewpoints of the participants, most of whom were middle-management personnel from business and industry, were summarized as follows:

> [The participant sees] his work world as more human and less impersonal; he sees clearer connections between how well interpersonal needs are met and how well the work gets done; he sees himself more clearly as the most significant part of his work problems; he sees no clear connection, however, between his new perceptions and how he translates these into action (Oshry & Harrison, 1966, p. 196).

Underwood (1965) investigated the effects of T-group experience on fifteen supervisors at the Radio Corporation of America, who volunteered for sensitivity training, and who were compared to fifteen recruited control supervisors matched for age, sex, department, and supervisory level. Positive changes were shown in the area of personal and interpersonal behavior by the experimental group, and the changed behavior appeared to persist after the end of training.

Other research workers, such as Miles, Cohen and, Whitman (1959) have obtained highly inconclusive results. These investigators administered the Group Behavior Task to participants in a training program conducted by the Protestant Episcopal Church, at the beginning and near the end of the program. Variables measured were diagnostic ability, sensitivity to other participants, and sensitivity to group decisions. There was consistent improvement in the variable of sensitivity to the feelings of other participants, but the remaining factors changed in some subgroups, remained constant in others, and in some subgroups even showed decreases in diagnostic ability. The authors speculate that patterns of individual change may have been obscured by the use of median scores, or that overfamiliarity with the test may have introduced a factor of error when it was readministered.

Intrapersonal Studies

A T-group approach where the objective was intrapersonal change was reported by Gassner et al. (1964), who investigated changes in self-concept versus ideal self-concept, and self-concept versus image of the "average other." These investigators administered the Bill's Index of Adjustment and Values (BIAV) to New York City College undergraduates before and after a three-day training workshop. Forty-six of the students were assigned to an experimental group and twenty-one to a control group. The experimenters found that the BIAV indicated an increase in similarity between self-perceptions and ideal self-perceptions for *both* experimental and control groups and also found an increase in similarity between self-perception and average-other perceptions for *both* groups.

A more favorable study of the effects of sensitivity training utilized four of the FIRO scales (attitudes toward control, affection, power, and close personal relationships). Test results confirmed the author's prediction that more extreme control and affectional needs would tend to change toward more neutral or less need-expressive positions. FIRO attitude changes were accompanied by validated perceptions of these changes by participant peers. Control subjects who took part in discussion groups did not show FIRO changes (Smith, 1964).

Lohman et al. (1959) investigated the effects of training on participants' self-perceptions and their perceptions of their trainers. The subjects were sixty-five college students in three sensitivity training classes which met for sixteen weeks, twice a week, for two hours. Each subject was asked to complete the Gordon Personal Profile (GPP), first with reference to themselves, and then with regard to how they saw their trainer. The GPP was administered near the beginning and at the end of the lab.

The researchers report that at the end of training, participants tended to see the trainers as less adequate than they had been seen at the beginning. Student self-perception scores did not rise as a result of the laboratory experience; the students did not necessarily feel that they were more adequate as individuals at the end of training than at the beginning. The authors speculate about possible inadequacies of the GPP and the possibility that increased ability to see oneself honestly is not necessarily accompanied by improvement in self-confidence. They also suggest a confounding effect due to decreased idealization of the trainers.

A study by Culbert et al. (1968) investigated whether two groups of students undergoing sensitivity training would show changes in self-awareness (Personal Orientation Inventory—POI) and self-actualization (Problem Expression Scale—PES). One group changed on the POI; the other did not. Rank order of POI changes for individuals did not correlate in either group with individual changes on the self-actualization scale. The authors account for the equivocal results as follows: (1) the two groups were somewhat different to begin with; (2) an individual's change in values, concepts, and percepts (as measured by the POI) may not be a sufficient antecedent to actual behavioral changes (as measured by the PES). The writers try to bolster their explanation by suggesting that both groups received comparable sensitivity experiences even though they had different leaders. Since the leaders behaved in consort with the researcher, however, and were under instruction to be "more self-disclosing of personal feelings" or "less self-disclosing of personal feelings," there seem to be many relevant dimensions of trainer-participant interaction that were not held constant.[2]

Studies Using External Criteria

A number of different researchers have reported favorably on T-group effectiveness in an on-the-job setting, a finding which seems to have stimulated the proliferation of T-groups in many business and educational settings. Bunker (1965) studied 194 participants in six labs composed of individuals from industry, government, and religious, educational, medical, and social service organizations. The experimental groups changed in three respects in contrast to the control groups. First, they exhibited increased openness, receptivity, and tolerance of differences. Second, they showed increased operational skill in interpersonal relationships. The third cluster of changes was characterized by improved understanding and diagnostic awareness of self, others, and interaction processes in groups.

Kuriloff and Atkins (1966) report extensive observations of T-grouping in one firm, where meetings were worked into the Monday-to-Friday schedule of the participants. There were many examples of on-the-job changes, culminating in the company taking on a new contract that entailed innovative work, maximal cooperation, and an extremely tight time schedule. The authors contend that the resourcefulness mobilized

[2] The dimension of the leaders' degree of self-disclosure was varied for the purpose of another investigation. The authors justify this variation as irrelevant on the grounds that it represents between-trainer differences which in any case would occur naturally in sensitivity training groups. Such a basic experimental flaw, however, may well have contributed to the confused findings.

by the subjects in order to handle this project and beat the deadline should be credited to the T-group experience, in view of the company's previous history of poor efficiency.

The impact of a T-group on thirty-six supervisors and executives from a single plant was studied. Bass (1964) used three main measures of laboratory effects: (1) subjects' ratings of each other with respect to the amount of constructive influence they felt each had demonstrated by the end of the program; (2) the extent of each participant's awareness and sensitivity to the reaction of others within the group, as rated by psychology trainees; and (3) a sentence completion test administered to subjects after each of two showings of *Twelve Angry Men*.[3] The film was shown at the group's first and last meeting in the laboratory. Bass found that sensitivity seemed to increase as a result of the management training lab, and that this improvement was positively correlated with peer group appraisals of the influence of individuals upon the group.

The importance of follow-up study for a realistic evaluation of laboratory training should not be overlooked. Argyris (1962) studied the effects of the T-group on a horizontal organizational slice of ten individuals from one firm. He used interviews, questionnaires, and personal observation in order to evaluate the group's effectiveness and also provided a matched control group. Data was obtained before, immediately after, and several months after the laboratory. The results of this study were very positive. One month after the program, participants reported increased awareness of their impact on others and others' impact on them, on the group, and on the organization. They reported that several concrete organizational changes had already been made as a result of the lab experience. They also reported increased trust and confidence in themselves and their group.

During a final evaluation nine months after the laboratory experience, several executives admitted to a "fade-out" effect (the disappearance over time of positive training impact). Since justification for group experience of any kind is intimately related to maintaining and applying immediate results, the "fade-out" effect is an important phenomenon. Argyris distinguishes two dimensions of "fade-out." The first of these, he says, may be described in terms of the frequency of the use of the new learnings. The second may be seen in terms of the potential or capability of each person to practice what he has learned. Argyris noted that the frequency of use the new learning had decreased much more than the capability to use it and hypothesizes that the fade-out effect may actually be only the dormancy of newly learned skills.

---

[3] This film depicts the interaction of a jury for a murder trial, in which a single juror insists upon the innocence of the defendant and eventually succeeds in obtaining acquittal. Perception and comprehension of the feelings and attitudes of the various jury members were taken as an index of sensitivity.—E.E.M.

Encouraging results utilizing external criteria are common to the following two studies of educational personnel. Miles (1960) investigated T-group effects on thirty-four NTL participants (mostly elementary school principals). Thirty-four criterion measures included associates' description of on-the-job behavior, the Leader Behavior Description Questionnaire, the Group Participation Scale, and an open-ended perceived-change measure developed by the author. Content analysis of changes reported by subjects and job associates indicated changes in sensitivity and behavioral skill ("listens more," "communicates better," "shares decisions more," "gives help to teachers").

A two-week laboratory learning experience was held for a group of thirty-five strangers who were to comprise the staff of a new high school. The basic objectives of the lab were to expedite an effective social system characterized by improved communication, decision making, problem solving, and conflict management, and to create an atmosphere of openness, trust, and freedom for innovation and experimentation (Keutzer et al., 1969).

Assessment by several independent means including observation by consultants all indicated significant and positive changes, in contrast to similar measures obtained from a control group.

Examination of these research articles, which are fairly representative of the T-group experimental literature, reveals many serious methodological problems. Several of the studies cited lack adequate controls (Miles et al., 1959; Gibb & Gibb, 1967); the research designs do not rule out confounding and misleading variables (Lohman et al., 1959; Oshry & Harrison, 1966; Culbert et al., 1968); and test instruments are often used that are of questionable reliability and validity. Many studies seem to minimize the significance of the therapist's skill, training and style, individual personality factors, the mental set of the subjects, group composition, group process variables, and the desirability of outcome criteria that include objective measures of long-range behavioral changes.

The growing interest in doing controlled research that is in keeping with the scientific tradition has been colored by the struggle to do justice to the complexity of real life experiences. Loevinger (quoted by Holt, 1965, p. 44) makes the point that "the fundamental problem of experimental research in the social sciences is how to discipline observation so that questions can be answered with some degree of confidence without abandoning a commitment to ask humanly important questions." Humanistic psychologists, with an interest in growth, observing life in natural settings, the inner subjective experience, and viewing man as a whole, tend to resist objective research strategies that oversimplify and reduce the human condition.

The blame for many of the inadequacies in experimental studies rests with the experimenter, according to Argyris (1969), who suggests a parallel between the typical behavior of individuals as they function in various group settings and current patterns of psychological researchers. He finds in the "typical world" (Pattern A) a tendency toward minimal expression of feelings, minimal openness to feelings, and minimal risk taking with ideas or feelings. The most frequently observed norms are concern for ideas (not feelings) and conformity. The norm of mistrust also tends to be high but must be inferred indirectly, since individuals do not feel safe in openly showing their mistrust. In contrast are Pattern B groups, in which "feelings are expressed and risks are taken; . . . and in which the norms of conformity and antagonism become less potent while the norms of individuality and trust become more potent" (p. 898).

T-groups, according to Argyris, begin with Pattern A; if successful, they move toward Pattern B interaction. Argyris holds, however, that only a minority of T-groups develop toward Pattern B successfully, a conservative viewpoint which does not accord with most published research on T-groups.

Argyris further points out that, in themselves, feedback and the desire to alter the interactional patterns which already exist may not be enough to affect change. He offers a study of two industrial groups, in which serious communication difficulties had been brought to the attention of the group members. Wishing to change, they did their best to alter their existing modes of communication, without T-group meetings and without the help of trainers. After two months, they decided their efforts were a failure and gave up. The inference is that motivation and unguided, unstructured efforts toward change are less likely to be effective than the T-group in a laboratory setting, which offers methods by which new patterns of interpersonal behavior can be exchanged for the old.

Argyris maintains that the pervasiveness of Pattern A behavior extends to psychological thought and practice which, he asserts, in its rigid, rule-bound context and preoccupation with hard data, makes much of the research today meaningless. However, there are also difficulties in humanistic research in that it is predominantly based on a population rarely available for empirical study (those individuals utilizing Pattern B behavior). In spite of Argyris's somewhat pessimistic view, there is a growing coalescence of the "holistic-experiential" and "dissectionist-scientific" views in an effort to make experimental material relevant and stimulating.

MARATHON RESEARCH

As is probably the case with many new approaches, those who are in the forefront of the marathon movement seem to possess a certain pioneering zeal. Therapists such as Bach (1966), Mintz (1969), Stoller

(1968), and Bindrim (1968) have adopted the marathon for use in a variety of settings and all report that defenses drop away, there is more open disclosure and sharing, there is less anxiety about and increased acceptance of self and others, and significant personal growth and behavior change seems to occur more readily than in regular therapy groups. These enthusiastic statements have been met by such criticisms as:

> To feel exhilarated and renewed is not invariably therapeutic. The dropping of masks and "learning that the masks are not necessary" disregards the fact that some masks are vitally needed ego defenses. Some patients are unable to build bridges until they have outgrown their need for barriers. In short, the primary shortcoming of this paper [Stoller's 1968 paper] is that it argues for the exposure of patients to an experience that may be desirable for some and undesirable for others without establishing any objective criteria for participation. A selection of candidates for accelerated interaction based primarily on "the feelings of the group leader" seems to me rather a hit or miss policy (Spotnitz, 1968, pp. 236–7).

Similarly, Anthony (1968, p. 253) notes:

> In the area of acceleration therapy, acting out becomes the rule rather than the resistance. . . . Ideally, as I see it, affect and cognition should go hand in hand, sensitively balanced to fit the need of the passing therapeutic situation. . . . There is a need to know as well as to feel, and both should find a place in the balanced therapeutic process.

A dissenting attitude is also held by Burton (1970), who feels that the principles of spaced learning with time between sessions for integration and working through of newly-acquired behavior is ignored by marathon advocates; he calls it an "hysterical form of encounter." The spaced versus massed learning controversy is not a new issue for psychologists, particularly those involved in education. However, Vernallis (1969) theorizes that the time between sessions in traditional groups may be utilized nonproductively. He feels that it allows the patient time to reinforce old modes of behavior in order to reduce the anxieties stimulated by the group. In a marathon, a participant must try to handle his interpersonal stress reactions within the group setting. Here, it is presumed, only the more effective ways of dealing with interpersonal problems will be reinforced.

Another qualifying note is added by Ellis (1970). After experimentation with a variety of techniques, he has settled upon the therapist-centered rational marathon encounter. Ellis criticizes the basic encounter group and human potential movement as "gimmicky," "hedonistic," "diffuse," and "inefficient." Although he concedes that the rational encounter marathon may not be the last word in the field, he asserts that it has yielded superior temporary and permanent results.

These conflicting viewpoints emphasize the need for empirical research. However, since the clinical practice of marathon therapy is still in its infancy, it should not be surprising that the majority of published reports tend to be anecdotal. Esalen in California, which is easily the most publicized growth center in the United States, and where literally hundreds of time-extended encounter sessions take place each year, is a good example of the lack of research activity generated by this movement. It was not until quite recently that Esalen began to sponsor such studies as those by Silverman, Kamiya, and Ornstein (1970) on the psychophysiological correlates of subjective experience and behavior change (brain wave and heart rate control, chemical substances present in the musculature of schizophrenics). A questionnaire sent out by this writer to a large sampling of affiliate growth centers around the nation revealed not one organized research program, nor did there seem to be much interest in subjecting the marathon experiences of individual practitioners to controlled evaluation and analysis.

Very little formal research has been done, yet a data-based assessment is a crucial step toward establishing the marathon as a proven, widely acceptable form of treatment.

Following are some illustrative examples of the type of research that has been undertaken with respect to marathons.

Descriptive Studies

In an exploratory fashion, researchers need to know what general operations and broad dimensions help to make the marathon as successful as it is intuitively felt to be. Bach (1967a) reported that he had at that time conducted over thirty marathon groups, involving at least 400 participants of whom 90 percent evaluated their experiences as "one of the most significant and meaningful" of their lives. Furthermore, even those initially disappointed "marathonians" returned for another try. Bach, attempting to delineate those parameters of marathons which have constructive effects, tested "helpfulness" or mutual aid by means of a self-report assessment checklist filled out by marathon participants after a session. The questionnaire was of a multiple-choice type; the items were compiled from frequently used words in essays written by former group members about their experiences. The data was collected from 135 persons, participating in nine different marathon groups.

The items in the questionnaire involved concepts of (1) empathic identification (similarity); (2) acceptance-warmth (affectional inclusion);

(3) self-understanding (insight mediation); (4) problem solving (reality orientation); and (5) aggression-confrontation (conflict acceptance). The subjects checked items from the list which they felt characterized the way they received help and the way they offered help. Most respondents checked several items. For helpfulness offered to others, self-understanding was cited in 25 percent of the items checked; aggression-confrontation 20 percent; acceptance-warmth 19 percent; and empathic identification and problem solving 18 percent. For helpfulness received, self-understanding totaled 25 percent, empathic identification 21 percent; acceptance-warmth, 18 percent (this dimension, thought by Carl Rogers to be the greatest factor contributing to effectiveness of encounter groups, made a relatively poor showing, according to Bach); problem solving 18 percent, and aggression-confrontation 17 percent.

Analysis of the results show that helpfulness, when received, was perceived as insight mediation. There was, according to Bach, a triple meaning to this category: (1) self-insight, (2) insight into others, and (3) insight into the effect one has on others. The marathon is considered to help develop these qualities by means of constant and prolonged feedback information. The dimension perceived most helpful when rendered was aggression-confrontation. This category together with insight was the most chosen combination. However, aggression was included by an impressive 96 percent of the subjects; it was, therefore, the most frequent additional or qualifying dimension of helpfulness *rendered*. Bach's results are interesting in the paradoxes exposed; the confrontation, experienced by members as helpful to others, did little to facilitate the dimension perceived as most helpful to themselves—insight. However, therein may lie a rationale for time-extended groups. That is, the confrontation is not assimilated by the confronted person at first, but repetition over a period of time, with others more empathically and gently speaking to the same point, allows the target person to accept the original feedback. Bach deems this insight, not confrontation, because it has become more palatable and there has been time for a more subtle kind of integration to take place.

Bach (1967b), using the same population, researched disjunctive contacts, i.e., "least helpful" types of interaction. The results supported Bach's theory about the regency of aggressive confrontation: avoidance of this dimension was seen as disjunctive by 26 percent of the participants and was substantially more often checked than most other categories.

One can raise some issue about the frequency with which the aggression-confrontation dimension was checked by the participants in terms of the possible expectations and preferences of the therapist. In a description of marathon procedures, Bach (1966) outlines a set of ground rules termed Marathon Commandments. These rules are made explicit to the group members by direct injunction or by the guidance of the group leaders. Among the expectations, aggressive confrontation is emphasized: (1) "Tact is out and brutal frankness is in"; (2) "Trying to feel better is NOT the purpose of the marathon. Self-appointed, tactful diplomats, amateur 'protectors' and Red Cross Nurses detract and dilute the levelling experiences" (p. 1001).

The efficacy of confrontation is supported by other writers. Stoller's (1968) view of the therapist's role is to evoke rather than alleviate anxiety. The extended time period is the important dimension which allows for a working through of the aroused anxiety. Stoller (1970), in order to foster confrontation, introduced videotape playback within the marathon session. The persons who were focussed upon during the tape playback react to themselves in a self-confronting manner; similarly, others in the group express their feelings. Stoller analyzed the exchanges between group members after a self-confrontation videotape playback in terms of Hill's analysis of group interaction. (Hill is referred to as stating that confrontation between group members, in terms of the relationships developed in the group, offers the greatest potential for therapeutic movement. Furthermore, Hill's studies show that this process is most infrequently engaged in and is difficult to sustain.) Stoller's findings revealed that video intervention induces and increases the therapeutic ingredient of personal confrontation.

Videotape feedback was found to be consistently and vividly effective during a nude marathon (Lawrence, 1969). The group consensus was that the playback added a valuable element to the nude marathon and provided the participants with a dramatically more accurate image of their own bodies.

In another report of characteristic feedback, Vernallis et al. (undated a) addressed himself to the question of what the therapist did over many consecutive hours of treatment during his extended marathon format, Saturation Group Therapy (SGT), in which groups engage in a series of twelve to sixteen consecutive weekend marathons. Using tape recordings taken during different periods of a sixteen week program, the samples revealed sustained attention toward one member of the group for at least twenty minutes. There were thirty-eight patients in the sample, comprising five groups who were led by four therapists. The twelve categories of therapist participation were taken from several theoretical and empirical sources, involving the utilization of psychodynamic, client-centered, learning, and group dynamic principles.

The findings and interpretations were as follows: (1) "Information Giving" was, by far, the most frequent type of participation by all therapists (42 percent). This was interpreted as being supportive to the patient, in that it allayed the high anxiety level the member experienced while scrutinizing himself under the critical eye of fellow group members. (2) "Goal Direction," which is an attempt to guide or influence the patient, particularly upon his request, accounted for 7 percent of the interaction and was translated as being similar to Bach's advice-giving dimension. (3) "Kindness" (3 percent), and (4) "Firmness" (5 percent), formed a subtest with "Goal Direction" as representative of leadership style.

Although Vernallis refers to the similarities between the modes of interaction used in his groups and those found helpful in Bach's (1967a) study, there are notable differences. For one, the patients reported those dimensions found most and least helpful in Bach's paradigm; Vernallis quantifies what the therapists did without actually indicating whether the participants did or did not consider it to be helpful. Patient-to-patient interactional modes were not assessed. Furthermore, the nature of the patient's illness or whether the participant is even defined as a patient, is an overriding factor which confounds any attempt to compare method and outcome; as we shall see later, Vernallis's group was relatively different diagnostically from most of the marathon groups.

Comparative Studies of Group Characteristics

The marathon format has been compared with traditional groups in a study of certain contributing processes, thought to be facilitative. Dies and Hess (1970), responding to the general agreement among investigators that effectiveness in a therapy or process group depends, to a great extent, upon cohesiveness, sought to investigate the degree of cohesiveness in marathon as compared to conventional group therapy. The authors hypothesized that (1) there would be a progressive improvement of cohesiveness as a function of time spent in therapy, and (2) marathon groups would produce a greater degree of overall cohesiveness than conventional groups. This latter contention was based on Stoller's assertion that the loss of time during traditional therapy when relationships have to be reestablished is eliminated during marathons and leads to a greater interpersonal involvement over a similar number of hours.

The subjects were thirty-four postnarcotic male patients accepted for treatment at the NIMH Clinical Research Center in Lexington, Kentucky, who expressed a desire for psychotherapy. They were assigned randomly into six groups: three marathon and three conventional groups. Three experienced therapists, who were naïve about the experimental hypotheses, conducted one of each type of group. The marathon groups met once for twelve consecutive hours, while the conventional groups met an hour each day for twelve consecutive weekdays. This procedure differs somewhat from the more usual time arrangements: 24–36 hours for marathon therapy and 1½ hours once or twice a week for traditional group therapy.

The testing instruments used were a semantic differential technique consisting of bipolar adjectives selected for their relevance to interpersonal behavior in groups (trusting-distrusting; cooperative-competitive, etc.); a rating scale indicating the extent of the patient's feeling of being an important member of his group (belongingness) and the degree to which he felt that his co-members understood him (understanding). Tape recordings were made during every fourth hour and rated for cohesiveness, characterized by verbal exchanges among group members. Indicators of cohesiveness were highly personal topics of conversation, evidence of emotional support, interpersonal trust, and shared participation by members. Noncohesiveness indicators included nonconstructive hostility and conflict, impersonal topics, and less interpersonal attraction. Following termination of the sessions, two additional measures of overall cohesiveness were administered: a brief questionnaire was given containing items to ascertain the subject's interest in maintaining group involvement and intactness; and all subjects participated in a "prisoner's dilemma game" to see whether the degree of trust was enhanced when the competitor was thought to be a member of their own group rather than another patient from the hospital population.

The results of this experiment strongly supported the hypothesized superiority of marathon group therapy over traditional modes for producing group cohesiveness. The use of several measurements adds to the credibility of the authors' conclusions that the rearrangement of time into an extended unit contributes to the amount of trust, personal disclosure, and emotional sharing among members.

Although Dies and Hess have made a substantial contribution with their work on the existence of greater cohesiveness in marathons, it highlights the absence of empirically tested theoretical notions; that is, it has yet to be conclusively proven that cohesion has a significantly enhancing effect on therapeutic outcome. For example, evidence to the contrary was presented in Weigel's study (1968), which showed no significant differences in outcome effectiveness between a marathon therapy group and a marathon discussion group, although there was little personal disclosure in the latter.

Myerhoff et al. (1970) conducted a study to substantiate the hypothesis that there is a heightened emotional intensity and a greater variability of emotions in marathon group therapy than in a traditional group. Also tested was the hypothesis that group cohesion would be greater in the marathon setting.

The subjects were selected from a hospitalized population of volunteers for a "more intense kind of group which has had outstanding success in helping people to get to know themselves better and in helping them become more able to help themselves; . . . treatment is not effective for people who feel . . . that their behavior has nothing to do with why they are here." (The latter is a quote from a notice posted in the hospital, to which patients responded. It is included here to give the reader a hint about the patient and therapist expectancies inherent in the statement.) All subjects were in-patients, half of whom were diagnosed as schizophrenic. The independent variable in this experiment was the arrangement of time. The marathon group (E) consisted of nine persons, eight of whom completed three six-hour sessions (eighteen total hours). The traditional therapy group (C) had thirteen patients with nine of them completing three two-hour sessions a week over three weeks (eighteen total hours). The Jacobs Adjective Check List (JACL) was administered after each two-hour treatment segment as the measurement of affective responses. Group cohesion was based on attendance rates and the expressed desire to continue therapy at the conclusion of the experiment. In order to control for therapist differences, the same therapist was used for both conditions, and an evaluation of the interaction in each format by means of the Hill Interaction Matrix revealed that therapist behavior in both groups was highly correlated.

The results of the JACL were analyzed along two dimensions for each group: positive emotion (activity, well-being) and negative emotion (anger, fear, depression, weakness). The marked difference of negative emotional responses between the marathon and traditional groups was dramatic. There was a rapid and regular decrease of reported negative emotionality for the traditional group in contrast to the sustained and irregular level of negative responses reported by the marathon group, which accounted for the overall higher level of emotionality expressed by the latter. Positive expressions were maintained at a steady, regular rate for both groups. The marathon group showed a greater cohesiveness than the traditional group.

These writers discuss their findings of greater variability and higher rate of occurrence of negative responses in marathon therapy as representative of the more intense emotional involvement which is supposedly characteristic of this type of treatment. The underlying theory for this phenomenon is that the longer, uninterrupted therapy period serves as a deterrent against maintenance of the defense system. A simplified explanation is that the individual is "too tired to be polite." [4]

No generalized statement can be made about this investigation in light of the severity of diagnosis of the research population. In a less disturbed population, for example, the highest level of negative emo-

---

[4] My preferred explanation for the emergence of sharp hostility in marathons is that a growing sense of safety and familiarity makes the participant feel secure enough to express his anger. Both explanations, however, are still conjectures.—E.E.M.

tional responses usually occurs during the middle of a marathon period, in contrast to the terminating period in which the greatest degree of positive emotionality occurs. An increase in cohesion would ordinarily be attributed to an increase of intimacy developing as a consequence of positive feelings after a sharing of negative affect. In this case, the typical pattern did not occur and the rationale for the higher cohesiveness scores for the marathon group was not offered.

This study was seen by the authors as important in that it demonstrated that hard data may be gathered on clinical material. In addition, the data served to corroborate clinical impressions made by the therapist and observers of the group.

Outcome Studies

A major concern of researchers is the testing of change in the feelings and behavior of the participant as a function of the marathon experience. Rogers (1967) makes the statement that outcome studies are the most important area of inquiry for innovative techniques. Weigel (1968), in an investigation of outcomes of marathon group psychotherapy and marathon topical discussions, utilized four groups composed of university students seeking assistance from the counseling center. Two groups of nine clients received eighteen consecutive hours of marathon therapy employing an encounter approach as well as more traditional modes. Another group of nine clients participated for the same number of hours in a topical, nonpersonal discussion. There were nine control subjects who were selected for participation and tested but who received no treatment. All participants completed an expectancy questionnaire, the MMPI, McKinney Sentence Completion Blank, and a revised Jourard Self-Disclosure Questionnaire.

Results of the experiment were not particularly illuminating. On the MMPI no scale changed significantly in either marathon therapy group; however, when data were pooled and compared to pretreatment scores there were some significantly positive changes. The McKinney Sentence Completion Blank revealed no changes for any group. In the Self-Disclosure Questionnaire there were significantly more changes for both marathon formats than for the untreated group. In general, there were few differences between the therapy groups and the discussion group. A two-week follow-up questionnaire yielded the information that 80 percent of the participants had positive feelings about the experience. Some difficulties in the sensitivity and appropriateness of the MMPI for a short term treatment outcome study is touched upon by Weigel; he had hoped to show results by the use of the newer research scales.

In a discussion about the poor showing of the marathon therapy group, the author places a great deal of responsibility on the two therapists. They reacted in a less than genuine manner and, for this reason, were the primary cause of the low level of intimacy. One therapist was protective and assumed a mental illness model role which stimulated angry feelings in the other therapist. The latter reacted by feeling discouraged and becoming passive. Interestingly enough, Smith (1970) reports that Weigel did a follow-up study which revealed that the "significant others" in the lives of twelve marathon participants expressed the feeling that the marathonians showed significantly more movement toward self-desired behavioral goals than did a control group of non-participants.

Saretsky (1970) reported on an eight-hour "minimarathon" conducted with theological students who were enrolled in a course designed to study social action as it related to urban problems. This class was divided into four seminar sections each comprised of fifteen students. One section was designated as the control group and received no marathon exposure; the three other sections did. It was hoped that a sensitivity experience might "improve communication skill, enhance self-awareness, sensitize the students to small group processes, and develop leadership potential."

Mixed results were obtained. Two of the sections showed markedly positive gains, as compared with the other experimental group and the control group, on both the Kingsley Group TAT and the Feeney Behavior Problem Checklist for Group Interaction. There was no significant difference between this last experimental group and the control group. Saretsky interprets this latter finding as a function of strong resistance patterns from the very beginning toward involuntary participation in the marathon (it was part of the course requirement). Another confounding factor was the therapist's lack of prior knowledge of the in-house power structure. One of the cooperating instructors was not entirely sympathetic to the idea of process groups operating on campus. His reluctance to allow issues emerging from the marathon to be freely discussed in his seminar section may have contributed to the negative results obtained with this group.

Another researcher utilized a minimarathon or long group therapy (nine hours) format in the treatment of married couples (Lewis, 1967). He hypothesized that (1) there would be greater congruency between the way clients feel they would like to be and the way they actually see themselves; (2) clients would make more accurate estimates about how their spouses feel about themselves; and (3) clients would rate their spouses as having improved on a list of pretreatment grievances. There were forty-eight subjects assigned to one of three conditions: (A) nine-hour group psychotherapy, (B) nine-hour educational, impersonal discussion group, or (C) no treatment condition. The writer used a Butler-Haigh Q-sort technique as the major instrument. A free response follow-up questionnaire was also administered. The data did not support the hypotheses. Although there were indications that the attitudes and feelings of the treatment participants were in a positive direction when compared to the control group, the long therapy group format showed no superiority over the long discussion group format.

An issue to be raised is the question of how much time is enough for measurable change. A nine-hour isolated experience (or the eight-hour minimarathon in Saretsky's case) does not fall into the usual marathon arrangement nor into the ongoing sensitivity group format. Perhaps a more efficacious approach would be the use of a nine-hour group as a facilitating process before beginning therapy or as an adjunct to treatment with couples.

Bach's assertion (1967c, p. 995) that the marathon group encounter is the most efficient "antidote to alienation, meaninglessness, fragmentation and other hazards of mental health in our time," led to a study designed by Guinan and Foulds (1970) to test this hypothesis. The experimental subjects were ten college students who volunteered to participate in a marathon "growth group." The untreated control group was an equal number of students who volunteered to "be in an experiment." The Personal Orientation Inventory (POI), a measure of positive mental health, was administered pre- and posttreatment, which, for the experimental group, was a weekend marathon experience.

Results showed significant changes in the mean scores of pre- and posttreatment assessment of the experimental group on the following scales: Inner Direction, Existentiality, Feeling, Reactivity, Spontaneity, Self-Acceptance, Acceptance of Aggression, and Capacity for Intimate Contact. The control group scores yielded no significant differences. However, a comparison of the treatment and control group POI pretreatment scores suggested that the two groups were significantly different in several areas, with a greater initial tendency toward mental health for the control group. Thus, a comparison of the two groups is spurious. No follow-up data was obtained.

A variation on the marathon approach yielded interesting and promising results. Vernallis et al. (undated b) designed an ambitious and innovative treatment format called Saturation Group Therapy (SGT). Reportedly similar to a number of intensive group treatments— T-group, sensitivity training, encounter group—it most closely resembles the marathon therapy of Bach. A notable difference is that SGT consists of an ongoing marathon weekend for sixteen consecutive weeks.

The participants in the experimental group consisted of four therapists, thirty-six patients who completed the treatment (there were ten dropouts), and a control group of forty-six persons. In marked contrast to most of the groups which are purportedly similar to SGT, the participants may definitely be labeled as patients. The members, all males, were classified by observation and psychometric testing as follows: fifteen as neurotic, ten as neurotic with detectable psychotic or personality disorder features, thirteen as psychotic, and eight as disordered personalities. Parenthetically, it is generally conceded that most of the testing instruments are not sensitive enough to pick up subtle changes; therefore, the presence of measurable pathology may have contributed to the firm and unequivocal test results in this study. Several assessment measurements were employed: the MMPI, Rotter's Incomplete Sentences Blanks, Symptom Rating Scale, and a Report of Social Adjustment. In addition, treatment changes were rated by peers, therapists, and participants on a scale from minus four to plus four.

Strong positive gains were reflected on several levels. There was solid psychometric evidence, in that several MMPI scales were significantly different in a positive direction from the control group, as was the Symptom Rating Scale. In addition, there were favorable gains in pre- and posttreatment and six month follow-up measurements. External criteria confirmed the gains shown on psychometric data. Treatment ratings by families, peers, self, and therapist showed improvement in varying degrees. The most impressive measure by objective means, however, was in a positive comparison with the control group on the number of problems with the law. Although both groups had previously had acting-out difficulties prior to treatment (sex offenses, drug offenses, drunkenness charges, etc.), the experimentals could claim only two traffic tickets as the sum total of their involvement with the police at termination of the study.

This experiment was fraught with many confounding complications —some patients were taking drugs and/or had additional therapy experience during the SGT; some of the control group sought and received treatment elsewhere; there were many outside variables, such as twice-a-week counseling by a social worker with a member of the patient's family; and there was socialization between patients and their families during the week, all of which may have contributed to the final outcome results. In spite of these problems this study makes a major contribution in the psychotherapy field in that it opens up an area rich in research potential. The short term intensive format could be replicated by other workers; various aspects of the format, such as group size and number of weeks in treatment can be varied and tested; and experimental use of SGT with different populations may be tried. Prison inmates, severely disturbed college students seeking counseling, and persons on parole were among the groups suggested by Vernallis as potential candidates for the saturation method.

One cannot confidently generalize the results from this patient population to less disturbed groups. Perhaps an abbreviated version would be helpful to less severely neurotic individuals, and further, a weekend marathon experience may facilitate growth and problem-solving operations for "normals."

We addressed ourselves earlier to general methodological, statistical, and evaluative problems inherent in the study of psychotherapy groups and T-groups. These same difficulties are applicable, of course, to research with marathon groups. However, there are some specific confounding and misleading variables present in the cited marathon studies that should be touched upon.

The nature of the therapist's influence upon the group is important. Weigel (1968) reported that the failure of the therapists to be open and "real" contributed to his disappointing results. His model for the effective therapist is based on Jourard's (1964) belief that the success of the therapeutic relationship is contingent upon the leader serving as a model of authenticity for the patient. However, there are divergent opinions concerning the therapist's proper role: Gibb and Gibb (1967) find leaderless groups to be highly effective; Ellis (1970) calls for an authoritative and directive leader; and Lieberman et al. (1971) suggest a wide variety of helpful modeling roles for leaders. On the other hand, most studies give short shrift to the theoretical orientation and experience of the participating therapist, implying either that they do not consider this to be a significant variable or that it just has not been taken into account.

The time factor is another dimension of the marathon experience that needs further elaboration. To begin with, there does not seem to be any universally agreed upon length of time that defines a time-extended session as constituting a marathon. The most common practice is to meet between sixteen and thirty-six hours. Some therapists break this up with specific periods allotted for sleeping and for meals; others prefer to keep the session going with the members napping and eating on an informal basis. The fact that there is no standardized procedure introduces a contaminating effect in comparative studies. Lewis (1967) working with a group for nine hours and Saretsky (1970) reporting on an eight hour group offer mixed results. These so-called minimarathons frequently seem to yield gains in some areas with some groups, but not in others. This points up the need for follow-up studies to ascertain whether permanent movement does take place in a relatively short, isolated span of time and to specify those variables that account for failures.

It has been noted in the literature (McGrath & Altman, 1966) that researchers are prone to using labels in order to designate variables. However, different investigators use the same label for operationally and conceptually diverse variables. In this review the term "cohesiveness" meant personal disclosure and shared emotional support to Dies and Hess (1970), and it meant attendance rate and desire to continue treatment to Myerhoff et al. (1970).

An illustration of still another difficulty in the comparability of the various marathon studies is the researcher's tendency to classify participants as disturbed versus normal. It is not always clear what the terms mean in a particular experimental paradigm. For example, Guinan and Foulds (1970) defined their groups as normal in that they were well-functioning adults, yet the experimental and control groups differed significantly on the pretest criterion of self-actualization. Just which group constitutes the "normals" is open to question. Vernallis's (undated b) group consisted of the "psychiatric walking wounded," a term which also seems to characterize the individuals described by Myerhoff et al. (1970); other leaders are very vague and imprecise when mentioning the population of their respective groups. Along these lines, group composition is often quite diverse since it is common practice not to prescreen candidates for marathons. Not only is a direct comparison between groups meaningless because of this tendency, but one may infer different goals and expectations, often unstated, for the outcome of a marathon experience as a function of the population being worked with. It is incumbent upon the researcher, then, to define the participants by some objective measurement and to state the prevailing circumstances and goals.

A comprehensive study is now in progress which shows an in-depth awareness of the need to elucidate the exact conditions under which therapeutic learning takes place, what kind of learning occurs, and when, if indeed, this learning does occur.

Lieberman, Yalom, and Miles (1971) are currently evaluating the findings of an elaborate group experience project conducted at Stanford University. In brief, they compared ten experimental groups representing most of the major approaches in the encounter movement: (1) T-groups, (2) groups reflecting a Rogerian orientation, (3) Synanon groups, (4) transactional-analysis groups, (5) Gestalt therapy groups, (6) "nonverbal" groups, (7) psychodrama groups, (8) psychoanalytically oriented groups, (9) marathon groups, and (10) leaderless tape groups. These groups were run by ten leaders experienced in one of the orientations just outlined. Two control groups were also employed. A time limit (thirty hours) was set as the total duration of the group experience. Only the leader selected to conduct marathons could utilize the time in a continuous manner. Some nonmarathon leaders chose to meet twice a week for ten weeks, others began with a six-hour session followed by weekly sessions and a six-hour final session. All subjects were tested several weeks before assignment, about two months after the pretest, and six months after termination.

The ambitiousness and level of complexity of the research strategy involved assessment of: (1) peak experiences, (2) interpersonal construct systems, (3) self-ideal discrepancy, (4) value reorientation, (5) the effect on life decisions, (6) learning new ways of dealing with personal dilemmas, (7) interpersonal changes, (8) leader ratings of participants, (9) social network ratings of change, (10) identification of psychological casualties resulting from the group experience, and (11) a study of group processes (i.e., are some groups more effective than others and, if so, what are the characteristics of an effective group?).

A preliminary report by the authors addresses itself to the following questions: Does an encounter group affect its members? Do the various types of approaches create different effects? Are there differences in the style and personality among the leaders that may be associated with the differences in results? Do different groups have unique properties? Do the participant's phenomenal experiences differ from group to group?

An overwhelming majority (75 percent) of the participants saw their group as constructive. This positive feeling was not matched by the degree of measured change in the individual (only about 35 percent of the experimental population "improved"). Most striking were the significant differences between groups—some groups had almost no overall effect on members while in other groups almost everyone was strongly affected. The groups differed sharply in the number of dropouts, ranging from a high of 40 percent to a low of zero percent. "Group characteristics associated with drop-outs were those that emphasized attack, challenge, and confrontation with few visible means of support. High drop-out rates, however, also occurred in groups that had very little stimulative input by leaders" (Lieberman, Yalom, and Miles, 1971, p. 38). The findings suggest that encounter leaders differ widely in their approach. A factor analysis of observer ratings of leader behavior yielded seven variables that may have a significant influence on individual and group impact: (1) Intrusive Modeling (challenging, confronting, revealing self and values, focussing on self, behaving as a participant), (2) Command Response (inviting, eliciting, questioning, suggesting procedures, facing the group with a decision task), (3) Drawing Attention (reflecting, calling on, comparing and contrasting, focussing), (4) Cognitive Inputs (explaining, interpreting, providing frameworks, providing concepts), (5) Setting Limits (group management maneuvers), (6) Mirroring (reflecting and summarizing), and (7) Support (protecting, showing love and affection, support and encouragement, and inviting feedback).

The authors concluded that since groups markedly differ in the amount of change, type of change, leader behavior, and a number of basic group characteristics (e.g., norms), it is likely that meaningful relationships can be established between such characteristics and outcome. In view of such contradictory experiences, it appears that in studying encounter groups there is no uniformity as implied in most studies; rather, there is a wide range of operations by leaders and participants that can lead to many different kinds of learning. Specific reference to the relative effectiveness of the marathon group is not included in this preliminary report. When the data analysis is finally completed, it should offer some interesting leads to a question that will interest many therapists, namely, what is the best use one can make of a finite amount of time spent with a group of patients. A corollary to this issue is what should happen during that span of time to facilitate positive change. Further research will be necessary to evaluate the application and generalization of Lieberman's findings to other groups with different populations.

Underlying other considerations in the study of groups is the need for strong theoretical postulates which can be operationally defined and tested. Jack and Lorraine Gibb have built a systematic theory of group development and group leadership called TORI. Using central concepts of climate, data flow, goal formation, and control, they have experimented with the different circumstances under which persons can move from fear to trust, from guardedness to openness, from strategies of persuasion and competition to realization and search, and from dependence-dominance to interdependence and emergence.

To conclude, there are many variables and interrelationships between variables which must be subjected to empirical research. As a first step, the characteristics of group members and the selection of those who would work best together in a therapeutic setting should be thoroughly explored. This could be in terms of psychological experience and sophistication, personality attributes, and attitudes about the marathon, other members, and the therapist. The composition of the group is another area which merits exploration. The size of the group, the goals of the group, the homo- or heterogeneity of the group have to be considered. The therapist's theoretical orientation may very well have a marked effect upon the success or failure of the marathon group. If one assumes competence, would a Gestalt therapy approach be more or less efficacious than a traditional approach? What of the newer encounter techniques, hypnotherapy, behavior modification, etc? The therapist's style—permissive, authoritative, peerish, nondirective, assertive, intellectual or self-disclosing—all these approaches should be tested. Group process and dynamics must be elucidated. Outcome studies (which imply the need for sensitive and appropriate instrumentation) are of utmost importance.

Follow-up studies are necessary, not just on the level of simply reporting subjective changes in feelings and attitudes. Mintz (1969), for example, has published the results of feedback from former marathon members (over 86 percent improved). This is valuable as a beginning orientation to the repercussions of the marathon experience, but only verification by explicit external criteria can demonstrate enduring effectiveness. How much transfer is there as experienced by spouses, other members of the family, associates at work, subordinates, and the boss? Is the marathon helpful or detrimental to ongoing treatment? There are no published studies dealing with this latter point, yet it is an issue of vital concern to clinicians. How are characterological resistance patterns transformed? What is the effect on transference towards one's own therapist after having a peak experience in another leader's marathon group? Amidst numerous reports of growth-producing regressions in the service of the ego, what happens after the marathon is over? Is the patient simply reconstituted at a higher level or is it possible that the high level of guilt and anxiety aroused by the marathon breakthroughs create new sources of primitive threat, the vicissitudes of which must be dealt with subsequently? [5] The marathon literature, thus far, has been deficient in describing how ongoing therapy could be best coordinated with marathon experiences.

To cite a clinical example, a therapist recently ran a marathon that he considered highly successful. When the patients returned to their regular group (eight of the marathon participants were drawn from one of the therapist's own groups), they seemed to have an air of smugness and complacency. This "flight into health" took the form of not wanting to buckle down and work things through. When it became evident that this attitude was not simply transitory and seemed to be contagious throughout the group, it was interpreted as resistance. Over a number of sessions, it developed that many patients had obtained a degree of intimacy and closeness during the marathon that was quite unusual for most of them and also very frightening. Their denial tendencies in the group were viewed as a last-ditch holding-on, a bartering for time, before they finally got around to surrendering the secondary gains of their neuroses. Once this resistance was confronted and worked through, many of the apparent gains made during the marthon again became evident. This summarizes the personal experiences of one therapist involved with a particular set of people "coming back home." The field would benefit if a large number of therapists would report on what the short and long term trends were for their patients who participated in marathons.

In addition to the various complexities which are entailed in conducting relevant, effective research on the effects of psychotherapy in general, research on the marathon must involve consideration of its

---

[5] These are important questions. It is hoped that some preliminary answers are provided in this book.—E.E.M.

specific purpose. Is it useful primarily as an adjunct to conventional therapy, as suggested by Fagan (1970) and Warkentin (1970)? Is it a type of therapy in its own right? Or is it a means of providing growth and insight to individuals who are not primarily interested in undergoing therapy? And in what ways should the conduct of a marathon differ in relation to its stated purpose? The values of this promising innovation, as well its limitations, still await further research to provide a conceptual background and technical information for marathon practitioners.

REFERENCES

Anthony, E. J. Discussion. *International Journal of Group Psychotherapy*, 1968, *8*, 249–255.

Argyris, C. *Interpersonal competence and organizational behavior.* Homewood, Ill.: Irwin, 1962.

Argyris, C. Incompleteness of social psychological theory. *American Psychologist*, 1969, *24*(10).

Bach, G. R. The marathon group: Intensive practice of intimate interaction. *Psychological Reports*, 1966, *18*, 995–1002.

Bach, G. R. Marathon group dynamics: Dimensions of helpfulness. *Psychological Reports*, 1967, *20*, 1147–1158. (a)

Bach, G. R. Marathon group dynamics: Disjunctive contacts. *Psychological Reports*, 1967, *20*, 1163–1172. (b)

Bach, G. R. Marathon group dynamics. *Psychological Reports*, 1967, *20*, 995–999. (c)

Bass, B. M. Mood changes during a management training laboratory. *Journal of Applied Psychology*, 1964, *46*, 361–364.

Bednar, R. L. Group psychotherapy research variables. *International Journal of Group Psychotherapy*, 1970, *20*(2), 146–152.

Benne, K. D. History of the T-group in the laboratory setting. In L. P. Bradford, J. R. Gibb, & K. D. Benne (Eds.), *T-group theory and laboratory method.* New York: Wiley & Sons, 1964.

Bindrim, P. A report on a nude marathon. *Psychotherapy: Theory, Research and Practice*, 1968, *5*(3), 180–188.

Buchanan, P. C. Evaluating the effectiveness of laboratory training in industry. In *Explorations in human relations training and research.* No. 1. Washington, D.C.: National Training Laboratories-National Education Association, 1965.

Bunker, D. R. The effect of laboratory education upon individual behavior. In E. H. Schein & W. G. Bennis (Eds.), *Personal and organizational changes through group methods: The laboratory approach.* New York: Wiley & Sons, 1965.

Burton, A. Encounter, existence, and psychotherapy. In A. Burton (Ed.), *Encounter.* San Francisco: Jossey-Bass, 1970.

Campbell, J. P., & Dunnette, M. D. Effectiveness of T-group experiences in managerial training and development. *Psychological Bulletin*, 1968, *70*(2), 73–104.

Culbert, S., Clark, J., & Bobele, H. Measure of change toward self-actualization in two sensitivity training groups. *Journal of Counseling Psychology*, 1968, *1*, 53–57.

Dies, R., & Hess, A. Cohesiveness in marathon and conventional group psychotherapy: An empirical investigation. Paper presented at Eastern Psychological Association, Atlantic City, April 1970.

Ellis, A. A weekend of rational encounter. In A. Burton (Ed.), *Encounter*. San Francisco: Jossey-Bass, 1970.

Fagan, J. The tasks of the therapist. In J. Fagan & I. L. Shepherd (Eds.), *Gestalt therapy now*. Palo Alto, Calif.: Science & Behavior Books, 1970.

Gassner, S., Gold, J., & Sandowsky, A. M. Changes in the phenomenal field as a result of human relations training. *Journal of Psychology*, 1964, *58*, 33–41.

Gibb, J. R., & Gibb, L. M. Humanistic elements in group growth. In J. Bugental (Ed.), *Challenges of humanistic psychology*. New York: McGraw-Hill, 1967.

Gibb, J. R., & Gibb, L. M. Role freedom in a TORI group. In A. Burton (Ed.), *Encounter*. San Francisco: Jossey-Bass, 1970.

Guinan, J. F., & Foulds, M. L. Marathon group: Facilitator of personal growth? *Journal of Counseling Psychology*, 1970, *17*(2), 145–149.

Harrison, R. Cognitive change and participation in a sensitivity training laboratory. *Journal of Consulting Psychology*, 1966, *30*, 517–520.

Hill, W. F. *Hill interaction matrix*. Los Angeles: Youth Studies Center, 1965.

Holt, R. R. Experimental methods in clinical psychology. In B. J. Wolman (Ed.), *Handbook of clinical psychology*. New York: McGraw-Hill, 1965.

House, R. J. T-group education and leadership effectiveness: A review of empirical literature and a critical evaluation. *Personnel Psychology*, 1967, *20*, 1–32.

Jourard, S. M. *The transparent self: Self-disclosure and well-being*. Princeton, N.J.: Van Nostrand, 1964.

Keutzer, C., Fosmire, F. R., Diller, R., & Smith, M. D. Laboratory training in a new social system: Evaluation of a two-week program for high school personnel. Paper presented at Western Psychological Association, Canada, 1969.

Kuriloff, A. H., & Atkins, S. T-group for a work team. *Journal of Applied Behavioral Science*, 1966, *2*, 63–94.

Lawrence, S. Videotape and other therapeutic procedures with nude marathon groups. *American Psychologist*, 1969, *24*(4), 476–479.

Lewis, R. W. The effect of long group therapy sessions on participant perceptions of self and others. Ph.D. dissertation, University of Oregon, 1967.

Lieberman, M. A., Yalom, I. D., & Miles, M. B. The group experience project: A comparison of ten encounter technologies. In L. Blank, G. B. Gottsegen, & M. G. Gottsegen (Eds.), *Confrontation: Encounters in self and interpersonal awareness*. New York: Macmillan, 1971.

Loevinger, J. Conflict of commitment in clinical research. *American Psychologist*, 1963, *18*, 241–251.

Lohman, J., Zenger, J. H., & Weschler, I. R. Some perceptual changes during sensitivity training. *Journal of Educational Research*, 1959, *53*, 28–31.

McGrath, J. E., & Altman, I. *Small group research*. New York: Holt, Rinehart, & Winston, 1966.

Miles, M. B. Human relations training: Processes and outcomes. *Journal of Counseling Psychology*, 1960, *7*, 301–306.

Miles, M. B., Cohen, S., & Whitman, F. Changes in performance test scores after human relations training. Mimeographed manuscript. New York: Horace Mann-Lincoln Institute of School Experimentation, Teachers College, Columbia University, 1959.

Mintz, E. E. Marathon groups—A preliminary investigation. *Journal of Contemporary Psychotherapy*, 1969, *1*(2), 91–94.

Myerhoff, H. I., Jacobs, A., & Stoller, F. Emotionality in marathon and traditional psychotherapy groups. *Psychotherapy: Theory, Research, and Practice*, 1970, *7*(1), 33–36.

Oshry, B. I., & Harrison, R. Transfer from here-and-now to there-and-then: Changes in organizational problem diagnosis stemming from T-group training. *Journal of Applied Behavioral Science*, 1966, *2*, 185–198.

Richard, H. C. Selected group psychotherapy evaluation studies. *Journal of General Psychology*, 1962, *67*, 35–50.

Rogers, C. R. The process of the basic encounter group. In J. Bugental (Ed.), *Challenges of humanistic psychology*. New York: McGraw-Hill, 1967.

Saretsky, T. Uses and abuses of T-groups. Paper presented at American Group Psychotherapy Association, New Orleans, 1970.

Schutz, W. C., & Allen, V. L. The effects of a T-group laboratory on interpersonal behavior. *Journal of Applied Behavioral Science*, 1966, *2*, 265–286.

Silverman, J., Kamiya, J., & Ornstein, R. Esalen research. Panel discussion presented at Esalen Benefit, New York, 1970.

Smith, P. B. Attitude changes associated with training in human relations. *British Journal of Social and Clinical Psychology*, 1964, *3*, 104–113.

Smith, R. J. Encounter therapies. *International Journal of Group Psychotherapy*, 1970, *20*(2), 192–209.

Spotnitz, H. Discussion. *International Journal of Group Psychotherapy*, 1968, *28*, 236–239.

Stock, D. A survey of research on T-groups. In L. P. Bradford, J. R. Gibb, & K. D. Benne (Eds.), *T-group theory and laboratory method*. New York: Wiley & Sons, 1964.

Stoller, F. H. Accelerated interaction: A time-limited approach based on the brief, intensive group. *International Journal of Group Psychotherapy*, 1968, *18*, 220–235.

Stoller, F. H. Therapeutic concepts reconsidered in light of videotape experience. *Comparative Group Studies*, 1970, *1*, 5–17.

Underwood, W. J. Evaluation of laboratory method training. *Training Directors Journal*, 1965, *19*(5), 34–40.

Vernallis, F. *Saturation group therapy*. Los Angeles: Human Interaction Research Institute, 1969.

Vernallis, F., Shipper, J. C., Butler, D. C., & Holson, D. G. Therapist participation in saturation group therapy. Submitted to NIMH, (undated). (*a*)

Vernallis, F., Shipper, J. C., Butler, D. C., Tomlinson, T. M. Saturation group psychotherapy in a weekend clinic: An outcome study. Submitted to NIMH, (undated). (*b*)

Warkentin, J. Intensity in group encounter. In A. Burton (Ed.), *Encounter*. San Francisco: Jossey-Bass, 1970.

Weigel, R. G. Outcomes of marathon group therapy and marathon group topical discussion. Ph.D. dissertation, University of Missouri, Columbia, 1968.

11 THE PRESENT SCENE

Specific data is still to be gathered under rigorously controlled conditions regarding the efficacy of the encounter marathon and similar groups, the circumstances under which they are maximally efficacious, and the ways in which group interaction affects the individual members. The difficulties of conducting such rigorous research became evident in the preceding chapter. Yet in another sense, the verdict on the value of these groups is already given by society itself. Wherever the philosophy and procedures of encounter groups become known, they are likely to flourish and proliferate to an extent which indicates that they are meeting basic needs of our culture.

A complete survey of the ways in which encounter methods are being used and the situations to which they are being applied would reach encyclopedic proportions. Early in 1970, the Manhattan Board of Mental Health estimated that about five thousand experiential groups already existed in this borough alone (Franke, 1970). Articles on the encounter group phenomenon, some critical and some enthusiastic, appear in the popular press almost continually, with a rapidity which unquestionably goes beyond the ability of research workers to provide justification for either the criticism or the enthusiasm. Reactions range from an appraisal of sensitivity training by an extremely conservative journalist as "emotionally and morally destructive" (Allen, 1968), to an evaluation of it by a respected psychologist as a basic social development which shows promise of solving many of the major problems of our time (Rogers, 1969).

The encounter approach is being applied to an increasing variety of situations and integrated with a variety of new techniques. Many variations of the extended time format are being used in diverse settings. This chapter provides a sampling of some of the new techniques, the current problems, and the widely varying applications of the encounter marathon which are a part of the contemporary scene.

Viewpoints on Leadership

Among acknowledged leaders in the behavioral sciences, opinions differ sharply as to whether the responsibility of conducting an encounter group should be confined to those who have a professional background plus specialized training; whether personal attributes are of primary importance regardless of training; or whether indeed a group may not function best as a peer group without any leadership at all.

Even before the development of the encounter group movement, the shortage of mental health professionals was generally recognized, and experiments were being undertaken to provide therapeutic services to the community by short-term training of people without a formal professional background, known as paraprofessionals (Milman et al., undated). As popular interest in encounter groups increases, many leaders with minimal background and experience, sometimes with none, offer themselves as leaders, usually choosing some variation of the marathon format. These groups can legally be advertised if they are not described as offering psychotherapy and hence do not come under the jurisdiction of state regulations. Personal charisma and familiarity with a few encounter techniques may be the sole qualifications of these practitioners, and there is concern both in professional organizations and among informed laymen about the extent of their usefulness.[1]

The American Psychiatric Association and the American Psychological Association appear to be moving toward similar official positions. The psychiatric organization has reported the findings of a Task Force on Recent Developments in the Use of Small Groups (Yalom et al., 1970), which points out the sparsity of research data as to either the dangers or the values of encounter experience; acknowledges that the proliferation of encounter groups must represent a response to the prevalent social starvation for intimacy; and regards skillful and responsible leadership as the critical factor in determining whether encounter experiences will be valuable or dangerous.

Similarly, the American Psychological Association has formed several committees, including a special subcommittee of the APA Committee on Scientific and Professional Ethics and Conduct, to develop a set of standards and ethics for innovative group procedures (Lakin, 1969). The American Group Psychotherapy Association has devoted several panels and symposia at its annual conferences to the discussion of appropriate training and ethical standards for encounter group leaders.

Yet, ironically, if professional organizations set up standards of training and conduct for the leaders of marathons and other encounter groups, these regulations will affect only the practitioners who are already members of the organizations, and who are therefore already accredited in a basic psychotherapeutic discipline. Untrained leaders without professional status can safely disregard the threat of sanctions

[1] Contemporary journalism recognizes this problem. For example, an article headlined *Playing Instant Joy to the Lonely Crowd* (Chesler, 1969) describes "an all-night group thing" conducted at $10 per person by a leader with vague or nonexistent qualifications, who utilized powerful nonverbal techniques to achieve "a manic, impersonal intensity . . . of pretended intimacy."

from professional organizations to which they do not in any case belong.

Perhaps the establishment of standards by professional organizations will be most effective through public education which would encourage people seeking encounter group experience to examine the qualifications of the leader. Yet some behavioral scientists are seriously questioning whether it is necessary, or even desirable, for the leader to function as a trained professional specialist or even to undergo formal professional training.

Gibb and Gibb (1968a & b; 1970), after several years spent in observing groups of various sizes in a wide number of settings, conclude unequivocally that the interaction within the group is a growth force so potent that the presence of a leader is unnecessary and may even be undesirable. If there is a leader, his contribution to the group should consist of being "personal, human, open, self-determining, and interdependent. . . . He will meet his role responsibilities as a therapist or professional trainer by being as fully a person as it is possible for him to be" (1970, p. 50). This is in sharp contrast to the prestructured programming of Bindrim (1968); the "fight training" of Bach (1969); and the highly structured rational approach of Ellis (1970), who assigns a specific therapeutic, directive function to the leader.[2]

According to Gibb and Gibb, only in a leaderless group or in a group with a "role-free" leader can the attributes of Trust-Openness-Realization-Interdependence (their formulation of the qualities which emerge in groups, termed TORI) develop. They recommend that leaders should seek to form their own "autogenic" groups, preferably beginning with some variation of the marathon time format, and maintain that "any group of people who have enough motivation can get together and form an intensive, intimate, compelling, and meaningful learning group" (1968a, p. 108).

The suggestion that readers form autogenic groups, in the absence of accumulated data, can be discussed only speculatively. To me it seems that anyone who takes the responsibility of organizing such a group would automatically be regarded as its leader, at least in the initial stages. Such an organizer might seek to avoid official leadership and try instead to help create a climate of trust and openness. Yet it would seem that the ability to organize a group, to help establish the sought-for atmosphere of openness and trust, and at the same time avoid imposing leadership upon the group, might be rarer among laymen than among professionals. If continuing research clearly establishes the desirability of nondirective, nondogmatic, nondidactic group leadership, then training for group leadership will be likely to implement these findings.

---

[2] The sharp contrast among these workers, all of whom tend to prefer the marathon time format, indicates once more that research on marathon groups cannot safely disregard the orientation of the leader.

However, some evidence does exist that under appropriate circumstances effective groups may develop with a minimum of formal leadership. Three therapists (Bloomberg et al., 1969), impressed by the strong relatedness which developed in their marathon groups, invited former participants to take part in bimonthly meetings. At the beginning, the therapists directed these groups actively, for instance insisting that only one interaction should go on at a time. However, after a year the group became so large that it divided into subgroups, and natural leaders emerged who facilitated interaction in the independent groups, which chose to have no formal leadership.

Two years after this "experiment in community development" began, the therapists no longer took responsibility. The group itself, now continually growing by word-of-mouth, initiated a series of projects, including a body-awareness subgroup, a Summerhill-type school, and the development of intensive leaderless groups in a neighboring city by participants who had originally attended the first therapist-led marathons.

After the therapists moved to another state, the activities of the original groups continued. The authors believe that their emphasis on honesty, openness, and permissiveness enabled a community to develop on the basis of positive human qualities. They contrast this basis with that of communities which are temporarily drawn together by facing a common disaster (war or natural catastrophe) or which are based on a common Utopian ideal which separates them from the rest of society as superior.

A variation on the leaderless group has been developed by behavioral scientists who utilized taped instructions or printed instructions to facilitate interaction. At the Human Development Institute in Atlanta, a method was worked out to employ printed booklets for the instruction of leaderless groups engaged in the development of management skills (Berlin, 1965). The development of PEER (the acronym of Planned Experiences for Effective Relating), a program of taped instructions for small groups worked out at the Western Behavioral Sciences Institute, represents seven years of experimentation and research (Berzon et al., 1969).

PEER began with efforts to increase the employability of clients for vocational rehabilitation being served by a California state social agency. Its general purpose was "to help people learn to relate more fully and effectively to the world around them" (Berzon et al., 1969, p. 73) by offering a series of structured opportunities for interaction. Various intensive time schedules were used, such as two weekend workshops each including five two-hour sessions, or two two-hour sessions each day for five consecutive days. In response to taped instructions, participants began with initial encounters, such as having each participant in turn move around the circle of members, touching and looking at each one, and sharing the initial impression. The exercise of passing each member in turn physically around the circle was used to develop mutual trustfulness. Taped instructions also emphasized the importance of sharing experience in the here-and-now. In later sessions, the groups focussed on becoming more aware of their own strengths and of the strengths of other people, on nonverbal expressions of positive feelings, and similar experiences designed to identify and enhance personal resources rather than to focus on emotional problems. For each activity, the tape offered each participant an opportunity to decide privately whether or not to participate, so that each group member could freely decide what degree of involvement he wished. In tests of the PEER program with two highly diverse groups, the inmates of a prison honor camp and summer session students at the University of California at Berkeley, significant positive changes on a self-concept scale were found, and personal reports of the experience were positive also. The authors suggest that similar programs might be developed for special groups such as children, families, and parties to a controversial negotiation. It may be conjectured also that the PEER audiotape technique might be modified for groups which would presumably require specialized leadership, but for which specialized leadership in proportion to the population demand might be particularly difficult to find, such as geriatric groups, handicapped groups, and prison populations.

Self-help groups, formed for the purpose of mutual aid for a mutual problem, also work without leaders (Hurwitz, 1970). They focus on common problems such as gambling, obesity, drug addiction, and alcoholism. They are known to be effective for a high proportion of the participants; for instance, Ruth Fox (quoted by Hurwitz, p. 70), a specialist in work with alcoholics, regards Alcoholics Anonymous as probably the most helpful medium of treatment. Some of these groups, especially those which are composed of drug addicts, make use of the marathon encounter approach, others prefer weekly meetings. New groups spring into existence when a local group decides that it is of optimum size and sends a delegation to form a new group in another community; or when someone is interested in starting such a group and asks for assistance from another group of the same type. These peer self-help groups focus on a single problem and typically emphasize self-control and conformity to group norms but resemble encounter groups in their stress on personal honesty and mutual helpfulness.

Innovative Techniques

As the encounter group movement expands, a variety of new techniques make their appearance. As described in preceding chapters, the encounter marathon is especially appropriate for the utilization of sensory-awareness techniques, the Gestalt approach, psychodramatic scenarios, and nonverbal encounters. Among more recent developments may be cited the use of videotapes, the employment of the "second-chance family," [3] and the introduction of nudity.

Recent technological developments have made it possible to introduce into a group a closed circuit television camera which can record the events of the group, and which can then be played back so that the group can scrutinize and react to its behavior. Stoller (1967, 1971), who has used this technique in marathon groups and a variety of other situations, warns that special leadership skills are required so that the interaction of the group will not become subordinate to the fascination of watching itself on television. He recommends that a videotaped group be conducted by two leaders, who may take turns in operating the television camera, since the selection of which aspects of the group interaction should be screened at any given moment may require considerable therapeutic sophistication.

The value of videotape techniques in encounter groups is primarily that it offers a direct, immediate opportunity for self-confrontation and may enable an individual to perceive discrepancies between the way in which he thinks he is behaving, or wishes to behave, and the way in which he actually is behaving. Traits of which the group member is genuinely unaware, such as tendencies to be provocative or domineering or evasive, may appear on the camera so clearly that it is no longer possible to deny them. As in any other type of group, the participant is then given an opportunity to discuss his behavior, compare it with his previous picture of himself, and perhaps experiment with different ways of behavior. The subtle, complex interrelationships of couples and of families can often be revealed with special clarity in a relatively short period of time if they are enabled to view themselves on the screen, subsequently discussing their interaction.

This technique has also been found useful for the ongoing treatment of hospitalized psychiatric patients (Lawrence, 1971). About two hundred patients, all volunteers, participated in groups which were viewed by the remainder of the hospital population on closed-circuit TV. It was found that group members were able to become involved with one another and with the therapist despite the distractions of camera, crew, and lights. An unexpected bonus for this technique occurred when the televised group members returned to their respective wards, where their wardmates had observed the program; they were greeted with great

[3] I am indebted to Drs. Leonard Blank, Gloria B. Gottsegen, and Monroe G. Gottsegen for providing me with material on innovative techniques which appears in more expanded form in their book *Confrontation: Encounters in Self and Interpersonal Awareness* (1971), New York, Macmillan.

warmth and interest, indicating that the experience had stimulated a feeling of personal contact among the ward inmates.

Videotape, it may be conjectured, may prove of special value in the treatment of psychosis, not only because of its intrinsically stimulating quality, but also because a vague body image and a confused sense of personal identity are usually part of the psychotic state. An opportunity for the patient to observe himself in immediate, lively interaction with others might well be helpful in stimulating ego development in these respects.

The technique of the second-chance family was developed by Malamud (1971) in his New York University workshop classes on self-understanding and has been adapted by several marathon therapists. Here the group creates its own families, "the family that might have been, the 'now' family that cherishes human value, allows for individuality, and encourages warmth and closeness."

Family members are not grouped together arbitrarily but are chosen after group members have had ample opportunity to know one another through the use of encounter techniques which are focussed primarily, though not exclusively, on feelings about family membership. Attention is paid to feelings about birth order, siblings, and the relative dominance of mother or father. Preliminary choices of second-chance families are then made, and the participants have an opportunity to experience and ventilate their early anxieties about being chosen or not chosen. Ample time is allowed for discussion so that no group member is left without a chance to deal with whatever early family anxieties are evoked by the experience. Finally, family groups are formed, and each group is assigned its own "home area" in the classroom, to be kept until the fifteen-week course comes to an end.

A family relationship of mutual support is encouraged. Family members exchange phone numbers, plan alternate meetings for self-exploration or for reaction, and support one another in their outside life situations. They are given exercises which may help to develop their ability to listen to and understand one another, to share their feelings, and to deal with family crises. It is believed that this experience may help dispel the traumatic aftereffects which are left over for most people from early family experience and may enable the participants to relate more satisfyingly to their actual families of the present time.

Nude marathons, pioneered in 1967 by Paul Bindrim on the basis of a suggestion by Abraham Maslow, have since been conducted by a number of marathon therapists. They are of special value for people who are insecure about their physical appearance. In a nude marathon conducted by myself, a man who had always been ashamed to have a woman see his genitals, because one of the testicles was slightly smaller than the other, recovered completely from this anxiety and reported a great increase in his feelings of sexual freedom and enjoyment. It is possible to conduct a nude marathon in the same way that any other marathon would be conducted, except that the setting must be selected for privacy and appropriateness, and that the participants must clearly understand that nudity is encouraged although not required. Under these circumstances, self-consciousness disappears rather quickly, and inappropriate or embarrassing sexual arousal, which is usually feared by the participants, does not occur.

Bindrim's marathons, however, have a special format which has been followed in a series of over sixty such groups, although the format is always modified if special needs emerge within the group (Bindrim, 1968, 1969). They continue for about twenty hours and are conducted in a secluded setting with a heated swimming pool. Participants sign a preliminary agreement which indicates their understanding that the group is to be nude; that disrobing is voluntary; that they will abstain during the session from alcohol or psychedelic drugs; and that they will not engage in overt sexual expression, defined as any activity which would generally be considered socially unacceptable in a similar group wearing clothing.

The marathon begins with a get-acquainted period in which the participants remain clothed and are given a chance to express their anxieties about nudity. Members then retire to separate dressingrooms and remove their clothing. After this there is a period of nude encounter and experience which includes bodily contact, humming, music, and the use of stroboscopic light. This period lasts for about eight hours, after which a four-hour period of silence is enjoined, during which the participants sleep, rest, or meditate. Wine may be served ceremonially at the beginning of the silence.

After the rest period, the group enters the swimming pool and participates in physical procedures designed to encourage regression through massage, holding and rocking one another in the water, and occasionally by feeding a participant with a baby bottle. It is reported that strong feelings of rage, terror, and dependency often emerge through the use of these techniques. Thereafter, several hours are allocated during which the participants discuss their experiences. A three-hour follow-up session is scheduled for the same group a month later.

Bindrim states that about 50 percent of his participants report major positive changes in their lives and in their feelings toward themselves and others. No negative results are reported, a finding which presumably is related to the fact that participants in the nude marathons are self-selected, are aware of what to expect, and are consistently given options as to the extent of their participation.

My own feeling, based on speculation and awaiting confirmation or disproof through the eventual accumulation of research data, is that the most controversial feature of Bindrim's approach is not the nudity, but the predetermined structuring of group interaction, such as the enforcement of a period of silence. There is a sharp contrast between Bindrim's clear-cut leadership and the encouragement of spontaneous interaction which characterizes most other types of encounter groups. Nudity, as Bindrim sees it, enhances "the freedom to disrobe emotionally"; assists participants to explore their own unresolved distortions in relation to their bodily self-images, especially their distortions about their sexual identities; and facilitates a regressive experience which may lead to a major cathartic breakthrough. These same values, it seems to me, might be obtained in a more spontaneous marathon encounter group in which nudity would simply offer another dimension of self-revelation.

Growth Centers

The proliferation of growth centers is probably the most dramatic single index of the existence of a need for intimate, spontaneous experience which is not met in conventional social settings. Early in 1970 the Association for Humanistic Psychology listed well over a hundred growth centers, and probably this number doubled a year later.

The prototype of the growth centers is Esalen, which began in 1962 when its president, Mike Murphy, in cooperation with Richard Price, decided to use his coastal land at Big Sur for the establishment of "a forum to bring together a wide variety of approaches toward the enhancement of the human potential" (*Esalen Newsletter*, 1968). The dramatic beauty of the natural setting, the hot springs in which men and women bathe nude, and its openness to experimental approaches toward widening human experience have all contributed to a popular impression of Esalen which is sometimes misleadingly sensational, as in *Time Magazine's* repeated references to "the feelie groups of California."

Actually, in addition to its experimental activities, Esalen is a stimulus and source for research in education, psychopathology, and other areas. The Ford Foundation has financed an Esalen project for the development of educational techniques to integrate emotional experiences with cognitive experiences. The California Department of Mental Hygiene and the National Institute of Mental Health are collaborating with Esalen to explore nontraditional methods of treating schizophrenia, which seem to hold out the promise of helping at least some schizophrenic individuals achieve a level of functioning and awareness superior to the previous nonpsychotic personality. Esalen has also drawn the interest of theologians, and the National Council of Churches has sponsored a series of Esalen workshops entitled Theological Reflection on the

Human Potential, in which theologians of various sects have participated in groups with Esalen leaders in an effort to integrate religious experiences with other means of facilitating growth and awareness.

The principal activity at Esalen is a year-long series of workshops, most of them conducted over a weekend in the time format of the marathon or the workshop, some lasting for a week or even a month. Esalen is usually identified with the Gestalt therapy of Frederick Perls, the encounter games of William Schutz, the sensory-awareness work of Bernard Gunther, and the family therapy of Virginia Satir, all of whom spent some years in residence there and have used the resources of Esalen not only to work with participants who may come from all over the country, but also to offer professional training in their specialized approaches. Esalen, however, is highly eclectic. Within a few months, it may offer seminars with "a Protestant theologian, an advocate of LSD, a Carmelite monk, an existential psychotherapist, the president of the American Psychological Association, a historian, an authority on extrasensory perception, a Zen scholar, an architect, or a Hindu mystic" (Murphy, 1967, p. 35). Other weekend workshops may focus on spontaneous dancing, massage, the development of personal creativity, or interracial encounters. Esalen has also developed branch centers at which similar programs are offered. Some workshops are open to qualified students only, but most of them accept couples, families, and any individual who wishes to broaden his personal horizons. Emphasis is primarily on experience rather than on theory, but not exclusively so. Murphy (1967, p. 35) writes, "Our primary concern is the affective domain—the senses and feelings, although we certainly are interested in the cognitive."

Other growth centers have in common with Esalen a primary interest in offering a wide diversity of experiences for the stimulation of personal growth, but in other ways they differ widely in structure and purpose. Some, like Oasis in Chicago which was founded by a group of psychotherapists and businessmen, were created for the purpose of bringing to the community specialists from all over the country, to offer workshops ranging in content from the demonstration of special psychotherapeutic techniques to the consideration of social problems. Other growth centers have been founded and staffed by a small group of people interested primarily in creating an opportunity for themselves to lead encounter groups.

Training is also offered at some of the growth centers, such as GROW (Group Relations Ongoing Workshops) in New York. Announcements of training in some growth centers require an advanced degree in behavioral science; others state specifically that no academic qualifications are necessary. Some group centers offer their own certification and seek to provide leadership for such community problems as drug addiction, mental retardation, child care, and geriatric needs. These programs represent an effort to meet community demands for which there are not enough academically qualified leaders available. They are open to the questions which have already been raised, although not answered, as to the appropriate training for an encounter group leader. The growth centers would seem to provide an excellent source for research data in this area and others, although Saretsky's sampling of these centers, as reported in the preceding chapter, yielded no data about ongoing research programs except at Esalen.

Couples and Families

Many writers on marital problems and marriage counseling have noted that a frequent problem is the congealment of a couple into a more-or-less unconscious mutual arrangement in which each accepts and maintains a specific role in regard to the other, which may leave little room for spontaneous relating or for growth within the marriage (Haley, 1963; Satir, 1964; Bach & Wyden, 1969). This unwritten contract sometimes includes "an implicit acceptance of a mutually unrewarding arrangement between husband and wife" (Schwartz & Schwartz, 1970, p. 8). The marathon time format, as discussed in preceding chapters, offers a unique opportunity for the individual participant to become aware of overcontrolled or artificial ways of behavior, to identify the underlying anxieties which keep him from fuller self-expression, and then try out more spontaneous and meaningful ways of being with others; similarly, the extended time format offers the same opportunity to a married couple.

Therapists who specialize in working with married couples may choose to limit the attendance at a marathon to couples only, in which case the focus of the group is likely to be entirely on problems existing within each marriage. This may make it difficult for the marriage partners to recognize the extent to which, as individuals, each of them may be unconsciously accepting or even seeking to perpetuate their marital dissatisfaction. Moreover, in a group focussed solely on marital tensions, it is extremely difficult to avoid an atmosphere of trial by jury, in which the group concentrates on determining which partner in each marriage is more at fault. My preference is to offer each marriage partner an opportunity to attend a marathon separately, as an individual, after which the couple together may attend a marathon in which the other members may be either married or single. This approach, with which Schwartz and Schwartz concur, gives each partner "maximum opportunity to experience their own individuality and hang-ups without having to perceive their partners as inhibiting or enhancing agents. Also, the partner who doesn't attend the marathon has an opportunity to experience his feeling of left-outness and deprivation . . . and the left-out partner's reaction will help both husband and wife realize how much they need and use their partner's dependence." [4]

Encounter techniques, in which an interpersonal problem is translated into physical or psychodramatic terms, are especially valuable for couples. A psychodramatic exchange of roles is often fruitful. Schwartz and Schwartz (1970, p. 8) offer several examples of how physical interaction can be used to clarify the nature of a marriage impasse, to "induce authentic response rather than stereotyped behavior," and to create a relaxed and playful atmosphere which tends to make group members less defensive. For instance, a couple who has fallen into the pattern of constant, repetitious argument is asked to stand in the middle of the floor and walk around one another in unending circles without speaking, in the hope of helping them perceive the pointlessness and absurdity of their behavior. A couple who were afraid of confronting one another directly with their hostility were accused of being "too chicken" to fight openly and were asked to have a chicken-fight in which each was to hold one foot while they hopped about on the other foot and tried to throw the other down. Hesitant at first, the husband was finally able to get his wife down without hurting her, with the result that she was relieved that at last there was some conclusive action and he was relieved that he did not feel like a bully. Still another man and wife, each of whom was trying to limit the freedom of the other, were tied together with a fifty-foot rope; instead of recognizing that the rope was long enough to enable him to move about the room freely, the husband shortened the rope to such an extent that it threatened to choke his wife, and the group was able to perceive vividly that both of them needed more room and that the wife needed permission to be more independent. Such techniques as these not only can enhance self-understanding but tend to introduce humor and perspective into a marriage partnership which has often been deadened by mutual blame and self-righteousness.

The extended time format also lends itself well to work with total family units. The two-day continuous marathon is too demanding for young children, but most families can adapt to the extended time workshop, in which therapy sessions several times a day are interspersed with

---

[4] Personal communication, Schwartz and Schwartz, 1970. In working with married couples who attend marathons together, I have been deeply impressed by the extent of the mutual dependency which seems especially noticeable with unhappy couples. Typically, an unhappily married couple enters the room together, sits side by side without changing position during the entire course of the marathon unless requested to change, and takes part in the group almost entirely by blaming the partner or expressing marital unhappiness. In contrast, a couple who are enjoying the marriage and are attending the marathon together primarily to share a worthwhile emotional experience are likely to show spontaneity and individuality. In one marathon, a happily married couple showed so much freedom and ability to relate to others that the group did not even realize they were married until the husband began to weep over a deprivation in his childhood, at which the wife instantly and warmly offered him loving comfort.

periods of free time. Many therapists work with several families at once, not only over a weekend, but also in settings where the families can live together for a week or more, an approach pioneered by Virginia Satir at Esalen and by Frederick Stoller at the Western Behavioral Sciences Institute. The Gestalt Institute of Canada, at Vancouver, offers month-long workshops for families, in a setting which combines recreational opportunities with treatment.

The approach to a family workshop may vary widely. Stoller, for example (1967), insists that every member of the family take part in all sessions, and that nobody should be discussed in his absence with the exception of young children, who need ample time for rest and play. Other family therapists utilize the prolonged time span to bring family members together in various combinations. A week-long workshop allows an opportunity for single families to work together as separate units; for sessions which bring several family groups together; groups for younger children in which play techniques can be used to help the children deal with feelings about their families and themselves; adolescents' groups; wives' groups; husbands' groups; and couples' groups. Thus each member of the family can obtain perspective on the way in which he interacts with his family and also on himself as an individual and with his peers. Ann Dreyfuss of the Center for Human Communication in California, who has offered a series of family workshops at various growth centers, has found it possible to work with an almost indefinite age range; one such group included a three-month-old baby and an eighty-eight-year-old grandmother. These workshops "are designed for families which are functioning reasonably well but express some dissatisfaction and wish to open up and explore new challenges of communication." [5] Joint leadership is offered by a man and a woman.

Use of a videotape machine, which enables group interaction to be recorded live and then played back on a television screen, lends itself especially well to the revelation of unacknowledged relationships within the family, which may be discussed after the playback. For example, a mother who complained bitterly that her family was overdependent on her and looked to her for all decision making was able to see through a video playback that in subtle ways she insisted upon maintaining control and was then able to explore this need with the help of the leader. This is a representative example of the way in which family relationships may be governed by implicit rules which are unwritten and may be unconscious.

The growing literature on family interaction [6] indicates the frequency with which families assign to one another and maintain pretended official roles which may differ greatly from the actual way in

_____

[5] Personal communication from Ann Dreyfuss, 1970.

[6] Students who wish to explore this field further are advised to begin with Satir (1964). Literature on communication (Haley, 1963) is also relevant.

which they deal with one another. For instance, either father or mother may ostensibly be held responsible for disciplining the children or planning a vacation or allocating family funds; yet the final decision may remain subtly in the hands of the other parent in a way which confuses the entire family. Rather often, one member of a family is selected as a scapegoat and family problems are ascribed to a delinquent adolescent, an overbearing father, or a demanding mother; yet covertly the family not only accepts the scapegoat's behavior but does everything possible to perpetuate it. In the workshop, these unwritten yet powerful rules are exposed so that they can be dealt with openly and superseded by more rewarding methods of family interaction. The workshop is "a microcosm of the difficulties that families experience at home" (Stoller, 1967, p. 33).

Special techniques for family treatment have been developed. For example, a family may be given a large sheet of paper and crayons and asked to draw a picture together in silence. In this simple exercise, it is sometimes possible to identify a family member who fights for space, a family member who takes his cue from what is done by others, or a family member who wishes to pursue his own ideas without joining in the cooperative effort. These roles often represent the true functioning of individuals within the family unit and differ from the official family roles to which the family has assigned them.

Another technique is to create a play situation, such as improvised hand-dancing or hand-clapping, and ask the family members to take part playfully without maintaining their usual positions in the family hierarchy. Such a game may bring to light the fact that a mother feels overburdened and longs to play like a child; or that a father needs to maintain a dominant position and does not wish to demean himself by playing; or that the children see their parents as overpowering, unreachable creatures who cannot be viewed as playmates or human beings, even temporarily. After every game, discussion follows, sometimes by the family group and the leader, and sometimes including several other families who may have been observing and who perhaps obtain fresh light on their own interaction through the observation.

Special Populations

The encounter technique, with various modifications of the extended time format, has been used extensively and effectively with drug addicts and shows promise of being highly efficacious with hospital, prison, and geriatric populations.

Prolonged encounter groups, sometimes extended for as long as three consecutive days with little sleep, were used at Synanon (Casriel, 1963; Yablonsky, 1965) and Daytop (Maslow, 1969) almost from the inception of these centers, which are voluntary residences for drug addicts wishing to cure themselves. These groups are usually conducted not by an academically trained leader or other outsider, but by an ex-addict who knows from firsthand experience the pleasures, the horrors, and the destructiveness of drug addiction, and the difficulties and rewards of abstention. These groups are noted for their brutal, tough assaultiveness, which participants appear able to accept, in part because the attacks come from peers and in part because they represent genuine concern. Verbal abuse is the norm rather than the exception, although physical violence is prohibited. Genuine grief is recognized, but self-pitying or evasive weeping is ruthlessly criticized. Emphasis is consistently placed on cooperative behavior and on self-control rather than on self-understanding. Explanations for self-destructive or uncooperative behavior in the group are regarded as evasions and excuses. One of the Synanon leaders (Yablonsky, 1965, p. 149) is quoted as saying, "We don't really give a damn if your grandfather was an alcoholic, your mother hustled, and your father slugged you daily. None of it is an excuse for bad behavior at Synanon." The leader makes no pretense of superior knowledge and is not exempt from the group's attack. The percentage of drug addicts who are permanently rehabilitated at these centers is estimated at 60 percent (Yablonsky, 1965, p. 398). This impressive record may be viewed as in part due to the fact that admissions at these centers are all voluntary and are restricted to addicts who must prove their wish to abstain by going through a difficult and challenging period of probation. However, more than 90 percent of Synanon residents have previously attempted to give up using drugs, voluntarily or involuntarily, in other settings, including prison, outpatient clinics, and hospitals, without success. The part played by the leaderless, unstructured encounter marathon in this record of success would be difficult to partial out in an effort to identify what factors make for the effectiveness of this approach, but most centers for narcotic addiction are currently using the marathon approach as part of their program, including Daytop, Exodus House, Odyssey House, Topic House, Phoenix House, Reality House, and others.[7]

An especially urgent social and scientific need is for a comprehensive survey of the application of the marathon time format and of the encounter-group approach in general to psychiatric and prison populations. Several reports already suggest that, even though an extended time format places special demands on the personnel in psychiatric hospitals, its results may justify the effort. My impression is that, in hospitals which are funded in such a way as to enable them to offer treatment

---

[7] Personal communication, David Deitch, formerly director of Daytop Village, now at the University of California in San Diego, 1970.

rather than primarily custodial care, this approach is being used more widely than has yet been reported in the literature. For example, the Pine Rest Christian Hospital [8] is currently offering encounter groups, some of which meet weekly and others of which follow the marathon format, both for inpatients and for those who are in the process of returning to the community. Marital groups are conducted which are attended by patients and their spouses, for the purpose of helping the patient and his family make an improved adjustment to one another. Participation is voluntary, groups number from ten to eighteen members, and they are conducted by psychiatrists or psychologists with group experience. This hospital adopted the policy, which most psychotherapists would regard as an optimum way of beginning an encounter program, of initiating the total experience with a marathon in which staff members participated.

A special variation of the marathon technique has been developed at the Veterans Administration Hospital in Topeka, Kansas (Vernallis & Reinert, 1966). Employed veterans, including formerly hospitalized patients and also including some who were seeking help for the first time, were offered an intensive weekend treatment program for a series of twelve consecutive weekends, continuing to work and to live at home during the week. The typical pattern was for a group of eight patients to remain together for forty-eight hours each weekend with two therapists. About sixteen hours each weekend were spent in intensive group therapy sessions, oriented toward the exploration of specific life problems, and the rest of the time was spent in recreational activity decided upon by the group. A preliminary follow-up, conducted independently (Marlar, 1964), showed improvement in approximately half the patients. The authors report a high degree of enthusiasm and emotional involvement by the patients, a finding which has also been reported by other therapists conducting marathons with psychiatric patients (Myerhoff, Jacobs, & Stoller, 1970).

Surprisingly little published data exists on the application of encounter techniques among prison populations.[9] If the purpose of imprisonment is regarded as rehabilitative rather than punitive, the encounter approach, with its emphasis on mutual helpfulness and confrontation among peers, would seem more promising than the traditional one-to-one psychotherapeutic relationship, which is more likely to evoke the rebelliousness against authority often regarded as an important factor in crime and delinquency. The approach developed at Synanon, in which

[8] In Grand Rapids, Michigan. This is a private, nonprofit, church-sponsored hospital with 650 beds. Their program is described on the basis of a personal communication from Dr. William Hiemstra, the head chaplain, 1970.

[9] The Information Center of the National Council on Crime and Delinquency was unable to provide additional references on this subject.

the leaders function as peers regardless of any official status they may possess, would seem especially appropriate for a prison population. One such report comes from the Colorado State Penitentiary (*New York Times*, March 30, 1970) in which three members of the prison psychiatric staff participated as peers with nine convicts, including men serving sentences for murder and armed robbery, in a twenty-four hour marathon. Truth-telling and abstention from physical violence were the only rules. The prisoners were generally enthusiastic about the results.

Another application of the marathon time format was made at Lewisberg Prison in Pennsylvania,[10] initiated by the prison chaplain after attendance at a week-long laboratory workshop given at NTL. The group consisted of thirty-six prisoners, eight professors from Bucknell University, the chaplain, the head of the prison guards, and two prison psychologists. Prisoners were self-selected. Divided into four groups, the participants were introduced to the "fishbowl technique," in which an inner group engages in encounters and discussion while a larger, outer circle observes them, after which the entire group engages in discussion. This marathon continued for seventy-two hours, with time off only for sleep. Similar marathons were held subsequently, one of which included some life-termers and some parolees. Results were reported as positive, and were regarded as helpful to several participants who reentered society successfully after being discharged.

A somewhat more extensive, though still limited, use of encounter techniques is being made by social group-workers in field services to probationers and parolees (Keve, 1967). The paucity of data in this field reflects the tendency of society to disregard the needs of its socially or emotionally crippled members and perhaps also reflects the preference of most encounter group leaders and psychotherapists to work with well-educated, well-functioning, middle-class peers.

Industry

In contrast to the sparsity of reports on the use of encounter techniques with prison populations, the reports of their application to industrial problems and management training are so numerous that a complete bibliography would probably constitute a book in itself. Many businessmen who have been directly or indirectly influenced by the vision of a humanistically oriented technology (Maslow, 1965; Fromm, 1968) see in this approach a practical method of increasing productive efficiency by

[10] Personal communication from the Reverend Otto Kroeger, an NTL associate who conducted the workshop with the assistance of the prison chaplain, William Zell, 1970.

developing better ways of communication in their organizations and by recognizing that organizational morale is related to personal satisfactions which individual employees derive from their jobs, in addition to acceptable hours and remuneration.

The use of encounter techniques in industry is usually known as sensitivity training and was pioneered by the National Training Laboratories, which now offers a vast program including many laboratory groups designed to increase the interpersonal effectiveness of executives and managers at all levels. Many business and industrial firms send their key men, or younger men who show the promise of developing executive ability, for training at NTL in workshops which may meet for a weekend, for two weeks, or even for a month. The wide range of industrial problems for which NTL offers workshops is suggested by two workshop descriptions from their 1970 brochure: one is entitled "Dynamics of International Business" and offers an opportunity for "representatives of European and American firms to work together to develop understanding of their own managerial styles, the processes of change, and the special dynamics of international teams"; another offers a seminar "for middle managers" directed toward "the human side of getting the job done . . . to examine their images of their roles and learn how others react to them."

Although NTL dominates the national scene, a number of smaller groups of psychological consultants have arisen that work largely with their own communities in the areas of industry, education, and community tensions. An example is Princeton Associates for Human Resources (PAHR) [11] which is developing methods of dealing with interpersonal problems and learning difficulties of people usually considered as the hard-core unemployed. For example, a program was designed to meet the needs of a large manufacturer of rubber goods who was faced with the problem of a 78 percent rate of turnover of employees from disadvantaged backgrounds and an overall turnover of 58 percent. This manufacturer, under a program sponsored jointly by the National Alliance of Businessmen and the U.S. Department of Labor, hired another 100 workers from substandard socioeconomic background and used the services of PAHR to help the new employees adjust to their jobs.

The PAHR training program for these men lasted four months. It was based in part on a buddy system in which each new employee was given as a partner another employee who had been successful in his job for some time, but who also came from a disadvantaged background. The senior buddy had the responsibility of serving as a liaison between the new employee and his supervisors and helping him with personal

<hr>

[11] This material, described more fully in *Confrontation: Encounters in Self and Interpersonal Awareness* (Blank et al., 1971) was provided by Leonard Blank.

problems related to his employment. For twelve weeks, the new employees met in small encounter groups with their buddies and with two foremen. The turnover in this plant, after the adoption of this program, dropped to less than ten percent.

Religious Groups

Religious leaders of various denominations frequently elect of their own accord to participate privately in marathon groups, for the purpose of enhancing their ability to communicate. Many training institutes also offer marathons and other forms of sensitivity training as part of their program; for instance, Drew Theological Seminary in New Jersey has provided opportunities for its students to take part in marathons, and one Catholic order of nuns arranged a marathon for its novices in which they could explore the genuineness of their wish to take perpetual vows. In Chicago, a group of Catholic priests have formed the Growth Resources Organization and participate regularly in personal growth laboratories (Fiske, 1970). Most of the major Protestant denominations maintain national directors of sensitivity training, who may make use of the resources of NTL and of Esalen to provide ministers and church leaders with a personal growth experience. The Episcopal Church sponsors its own program for sensitivity training within the church, using the NTL-trained staff. The Union of American Hebrew Congregations, as of 1970, had no national encounter director but reports that some encounter work is being done on the congregational level.

An intensive one-week residential program, sponsored by the Church Executive Development Board, is reported by Shapiro (1969). About seventy participants, many of them in their fifties and sixties, included bishops, administrative officers of synods and dioceses, finance directors, and district Sunday School directors. Typical individual conflicts within the group included difficulty in acknowledging and expressing aggressiveness in constructive ways; conflicts between their actual social powerfulness and their ideals of Christian humility; and a sense of confusion and perhaps even of opposition between traditional religious values and ceremonies and contemporary demands on the churches for helping parishioners with difficult contemporary problems.

It was found that despite these special conflicts, the group responded with increasing enthusiasm to techniques for facilitating self-disclosure and communication. After the laboratory had been in session for several days, and the group members were at home with one another, they were divided into small subgroups, each of which was given the task of expressing in some new way an accepted religious ideal. The most meaningful demonstration came from a group which invented a pantomime designed to express the ideal of moving the church out into the world:

> The only words they used were "This is the church," pointing to a small circular rug . . . barely large enough for all six people in the group to sit on it, and they began a rather animated nonverbal communication which represented first the business and then the worship services of the church. Soon one member was singled out and pointed at because he did not conform to the group ritual. Fingers were shaken in his face and he was driven out of the church, onto the bare floor of the large room . . . while the in-group church members went back to their rug church. . . . They were suffering considerable guilt. They quickly agreed to send someone out into the world and to bring the maverick back to the fold . . . but he was rebuffed by the outcast. . . . The church group held a meeting—and they decided to move the whole church "out into the world." They did this by picking up the rug and carrying it to the man outside. Then they invited him in again—and this time he accepted (Shapiro, 1969, p. 182).

Many ministers and pastors who have experienced encounter groups have developed similar groups to serve their congregations.[12] For example, weekend retreats for church members are likely to allocate less time for silence and meditation and more time for group encounters. Other churches offer weekly encounter workshops, some of which are directed primarily toward young people. The values of mutual acceptance and mutual concern which are usually stressed in encounter experiences are seen by many church leaders as essentially religious.

Some opposition, however, exists within religious groups. One denominational group in Oklahoma has banned its local churches from taking part in sensitivity training. Concern has also been expressed by an executive of the National Council of Churches about the need for an adequate background in order to conduct encounter groups (Fiske, 1970).

Within the Roman Catholic Church, differences of opinion exist as to the value of the "Cursillo," a name which in Spanish means "little course," and which has its antecedents as a spontaneous, emotional religious movement in Spain rather than in the American encounter group movement (*New York Times*, Jan. 8, 1970). Part of the Cursillo is a three-day conference of thirty or forty people who "talk, eat, pray, think, laugh, and sometimes cry together," followed by a continuing series of hour-long weekly meetings. The exhilaration reported as a result of these

---

[12] In a personal communication (1970), the Reverend Eli Wismer of the National Council of Churches wishes to make it clear that these religious leaders do not seek to deal with serious problems of personal psychopathology except by appropriate referrals.

groups is similar to what is reported by most marathon participants. Some Catholic leaders believe that the Cursillo offers a genuine emotional experience as a "workshop in communal Christian living." However, it is not an officially sanctioned church activity, and other Catholic theologians question the difficulties of integrating the intense emotional experience of the Cursillo with the demands of everyday life—the same problem which is often raised by behavioral scientists regarding the integration of marathon experience with ongoing daily relationships.

Education

The application of encounter techniques to teacher training, to furthering cooperation within school systems and to the actual classroom program, is already so extensive that it could be fully reported only in a separate volume, even if confined only to groups sponsored officially as part of educational programs. To describe the extent of spontaneous participation in encounter groups on college campuses in which students select their own leadership would probably be almost impossible; for instance, it is estimated that well over a thousand students have taken part in these groups at Stanford University alone. The City University of New York is conducting a project known as Triple-T, which refers to Training the Trainers of Teachers, such as deans and department heads of education. Sensitivity training is offered as an in-service course for New York City Public School teachers. Personal growth groups are provided for students, faculty, and staff at the University of Lethbridge in Canada. T-group training is offered to graduate students of clinical psychology in many universities, including Teachers College of Columbia and City College of New York. The National Training Laboratory, as part of its comprehensive program, gives workshops described as Conflict Management in the Schools; Inducing Change as a Classroom Teacher; Race Issues in the Schools; The Teacher as Manager, which aims to develop management skills for teachers, principals and supervisors; and Black Faculty in the University Structure.

At Esalen, in a project funded in part by the Ford Foundation, a staff of teachers familiarized themselves with the experiential growth techniques of Esalen, selected those which seemed appropriate for incorporation into the curriculum, and adapted them to use in the classroom. At the Western Behavioral Sciences Institute, Carl Rogers worked with the school system of the Sisters of the Immaculate Heart, in an encounter program which included students, faculty, parents, administrators, dropouts, and community leaders. The use of encounter techniques in educational methods is usually seen as an aspect of the growing influence upon education of humanistic psychology, with its emphasis upon creative thinking rather than on the acquisition of knowledge by rote, upon individual self-actualization, and upon the development of a society which can provide more human satisfactions rather than upon conformity to the society which exists. The vision of humanistic education in the future has been vividly and imaginatively described in Leonard's *Education and Ecstasy* (1968). Most applications of encounter techniques to educational problems involve use of the intensive workshop technique, in which several sessions of approximately two hours are conducted on several consecutive days.

Education and Race Conflict

Since the secondary schools and college campuses are among the primary locations of violent interracial conflicts, and since many students and teachers are willing to participate voluntarily in interracial encounter groups even despite initial skepticism, black-white groups in the school system offer an opportunity to deal with this immensely important social problem. As with industry and with education in general, work in this area is so extensive that only a representative sample can be described.

With a staff drawn from the Princeton Associates for Human Resources, a five-day residential workshop was offered to students from Trenton State College in New Jersey and from the Trenton school system, together with teachers and faculty members, with an approximately equal number of black and white participants. The primary purpose of the workshop was to explore the extent to which the teaching curriculums were relevant to the needs of black students.

Various encounter group techniques were used to overcome mistrust and facilitate communication. Task groups to develop specific proposals for changing the curriculum were also formed. The entire workshop began by dividing itself into two unofficial subgroups, black and white, after which it veered off toward another polarization, of students and faculty. Halfway through the workshop, the PAHR staff members challenged the participants to plan changes in the school program without technical assistance from outside, taking full responsibility for implementing these changes. The workshop participants were able to respond with a plan which was at least partially satisfactory to the various factions, and almost a year later, workshop members continued to meet voluntarily to discuss their common problems.

NTL in 1970 inaugurated a program directed toward reducing racism, especially in schools, colleges, and other institutions as well as in industry. In cooperation with the Race Institute of Washington, D.C., the program, known as PRIOR (the acronym for Program to Reduce

Individual and Organization Racism), attempts to deal with such issues as possible racial bias in allocating organization power and promotion; tolerance of differences among races in personal styles and working styles; and recognition of the possibility that different racial value systems may be valid.

All of these intensive group experiences, whether conducted for personal growth as in therapeutically oriented marathons, or for dealing with broader social issues such as education, religion, and racial tensions, present most of their participants with the same problem—the difficulty of returning to a family, a job, and a community in which the values of openness, mutual trust, and mutual concern are accepted only partially.

A black participant in a black-white encounter group may, for example, undergo experiences which diminish his antagonism toward whites and may attempt to try out his tentatively friendly feelings, only to find that his friendliness is not reciprocated. A white participant may develop new respect and acceptance for blacks and may attempt to carry over his positive attitudes into the community, only to be met by withdrawal. A school superintendent may return from a laboratory experience full of enthusiasm for the ideals of openness and self-expression, to find that his teaching staff not only considers these ideals impracticable but views his attempt to share his enthusiasm with downright suspicion. Indeed, a training center for high-level federal executives recently dropped an optional one-week sensitivity training course because, according to the director of the training center, "the openness of the group can flourish at the institute [but] is often frustrated when executives return to the system" (*Behavior Today*, June 8, 1970).

It is therefore a sound policy for anyone who attends a marathon or any type of encounter group to give adequate consideration, toward the end of the group and after its conclusion, to the need for finding appropriate and practical ways of integrating his sense of being a part of the human community with the everyday world outside. It is even more the responsibility of a marathon leader to help prepare the participant for possible disappointments if he expects everyone in his environment to respond easily and immediately to his enhanced awareness of the rewards of trust, openness, and intimacy. Realistically, however, it is not overoptimistic to expect most families, most friends, most job associates, and even the community itself to respond, though perhaps gradually and only to a limited extent, to an individual's effort to achieve a more authentic and honest kind of communication. Perhaps, indeed, part of the equipment of a well-qualified marathon leader should be the conviction that, even if only to an infinitesmal degree, an individual may be capable of affecting society in such a way as to bring it closer to the ideals of humanism.

REFERENCES

Alger, I., & Hogan, P. Videotape recordings in conjoint marital therapy. In M. M. Berger (Ed.), *Videotape techniques in psychiatric training and treatment.* New York: Basic Books, 1971.

Allen, G. Hate therapy. *American Opinion,* January 1968.

Bach, G. R., & Wyden, P. *The intimate enemy.* New York: W. M. Morrow, 1969.

Berlin, J. I. *Management improvement program.* Atlanta: Human Development Institute, 1965.

Berzon, B., Reisel, J., & Davis, D. P. PEER: An audio-tape program for self-directed small groups. *Journal of Humanistic Psychology,* Spring 1969, 9(1).

Birnbaum, M. Sense about sensitivity training. *Saturday Review,* 15 September 1969.

Blank, L., Gottsegen, G. B., & Gottsegen, M. G. (Eds.), *Confrontation: Encounters in self and interpersonal awareness.* New York: Macmillan, 1971.

Bloomberg, L., Bloomberg, P., & Miller, R. L. The intensive group as a founding experience. *Journal of Humanistic Psychology,* Spring 1969, 9(1).

Casriel, D. *So fair a house.* Englewood Cliffs, N.J.: Prentice-Hall, 1963.

Chesler, P. Playing instant joy to the lonely crowd. *Village Voice,* 25 December 1969.

Ellis, A. A weekend of rational encounter. In A. Burton (Ed.), *Encounter.* San Francisco: Jossey-Bass, 1970.

Fiske, E. B. American churches are turning to sensitivity training. *New York Times,* 26 March 1970.

Francke, L. The encounter group explosion. *New York,* 25 May 1970.

Fromm, E. *The evolution of hope.* New York: Harper & Row, 1968.

Gibb, J. R., & Gibb, L. M. Emergence therapy. In G. M. Gazda (Ed.), *Innovations to group psychotherapy.* Springfield, Ill.: C. S. Thomas, 1968.

Gibb, J. R., & Gibb, L. M. Leaderless groups: Growth-centered values and potentials. In H. Otto & J. Mann (Eds.), *Ways of growth.* New York: Grossman, 1968.

Gibb, J. R., & Gibb, L. M. Role freedom in a TORI group. In A. Burton (Ed.), *Encounter.* San Francisco: Jossey-Bass, 1970.

Haley, J. *Strategies of psychotherapy.* New York: Grune & Stratton, 1963.

Harrison, C. H. Schools put a town on the map. *Saturday Review,* 21 February 1970.

Hurwitz, N. Peer self-help psychotherapy groups. *Psychotherapy,* Spring 1970, 8(1).

Keve, P. W. *Imaginative programming in probation and parole.* Minneapolis: University of Minnesota Press, 1967.

Lakin, M. Some ethical issues in sensitivity training. *American Psychologist,* October 1969, 24(10).

Lawrence, S. Televised encounter groups. In Blank, L. B., Gottsegen, G. B., & Gottsegen, M. (Eds.), *Confrontation: Encounters in self and interpersonal awareness.* New York: Macmillan, 1971.

Leonard, G. B. *Education and ecstasy.* New York: Delacorte, 1968.

Malamud, D. The second-chance family. In Blank, L. B., Gottsegen, G. B., & Gottsegen, M. (Eds.), *Confrontation: Encounters in self and interpersonal awareness.* New York: Macmillan, 1971.

Marlar, D. C. Follow-up study of a weekend hospital program. *Mental Hospital,* 1964, 15.

Maslow, A. *Eupsychian management.* Homewood, Ill.: Dow-Jones-Erwin, 1965.

Maslow, A. Synanon and eupsychia. In H. M. Ruitenbeek (Ed.), *Group therapy today.* New York: Atherton, 1969.

Millman, L. I., & Chilman, C. S. *Poor people at work, An annotated bibliography.* Washington, D.C.: U.S. Department of Health, Education, & Welfare, n.d.

Murphy, M. M. Esalen, Where it's at. *Psychology Today,* December 1967, *1*(7).

Myerhoff, H. L., Jacobs, A., & Stoller, F. Emotionality in marathon and traditional psychotherapy groups. *Psychotherapy,* Spring 1970, 7(1).

Rogers, C. The T-group comes of age. *Psychology Today,* December 1969, 3(7).

Satir, V. *Conjoint family therapy.* Palo Alto, Calif.: Science & Behavior Books, 1964.

Schwartz, J. J., & Schwartz, R. Growth encounters. *Voices,* Fall–Winter 1969, 5(3).

Shapiro, S. B. Tradition innovation. In A. Burton (Ed.), *Encounter.* San Francisco: Jossey-Bass, 1970.

Stoller, F. H. The long weekend. *Psychology Today,* December 1967, *1*(7).

Stoller, F. H. Group psychotherapy on television: An innovation with hospitalized patients. In M. M. Berger (Ed.), *Videotape techniques in psychiatric training and treatment.* New York: Basic Books, 1971.

Vernallis, F. F., & Reinert, R. E. Group treatment methods in a weekend hospital. *Psychotherapy,* May 1966, 3(2).

Yablonsky, L. *The tunnel back.* New York: Macmillan, 1965.

Yalom, I. D. *Encounter groups and psychiatry.* Washington, D.C.: APA Publications Services Division, 1970.

APPENDIX

SUGGESTIONS FOR MARATHON LEADERS

The first task of anyone interested in conducting marathons or other types of encounter groups should be a scrutiny of his own personal qualifications. It has been pointed out elsewhere in this book that some behavioral scientists are currently questioning whether or not formal training and accreditation in such disciplines as psychiatry or clinical psychology are necessary in order to become a capable encounter group leader, a question which is still open to debate. Perhaps a preliminary answer, for each individual who is interested in offering marathon groups, should include a consideration of exactly what purpose the group is intended to serve, and what type of participants will be selected.

Groups may in general be regarded as serving any one of several purposes, although these purposes overlap. They may be intended to deal with a specific problem, such as decreasing interracial tension or enhancing industrial efficiency or increasing the effectiveness of school teachers. They may be directed toward making their participants more capable of communicating with one another, without necessarily involving the exposure of deep emotional problems. Or they may be essentially therapeutic in their intention, aiming toward the exploration and resolution of basic personal conflicts. It is important for the group leader to be clear about the purpose of the group and to make its purpose equally clear to the participants.

The necessary background of the group leader depends in part on the purpose of the group. Minimal background for the leadership of any group, in my opinion, should include:

1. General knowledge of group dynamics. This may be obtained through training and experience as a group therapist, or through training and experience at accredited institutes such as the National Training Laboratories or the Workshop Institute for Living-Learning.

2. Sufficient knowledge of individual psychodynamics to be able to recognize and deal with anxiety reactions in the group in such a way that neither the group's function nor the individual participant is damaged.

3. Special knowledge which is appropriate to the specific purpose of the group. For example, a belief in the value of an encounter approach to interracial tensions is probably not sufficient to qualify a group leader

to deal with black-white community tensions; his effectiveness would also require adequate information about the black-white situation in the community. Similarly, familiarity with encounter games is not enough to qualify a group leader to deal with emotional problems in depth. If the purpose of the group is to explore and resolve deep individual anxieties, then the leader's background should be equivalent to what is required for the ethical practice of individual psychotherapy. A leader who is personally enthusiastic and who is familiar with encounter techniques can often elicit strong emotional reactions but may not be able to deal constructively with the powerful feelings which may be evoked in a marathon group.

4. Finally, it is strongly recommended that anyone who wishes to conduct a marathon group should begin with a preliminary experience as a participant. To me this seems analogous to the requirement of most psychotherapeutic training institutes that anyone who wishes to practice psychotherapy should go through the experience of being a patient. The anxiety about self-disclosure, the difficulty in working out reactions toward a leader, and the growing awareness that self-disclosure does not bring catastrophe can only be understood when they have been experienced.

The next task of the marathon leader is the selection and screening of participants. Here there is a sharp dichotomy between a situation in which the participants are required to attend the group by an employer or by some other authority and a situation in which the participants decide voluntarily that they wish to participate for their personal growth. If, for example, a school superintendant decides to insist that all the guidance counselors in his district must attend an encounter group in order to increase their effectiveness, it is likely that several participants will be there against their will. Although, theoretically, a group such as this is composed of people regarded as socially normal, the statistical probability is that several of the participants may be wrestling with personal problems which will interfere with their participation in the group. Moreover, they may be resentful over enforced participation. An encounter group leader who is working for an industrial organization, or who has undertaken the task of handling an encounter group which has been set up for training purposes in a school district, or who has been given the responsibility of dealing with community tensions of any type, is advised to allow each prospective member of the group to choose for himself whether or not he wishes to participate. Enforced participation may evoke deep-lying resentment toward quasi-parental authorities, and the resentful member may impede the work of the group. If the group is regarded as training and the organizational authorities insist upon participation, the disadvantages of enforced group membership may to some extent be overcome if the leader begins by giving the members an opportunity to express their resentment.

There is another type of problem which can arise in a group which is offered for the purpose of enhancing communication or improving performance in a social organization (school, church, industrial plant, community) which already exists, as opposed to a group which is offered simply as a worthwhile experience for the individual participants. Most responsible growth centers, and training organizations such as NTL, usually announce specifically that their groups do not meet for the purpose of dealing with the deep emotional problems of individuals. Despite this precaution, many individuals who attend such groups entertain the hope, consciously or unconsciously, that their emotional problems will be solved without the necessity of admitting to themselves or to society that these emotional problems exist. They may regard the encounter group as an unembarrassing alternative to entering psychotherapy, which in many communities is still regarded as an admission of being weak or crazy. Such participants, also, may impede the work of the group by attempting to focus its attention on their individual difficulties.

And, finally, there are many individuals who enter a nontherapeutic encounter group, voluntarily or involuntarily, without being aware that its challenge may precipitate emotional difficulties which they have heretofore denied or ignored.[1] The group leader must be vigilantly sensitive to signs of personal crisis, such as trembling, weeping, flushing, irritability, withdrawal, or even subtler indications. Again, these crises may not only represent some degree of psychological risk to the individual but may hamper the group. An encounter leader must be capable of recognizing an individual emotional crisis and dealing with it on an emergency basis. Usually, sufficient relief is obtained if the distressed participant is encouraged to express his feelings, and in a nontherapeutic encounter group it is seldom necessary, or even appropriate, to work out the problem in depth. Dual leadership offers a special safeguard for these situations, since, if necessary, one of the leaders can devote his full attention to the distressed participant while the other leader continues with the group.

Technically, it is of great importance that if an encounter group meets to deal with social or educational problems, the leader should avoid probing into personal difficulties except insofar as they are related to the goal of the group. Encounter games, nonverbal communication, and psychodramatic scenarios should be selected in terms of their appropriateness for the specific orientation of the group. Suppose, for example, that the supervisors of various departments in an industrial plant are attending an encounter group designed to increase their ability to understand one another's practical problems. It would be highly ap-

---

[1] An example of this type of situation, which also illustrates the need for skill on the part of the leader, is found in Haigh (1968).

propriate to offer feedback as to their here-and-now communication in the group; to use the device of exchanging roles and impersonating one another so that each of them might better comprehend his individual manner of communicating; and perhaps even to use nonverbal techniques such as arm-wrestling to bring latent rivalries to the surface and deal with them. It would be highly inappropriate to insist upon the exploration of childhood traumata or current family conflicts, unless material of this type is spontaneously brought into the group by a participant who believes that his childhood background or his present family situation is directly relevant to the immediate problem. The leader of an encounter group which has a specific, limited goal is urged to accept whatever personal data is brought into the group by its members, but not to push for any self-revelation beyond what they choose voluntarily to share.

If the basic purpose of the group is individual growth, or psychotherapeutic treatment, the selection of participants poses quite a different problem.[2] The selection and screening of participants for these groups, in which emotional involvement may become spectacularly intense and in which deep characterological changes may begin, awaits further research. Stoller (1968, p. 233) suggests that possibly the best screening procedure is "the feelings of the group leader toward a prospective participant, whether he finds he wants to spend a long period of time with him." This method of screening is perhaps not as subjective as it may appear, since presumably a willingness to spend time with the prospective participant is based on his showing some capacity to communicate and to respond on an emotional level, which would seem minimally necessary for effective group membership. Certain personality types, however, probably should not be admitted to a marathon encounter group, not only because of a potential risk to the individual participant but because a seriously disturbed individual tends to absorb the time of the group disproportionately. On an *a priori* basis, I would exclude: people whose reality-testing is so seriously disturbed that they might find it difficult to discriminate between fantasy and reality in the group; people who are currently showing overt psychotic symptoms such as hallucinations and delusions; and people who are consistently so withdrawn and frightened that group participation would seem impossible.[3] Such people almost never apply voluntarily for par-

---

[2] The function of the leader in such groups is not discussed here, since it is covered extensively throughout the foregoing chapters.

[3] These exclusions apply to marathons conducted outside institutions. Modified marathons can be conducted in a hospital setting, where most of the participants would be too seriously disturbed to participate in the usual type of intense encounter marathon. Ample time for rest must be allowed under these circumstances, and technical procedures must be modified in accordance with the vulnerability of the

ticipation in a marathon, since the prospect is extremely threatening. In general, an applicant who knows the nature of a marathon is capable of self-selection and self-screening. If the marathon therapist decides to refuse an application for marathon therapy, he is ethically obliged to explain his reasons tactfully and to make specific suggestions as to where and how the applicant can arrange for individual psychotherapy. Under no circumstances should anyone in individual treatment be admitted to a marathon without the knowledge and consent of his therapist, who must agree to his patient's participation even though he need not necessarily be optimistic about the possible benefits.

If there are physical symptoms, it is urgently recommended that a medical checkup be conducted within a few weeks before the marathon takes place. For example, a prospective group member has a history of heart symptoms which, a year ago, were diagnosed as having no organic basis. Since marathon participation involves a physical strain, it is desirable to insist upon another cardiac examination shortly before the participant is admitted.

The question of whether a homogeneous or a heterogeneous group functions best also awaits specific investigation. My observation, in general corroborated by other marathon leaders, is that it is desirable to have an approximately equal number of men and women; that youngsters under twenty do better in groups of their age peers; and that the group should be sufficiently homogeneous in educational level and general intelligence so that they can communicate easily. Otherwise, heterogeneity is distinctly preferable. An age range of twenty years and up gives various generations an opportunity to come to terms with one another. Black-white marathons have an extra dimension of intensity and richness which appears even without the specific exploration of racial problems. Homosexual participants often give and receive a great deal within the group (Mintz, 1966). Ideally, a group should consist of some relatively quiet, passive members and some talkative, excitable members, but usually chance itself brings about this optimal balance. A sole exception is that, in general, I find that professional psychotherapists work better in a group of colleagues, not because they are more intelligent or less troubled, but because the attitude of attempting to be helpful becomes so deeply ingrained through the years that it is inevitably elicited in almost any group, even if the psychotherapist attempts sincerely to avoid this. In a group of colleagues, where everyone is identified as a member of the "helping professions," this problem is less likely

---

participants. Since individual attention to group members almost certainly becomes necessary from time to time with hospitalized patients, leadership by two or three therapists, one of whom should be prepared to render emergency psychiatric treatment, is strongly recommended.

to arise. In such a group, of course, the leader must actively discourage shop talk and theoretical discussion.

My own procedure is to accept, sight unseen, any prospective participant who is referred to me by a trustworthy colleague or friend who knows the applicant well and who also understands the nature of a marathon. Applications by mail or phone from unknown people are not accepted without some preliminary information. A detailed letter, a long telephone conversation, or a twenty-minute screening interview usually provide an adequate basis on which to accept or reject the participant. In the rare instances in which a prospective participant has been rejected, it is usually because he has misunderstood the nature of a marathon, regarding it perhaps as a purely recreational weekend, or—at the opposite extreme—as a psychotherapeutic experience which will transform neurosis into health in two effortless days.

The time format of the marathon, as discussed in Chapter 9, should depend to a considerable extent on the physical and personal needs of the leader. My preference is to set the beginning and the ending time very sharply, but to decide with the group what time to break up at night and when to start again in the morning. It is advisable for the leader not to join the group members until the official starting time, since an atmosphere of social small talk is likely to be established if the leader participates in preliminary socializing before all members of the group arrive. Since it is part of the total group experience to face and overcome separation anxiety at the end of the group, it is even more important to break up at precisely the appointed time. My policy is to warn the group a half-hour before the ending time and to ask them to express any pent-up resentments, in order to facilitate a sense of complete closure.

The physical setup of the marathon encounter group is important. Ideally, the room should provide sufficient space for free dancing and every variety of encounter game. Since this is not always practical, there should at least be heavy cushions or a couch for the release of anger through pounding, and gymnasium mats or mattresses on the floor. Delicate ornaments should be removed. Floor cushions are more comfortable than chairs for long periods of time and create a more informal atmosphere. Participants should be advised to wear comfortable clothing, and women are usually more comfortable in slacks.

My strong preference is for the marathon participants to remain together at all times, rather than to separate at mealtime. The preparation and serving of food must be carefully thought out. It should be simple and plentiful. My custom is to keep apples, oranges, cheese, and crackers available at all times, with a large coffeepot of hot water, so that participants can serve themselves instant coffee or tea at will. The availability of food at any time helps create an informal atmosphere. Sometimes the giving and acceptance of food has a symbolic meaning; for example, in one marathon a woman who had made herself a servant to her family for years was instructed never to wait on herself during the course of the weekend but to ask the nearest person to bring her coffee or fruit when she wanted it. This became a game which she enjoyed, and which helped her gain a better perspective on her inability to receive and her need to place others under obligation to her by incessant giving.

Paper plates, cups, and napkins are recommended. Several boxes of cleansing tissues are necessary. Large paper bags are convenient for collecting the debris which accumulates. Some group leaders forbid smoking; I prefer to allow participants to make their own decision, since a habitual smoker who is asked to give it up for a weekend may be so preoccupied with his unsatisfied craving that he finds it difficult to deal with other problems. Liquor is not served during the marathon, even though participants may request it if the first few hours are slow and dull. Occasionally, in a mature group, I offer participants a drink immediately before we separate for the night, with the understanding that we will now relax together for a half-hour before separating.

Part of the responsibility of a marathon therapist is to provide closure for the participants, which is not possible for every participant in every marathon. Anyone who is not currently in individual therapy should be informed that, if he should want a follow-up session during the week, he may have an appointment either with the marathon leader or with a capable therapist who has agreed to be available. This is desirable not only because an emergency follow-up session may be needed, but because some participants wish to consolidate and reaffirm whatever insights they have gained during the marathon.

During the second day of an encounter marathon, which is often marked by strong feelings of elation and even euphoria, it is advisable to spend some time discussing what the various participants plan to do on the evening after the marathon. They should be warned that, upon returning to family and friends, they may have difficulty in carrying over the openness and spontaneity of the marathon, and they may appropriately be informed that a temporary letdown often occurs but lasts for only a day or two. Usually I find myself saying something like, "You won't take all this with you. You'll lose some of the good feelings. But you'll keep some of them too." Since members often become enthusiastic about one another, and wish to exchange telephone numbers, they should be informed that while enduring relationships sometimes begin in a marathon, it is also possible that the intimate and intense atmosphere of the group may cause people to commit themselves prematurely to a frendship or a sexual relationship which is not realistically appropriate to their life situation.

Finally, the marathon leader must plan for his own postmarathon needs (see Chapter 9). Some leaders need solitude, others need companionship, but nearly everyone needs to be free from responsibility the evening after conducting a marathon.

The question of co-leadership also needs careful preliminary consideration. It is wise for a leader to undertake his first marathon with a co-leader who is already known and trusted. Close personal friendship is not necessary, but some preliminary experience of working together on a professional level is helpful. If there are personal or professional tensions between the two leaders, they should spend several hours together well ahead of the marathon and talk them out, sharing their feelings with one another as honestly as possible. Unresolved tension between co-leaders can damage a marathon, since it is invariably sensed by the participants. If tension does exist and is questioned by the participants, the leaders are advised to acknowledge the tension; whether or not they wish to share their differences fully with the group and to work them out in the group situation depends on their individual temperaments and their theoretical orientation.

REFERENCES

Haigh, G. The residential basic encounter group. In H. Otto & H. Mann (Eds.), *Ways of growth*. New York: Grossman, 1968.

Mintz, E. E. Overt male homosexuals in combined group and individual treatment. *Journal of Consulting Psychology*, 1966, *30*(3).

Stoller, F. H. Accelerated interaction. *International Journal of Group Psychotherapy*, April, 1968, *18*(2).

NAME INDEX

SUBJECT INDEX